Library of
Davidson College

Socialist Korea

Socialist Korea

A Case Study in the Strategy of Economic Development

Ellen Brun and Jacques Hersh

Monthly Review Press
New York and London

Copyright © 1976 by Ellen Brun and Jacques Hersh
All right reserved

Library of Congress Cataloging in Publication Data
Brun, Ellen.
  Socialist Korea.
  1. Korea (People's Democratic Republic) —Economic
conditions. 2. Korea (People's Democratic Republic) —
Economic policy. 3. Socialism in Korea (People's
Democratic Republic) I. Hersh, Jacques, joint author.
II. Title.
HC468.A2B78   330.9'519'3043   76-1651
ISBN 0-85345-386-1

Monthly Review Press
62 West 14th Street, New York, N.Y. 10011
21 Theobalds Road, London WC1X 8SL

First printing
Manufactured in the United States of America

"Therefore mankind always sets itself only such tasks as it can solve."

—Karl Marx, Preface to the *Critique of Political Economy* (1859)

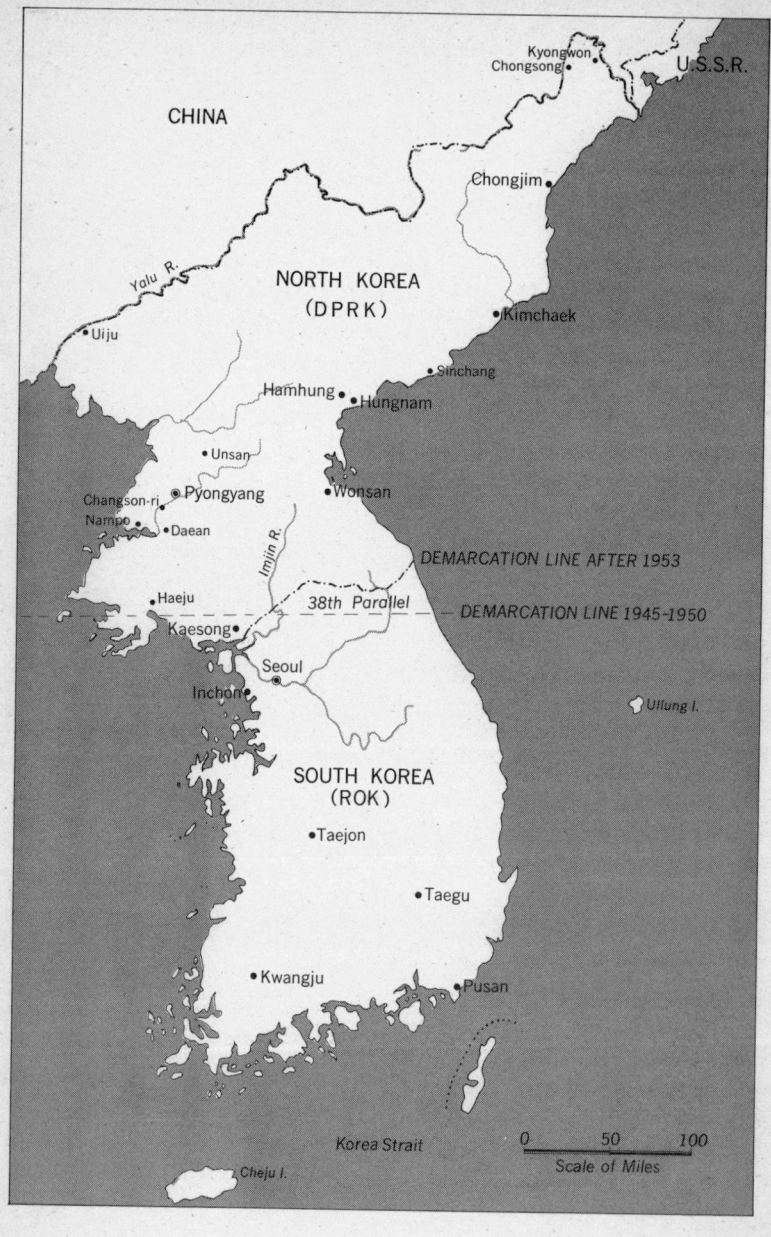

Contents

Introduction   11

Part I: The Historical Tradition

1. The Historical Roots   25
2. Japanese Colonialism   39
3. Anti-Imperialist Resistance   66

Part II: Building an Independent National Economy

4. The Genesis of Korean Socialism   109
5. Priorities in Postwar Reconstruction   163
6. Socialist Methods of Economic Development   194
   A. Agriculture
   B. Revolutionizing the Education System
   C. Socialist Industrial Construction
7. Economic and Social Achievements   279

Part III: Problems of Socialist Transition

8. The Need for a Socialist Political Economy   303
9. Administration and Planning in the DPRK   326
   A. Organizing Socialist Agriculture
   B. Transforming Relations of Production
      in Industry
   C. The Task of Socialist Planning

10. Contributions to Theoretical Questions   373

Appendix

The Ten Point Program of the Association for the
  Restoration of the Fatherland (1936)   419
The Twenty Point Platform (March 23, 1946)   421

Charts   423

Introduction

In this presentation of the development of the Democratic People's Republic of Korea (DPRK), the authors have been guided by one fundamental principle: to contribute to the struggle against economic underdevelopment. This commitment is based on our awareness that mankind has reached a stage where the means of production and technical knowledge capable of liberating humanity from material want are, indeed, at hand.

A basic weakness of the social sciences lies in the fact that they have not lived up to their responsibility of projecting social forms of organization which could spread the benefits of this liberation. Today, it is more vital than ever before not to remain on a descriptive level which exposes merely the symptoms of underdevelopment—as is the fashion among specialists—but to point out the roots of the evil and promote the search for solutions. Karl Marx, in his day, emphasized the need for such an active engagement in the process of change on the part of scientific analysis: "The philosophers have only *interpreted* the world, in various ways; the point, however, is to *change* it."[1]

This ambivalence on the part of the social sciences may be related to the fact that economic development in our era is not simply a process of controlling nature but, even more, a struggle against a world order in which the means of production are directed toward the satisfaction of the needs of a minority, to the detriment of the majority. Yet we can also observe a movement toward the transformation of this old order, particularly in the evolving social practice of several newly independent nations.

Historical circumstances have given Korea a central position in this entire problematic. First, it is a country whose background and present situation have been either distorted or ignored in our part of the world. Second, the Democratic People's Republic of Korea in the north, in contrast to most other Third World countries, has been undergoing a remarkably rapid and efficient process of economic development. Korea's size and former colonial status provide a basis for comparison with quite a few countries of Asia, Africa, and Latin America. What is obviously needed, then, is an effort to throw more light on the means and social forces involved in Korea's achievement of such different results.

In order to establish at least a preliminary basis for understanding the scope of the socioeconomic transformation of Korean society, this study begins with an attempt to evaluate the country's assets and liabilities as they existed at the point of departure, in 1945. In these first chapters, an account of Korea's earlier history is followed by a brief exposition of the main characteristics of Japanese colonialism, an examination of the events leading to the partition of the country and the Korean War, and an attempt to situate Korea in an international context.

However difficult it may be to trace the path of Korean evolution, an historical survey does bring to light the basic fact that in the final analysis all political struggle is related to the control of the means of production as well as to the appropriation and utilization of the social surplus. In the Korean case, where the principal means of production were land and human beings, we see a history of political struggle in the form of both violent peasant upheavals and almost uninterrupted factional strife within the ruling elite. Not until the 1946 land reform in the DPRK do we see a realistic attempt to solve this basic social contradiction.

Another dimension of Korea's history is its persistent struggle to retain national independence and identity. As a small country surrounded by powerful and at times expansionist neighbors, Korea developed a nationalism with deep cultural and geopolitical roots. This nationalist tradition, born of a centuries-long struggle against foreign domination, was to play an important progressive role in contemporary history and is even today a pervasive element of Korean socialism.

Korea, furthermore, offers a classic example of the complex process of capitalist development and underdevelopment. Its internal evolution toward the development of capitalism was arrested: it was subjected to colonialism before it had even overthrown feudalism. For a half century the country was kept in a state of economic backwardness, suffering under both colonialism and feudalism, with national capitalism an extremely weak element (a state of affairs which resembles the situation in many present-day Third World countries). On the other hand, Japanese colonialism had the effect of promoting a new popular consciousness. The people—to use Lenin's famous phrase—were economically backward, but politically advanced. During the 1920s and 1930s Korean revolutionaries became known for their militancy and political awareness as well as for their internationalism. This element played a positive role in the protracted Korean anticolonial and antifeudal struggle in the period both before and after liberation.

The mechanisms involved in establishing the uneven relationship between Japan and its colony in turn exemplify a phenomenon which had already become universal in other parts of the world dominated by Western imperialism. In this case, such mechanisms may have been even more pronounced due to the intensity and rapidity with which relations between Japan and Korea transformed themselves into a process leading to capitalist industrialization of the former and colonial deformation of the latter. Japan, in order to avoid becoming a victim of colonialism itself, was engaged in a race to catch up to the other advanced nations expanding in the Far East. Its colonial relationship to Korea was thus a major element in what is usually recognized as the most rapid process of capitalist industrialization ever to have occurred, and the only one outside the Western world.

In modern times, even though formal colonialism has become a kind of anachronism, it is increasingly recognized that the unequal relationship between the industrial capitalist world and what has been termed the Third World may still be regarded as a determining factor in the latter's situation. Under the guise of a so-called free world market, economic mechanisms originating in classical colonialism continue to reproduce themselves. There is growing awareness of this situation among political elements in the Third World—take, for example, the declarations of Third World representatives at the United Nations Conference on Raw Materials and Development, held in New York in the spring of 1974. This is not the place for a discussion of the legitimacy of each one of these declarations; taken together, however, they do indicate that a change in consciousness is taking place in an important region of the world.

Since ideas affect people's actions, great changes can be expected in the coming generations. If political forces in the Third World are true to their understanding of the cause of their underdevelopment, they will have to move from verbal pronouncements to positive actions in order to struggle against it. In choosing such a road, these nations will have to be on guard against pressures and advice not only from the developed countries—whose socioeconomic system ultimately depends on the present (unequal) international division of labor—but also from internal elements who prefer the present status quo to a new system which might endanger the privileges this minority has drawn from contact with the imperialist world. Hence the problem of economic development reveals itself as a highly political question. C. Wright Mills points this out in an essay on problems of industrialization:

> No population is going spontaneously to industrialize itself. We must determine the *agencies* of industrialization, for anonymous economic forces in the world today, both internal and external to the underdeveloped world, are now rather set against rapid structural industrialization. In brief, I believe that the agency today can only be political. Our problem is basically a political problem.[2]

Industrial development under present condition—in contrast to previous historical examples—thus implies a *conscious* process of social transformation, i.e., a strategy based on scientific methods. And even more important, it involves a recognition of the social forces which may become the tools for such a strategy—those with the greatest interest in radical change, those "with nothing to lose but their chains." In his address on the occasion of the visit to North Korea by President Houari Boumedienne of Algeria, President Kim Il Sung expressed the problem succinctly:

> Historic experience shows that if newly independent peoples are to defend the gains of revolution and attain the prosperity of their countries and nations, they should destroy the old colonial ruling machine and set up a new progressive social system, smash the subversive machinations of the foreign imperialist and domestic reactionary forces and deprive them of their economic footholds, and build an independent national economy and national culture.[3]

The entire experience of North Korea from 1945 to the present may be characterized as precisely such an attempt to combine the political mobilization of social forces most interested in change with a conscious strategy for economic development. In order to accomplish this, the DPRK had to choose the road of socialism—in part because in Korea capitalism had already discredited itself by its inadequacy and weakness, but also because it is the poor and exploited peasants and workers who objectively have the greatest interest in change, and a policy of egalitarianism and reform is the one most apt to mobilize their initiative and enthusiasm. Moreover, in an economically underdeveloped country which has not yet been able to reap the benefits of industrialization, human beings constitute the most important means of production. In fact, socialism itself is closely connected to the historic task of gradually removing all the socioeconomic, political, and cultural fetters which under the old system prevent mass initiative and creativity.

This in turn leads to another problem: from its inception, socialism was conceived in Marxist terms as the culmination of the development of productive forces under capitalism: "No social order ever perishes before all the productive forces for which there is room in it have developed; and new, higher relations for production never appear before the material conditions of their existence have matured in the womb of the old society itself."[4] This famous observation by Marx was originally interpreted to mean that social revolutions would tend to break out first in the highly industrialized countries. However, history turned out differently. Due to the rise and expansion of imperialism, the breakdown of capitalism occurred first in those countries which had been prevented by imperialist intervention from developing along traditional capitalist lines. Under these conditions, the choice between waiting until capitalism could develop the productive forces of the regions of Asia, Africa, or Latin America, or attempting to bypass this system and lay the foundations for a new socioeconomic mode of production, has become a very immediate one for a majority of humanity. In the words of of C. Wright Mills, "The world default of capitalism, in failing to industrialize the world, is one of communism's conditions of success."[5]

Thus, historical circumstances have made it necessary for countries such as Korea to embark upon the road of economic development while at the same time constructing socialism. Kim Il Sung explains the logic behind the Korean decision in the following manner:

> As we did not go through the normal course of capitalist development, we have the task of developing the productive forces in our socialist era today—a task which we should have tackled under capitalism. There is no need to make society capitalistic and go to the trouble of fostering the capitalists just to smash them and then build socialism, on the plea that we could not discharge the task which we should have done in the capitalist stage.[6]

But socialism is much more than a society in which the means of production are developed. It is a stage on the way to a higher form of social organization with radically different norms than those existing in the capitalist world. It seems to us that certain historical circumstances have made the Korean case of particular interest in this regard. Korea's opportunity to draw lessons from past and present experiences in fraternal socialist countries, combined with the continual external pressure exerted upon it, helped to promote a process of efficient and rapid socialist development.

In dealing with this process we have divided our work into three parts. The first, described above, deals with the historical dimensions of Korean development. The second is an attempt to identify the main forces and laws governing the process of rapid economic development as revealed by the Korean example. The third and last part addresses the particular problems of a transitional society, especially on the superstructural level, including changes in planning and management systems, social priorities, and motivations. This is an area in which, historically, the peoples of Asia are the pioneers, yet the questions it raises are ones the developed world may also have to come to grips with sooner or later.

In our presentation of the case of Korean development we have been principally concerned with drawing lessons which may be useful for other countries which are or will be embarking upon a search for solutions to similar problems. Thus we have drawn comparisons not only with the methods used and promoted by Western development experts, but also with the policies followed in other socialist countries. Korea does not exist in a vacuum. It is part of the Third World as well as one of a group of nations engaged in socialist construction, and it is within this context that its achievements must be viewed.

Painfully aware of the difficulties involved, the lack of unbiased material, and the many unsolved riddles of the development of the Korean revolutionary movement, we have tried to remain as openminded as possible. We have tried to avoid digressions into areas secondary to our central purpose and to concentrate our attention on the principal function of human activity, the struggle for material survival, and the sociological factors, such as political organization and economic development, on which it depends. Given the nature and scope of the issues involved we cannot make any claim to infallibility. Although general political lines and priorities are major topics in our study, it would be unrealistic for any foreign student of Korean reality to claim an intimate and detailed knowledge of the manner in which Korean socialism is practiced at the grass-roots level. In view of the Korean situation, whatever contradictions are bound to emerge in the process of transformation are only partly revealed to the foreigner. These limitations notwithstanding, we feel that the result of our discussions in Korea and the material we do possess do permit us to get at least a preliminary outline of what seems to be a highly relevant experiment. It should further be kept in mind that few countries are as difficult to get throughly acquainted with as the DPRK: it was never under Western influence in the past, and today it is characterized by social norms entirely different from those of capitalist states.

Very few of the arguments in this study have been based exclusively on statistical material. But where we do use data of this sort, we have tried whenever possible to give preference to sources other than North Korean ones. This is because in the eyes of many people the use of such outside sources make the case even stronger. Social sciences in our part of the world still have a tendency to regard statistical material originating from official sources in socialist countries as unreliable, while often accepting at face value statistics emanating from other countries (a case in point: South Korea!). And yet, according to an American-educated Korean who has studied the economy of North Korea, there are some sound reasons for trusting the reliability of North Korean economic statistics. Among these are the following: (1) planned economies need more reliable data than market economies; (2) there is no difference between data published for domestic use and that used for propaganda purposes abroad (this is also the case for China and the Soviet Union); (3) cross checking reveals no internal inconsistencies; (4) since the targets of plans are determined by the results reported by enterprises and agencies to higher authorities, any tendency toward exaggeration could be discerned; (5) omission rather than direct falsification is the method usually employed in concealing unfavorable results; (6) according to the "law of equal cheating" (compensating errors), all relative data such as growth figures are not affected as long as the extent of falsification, omission, errors, etc., remains constant—and this is assumed to be so; (7) foreign trade figures can be checked against the data of trading partners. This Korean economist further notes some factors that tend to produce upward biases in official data, including increased statistical coverage, inclusion of traditional products and output which are newcomers to the exchange circuit, etc. But such factors are at work in any developing economy.[7] No doubt the main source of difficulty is the preference given to relative indices rather than absolute figures. Furthermore, information concerning the base year, aggregation, etc., may be lacking, or else the base year seems to be chosen in order to create the most impressive effect. But since statistics have been used in this study only to illustrate certain important trends, for our purposes the aforementioned reservations do not substantially weaken their validity.

Another point which may require clarification is our method of dealing with policy statements. When highly placed politicians in Western countries make pronouncements on their political objectives and projects, only the most foolish observer accepts them at face value; it is assumed that the corresponding political "practice" will in some way fall short of the announced goals. This is quite a normal and accepted state of affairs in the so-called parliamentary democracies. In a socialist state such as the DPRK, the situation is very different. Not only do the various speeches and writings by Kim Il Sung reflect the decisions and political aims of the highest political authority of the country, the Central Committee of the Workers' Party, but they are studied intensively by rank-and-file members of the Party and used as guidelines to political mobilization and economic construction. Often these documents include severe criticism of past and present errors. Political statements in the DPRK thus in a very real sense reflect the aims and objectives of the regime. This may serve to explain why no realistic presentation of Korean priorities and strategies for development and socialist construction is possible without reference to such speeches and writings. As the timing and general context of these pronouncements may be significant, all notes have been supplied with dates.

The scarcity of material concerning the development of the DPRK is another argument for studying the documents published by the Koreans themselves (some of which are obviously printed for propaganda purposes). This lack of material was extremely pronounced until very recently and explains why certain important events —for example, the Korean Chollima Movement of the 1950s—have remained largely unknown to the outside world. Since 1968, a number of works have been published which have been of assistance in our study. Paradoxically, the fact that many Western students of North Korea have been biased against the regime, and have tried to build their case on whatever omissions or ambiguities could be found in the official interpretations, has proved particularly helpful. Proceeding from an attitude of Cold War scepticism, these works often grudgingly confirm the very trends we consider most essential.

In conclusion, although we should not consider the DPRK a "model" which can be copied mechanically by other countries, the methods and mechanisms which emerge from a study of its social development do constitute the outline of an alternative development theory which turns upside down all the accepted premises of Western economic thinking. With a unique singleness of purpose and in a very brief span of time, the DPRK traveled the road which took other socialist countries several decades to complete. Perhaps this is why theories and methods emerge with greater clarity in the Korean context, thus contributing on the empirical level to the political economy of socialism—a work which remains to be written.

As to our own qualifications for making this study, our background is in the area of problems of economic development and underdevelopment. In 1969 one of us visited the DPRK for the first time. Following that, we studied the relevant available literature on Korea and together paid a second visit to the country in 1971. This time we stayed about two months and our visit took the form of a systematic investigation, including numerous visits to institutions and enterprises, as well as extensive talks and interviews with highly placed functionaries and experts in planning, management, and economic construction. Considering the scope of the subject, which transcends any single social scientific discipline, our own contribution should be considered simply an attempt to open up the discussion. Further studies would obviously prove highly relevant to an elucidation both of the particular problems of the Third World and the problems of transition from capitalism to socialism. If this book inspires others to proceed with further studies along these lines, we would feel that we had achieved our main objective.

One final motivation should be mentioned. As is well known, Korea is in the peculiar situation of having introduced socialism in one part of the nation, while at the same time the national liberation of the other part has not yet been carried to a successful conclusion. This fact accounts for certain features of Korean socialism which would not otherwise have existed. It also serves to explain —at least to a large extent—the "conspiracy of silence" which has enshrouded this small Asian nation for so many years. Not the least of those kept in the dark with regard to developments north of the 38th Parallel—probably the most efficient "curtain of ignorance" ever established— are the South Koreans. We would like to dedicate this book to them, for we feel that traditionally the Korean people have shown not only an unequaled capacity for suffering, but also a political maturity and sense of combativity which are sure to guarantee coming generations a better future.

—Autumn 1974

Notes

1. Karl Marx, *Theses on Feuerbach,* in K. Marx and F. Engels, *Selected Works in Two Volumes,* vol. II (Moscow: Progress Publishers, 1958), p. 405.
2. C. Wright Mills, *Power, Politics and People* (New York: Oxford Univ. Press, 1963), p. 144.
3. Kim Il Sung, *The Peoples of the Third World Who Advance Under the Uplifted Banner of Independence Will Certainly Win Their Revolutionary Cause,* March 4, 1974 (Pyongyang, 1974), p. 4.
4. Karl Marx, "Preface to A Contribution to the Critique of Political Economy," in Marx and Engels, *Selected Works in Two Volumes,* vol. I, p. 363.

5. Mills, *Power, Politics and People,* p. 152.
6. Kim Il Sung, *On the Questions of the Period of Transition from Capitalism to Socialism and the Dictatorship of the Proletariat,* May 25, 1967 (Pyongyang, 1969), pp. 12-13.
7. Cf. Joseph S. Chung, *The North Korean Economy: Structure and Development,* (Wayne State Univ. Doct. Diss. Series No. 65-7720, unpub. diss. 1964), pp. 10-14.

Part I
The Historical Tradition

Chapter 1
The Historical Roots

Geographically, Korea is formed by the peninsula stretching out of the far eastern part of the Asian continent, with some 3,300 islands scattered around its coasts. The total area is slightly more than 220,000 square kilometers, with a current population of some fifty million. Despite its long recorded history, Korean civilization is little known to the West. A number of elements have conspired to make Korea less accessible to the Western scholar than most other countries. Few experts have concentrated their efforts on Korea and even fewer have taken the internal situation of the country as their point of departure. The proximity of a flourishing Chinese civilization on the one hand and a dynamic Japanese capitalism on the other, influenced many students of Asia to consider Korea a mere appendage of one of its powerful neighbors. The fact that the Korean nation was colonized by Japan and thus never came under the direct influence of the West is another reason for the scarcity of Western historical studies on Korea.

Korea's historical origins, like those of all ancient civilizations, are somewhat obscure. Korean archeologists refer to relics from the Palaeolithic Age and the area is said to have entered the Neolithic Age around 5,000 B.C. The first sociopolitical formation, ancient Chōson (Land of the

Morning Calm), took shape during the Bronze Age in the area between the Liao River in southern Manchuria and the Taedong River in the peninsula itself. For a long time there was a succession of various feudal states in Korea. According to the usual Western version, the unification of these states took place as early as the seventh century, but modern North Korean historians maintain that the total unification of the various kingdoms then in existence was not completed until the early tenth century. Nevertheless, it is a fact that from around the seventh century to the present day, the country has retained its essential integrity, both in terms of geographical extent and population, and in terms of a distinct language, culture, and set of traditions. Thus, it is one of the world's oldest nations. As pointed out by the American expert on Asia, Edwin O. Reischauer, "certainly none of the countries of Western Europe achieved both its modern boundaries and its present ethnic composition until well after Korea."[1]

During various periods of its recorded history, particularly in the early fifteenth century, Korea stood at the pinnacle of human civilization. There were traditions in painting, architecture, sculpture, philosophy, and literature. Especially noteworthy was the invention of the Korean phonetic alphabet, *Hangul*, in the fifteenth century. Later, during the period of Japanese colonialism, *Hangul* became a national symbol of the resistance. Even today, it is regarded as one of the world's most scientific and simple alphabets. Printing with movable metal type was invented and came into widespread use at least half a century before a similar process took place in Europe. Agricultural techniques as well as various industrial skills were highly developed.

Whether the socioeconomic structures of precolonial Korea should be characterized as feudal or not may still be a source of debate. Certainly the typical traits of vassality, fiefs, etc., characteristic of its European counterpart, were absent in Korean feudalism. In principle the royal dynasties had property rights to all lands, bestowing only various privileges upon the nobility and the class of officials. As a result of the introduction of hereditary rights as well as other institutional changes, however, local centers of power emerged at various times, giving rise to increased rivalries and disorganization of the state system not unlike the situation under European feudalism. This fluctuation between a highly centralized type of society and the more decentralized type occurred several times in Korean history.

Politically, the entire evolution was similar to that of other contemporary formations, characterized by a continuous struggle between the rulers and the peasantry who created the economic surplus on which society depended for its survival. On the other hand, the privileged classes often competed among themselves for the control and appropriation of this wealth. The rise and fall of the various dynasties bear witness to the dynamics of this basic contradiction. The most important question, whether or not, given the proper opportunities, Korean society might have evolved in the direction of capitalism, must in our opinion be answered affirmatively. External and internal conditions may have differed from those of the Middle Ages in Europe, but there can be no doubt that Korean society contained the same basic potential for capitalist evolution. The observation on China and India of English historian George Thomson, applies equally well to the case of Korea: " . . . there were marked divergences in the forms of pre-capitalist society as it evolved in Europe, China and India; yet, despite these differences, they are rightly regarded as parallel manifestations of a single process, marked by uneven development."[2]

External and Internal Threats to Korean Feudalism

The contact between the European and Asian civilizations was to have an important impact on the ensuing development of each. Western interest in Korea came at the time when the kingdom—under the Yi dynasty—had been weakened by foreign invasions and internal contradictions. Korea's geographical location had for centuries made it a target for the expansionist ambitions of its neighbors. Although it had succeeded in maintaining its independence, the Japanese onslaught of 1592 and 1597 had had disastrous effects on the country: towns had been plundered and sacked; famine and plague had decimated the population.

Coming so soon after these invasions, the Manchu attacks of 1627 and 1637, though lasting a shorter period of time, made an already desperate situation even worse. In reaction to these events, the Korean kingdom attempted to close itself to foreign penetration in subsequent decades. Frustration with these efforts to maintain independence led ideologists of the various imperialist powers—just then beginning their expansion into the Far East—to denigrate Korea as the "Hermit Kingdom." This name has been repeated by Western history books ever since.

The many years of foreign invasion and plunder had exacerbated Korea's internal conflicts and weakened the state to such an extent that the Yi dynasty never regained its former vitality. An important consequence of the conflicts with the neighbor states had been the destruction and loss of control over registered taxpaying lands. Opportunistic landlords used the nonexistence of land records in the invasion-racked country as an excuse to illegally get their hands on additional properties. Since income from land was the material basis for the functioning of the state, it was vital for the government to regain control over these areas. Only a radical transformation of the system of land tenure could have resolved the problem, but because of the interests involved such a course was impossible. The government was unable to do anything but raise taxes, which were then passed on to the peasant tillers. The result was a growing corruption accompanied by factional divisions which in turn led to growing dissatisfaction among the lower officials who suffered diminishing salaries and injustices. Thus the agrarian question and its corresponding form of social organization became the main sources of political instability.

Meanwhile, an ever greater change was taking place in an altogether different sphere of activity. In Seoul, the tribute contractors, charged with supplying the court and government, were beginning to transform economic life by gradually opening the way to the development of a money economy, despite the official bias against mercantile endeavors. After the foreign invasions, the government had had to discontinue handicraft production in the officially controlled shops. This meant that newly emancipated artisans had no recourse but to sell their goods on whatever markets they could find. At the same time the government started minting money, further facilitating commercial transactions. There were also attempts to commute the tax system to cash payment. This in turn stimulated the practice of money-lending at interest with many *yangban* (civil and military officials) joining in, not to mention wealthy merchants and even government officials, despite Confucian prejudices against it.. The result was a growth of commercial capital. As Professor Han Woo-Keun points out, an important change was taking place: "What was developing, in Western terms, was a laissez-faire capitalist economy, and what happened in the early stages of its development was a familiar phenomenon to economic historians: the rich get richer and the poor get poorer, and the traditional class structure of society was disrupted and confused."[3]

According to North Korean historians, in the first part of the nineteenth century feudalism was further weakened. A crack appeared in the structural caste system: impoverished peasants, no longer so frequently reduced to serfdom —i.e., subordinated physically to others—became "free" and moved to towns or found their way into mines. In addition, government offices started to employ hired labor. "Thus a 'free' labor force took shape at one end, and the transformation of the growing commercial capital into industrial capital went ahead, though slowly, at the other."[4] These trends were already well established prior to the "opening" of Korea by the imperialist powers.

Conditions were deplorable for peasants throughout this period of evolution. The introduction of improved methods of cultivation had, it is true, made the agricultural sector capable of supporting an increasing population. But the appearance of the two-crop system—whereby winter barley could be harvested before planting rice in the spring, thus alleviating the traditionally difficult few months until the rice harvest—also made it possible for a segment of the peasantry to bear the burdens of taxation. The growth of commodity-currency relations and the emergence of new capitalist elements generally served only to intensify the feudal oppression and exploitation of the peasants, whose situation was worsened by the emergence of usurious money-lenders. Because of the state's corruption, the government became less able to offer protection against overexploitation or poor harvests, and throughout this period famine was endemic. In its wake came pestilence and disorders: in 1811, a brief but massive peasant movement swept northwestern Korea, followed in 1862 by large-scale uprisings in both the north and the south. Yet these *jacqueries* fell short of threatening the existence of the dynasty.

The "Opening" of Korea

Parallel to this internal evolution, Korea's self-imposed isolation from external events was coming to an end. In 1842, after the Opium War, the West had forced China to open its doors, and twelve years later the seclusion of Japan was broken by the United States. Thus, the ancient civilizations of the Far East were facing growing pressures on all sides: England and France from the south, Tsarist Russia from the north, and the United States from across the Pacific.

These geopolitical movements set off a process of world-shaking impact, and it was only a matter of time before

Korea, too, would feel their influence. From the point of view of Korea the opening of Japan to Western influence was particularly significant. This Western penetration had the effect of favoring the overthrow of the Tokugawa shogunate in 1868 by the Meiji Restoration and the establishment of an imperial government.[5] These events were followed by a radical modernization process in which Western industrial methods were introduced, the country was initially almost completely closed to foreign interests, and a series of internal political reforms were implemented. At the same time, a social movement characterized by agrarian uprisings and people's rights movements was suppressed by the old feudal militarist caste. This latter group gained increased influence when they were given positions within the new government. Under the Meiji regime trade and industry were promoted and three main principles guided governmental policy: (1) keeping out the "foreign barbarians"; (2) introducing some reforms to promote development; and (3) charting aggressive designs on weak Asian nations. The implementation of this program could not fail to have grave consequences for the future of Asia. A nationalistic campaign was launched typified by such jingoistic slogans as "Enrich the nation and strengthen the Military!" As the Japanese scholar Takashi Hatada points out, these ideas were more widely accepted than is generally recognized: "This program was not simply the reactionary expression of a disgruntled military class, deprived of special feudal privileges, but had the general support of the liberals, who were promoting the development of Japanese capitalism."[6]

Korea was the chosen target of these aggressive designs. Thus, following unsuccessful attempts by France (1866) and the United States (1866 and 1871) to "open" the peninsula, in 1876 Japan imposed the first unequal treaty, the Kanghwa Treaty, opening Korea to intensive foreign penetration.

Within Korea, meanwhile, the crisis of feudal rule continued. Violent peasant uprisings took place while new political circles representing the interests of big merchants and other capitalists were beginning to acquire increasing influence. There was growing discussion of how the old feudal system could be liquidated and the nation modernized through reform. Such reformist ideas were advanced in the 1860s and 1870s by the so-called "practical school," which until then had been mainly anti-Confucian in tendency. After the opening of Korean ports to Japan in 1876, the political activities of this reformist group gained momentum and developed into a patriotic-radical movement. In 1884 the Korean reformists adopted the line that contradictions between the Chinese Ching and Japan should be used to carry out a coup d'état. A few days before the event, one of the rebellious leaders wrote, "I am worried to death, because if another few years go by without a reform in our country, it may be difficult for the Korean people to rule their own country any longer, even if there is a reform."[7]

Immediately following this so-called Kapsin coup a cabinet was formed with a political program meant to promote the process of capitalist development. For various reasons, however, this attempt at taking power failed,[8] and an internal structural reform—the only thing which could have saved the nation from foreign domination—was never carried out.

Although Japan had specific plans to make Korea its colony, all Western countries were interested in gaining concessions and expanding business relations there. For a time, American capital played an important role in the "opening" of the country. But the United States was not the only foreign concessionaire in the kingdom. Table 1 provides a picture of the interimperialist scramble in Korea at the turn of the century. The way had been prepared diplomatically for this inrush of foreign interests through a series of treaties of friendship and commerce with the United States (1882), Great Britain (1883), Germany (1883),

Table 1
Concessions and Concessionaires in Korea, 1896-1900

Year	Rights or privileges granted	Concessionaires
1896	Building of Inchon–Seoul railroad	American
1896	Exploitation of Kyongwon and Chongsong mines in North Hamgyong province	Russian
1896	Exploitation of gold mines at Unsan in North Pyongan province	American
1896	Building of Seoul–Uiju railroad	French
1896	Exploitation of forests in the Yalu River basin and on Ullung Island	Russian
1897	Exploitation of Tanghyon gold mines in Kumsong county of Kangwon province	German
1898	Building streetcar lines in Seoul	American
1898	Building the Seoul–Pusan railroad	Japanese
1900	Exploitation of the Unsan gold mines in Pyongan province	German
1900	Exploitation of the Chiksan gold mine in South Chumgchong province	Japanese

Source: Takashi Hatada, *A History of Korea* (Santa Barbara, Cal.: American Bibliographic Center-Clio Press, 1969), p. 105.

Italy (1884), Russia (1884), France (1886), Austria (1892), Belgium (1901), and Denmark (1902).[9]

Japanese penetration took the form of a growing emigration to the peninsula. At first the emigrants settled in Korean ports; then they gradually spread into the countryside. Taking advantage of the peasantry's ignorance of modern concepts of property, they accumulated great areas of land at a fraction of its true value. Similarly, Japanese manufactured goods flooded the country, outcompeting and ruining local handicraft industries. A further item on the debit side was the large quantity of rice exported to Japan.

As had been the case in China, the Korean government

found itself unable to oppose foreign penetration or carry out needed reforms. From the earliest days Koreans had been accustomed to paying their taxes in kind and according to the size of the harvest. Various attempts had been made to convert taxes into cash payments, but this had never been successfully carried out. When it was ordained in 1894 that payment be made in money, the change had great impact. After having lived so long under what was virtually a system of barter, the peasantry was suddenly drawn into contact with capitalism. The economy became thoroughly commercialized and gradually even simple necessities were imported in exchange for the export of rice. "The living conditions of the Koreans grew progressively worse as this sort of foreign penetration of the country increased, so it was not surprising that anti-foreign feeling emerged in Korea."[10]

The culmination of antiforeign feelings among the masses was the 1894 Farmers' War (also called the Tonghak Rebellion) which was comparable in scope and vigor to the Taiping and Boxer Rebellions in China. In Korea, however, two neighboring countries tried to take advantage of the revolt to further their own interests. Toward the end of the nineteenth century, while the Western powers were mainly occupied in other areas, Sino-Japanese rivalry over Korea had intensified. In order to put down the Tonghak Rebellion the Korean court appealed to China for help. Despite the fact that it had not been asked, the Japanese government sent six times as many soldiers as Korea's Chinese ally. Unhappy with the Korean attitude toward foreign penetration and wary of its relationship with China, the Japanese proceeded to attack the palace and start a war against China.

Interimperialist Contention and Collusion

The Treaty of Shimonoseki, signed in 1895, spelled final defeat for China. Through this treaty, China was forced to recognize the "full and complete independence and autonomy of Korea" and to cede to Japan certain territories and privileges (the Liaotung Peninsula, Formosa, and the Pescadores, as well as a promise that several ports on the Yangtse River would not be open to Japanese interests), which gave Japan a dominant position in Korea and southern Manchuria. These developments did not go unnoticed by the other imperialist powers. Only a week after the signing of the Sino-Japanese treaty, the so-called Three Power Intervention (Russia, France, and Germany) forced Japan to return the Liaotung Peninsula to China.

But this apparent sympathy was hardly motivated by philanthropic considerations. In fact, these events led to what has been called the "second partition of the Far East." China was now subjected to a savage renewal of Western aggression: Russia obtained the rights to mines, railroads, and police power in Manchuria as well as the lease of Port Arthur and Dairen; France was accorded special privileges in South China and the lease of Kuang-chou Bay; Germany was granted a dominant position in the Shantung Peninsula and occupied the Bay of Chiao-chou; England obtained Weihaiwei and the Kowloon Peninsula; and the United States announced its "Open Door" policy for China, meanwhile taking over the Philippines and Hawaii.

In the case of Japan and Russia, rivalry was particularly intense. As their divergences were not limited to Korea, but encompassed the entire Asian mainland, a war between them could not be avoided. For Korea, the Russo-Japanese War (1904–1905) was a traumatic experience—the second conflict between two foreign powers to be fought on its territory within one decade. The Russian defeat did not improve matters for Korea, since the peace treaty of Portsmouth (New Hampshire) established Japan's exclusive domination of the peninsula.

As far as relations within the imperialist "club" were concerned, Japan now became an accepted political, economic, and military member, recognized by all powers. In 1883, the United States had signed a treaty with the king of Korea providing for mutual aid in case of foreign intervention, thus making itself a kind of protector of Korean independence.[11] Even before the end of the Russo-Japanese conflict, however, President Theodore Roosevelt had sent his secretary of war, William Howard Taft, to Tokyo to conclude a deal with Prime Minister Katsura. In exchange for American recognition of the Japanese seizure of Korea, the United States requested Japanese acceptance of the American acquisition of the Philippines! Not only was the treaty of 1883 forgotten, but when the Korean king attempted to send emissaries to Portsmouth to attend the treaty session, the American president told him in effect that it was "none of his business."[12] For those Koreans who had considered American protection a shield against foreign domination, this came as a rather bitter shock.

With interimperialist competition in abeyance for the time being, there was no more international resistance to Japanese expansion. Korea's fate was sealed. On August 22, 1910, a formal treaty of annexation was signed, making the peninsula a Japanese colony. Yet the destruction of Korean independence between 1905 and 1910 did not take place without a struggle. The entire period was characterized by insurrections, demonstrations, disturbances, political murders, and guerrilla activities. According to Japanese sources, from July 1907 to the end of 1908 about 14,566 insurgents were killed, while 8,728 surrendered. (The population of Korea at the time was estimated at between 12 and 13 million.) According to Andrew J. Grajdanzev, it was a struggle in which medieval spears and swords were pitted against twentieth-century machine guns.[13]

From 1910 on, the Japanese strategy was to use the peninsula as a gateway to the Asian continent and to make Korea's economy completely subordinate to the needs of Japanese industrial and military capitalism. Subsequent political events were to demonstrate that this period marked a milestone not only in the history of Korea and

Japan—whose fates would henceforth be closely intertwined—but also in the course of world affairs.

Notes

1. Edwin O. Reischauer and John K. Fairbank, *East Asia: The Great Tradition* (Boston: Houghton Mifflin, 1960), p. 411.
2. George Thomson, *Capitalism and After* (London, 1973), p. 56.
3. Han Woo-Keun, *The History of Korea* (Honolulu: Univ. of Hawaii Press, 1972), p. 312.
4. Kim Suk Hyung, Kim Heui Il, and Son Yung Jong, *On the Grave Errors in the Descriptions on Korea of the "World History,"* edited by the U.S.S.R. Academy of Sciences (Pyongyang, 1963), p. 25 ff. (henceforth referred to as *On the Grave Errors*). This correction of a Soviet historical version is interesting as it contradicts many important points of the official Western interpretations.
5. The degree of Western influence in Japanese developments is described by Robert T. Oliver:

    > The opening of Japan to the West in 1854 by Admiral Perry was followed by the garrisoning of Western troops in Japanese cities and control of Japan's tariffs by the Western Powers. In 1868 the foreigners led by the British, fomented and supported the revolution that restored the Meiji dynasty from its seclusion in Kyoto, reinstituted Emperor worship, subordinated the 200 feudal principalities to the throne, and placed the Samurai warrior class in power. This was done in the interests of providing a single central government with which the trading powers could deal. They did not realize they had unleashed a dragon they would soon be unable to control.

    R.T. Oliver, *The Truth About Korea* (London, 1951), pp. 33-34.
6. Takashi Hatada, *A History of Korea* (Santa Barbara, Cal.: American Bibliographic Center-Clio Press, 1969), p. 92.
7. *Data on Negotiations Between Korea and Japan,* vol. I, pp. 291-292 (quoted in *On the Grave Errors,* pp. 29-30).
8. According to North Korean sources the Kapsin coup was carried out by a nationalist group motivated to protect their country from colonization, and not, as claimed by Western versions, instigated by the Japanese. (Cf. *On the Grave Errors,* pp. 30-31.)
9. Li Ogg, *Histoire de la Corée* (Paris: Presses Universitaires de France, 1969), p. 104.

38 *Socialist Korea*

10. Hatada, *History of Korea,* p. 99.
11. Oliver, *The Truth About Korea,* p. 34.
12. Ibid., p. 35. On July 29, 1905, in a private conversation between Count Katsura and the American envoy Taft, the Japanese statesman had already declared that "Japan does not harbor any aggressive designs whatever against the Philippines." This opened the way for American consent to Japanese plans in Korea: "President Roosevelt, through his personal representative, had given the Tokyo Foreign Office an assurance that the reorganization of Korea by the Japanese would meet no opposition from the United States." [G. Nye Steiger, *A History of the Far East* (Boston, 1936), p. 730, quoted by Andrew J. Grajdanzev, *Modern Korea* (New York: John Day, 1944), p. 32.]
13. Grajdanzev, *Modern Korea,* pp. 44-45.

Chapter 2
Japanese Colonialism

As the only example of a non-European nation "opened" by the West which was subsequently able to industrialize itself, Japan is of special interest. Not only does its development illuminate the mechanisms of capitalist industrialization but it throws a particular light on the historical role played by Korea, however involuntarily.

To understand Japan's unique situation, one has to take various elements into consideration. One of the determining factors paradoxically may have been the country's relative lack of natural resources. Without oil, with very little coal, iron ore, or other vital metals, the Japanese Islands were less attractive to Western imperialism than other nearby areas.[1] Moreover, the international rivalry between imperialist powers, which had at a certain time played a role in determining the fate of Korea, similarly affected Japan's future. A student of Japanese affairs explains this exceptional situation:

> The peculiar complexity of the international situation from 1850 right through to the end of the American Civil War and the outbreak of the Franco-Prussian War, and the stalemate resulting from the Anglo-French intrigues in Japan . . . gave Japan the vitally necessary breathing-space in which to shake off the restricting fetters of feudalism which had caused the country to rot economically and to be exposed to

the dangers of commercial and military domination from abroad.²

It was after having seen the damage inflicted by Western imperialism upon such great civilizations as India and China that Japan resolved to refuse to be subordinated to Western pressure and closed itself almost completely to foreign investments. As an indirect result, Western influence in that country had a different impact than it had in colonized areas. Paul A. Baran stresses the fact that Western sciences and knowledge were able to penetrate Japan and become accepted there with none of the extremes of xenophobia or antiforeign feeling so typical of countries that had been colonized.³

The convergence of these factors led to the use of Western science and methods in Japan, and to internal structural reforms which permitted domestic capital accumulation. Because Japan was not dominated by more powerful industrial nations, it was "allowed to invest its economic surplus in its own economy."⁴ This last element, together with the constant threat posed by the Western powers, determined the speed and direction of Japanese capitalist development. The Meiji Restoration ushered in a political and economic process which resulted in a concentrated, monopolistically organized industry, providing a base for military power that turned Japan into the West's most successful "junior partner" in the imperialistic game. Lenin recognized the influence of this external element on the Japanese model. "By their colonial looting of Asian countries, the Europeans managed to harden one of them—Japan—for great military exploits that assured it of an independent national development."⁵ Yet it is very unlikely that Japan could have developed as it did solely by means of adopting Western technology and utilizing its own internal surplus. A further element had to be added. Just as European territorial and economic expansion had helped the birth of industrial capitalism on the old continent, control of overseas areas—and not least the colonization of Korea—was to be a precondition for Japanese industrialization. The early development of militarism, the solution of the food crises at critical moments through the importation of cheap foodstuffs, the availability of foreign markets when internal consumption was slack, the utilization of cheap labor and investment possibilities overseas—all these factors were prerequisites for the dynamic development of Japanese industrial capitalism.

Japanese Development—Korean Underdevelopment

The mechanisms of industrialization, so familiar to us from European history, were more concentrated in Northeast Asia than anywhere else. In order to catch up with the other "advanced" nations, in the space of about fifty years Japan had to travel the path which it had taken Europe approximately four centuries to cover. In accomplishing this feat, Korea was of paramount importance for Japan. Thus, with remarkable rapidity the relationship between these two countries was transformed, following the typical dialectical process of furthering industrial development in the one and crippling the developmental possibilities of the other. The determining factor in this process was the historical conditions under which the capitalist mode of production was introduced.

Whereas capitalism in Japan was based on the confluence of an internal political process and the external influence of advanced Western technology, enabling it to become a center of capitalist development, the situation was entirely different in Korea. Here a deformed socioeconomic system was imposed from the outside, placing it in a tributary relationship to a capitalist center. Under such conditions only a peripheral and dependent form of capitalism could develop. The Egyptian economist, Samir Amin, has correctly analyzed this phenomenon: "The aggression of the capitalist mode of production from the outside on these (precapitalist) formations constitutes the essence of the problem of transition to peripheral capitalism."⁶

Whatever modernization did take place in the Korean economy came about through military, economic, and political intervention. As such, it was closely linked to Japanese needs and did not imply a true revolutionization of backward social structures. According to the American writer George McCune, who lived in Korea for many years, "In advancing their own interests in Korea, the Japanese in essence were expanding the Japanese economy, not replacing the medieval economy of Korea." He adds: "The old economy was pushed back where necessary to accommodate the new, but not supplanted. The age-old way of getting a living, the primitive agriculture under a feudalistic landlordism, persisted as the economy of most Koreans, but with the important difference of vassalage to Japanese economic interests."⁷

Monetarization of the Precapitalist Economy

On the political level, the imposition of Japanese colonial rule took the form of a military administration, with the establishment of a large number of gendarmes and police stations all over the country. On the economic level, the replacement of taxes in kind by fixed money payments was only the beginning of a thoroughgoing monetarization of the society.⁸ Even the old system of weights and measures was abolished and replaced by Japanese standards. The necessity of such changes may be attributed to the fact that when a monetary and commercial economy is introduced into a precapitalist formation from the outside it is generally *not* strong enough at first to prevail over the traditional social structures. Discussing this aspect in more theorectical terms, Samir Amin points out that whereas competition played a determining role in the European transition from feudalism to capitalism, in many precapitalist formations the vitality of communal life—the villagers' right to use the soil, for instance—

makes the simple mechanism of competition ineffective. This is why the colonial power has to intervene actively, sometimes by force, to monetarize the primitive economy.[9]

Since land is the main means of production in agrarian societies, the right to private property had to be institutionalized in order to make colonization effective. The outright seizure of land from native Koreans would not have served the purpose. On the economic level the buying and selling of land plays a key role in the formation of capital, and on the psychological level the population has to be made to accept their condition if the system is to be workable. Prior to the Japanese era, agricultural areas had been attached to royal houses, administrative offices, and to *sowon* and *yangban* families. Even though the official class had had formal claim and control over these lands, they had not administered them directly. All they cared about was the revenues they received from their share of the harvest. The actual management was carried out by a kind of middleman between the peasant tillers and the caste of officials. Over time these *saum* (land agents) had become rather numerous. On the other hand, those who tilled the soil might have been on a piece of land for generations, with a time-honored right to use it, yet have no formal claim to it. According to Hatada, "the concept of land-ownership simply had not developed."[10] Even though this interpretation might be somewhat too categorical, one may safely assume that property rights had generally been vague.

Even before formal annexation, an extensive land survey had begun. In 1906, the Japanese institutionalized the right to private ownership of land through a special order requiring that ownership of all lands and buildings be proven and registered. In order to overcome resistance to this measure, a certain time limit was imposed during which proprietors could make their claims valid. The abrupt reorganization resulted in widespread speculation whereby clever individuals obtained lands to which they were not legally entitled. In addition, the government took over much of the communal land which had formerly belonged to the villages. The Decree of Land Survey declared all lands on which the organs of the feudal state, the court, and royal tomb-maintenance offices had had the right to taxation to be the "national lands" of Japan, taking them over without compensation. Furthermore, under the Law on Forests of 1911 the bulk of forests in Korea were declared "state-owned forests." Some of the areas thus acquired by the Japanese government were sold at favorable terms to Japanese land companies, such as the notorious Oriental Development Company, or to Japanese immigrants. By 1910, the Oriental Development Company alone had already taken over 11,000 *chongbo* of land; by 1918 it had increased its holdings to 77,000. (1 *chongbo*= 0.992 hectares.) In the same period the number of Japanese landowners swelled from some 2,000 to over 10,000 and their holdings increased from 87,000 to about 200,000 *chongbo*.[11] In this violent manner modern property rights were established, legalizing Japanese ownership of Korean land.

The loss of their traditional land rights profoundly affected the Korean peasants. Shannon McCune describes its impact as follows:

> The holding of farm land by landlords had been common practice before 1910. However, at that time the system was operated rather benevolently. By the force of public opinion tenant farmers were given virtual rights to control the land they rented and to renew their leases every year. Furthermore, landlords had the responsibility of helping their tenants in poor crop years. However, with the "commercialization" of agriculture under the Japanese much of this benevolence went by the board. Moreover, many small landholders lost their fields because they could not pay for the land reclamation and irrigation improvements which were virtually forced upon them.[12]

The latter activities were part of a program to increase rice production which the Japanese had initiated after

World War I. In the years following, "irrigation associations" were set up in the main plain areas, where what were once dry fields were turned into rice paddies. Korean peasants not only were used as forced labor in the irrigation works, but were later made to pay for these projects in the form of heavy water taxes. Apart from the direct expropriations involved, countless peasants became impoverished during this process, forced to become tenant farmers or hired farm hands while their property passed into the hands of the Japanese. The pattern of landownership toward the end of the period of Japanese rule is shown in Table 2.

Table 2
The Number of Landowners (in 1937)

No. of chongbo	Over 5	Over 10	Over 20	Over 50	Over 100	Over 200
Koreans	106,162	30,332	12,701	1,571	385	49
Japanese	6,901	3,504	2,958	749	561	181
Total	113,063	33,836	15,659	2,320	946	230

Source: *The Historical Experience of the Agrarian Reform in Our Country* (Pyongyang, 1974), p. 7.

Twenty-five Japanese held over 1,000 *chongbo*. In spite of the Japanese interest in increasing rice exports from Korea, little capital was invested in the modernization of this sector. Because of growing poverty among the peasants, farm tools and draft animals became scarce, and human power gradually replaced animal power in nearly all work processes. North Korean sources cite data released by the Government-General in 1940 as to the number of farm implements owned by each peasant household, excluding hired hands and firefield tillers: traditional ploughs, 0.29; hoes, 1.81; sickles, 1.48; and long-handled spades, 0.15. There was only one improved plough for every 17 households and one treadle thrashing machine for every 19 households, with the owners of these tools obviously coming from the small number of Korean "rich" peasants.[13]

Thus, the fact that land had become a commodity did not fundamentally modify production relations in the rural sector. The new relationship between the growing number of tenants and those who owned the land in many ways resembled the earlier system of slavelike peasants working under overseers—but with some basic social changes which made life still more difficult for the tillers. The fact that taxes and rent now had to be paid exclusively in money made farmers dependent on the sale of their agricultural produce. This gave free play to the forces of the market—which meant low prices at harvest time and high prices in the spring—and opened the way to usurious money-lending, land speculation, and hoarding of rice. Numerous peasants were forced to give up their modest holdings. George McCune describes the benefits of this system to the colonial power:

> The Japanese found that landlordism was a convenient device for furthering their own principal interests in Korean agriculture, which no doubt accounts, in part at least, for the lack of interest in reform. Landlordism was useful for pumping rice out of Korea to Japan. Korean tenants, after paying rent and taxes, were left with only a small share of the rice which they produced, while the system put into the hands of the landlords large surpluses to be marketed in Japan.[14]

Those fortunate enough to hold on to their farms throughout the colonial period, despite these conditions, gradually saw their purchasing power shrink to nothing, forcing the Korean village to return to almost a natural economy. Actually, by the late 1930s only about 18.1 percent of Korean farmers owned their own land, while the remainder lived mostly as tenant farmers, poor farm hands, or squatters on firefields. Takashi Hatada quotes the Japanese Governor General Ugaki Issei who in a speech in January 1934 referred to the fearful misery of the peasantry: ". . . every spring the number of wretched farmers lacking food and searching for bark and grass to eat, approached 50 percent of the total peasant population."[15] Once driven from their land, these peasants were hard put to survive: "Words in current use at the time such as the 'spring and autumn poor,' 'uprooted wanderers,' 'stowaway,' 'firefield agriculturists,' and 'dwellers in earth mounds,' indicate the seriousness of the conditions." As these terms suggest, people suffered constantly from starvation, groups of Koreans who in desperation crossed over to Japan and Manchuria, peasants who lived in earth caves on the outskirts of large cities like Seoul.[16] Many of the destitute were forced to seek a livelihood through the practice of so-called firefield agriculture, leading a nomadic existence in the mountainous regions of the country. Although the system of burning and cultivating land had previously existed, it had not been practiced on such a scale since prehistoric times. In 1936, about one million acres were taken up by this type of primitive agriculture, coexisting with a modern agricultural sector catering to the needs of the metropolis. According to a Japanese description of the wandering peasants or *kadenmin* who roamed the country and lived from firefield cultivation, "These poor people are driven by hunger from place to place, making shelters in log cabins and keeping their bodies and souls together by planting grains and vegetables on the hillsides."[17]

Subordination to Japanese Needs

The relationship between the metropolis and the satellite economy intensified exploitation in those sectors catering to Japanese demands, while neglecting those which could have served the needs of the Koreans. The fluctuating policies followed with regard to rice cultivation may serve as an illustration.

At the beginning of the colonial period, the appropriation of rice was the main focus of economic interest, particularly after the rapid growth of Japanese capitalism during World War I had caused a serious food crisis in the country. In 1918 there was an acute rice shortage, and riots broke out throughout Japan. As a result of these rice riots, the Japanese government worked out a thirty year plan to increase rice production in Korea to meet Japanese needs.

In the years following, efforts were made to expand the paddy area by promoting irrigation and the utilization of fertilizer. But since the peninsula was considered simply a source of raw materials and foodstuffs for the Japanese, even this increased production had a detrimental effect on the conditions of the common people of Korea. While in 1916-1920 about 14 percent of the rice crop was exported to Japan, the percentaged jumped to 48 percent in 1931-1935. In the meantime domestic consumption had decreased 45 percent.[18] For Koreans this meant producing more but actually consuming less. As the years went by, people were forced to subsist on millet from Manchuria. This represented a change of dramatic significance, since rice is the Koreans' staple food. Indeed, the common word for food in the Korean language is "rice." Table 3 illustrates the decline in rice consumption under Japanese colonialism.

In Japan itself the results of this policy were quite the opposite. The availability of a continuous supply of low-priced foodstuffs made it possible to alleviate the effects of the inherent contradictions engendered by accelerated industrialization. Without such access to cheap food Japan's economy might have been threatened by inflationary tendencies, thus affecting the up-and-coming industrial power's ability to compete as well as endangering internal social stability.

In Korea, a byproduct of Japan's exclusive emphasis on rice production was a lack of agricultural diversification. Thus, despite an abundance of labor, vegetables repre-

Table 3
Per Capita Consumption of Rice in Korea
(in koku[a])

Average for	Amount	Index
1915-1919	0.707	100
1920-1924	0.638	90
1925-1929	0.512	72
1930-1933	0.449	63
1934-1938	0.396	56

Source: Andrew J. Grajdanzev, *Modern Korea* (New York, 1944), p. 118.
[a] One koku = 5.12 U.S. bushels, or 4.96 imperial bushels.

sented only 8.4 percent of total agricultural output and fruit only 1.2 percent, while the share of industrial crops was equally low—this in spite of the fact that rice is much more vulnerable to fluctuations in the weather.

The efforts to increase rice output were continued only until about 1930 when, as the result of an international crisis of overproduction of foodstuffs, Japanese agricultural producers began to feel threatened and demanded restrictions on imports. "In 1933 the Korean Government-General—under pressure from Japan, where the landlords clamored for protection against the flood of Formosan and Korean rice and complained that the Japanese government was financing this competition—cancelled all plans for the increase of the rice production, and in May 1934 even discontinued works in progress."[19] This led to the introduction of a new Japanese plan to make Korea a source of industrial raw materials for the empire, with particular emphasis on cotton. It was explicitly pointed out at the time that Korean cotton production would pose no threat to Japanese domestic interests. But plans for the "intensification and diversification" of Korean agriculture were soon revised when in 1938-1939, the Japanese war with China caused a renewed rice shortage. From that time on, the Japanese attempted to mobilize the forces of the empire through a single plan encompassing both the metropolis and its dependencies. According to a Japanese publication, "Because of her geographical position—being a military base for the continent—the part of Korea as a supply depot for military materials and foodstuffs is very important. Her contribution to the Empire's demand for rice . . . is also very great."[20] The wartime conditions further increased exploitation, making agricultural production difficult. As a result of this and a severe drought in 1939 the area under cultivation dwindled by more than 376,000 *chongbo* between 1938 and 1943, and the grain output suffered accordingly.[21]

The same disregard for the interests of Koreans could be observed in other branches of the primary sector. Under colonial rule, fishing underwent a rapid development. According to Japanese estimates the volume of the catch in Korean waters quadrupled between 1912 and 1938. But as Grajdanzev so pointedly remarks, "the question remains, however, whether this remarkable growth has resulted from the reckless plunder of fishing resources without any thought of the consequences."[22] In the late thirties, in fact, there were signs of a sharp decline in the availability of fish. Furthermore, only a small share of it was destined for direct human consumption. Approximately 91 percent of the main fish catch in 1937 was processed into oils, glycerine, fatty acids, gunpowder, medicines, soap, candles, fertilizer, or margarine. Thus, only 54 percent of manufactured marine products were used as food, while some of them served the military sector. Besides, as Grajdanzev points out, the actual increase in the volume of fish output benefited Koreans very little, since five-eighths of all marine products were exported.

A similar pattern could be seen in the practices of the colonial power with regard to the timber industry. As the Japanese war effort gained momentum, the demand for wood increased and the felling of trees in Korea was intensified, with little concern for future generations. As a matter of fact, in the forest areas of the far north of the country, tens of thousands of old tree stumps can still be seen—a present-day reminder of this past spoliation.

Better Infrastructure—Better Exploitation

In spite of the sufferings of the Korean people, Western observers at the time were often positively impressed by Japanese "efforts" in Korea. This judgment was based on purely technocratic considerations: the infrastructural improvements which had been made in Korea in the form of port facilities, railways, roads, etc. According to George McCune such evaluations were for the most part dictated by ideological bias: "When Japan gained a free hand in Korea in 1905, it was complaisantly accepted in Western countries that the Japanese were performing yeoman's service to the rationalized ideals of Western imperialism, and that Japan by her precociousness had demonstrated that she could be deputized to carry part of the white man's burden in the Far East."[23]

In fact, the devastating effects of the relatively highly developed infrastructure introduced in Korea by Japan demonstrate precisely the fallacy of many past as well as present-day concepts concerning development in the Third World. When inadequate infrastructure is cited as the main reason for economic underdevelopment it is often forgotten that the exploitation of a colony—turning it into a satellite—also requires the creation of a certain infrastructure. Objectively, such an infrastructure may of course at a later date have a definite value for the population in question. But in the short run it mainly benefits foreign firms, facilitating the economic infiltration of these countries.

Infrastructural development in Korea not only was considered important for Japanese exploitation of agriculture, forestry, and mining industries, but also was motivated by geopolitical considerations. Japan's plans for the conquest of Manchuria made a developed communication system more necessary than was the case in most other colonial areas. In 1936, the director of the Government-General Railway Bureau made the following revealing statement:

> With the advent of Manchoukuo as the turning point, there has taken place . . . an almost phenomenal economic development, naturally followed by the spectacular growth of general transportation means. Thus the mighty trio of Government railway lines, private lines and motorcar routes, coupled with the Japan Sea routes . . . has elevated the peninsula to a position more valuable as a land-bridge connecting Japan with the continents of Asia and Europe. Inasmuch as Chōsen constitutes Japan's barricade and life-and-death line of vital importance from a viewpoint of national defense, it is all the more significant to complete the network of transportation in the peninsula.[24]

Since the formal decolonization of Africa and Asia, infractructural projects in the Third World have often been financed by international institutions with motives not very different from those just described in the case of Japan. Such examples as the World Bank's financing of highways in Thailand and the Mekong Delta Project in Southeast Asia (at the time of the American Indochina war in the 1960s) show a strong tendency to let military and strategic factors influence decision-making. On the other hand, these international financial bodies seem to shy away from projects which could make Third World countries more self-reliant and economically independent.[25] Infrastructure, in short, is not a neutral element of modernization, as foreign-aid officials tend to imply. Its character depends entirely on the underlying political motivations.

Absorbing Surplus Capital and Goods

In the sphere of industrialization, European and Japanese capitalism began by investing domestically the surplus generated at home or abroad. This led to the creation of a manufacturing base the products of which soon replaced those supplied by the old handicrafts system.

But in the case of the colonial world (dependent capitalism) the process was completely different. In those countries, the internally generated surplus, instead of being invested locally, was extracted and utilized in the development of the industries of the "mother country." At the same time the introduction of finished manufactured goods into these economies from the outside displaced the small domestic artisans, who were unable to compete with modern means of production. While on the one hand handicraft production was fatally weakened by this influx of mass-produced goods, no local industrial development took place which could have reabsorbed the ruined artisans and peasants, whose situation became desperate. In the cases of Europe and Japan it was, on the contrary, precisely from among the large numbers of ruined artisans that the new industries initially recruited their labor force.

Here, in a nutshell, lies one of the fundamental differences between capitalism in the metropolis and the dependent capitalism of the colony (in the words of Samir Amin). This classical pattern was also followed in the Japanese-Korean relationship. Japan's extraction of a surplus from the Korean agricultural sector and, simultaneously, its opening of Korea as an overseas market for its own manufactured goods, was bound to be damaging to the Koreans:

> A huge army of indigent persons grew up in Korea, for their land was gone and there was no modern industry to absorb them. At this point, Japan had neither time nor money to develop an industry in Korea because Japan had its hands full developing her own industry, which experienced a phenomenal growth during the First World War supplying the allies with war goods. She was importing agricultural products, especially foodstuffs, from Korea, and exporting industrial products to Korea. Her complete control of Korea's economy through trade, after annexation, made it possible

for her to promote more forcefully in that country a typical colonial economy[26]

Japanese investment policies in Korea in the industrial sector, as in agriculture, followed a fluctuating course—a function of their complete subordination to the needs of the metropolis. In order to prevent any competitive industrial development in Korea, in the first decade of Japanese domination only activities necessary for Japanese commerce and transportation were allowed. In that period repair shops, production of bricks, and some food processing were among the few manufacturing activities in the peninsula. After formal annexation in 1910 restrictive laws were passed which made the establishment of new businesses almost impossible. The intention was to preserve a substantial amount of capital for the development of Japan itself. Even the chief of the department of industry was critical of this policy, pointing out that Japanese enterprises could establish branches in Korea only with "extraordinary difficulties" and that "after annexation of Korea its industrial development was consciously checked."[27]

After World War I, however, Japan began to look around for profitable investment possibilities and the value of Korea in this respect became apparent. At the urging of financial interests, a policy of complete freedom for the establishment of Japanese firms in Korea was now put into effect. Following the abolition of investment restrictions in Korea in 1920, the system of tariffs and customs duties was reformed. From the Strait of Korea to the Yalu River, Japanese financiers and manufacturers now had a freer hand than ever before. At first, however, Japanese capital was drawn not to industries requiring large outlays but to such small-scale commercial activities as investment in food processing, land, or agriculture. Only in the harnessing of hydroelectric power in northern Korea did Japanese capital play a preponderant role. The relatively favorable conditions for the generation of hydroelectric power led in time to the establishment of chemical industries which were vital for Japanese activities in Korea as well as in Japan itself.

As mentioned above, World War I played a decisive role in Japan's industrial development as well as in its colonial policies. The world depression in the late twenties, similarly, was bound to have consequences for Japan and, indirectly, for Korea. In order to solve the problem of capital absorption, capitalists in Tokyo now became eager to find profitable investment outlets. Besides providing additional sources of revenue, the export of capital served to stabilize the rate of profit in Japan by relieving the internal market of surplus funds. By fulfilling this role as stabilizers of the capital markets of countries with surplus capital, colonies have, at times, helped to harmonize the development of the "mother countries" in the field of finance.

Nipponese Military Efforts and their Effects on Korea

The development of militarism was another aspect of Japan's attempt to overcome the effects of the world crisis. Economic and military expansion went hand in hand, and this process was accelerated by the Japanese intrusion in China, resulting in the so-called Manchurian Incident.[28] With the establishment of Manchoukuo as a Japanese puppet state and the creation of a garrison state in Japan, Korea's strategic raw materials gained increased importance.

Table 4 illustrates the fluctuations of the mining industry in accordance with the needs of the colonial power. Grajdanzev sees these figures as corresponding to three distinct periods: (1) the rather slow development before the Mukden Incident, (2) a fall in production in 1921-1922 and 1930-1931 due to the international depression, and (3) a rapid increase in output after 1931 with the militarization of the Japanese economy. A further indication of the importance of Korean natural resources for Japan's eco-

Table 4
Value of Mining Products Including Coal
(in 1,000 yen)

1910	6,068	1929	26,488
1915	10,516	1931	21,746
1920	24,205	1936	110,430
1922	14,503	1937	150,000

Source: *Chosen Keizai Nempo,* 1939 (quoted in Grajdanzev, *Modern Korea,* p. 139).

nomic and military build-up was the increase of the mining labor force from 36,000 to about 220,000 between 1931 and 1938.

Throughout Japan's development, utilization of Korea's natural wealth had also been important in a more indirect manner. Thus, while Japan sought to achieve a high degree of autarky, certain products were still unavailable within the empire and had to be obtained through exchange with foreign countries. Many Korean resources were exported to foreign markets in order to pay for Japan's import of needed goods. It was with this objective in mind that tax exemptions and government subsidies were granted to Japanese firms engaged in the extraction of minerals in Korea between 1934 and 1939. Since Korean gold was a source of foreign exchange, with which Japan could obtain iron, oil, copper, and other materials from the United States, production of this precious metal was given high priority by the colonial authorities.[29] But when in 1941 Japan was cut off from the world market by the war, gold production in Korea declined and the mining machinery, which could be used in the war effort, was dismantled.

Japanese war preparations gave rise to an increased development of Korea's heavy industrial sector. In 1936, the production of chemicals, machine tools, iron, and steel represented only 28 percent of the value of total industrial production. By 1939, this figure had reached 47 percent.

> But this industrialization of Korea did not bring about the development of Korean-owned industry, for nearly all large industries were Japanese enterprises, established for the most part with the capital of the big *zaibatsu* (cartels) such as the Mitsui, Sumitomo, Noguchi, and Mitsubishi. It was only through the investment of such monopolistic capital that Korea could be industrialized and turned into a military supply base.[30]

In Korea, the alliance of Japanese finance capital with militarism was complete.

To organize the war effort the Japan-Korea-Manchuria Resource Mobilization Plan was set up, thereby draining further resources from the colonies. At the same time, transportation and communication facilities took on increased importance for the Japanese and were developed, obviously for military purposes, to a point far in excess of local needs.

For large segments of the indigenous population this new aspect of Japanese economic policies brought further hardships. This was especially the case in the agricultural sector, where farmers had been forced by unfavorable conditions to supplement their meager earnings through the development of domestic industries. Textiles, household utensils, farm implements, oils, ceramics, bricks and tiles, paper, and furniture were produced as well as food, straw shoes, straw mats, baskets, and other grassware products. Besides giving farmers a much needed source of additional income, such activities served to make daily necessities accessible to the local population. These activities continued as long as raw materials were available. But with growing Japanese encroachment on the economy, resources were increasingly monopolized by the colonial power, squeezing out this form of domestic industry. In some cases, the Japanese authorities even applied legal sanctions against those household industries which, from the Japanese viewpoint, were considered undesirable.[31] As a matter of fact, by the end of the period of Japanese domination, consumer goods production had almost completely disappeared in Korea.[32]

Whatever industrialization did take place in the peninsula was entirely dominated by the relationship of interdependency between Japan and Korea. These industries were never meant to function independently, in fact, since most of them produced only semifinished goods. What they represented could hardly be called industrialization in any meaningful sense. According to McCune,

> industry in Korea was such an integral part of the economy of Greater Japan that most of the industrial plant existing in Korea at the end of the war was incapable of independent existence. For capital goods Korea relied almost wholly upon Japan, and certain important stages in the production of consumer goods also depended on Japanese parts or supplies . . . light bulbs were fabricated in Korea, but the tungsten filaments used in these bulbs were manufactured in Japan, even though Korea was a large producer of tungsten ores. The ore was shipped to Japan to be refined and manufactured into wire, which was then shipped back to Korea for use in the production of light bulbs.[33]

This particular division of labor, so well known from European colonialism, is the real foundation of economic domination. In fact, the conclusions McCune arrived at with regard to Korea may still be considered relevant to many countries in the Third World today:

> In summary it may be said that the development which took place during the period of Japanese rule in Korea hardly constituted a Korean economy. Koreans appreciably shared neither in the direction of this development nor in its benefits. The Korean economy was Japanese-owned and Japanese-directed and in no sense an entity in and of itself, but rather the geographical location of a portion of the wider configuration of the economy of Japan.[34]

This interdependence became especially pronounced in

the last hectic months of World War II, when industry in Korea was stripped of everything that could be used for military purposes. This rapacity reached a climax when, just before surrender, the Japanese destroyed machinery, sabotaged all important industrial and transportation facilities, and set underwater mines in the north in order to prevent Koreans from making use of these resources.

The Exploitation of Korean Labor

One of the preconditions for the Japanese geopolitical strategy in Asia was the availability of labor for Japanese enterprises not only in Korea, but in Japan itself. Thousands of Korean workers were sent to Japan to work under conditions of extreme hardship in mines, shipyards, and plants. "American forces who captured Japanese islands in the farflung stretches of the Pacific," Shannon McCune tells us, "almost invariably rounded up hosts of Korean laborers whose job had been to build fortifications and construct air-fields. They had been unwilling allies at best."[35]

In Korea itself working conditions were harder than any mere figures can express. Nevertheless, we can get some notion of the situation from the following statistics, yielded by Grajdanzev's patient investigations. Hours of work in small- or medium-sized enterprises—i.e., the majority—were as long as twelve to thirteen per day, exclusive of time for lunch. In large-scale enterprises men worked an average of ten hours, women and children about eleven hours. Due to the shortage of materials for nonmilitary production, from 1939 on working hours for women and children (employed mostly in light industry) were slightly reduced. In 1938, about 30 percent of all industrial workers were women and 10 percent were children (with the latter being distributed unequally—for example, chidren made up 22 percent of the work force in textiles). Wages, furthermore, were so low that only when several members of the same family worked could they subsist. "The Korean worker cannot support himself," writes Grajdanzev, going on to point out that since workers were usually brought up in farm families, the expenses of their rearing were often borne by the backward village economy.[36] The importance of this factor is further described by the Japanese historian Hatada:

> The poverty-ridden Korean farm villages were, at the same time, an important foundation for the industrialization of Korea inasmuch as they provided a source of plentiful, cheap labor accustomed to harsh conditions such as long hours and low wages. This labor pool was highly valued by Japanese capitalists, for it made possible large colonial profits. An ample supply of labor in all fields, much cheaper than the so-called cheap labor market of Japan, and the ability to oppress this labor force much more severely than was possible in Japan—these were important factors in the attraction of Japanese capital to Korea during its industrialization.[37]

Apart from these "normal" conditions of work, a great number of public works—roads, railroads, bridges, fortifications, etc.—were constructed by Korean forced labor—often without payment. It should be added that the land upon which the roads, etc. were built was usually confiscated without compensation. Although we are hardly likely to find the statistics to prove it, we may safely assume that many Koreans literally worked themselves to death.

In its undeclared war with China, Japan even used Koreans on the front line in a so-called volunteer system. These same troops were used inside Korea for propaganda and law-and-order purposes. In 1942 the "volunteers" were replaced by a draft system, which meant that "the mobilization of students, conscription, military training and other measures, identical with those in force in Japan, were applied in Korea to a colonial population that had no voice whatever in the matter."[38]

Korea's transition from a precapitalist stage to peripheral capitalism (a semifeudal, colonial economy) implied profound social changes. Thus the Japanese influx had the effect of changing the old Korean class relations. Not only was the old *yangban* rule replaced by an organized civil service backed by military power, but the *yangban* class soon became outnumbered by Japanese nationals. In 1940 Japanese nationals represented 3.2 percent of the Korean population.[39] This presence of a large Japanese ruling class in both Korea and Taiwan was a feature peculiar to Japanese colonialism, setting it apart from Western colonialism in other Asian countries.

Occupationally the greatest number of these Japanese (41.4 percent in 1937) were in government services, where they monopolized the most important functions. This compared with 2.9 percent of Koreans in similar jobs.[40] In industry and commerce the respective percentages were as follows in 1938:

	Japanese	*Koreans*
Industry	16.6	2.6
Commerce	23.4	6.5

Most Koreans (75.7 percent) were still in agriculture at this time. But just as important, perhaps, as the occupational divisions was the fact that a kind of physical separation had taken place, with 71 percent of the Japanese population living in urban areas, as opposed to 11.5 percent of Koreans. Gregory Henderson has called this a system of "de facto apartheid":

> ... differences tended to increase rather than narrow as expansion and war made the Japanese an increasingly prosperous elite while raising appreciably the living standards of only few Koreans. Koreans watched a rising tide of government and of economic modernization: from full participation in both they were separated by a thick layer of alien elite filling almost all important jobs. It was a phenomenon

not often found in colonialism—perhaps the rule of the French in Tunisia offers a rare parallel.[41]

Cultural Imperialism

From the first, resistance on the part of the Korean people had an influence on Japanese policy-making. Thus in August 1919, after the rice riots in Japan and huge demonstrations in Korea, the so-called cultural rule policy was adopted. The policy of trying to buy Korean cooperation, first applied only to a minority of the nobility, was now extended to larger groups among the upper and middle classes. The result was the creation of a pro-Japanese segment of the population who, as small capitalists and landlords, participated in the exploitation of the majority and developed a comprador relationship with the colonial power. Jon Halliday points out, "this stratum subsequently provided the link between Japanese and American rule" in the southern part of the country.[42]

War preparations intensified the need to win Korean allegiance. With this objective in mind, various new reforms were introduced in the cultural sphere. In 1938, the last remnants of Korean education were abolished, with all schools now required to follow the Japanese system. Three principles, all of them clearly intended for purposes of indoctrination, made up the basic educational policy: (1) "clarifying the national policy," (2) "Japan and Korea as one"—thus obliterating Korean culture—and (3) "training to endure hardship." Koreans were henceforth expected to behave as imperial Japanese subjects. After renewed Japanese aggression in China (1937) an oath of allegiance was drawn up. Students were forced to recite the following pledges in their classes each morning: "We are subjects of the empire of Greater Japan. We unite our hearts in striving to give loyalty and service to the emperor. We will learn to endure hardships and be strong upright citizens."[43] It was already the policy for all school principals, as well as almost all court magistrates, to be appointed by the Japanese.

To accelerate the transformation of Koreans into Japanese subjects, the use of the Korean language in schools was forbidden and Korean newspapers banned. Similarly, certain customs practiced in Japan were transferred to Korea. After 1939, on the first of each month a "Day of Service for the Rise of Asia" was observed. Koreans were made to alter their family names to conform to the Japanese style; by September 1940, 80 percent of the total population had actually been forced to change names. The policies of Japanese imperialism in Korea thus victimized nearly all sectors of the population economically, culturally, and politically.

This extreme colonialist exploitation and subjugation may account for the fact that the anti-Japanese nationalist movement in Korea, as we shall see, at an early date became oriented toward the political objectives of class struggle.

Notes

1. E.W. Zimmerman, *World Resources and Industries* (New York: Harper & Row, 1951), pp. 456, 525, 718.
2. E. Herbert Norman, *Japan's Emergence as a Modern State* (New York: Inst. Pacific Relations, 1946), p. 46.
3. Cf. Paul A. Baran, *The Political Economy of Growth* (New York: Monthly Review Press, 1962), p. 160. [Sociopsychological resistance to imposed modernization in colonial areas has often been interpreted as "backwardness" but, as demonstrated by Frantz Fanon in *Les Damnés de la terre* (Paris, 1966), is in reality part of an anti-imperialist reaction, the reverse aspect of colonialism.]
4. Baran, *Political Economy of Growth,* p. 160.
5. V.I. Lenin, *Sochinenya (Works),* vol. 15, 4th ed. (Moscow: Progress Publishers 1947), p. 161 (quoted by Baran, *Political Economy of Growth,* p. 161).
6. Samir Amin, *L'Accumulation à l'échelle mondiale* (Dakar, 1970), p.

168 [in English as *Accumulation on a World Scale* (New York: Monthly Review Press, 1974)]. In the following we use the terms "peripheral capitalism," "underdevelopment," and "colonial deformation" to describe what we perceive not so much as a condition but as a process based on the particular structure of production relations formed by colonialism and neo-colonialism. Cf. Paul A. Baran, *The Political Economy of Growth*; Yves Lacoste, *Géographie du sous-développement* (Paris, 1965); Andre Gunder Frank, *Capitalism and Underdevelopment in Latin America* (New York: Monthly Review Press, 1967); Pierre Jalée, *The Pillage of the Third World* (New York: Monthly Review Press, 1968); and Samir Amin, *L'Accumulation a l'échelle mondiale,* to mention only a few.

7. George McCune, *Korea Today* (Cambridge, Mass.: Harvard Univ. Press, 1950), p. 33.
8. Such violent intervention also characterized Western colonization of Africa. Cf. Mamadou Dia, *Réflexions sur l'Economie de l'Afrique Noire,* coll. "Enquetes et études" (Paris, 1953), pp. 27-30, and W. Rodney, *How Europe Underdeveloped Africa* (Dar es Salaam and London: Tanzania Publishing House and Bogle L'Ouverture, 1972).
9. Amin, *L'Accumulation,* p. 169.
10. Takashi Hatada, *A History of Korea* (Santa Barbara, Cal.: American Bibliographic Center-Clio Press, 1969), p. 113.
11. *The Historical Experience of the Agrarian Reform in Our Country* (Pyongyang, 1974), pp. 6-7.
12. Shannon McCune, *Korea's Heritage* (Rutland Vt.: Charles Tuttle, 1964), p. 86.
13. *The Historical Experience,* p. 13.
14. McCune, *Korea Today,* p. 129.
15. Hatada, *History of Korea,* p. 126.
16. Ibid., p. 127.
17. *The Annual Report on the Administration of Chōsen, 1934-35,* p. 116 [quoted by Andrew J. Grajdanzev, *Modern Korea* (New York: John Day, 1944), p. 108].
18. Cf. McCune, *Korea Today,* p. 36.
19. Grajdanzev, *Modern Korea,* p. 92-92.
20. *Toyo Keizai* (the *Oriental Economist*), October 20, 1940 (quoted by Grajdanzev, *Modern Korea,* p. 117).
21. *The Historical Experience,* p. 13.
22. Grajdansev, *Modern Korea,* p. 127.
23. McCune, *Korea Today,* p. 29.
24. Kon Yushida, "Overland Transportation in Chōsen," *Japan and Manchoukuo, 1935-36,* (Tokyo: Japan Publishing Co., 1936), p. 79 (quoted in McCune, *Korea Today,* p. 40).
25. One example was the refusal by the West to construct the Tanzam

Japanese Colonialism 65

railway between Tanzania and landlocked Zambia in West Africa. When China came forward with a proposal to carry through the project, it came as an unpleasant surprise to the industrial world. It is well known that the West has large economic interests in Rhodesia and thus could see no advantage in a project that could have enabled Zambia to export its copper via Dar-es-Salaam, bypassing white-ruled colonial areas.

26. Hatada, *History of Korea*, p. 114.
27. Grajdanzev, *Modern Korea*, p. 53.
28. The Manchurian (or Mukden) Incident refers to the Japanese attack on North China in 1931 which led to the establishment of the Japanese puppet state Manchoukuo in 1932.
29. The strong official U.S. criticism of Japan's attack on China in 1937 did not prevent the two countries from carrying on "business as usual": "during 1938 she provided Japan with 90.9% of her copper imports, 90.4% of her scrap iron and steel, 76.9% of her aircraft and plane parts imports, 65.6% of her petroleum needs, and many of her other sinews of war. This trade continued to the very eve of Pearl Harbour." [R.T. Oliver, *The Truth About Korea* (London, 1951), p. 37.]
30. Hatada, *History of Korea*, p. 122.
31. Grajdanzev, *Modern Korea*, p. 152.
32. McCune, *Korea Today*, p. 36.
33. Ibid., p. 140.
34. Ibid., p. 37.
35. McCune, *Korea's Heritage*, p. 105.
36. Grajdanzev, *Modern Korea*, p. 182.
37. Hatada, *History of Korea*, p. 127. Often the profits reaped in Korea were double those of Japanese firms in Japan. Furthermore, a survey published in the spring of 1940 showed Japanese ownership of 81.7 percent of the paidup capital of all industrial enterprises in Korea, ranging from an exceptionally low 36 percent in medicines and drugs to a high of 97 percent in the chemical industry. [Cf. Jerome B. Cohen, *Japan's Economy in War and Reconstruction* (New York: Oxford Univ. Press, 1949), p. 36.]
38. Hatada, *History of Korea*, p. 126.
39. Gregory Henderson, *Korea—The Politics of the Vortex* (Cambridge, Mass: Harvard Univ. Press, 1968), p. 75.
40. Ibid., p. 75, and Grajdanzev, *Modern Korea*, pp. 75-81.
41. Henderson, *Korea*, pp. 75-76.
42. Jon Halliday, "The Korean Revolution," *Three Articles on the Korean Revolution 1945-1953* (mimeographed publication from the Association for Radical East Asian Studies, London, presumably 1972), p. 4. Halliday adds that during the U.S. occupation (after 1945)

this process was promoted by the fact that many of these Koreans had been educated by Western missionaries in a Western language.
43. Hatada, *History of Korea,* p. 124.

Chapter 3
Anti-Imperialist Resistance

While imposing its colonial rule on Korea, Japan at the same time became the target of deep resentment on the part of the majority of Korean nationals. Actually, resistance began on the very first day of Japanese rule and never stopped. But poverty and political persecution forced many Koreans into exile during the years of Japanese domination. Some went to Manchuria and Siberia, others to China, Japan, and the United States. Even among these exiles, however, the flame of nationalism was very much alive; they never lost touch with events in their homeland.

International events also contributed to the development of Korean nationalism. The end of World War I had stimulated revolutions in Russia and in various Central European countries. At about the same time American President Woodrow Wilson had proclaimed the doctrine of national "self-determination." Probably this doctrine was prompted mainly by political considerations—the desire to hamper the unification of nationalities in revolutionary Russia as well as to take advantage of European postwar weakness to gain a foothold in the colonial world—still, its idealistic terminology raised the hopes of oppressed nations. For Koreans, among others, all these events were a subject of heated discussion and debate.

The March 1st Independence Movement

From the start, there was clearly a vital spirit of nationalism among the Korean people, and this widespread sentiment soon evolved into a mass movement. Although the main causes of popular unrest were the extreme, harsh, and medieval methods of the Japanese oppressors, the earliest massive demonstration of nationalism took place in January 1919, upon the death of the old Emperor Yi T'aewang. The disappearance of one of the last symbols of the Korean nation provided the spark for the Korean independence movement, whose strength and resourcefulness surprised the Japanese authorities. Basing himself on Korean and Anglo-Saxon sources, the American author Cornelius Osgood gives the following vivid description of an event which was to become the living symbol of anti-Japanese resistance:

> ... suddenly and without warning an extraordinary thing happened. On the afternoon of March 1, 1919, thirty of the most prominent Koreans in the country, having signed a proclamation of independence, sent a copy to the Governor-General with their compliments. After this the Central Police Station was called, the action explained, and the men awaited arrest which followed as soon as the astounded officers could arrive. While being driven to prison, great crowds cheered them from the streets. The people by this time were fully aware of the nature of the occasion for at two o'clock special copies of the proclamation had been read by appointed delegates in public places over the country ...
>
> The immediate spread of peaceful demonstrations over Korea was phenomenal and clearly the result of a carefully planned program. How such organization was achieved unseen by the hawklike eyes of the Japanese secret police soon became one of the most incredible aspects of the whole situation. ... A mimeographed sheet called "The Independence News" appeared on the day of the proclamation and daily for months thereafter. It is reported that the Governor-General found two copies on his desk every morning and that the Japanese were completely baffled by their almost spontaneous and universal appearance.

The popular action consisted primarily in meeting at a predetermined point . . . march[ing] down the streets shouting "Manse," the ancient national cheer, until dispersed by the police . . . The completely national character of the demonstrations was shown by the fact that coolies, nobles, scholars and preachers, children and aged, male and female, walked side by side. Some policemen who worked for the Japanese changed into civilian clothes and joined the crowd, stores and schools closed, and economic life came almost to a standstill.[1]

But those Koreans who had hoped that these actions would draw world attention to their plight got nothing but uneasy statements of sympathy. And since they were completely unarmed in the face of a merciless and modern Japanese army, the result was a veritable bloodbath. Tens of thousands were arrested, filling the jails to overflowing, while peaceful demonstrators were attacked in the most brutal manner. Week after week this terror continued; in some cases, entire villages in the countryside were burned down. Osgood concludes his narrative, saying, "There is reason to believe that Koreans gave one of the most extraordinary examples of passive resistance to foreign domination that the world has ever seen."

In order to discredit Korean nationalism, the Japanese authorities in their annual report blamed German as well as "Bolshevik" influence for these events. There was some truth to the latter accusation in the sense that the Soviet Revolution was undoubtedly an indirect source of hope and inspiration for many oppressed peoples. In any case, the March 1st Movement had shown a greater combativeness and readiness for action on the part of the masses than either its leaders or the Japanese had anticipated.

The Militancy of the Anti-Japanese Struggle

One lesson which the March 1st Independence Movement had taught nationalists was the need to rely on their own forces and not to expect aid from foreign nations.

While the March 1st Movement originally had been under the influence of petty bourgeois elements (officials of the Yi dynasty and intellectuals), the independence movement from then on became increasingly dominated by workers, farmers, students, and progressive intellectuals. The struggle against Japanese domination now developed along socialist lines with Communists playing an important role. The founding in 1925 of a Communist Party was an indication that revolutionary ideas had penetrated deep into Korea. Even though the Party was dissolved in 1928 because of repression, internal divisions, and a failure to become firmly rooted in the concrete situation, Marxist influence persisted. Nearly all social disorders and conflicts from then on directly or indirectly involved these new elements.

In the 1920s and 1930s there was a succession of militant strikes and demonstrations. In 1926, the June 10th Independence Movement developed into a mass demonstration against the Japanese. In 1929 a general strike took place in Wonsan, completely paralyzing industry and transportation in the area for several months and gaining support in all corners of the country. In the same year a nationwide student movement arose under the slogan "Down with Japanese imperialism!" In 1930 a strike of workers in the Sinheung coal mine set off militant actions throughout the region. In Canchun county, South Hamgyung province, 3,000 peasants raided the Japanese county office and the police station and a whole series of riots, demonstrations, and tenancy disputes broke out in Hamgyung, Kangwon, Julla and Pyungan provinces. Among the Korean minority across the border in the Chintao district of northeast China, great struggles such as the Autumn Harvest Riot and the Spring Famine Riot swept the countryside.

In all these movements, Communists played an active role. According to the liberal Korean writer Dae-Sook Suh, who can hardly be accused of harboring pro-Communist sympathies, their activities made them a more important political force in Korea than the other currents of anti-Japanese resistance:

> They [the Communists] succeeded in wresting control of the Korean revolution from the Nationalists; they planted a deep core of Communist influence among the Korean people, particularly the students, youth groups, laborers, and peasants. Their fortitude and, at times, obstinate determination to succeed had a profound influence on Korean intellectuals and writers. To the older Koreans, who had groveled so long before seemingly endless foreign suppression, communism seemed a new hope or a magic torch from which they hoped to gain revolutionary strength. To the young, it was a new approach to the solution of age-old social problems and stratification, from which their forefathers had suffered so long. Among the intellectuals, communism prompted a reappraisal, not of capitalism, but of traditional Korean society; they applied the new method of analysis to the difficulties facing Korea. For Koreans in general, the sacrifices of the Communists, if not the idea of communism, made a strong appeal, far stronger than any occasional bomb-throwing exercise of the Nationalists. The haggard appearance of Communists suffering from torture, their stern and disciplined attitude toward the common enemy of all Koreans, had a far-reaching effect on the people.[2]

As mentioned above, because of Japanese repression and miserable economic conditions, many Koreans had been forced into exile. And to the north, just accross the Chinese border, the struggle against the Japanese continued. In 1920 the Japanese, having been defeated by Koreans in an attack on Hunchun (a town on Chinese soil), "wreaked their vengeance upon wholly peaceful people in the Kando (Chientao) region. They slaughtered 4,000 Koreans and burned their bodies in the center of the principal town."[3]

The most important resistance activities were centered in these border regions. But inside China as well, the Korean minority was fighting the Japanese and their allies. A Korean column even participated in the Long March. There were also some very militant groups active in Japan. Thus, Koreans were being exposed to revolutionary ideas and experiences, and the Japanese could not put a stop to it. In 1933 the Japanese Governor-General Ugaki made a speech noting that communism and other subversive ideas were entering Korea from Japan: "What greatly concerns me are the Korean students and laborers crossing to Japan Proper who are apt to introduce various radical thoughts into Chōsen after being infected in Japan Proper."[4]

During the first decades of colonial dominance, individual groups had already been engaging in armed struggle. But after the Japanese overran Manchuria, attempts were made to step up the resistance by organizing these disparate groups and formations. Thus to a certain extent, the Japanese act of aggression worked to internationalize the conflict. For example, the United Association of Movements for the Revival of Korea under Kim Koo, with its seat in Chungking (China), had the support of the Kuomingtang government. Its importance has often been exaggerated by Western historians—in reality, it seems to have had little influence on the liberation struggle. By far the strongest resistance to colonial authorities came from the anti-Japanese movement that developed in the border area. The reasons for this were both political and geographical: a large proportion of the inhabitants were people who had earlier been forced by the Japanese to leave their native soil and who therefore nursed strong anti-imperialist sentiments. Thus, both class composition and political consciousness favored resistance in this area. Geographically, moreover, the steep mountainous terrain made possible sustained guerrilla activities. Finally, this border area was well suited for linking up the Korean resistance internally and internationally with that of the Chinese.

During this period an important role was played by the Anti-Japanese Guerrilla Army, a military organization formed in the early 1930s under the leadership of Kim Il Sung, which tried to coordinate the Korean liberation struggle with that of the Chinese. This was a logical course, as many Koreans at the time participated in the Chinese struggle, while not a few Chinese took part in the activities of the Korean resistance: Japan was the common enemy. From base areas in the mountains, Korean Communists not only carried out reforms among the peasants but organized and armed them for the struggle. The army's best-known exploit took place close to the Manchurian border during a raid on the enemy stronghold of Bochombo in 1937. Under the leadership of Kim Il Sung the attack resulted in a Japanese defeat. This victory on Korean soil became a symbol of the resistance movement and further increased the prestige of the Communists above all other political forces. Japanese papers at the time concluded that many of the strikes, revolts, and demonstrations inside Korea received their impetus and inspiration from tales of the exploits of the guerrilla army.[5] At the same time united front organizations were active all over Korea, some of them under the direct leadership of this center in the border area. Throughout the length of World War II anti-Japanese activities and political agitation were carried on.

Liberation and Division of Korea

Since the struggle against the Japanese was part of an international conflict, it was bound to be affected by events outside of Korea as well as by the success of the resistance movement. With the capitulation of Germany in May 1945, it became obvious that the day of Japanese collapse was fast approaching. A few months later, on August 8, 1945, the Soviet Union declared war against Japan and its Red Army attacked the Japanese Kwangtung Army in Manchuria.[6] On August 12, Soviet troops, together with Korean partisan units, marched into Korea as liberators.[7]

Although the United States was eager to get an early Japanese capitulation, the collapse of Japanese resistance came sooner than expected—an unwelcome surprise for American policy-makers. Since there was no American military presence in Korea which could have forestalled the liberation of the peninsula by the Soviet Red Army and Korean partisans, the U.S. government requested the Soviet Union to stop its advance at the 38th Parallel and await the arrival of the American troops. The implication was that there would be a temporary division of the country, with the Russians accepting the Japanese surrender in the North and the Americans in the South. This was agreed to by the Russian ally "as a military expediency and courtesy," according to D.F. Fleming.[8] Contrary to popular belief, this partition of Korea had never been the subject of discussions between the wartime allies, but was a unilateral American decision.[9] In view of the current situation it seems fair to conclude that the United States in fact wanted to prevent full Korean independence. It had been agreed that the Japanese colonies of Taiwan and Manchuria would be returned to China after the war. But the idea of independence for Korea was opposed by both the United States and Great Britain. At a meeting on February 8, 1945, President Roosevelt had declared to Generalissimo Stalin that he would like to see a trusteeship over Korea, stating "that the only experience the United States had in such matters was in the Philippines. He added that it had taken about 40 years for the Philippine people to be prepared for self-government, but 'in the case of Korea, the period might be from 20 to 30 years.' "[10] According to one source, Stalin's reply to this proposal had been "why was there any need for trusteeship if the Koreans could produce a satisfactory government?"[11]

However, a few months after liberation, during a conference in Moscow in December 1945, a joint commission was established to find a solution to the division of Korea and to work toward the independence of the country. The time limit for this trusteeship was set at five years. Under existing conditions this was seen as the best settlement possible between the two parties.

Anti-Imperialist Resistance 75

The Moscow decisions were first made known in a Moscow radio broadcast on December 27, 1945, followed by a Tass commentary explaining that American aims at the conference had been to secure a permanent division of the country and that the Joint Commission was the best compromise that could be salvaged at that time.[12]

The American attitude was shaped by events in Asia generally—and in Korea particularly—and the challenge they posed to Washington. From the United States point of view, it was feared that genuinely anticolonialist forces would take advantage of the new situation created by the breakdown of Japanese imperialism. On August 14, 1945, the 38th Parallel proposal was promulgated by Truman in the document known as General Order No. 1. Its purpose was to "avoid political defeat in the wake of the war and to counter the resistance in Asia" as it attempted "to redefine the distribution of power throughout the entire Far East."[13] As Jon Halliday points out, this directive "drew a new political map not based on military presence, and only imperfectly related to the international agreements between the powers," not to mention the interests of the peoples involved![14] As far as U.S. policy in Korea was concerned, the Order "commanded the Japanese to aid and assist the Allied takeover in the precise manner MacArthur dictated, and above all not to surrender to unauthorized local armed resistance groups."[15]

American worries centered on the fact that even though the Red Army had not crossed the 38th Parallel, in South Korea political forces were proceeding to disarm the Japanese and set up a new local administration. On August 28, 1945, a wire from the Japanese commander in Korea was received at MacArthur's headquarters stating that "Communists and independence agitators are plotting to take advantage of this situation to disturb peace and order."[16] In the face of such a situation, the American answer was unequivocal: "It is directed that you maintain order and preserve the machinery of government south of the 38th degree . . . until my forces assume those responsibilities."[17] Such interimperialist collaboration between former enemies when confronted with popular liberation movements was also practiced in Indochina and Indonesia. Above the 38th Parallel the course of events was quite different. Confronted with the advancing Soviet army and Korean partisans, the Japanese, as mentioned above, sabotaged all important economic facilities so that the means of production would not fall into the hands of the Koreans. Rather than face the consequences of their actions, the Japanese preferred to flee south and await the arrival of the American forces. Thus, while the relationship between the Japanese and the liberating forces in the north was a hostile one, "in the south the Japanese assumed an attitude of guileless cooperation towards the occupying authorities."[18]

The American Intervention

The different forms of liberation experienced by North and South were bound to influence subsequent developments. Two key factors were the American attitude toward Korean politics and the deteriorating relationship between two former allies, the United States and the Soviet Union, each of whom now occupied one part of Korea. Under these circumstances the partition of Korea, originally meant only as a temporary expedient, became solidified and developed into a source of tension:

> ... from virtually the beginning of occupation this demarcation was a far more effective dividing boundary than most national frontiers. As time went on the zonal division hardened all phases of Korean life into two separate patterns. As the Korean problem became lined with the dismal course of U.S.-Soviet relations, Korea was alienated against itself despite the fundamental homogeneity of the Korean people. This division came to be the dominant force in Korean political and economic affairs.[19]

Although the attitudes of the two big powers were thus

of great importance, internal elements were to play a decisive role. After nearly forty years of domination by a foreign power which had attempted to destroy the Korean identity, nationalism now re-emerged as a major political force. Koreans, unamimously hailed the Japanese defeat, viewing liberation as the beginning of a new era of independence and greater social justice. An unprecedented upsurge of political activity took place in the period between the Japanese capitulation and the arrival of American troops, with Korean nationalists and Communists expressing and organizing themselves openly. Political prisoners were liberated; collaborators were punished; preparations were even made for a future land reform. People's committees were formed throughout the country to replace the Japanese colonial administration. In the North these committees were able to operate under the benevolent eye of the Soviet Union. It would be wrong, however, to consider them mere "agents of Soviet policy" since they were made up of elements from the whole range of the political spectrum, including religious leaders and conservative politicians.

In the South the situation was extremely complex. Prior to the American entry, a government composed of various political tendencies had been formed in Seoul on September 6, 1945. Thus, when the U.S. forces, under the command of General Hodge, landed at Inchon two days later, they were met by a welcoming committee from the Korean government. But the weakness of this political body soon became apparent. Although it was ostensibly intended to create a so-called "People's Republic" consisting of both North and South, there is little evidence that it was truly representative. This "People's Republic" was supported by some Communists in Seoul, but it was not accepted in the North, where it was looked on as the work of a handful of people. This northern attitude was in part a reflection of complex factional disputes within the Korean Communist movement over which course to pursue. The North Koreans argue—perhaps with a certain element of self-justification—that two erroneous tendencies were threatening the entire political project at this time:

> The rightwing capitulationists headed by the spy, Pak Hun Yung, and his followers, speaking on behalf of the pro-Japanese landlords and capitalists, insisted that our country must be a "people's republic," by which he meant a bourgeois republic. The extreme leftist elements, ignoring the objective requirements of our society's development, asserted that the stage of democratic revolution should be skipped and that a proletarian dictatorship should be established to carry out a socialist revolution.[20]

The U.S. occupation forces at once proclaimed a military government. Not only were Japanese retained in their administrative positions but the people's committees were soon declared illegal. General Hodge even went so far as to rearm some Japanese, and there were incidents in which these armed Japanese opened fire on Koreans demonstrating for independence. Colonial property rights, which had dominated most of the economy, were reaffirmed. English was proclaimed the official language. Anti-American feeling began to spread as Koreans saw themselves robbed of their newly acquired independence. The people felt, as E. Grant Meade put it, that "The liberators had become the oppressors."[21]

Meanwhile, as far as the government of the "People's Republic" was concerned, internal strife, as well as its lack of mass participation and links with the people's committees in the countryside, robbed it of whatever significance it may once have possessed. As an American specialist in Korean affairs remarked, "The KPR organization in Seoul had its faults as well. It was quickly riven by factions and general disunity; some of this can be explained by Japanese and American pressure, but it is also true that its leaders had little experience with a political movement with strong roots in the countryside. They tended to think, incorrectly, that maneuvering in Seoul was the key to power."[22]

Simultaneously, ultra-conservative and former collaborationist elements within South Korea were strengthened by the U.S. presence. There was also an influx of rightist Korean politicians from China and America, including the seventy-year-old Syngman Rhee who returned from his exile in the United States on a U.S. air force plane.[23] Any objective evaluation of American policies at the time shows that Washington's refusal to reconcile itself to the post-liberation political evolution on the peninsula and its denial of recognition to these internal political forces through its outlawing of the "people's committees" amounted to blatant interference in the Korean independence movement. Later developments can invariably be traced back to this intervention. But as stated by the liberal Korean scholar, Soon Sung Cho, "America was not necessarily ready to grant Korea independence at the expense of its own national interests."[24]

Opposition to the American Efforts

From then on, development went in opposite directions on either side of the 38th Parallel. The Americans faced a political dilemma which was the direct legacy of colonialism: with all nationalist activities suppressed and the majority of the people reduced to poverty, under the Japanese a moderate nationalist movement had been unable to develop. As Takashi Hatada puts it: "The majority of the people had become paupers, and political activities had been suppressed. Under these circumstances, a moderate nationalist movement could not develop, and it was inevitable that Korean nationalism would be led by radicals and leftists." The fact that there had been no opportunity for the development of native Korean capitalism further influenced internal policies. And with liberation, the desire for complete independence and social reforms regained its full vigor. Going against the popular sentiment for reunification, the American military government pushed Syngman Rhee into power, since he was one of the very few political figures opposing all contacts with the North. From the beginning, and with U.S. backing, Rhee adopted an anti-Communist platform and suppressed all movements for the country's unification "because unification movements were not accepted at their face value but feared as fronts for revolutionary and destructive activities."[25] This type of political oppression, coumpounded by economic difficulties, could not fail to call forth resistance.

Resistance began as early as 1946, with the Taegu Rebellion. This revolt, which very soon reached "prairie fire" dimensions, was a consequence of the government's anti-Communist campaign and resulted in the killing of about fifty policemen and civilians. The *Chicago Sun* described it in the following terms:

> It was a full-scale revolution, which must have involved hundreds of thousands, if not millions of people. In Taegu alone a third of the 150,000 inhabitants took part in the uprising.... The railroad workers went on strike, followed by the phone and metal, textile and electric workers. As each strike was suppressed by the police, another took its place. Students went to the streets to demonstrate....
>
> From the city, the revolution spread into the countryside and was taken over by the share-croppers. The farmers refused to surrender their rice to the police. They attacked the homes of the landlords, and then the police stations. They tore jail doors to release arrested share-croppers, they burned the records and stole the weapons.[26]

An important source of difficulties—besides the nationalist feeling—was the economic situation. This was further complicated by the partition, each zone suffering from being cut off from its complementary part. The only remedy lay in economic and democratic reforms which could get the previously Japanese-centered economy moving again. But such reforms failed to materialize, chiefly because only extreme rightist circles were willing to cooperate with the occupation forces. Under such conditions the American attitude was dominated by two concerns: a policy of nationalization would have antagonized conservative elements in the United States itself, as well as in Korea, with no assurance that the state could perform such a task efficiently; on the other hand, handing over means of production and resources to private individuals who had had little to do with their development seemed to have ideological limitations. Accordingly, Koreans were temporarily appointed to manage firms "on behalf of the administrating military government agencies and responsible to them."[27] This lack of reformist resolve, along with the vacillations of American policy, produced a situation in which the flow of goods was diverted into black-market channels and inefficiency became the characteristic trait of Korean firms. Similarly, Japanese property transferred to private individuals usually landed in the hands of comprador elements, creating social tensions. "With half the wealth of the nation 'up for grabs' demoralization was rapid."[28]

The oscillations of economic policy solved none of the old problems and created many new ones. General MacArthur's Proclamation No. 1 was an effort to continue the old Japanese policy of economic controls—despite the fact that price controls and rationing had broken down. Since there was no personnel to enforce these controls, they were soon given up and a decision made to institute a "free market economy." The result was galloping inflation particularly in the price of rice, forcing yet another reversal in policy. A ceiling was imposed on rice prices but this, added to the shortage of manufactured products and the existence of a black market, was hardly conducive to increased agricultural production. To relieve this situation a food collection program was started, but it proved unable to cope with the demand: "The rice so collected was sufficient to provide only about one-third of the daily caloric intake. Many could not pay the inflated prices prevailing on the open market to obtain additional food, and food riots occurred."[29] At the same time, state revenues, due to the inadequacies of the tax system, were dwindling, resulting in an almost chronic crisis situation: "Widespread scarcities and the expansion of the currency supply to cover governmental budgetary deficits created a rampant inflation which had not yet abated more than four years after the end of the war."[30]

In the meantime, events were about to take place on the diplomatic level which would further affect the internal political situation in South Korea. There had been little progress in the work of the Soviet-American Joint Commission on Korea, established at the Moscow Conference of 1945 with the purpose of setting up a unified provisional Korean government and preparing for the unification and independence of the former colony. Following the failure to reach an agreement at the summer 1947 session, the United Stated unilaterally referred the matter to the United Nations. Despite Soviet and North Korean protests, the world body officially created a Temporary Commission on Korea (UNTCOK). Even though this commission was from the beginning refused entry into North Korea and in spite of considerable opposition by the Soviet Union and other U.N. members, UNTCOK decided to hold separate elections in South Korea. In the American zone, only the most extreme rightist elements were in favor of such a vote; the majority of people saw the measure as a step toward the permanent division of their country.[31]

Besides provoking widespread opposition in the South, this American initiative set off a political process which had far-reaching repercussions for the future of the Korean nation. In March 1948, in an effort to prevent the permanent partition of the country, all important political figures in the South—with the notable exception of Syngman Rhee—stated their support for Korean unification and independence and their opposition to the U.N.-sponsored election. Further, two nonsocialist nationalist politicians—Kimm Kiu-sic and Kim Koo—backed a leftist demand that prior to any election all foreign troops should be withdrawn. Early in 1948 North Korea had countered the U.N. plan with several proposals of its own: general elections should be held all over the country (this, in spite of the fact that two-thirds of the population lived in the South); if this proved impossible, then the two governments should temporarily be combined. As a third possibility it was proposed that there be a conference of representatives from all political parties and organizations, North and South. Such a conference was in fact convened in Pyongyang in April 1948 with the participation of 240 southern delegates, representing every noteworthy political party or organization, excluding only the pro-American Syngman Rhee group.[32] But the opponents of this conference later took revenge on its well known participants; following the election and the subsequent repression in the South, Kim Koo was assassinated by an army officer.

Opposition to U.S. policies in South Korea—as well as to these diplomatic maneuvers—also took the form of mass upheavals. As early as April 1948, while preparations for the election were being made by the U.N. Temporary Commission, an uprising started on Cheju Island. The events there bear witness to the strength of nationalist feelings among the people and to their understanding of the implications involved. "The revolt was quickly joined by military units who had been sent to suppress it as well as by local Communists and large numbers of students. The rebellion rapidly spread to the towns of Posong, Kwanyang and Polkyo."[33] The American occupation authorities sent advisers to supervise the repression, but could not prevent successive defections of entire Korean military units. Before leaving the towns the rebellious revolutionaries had set up people's tribunals and punished government officials. A month later another revolt broke out in Taegu where a popular uprising was again joined by the military. After the rebellion was suppressed, "maintenance of law and order became extremely difficult as many civilian Communists joined the guerrilla forces.

In many rural areas the central government may have ruled during the day, but Communist guerrillas ruled at night."[34]

Once unleashed, this armed struggle grew to enormous proportions. There is a striking similarity to later events in Vietnam, as will be apparent from the following description of the situation up to the outbreak of the Korean War:

> From [the time of the rebellion of Cheju Island] guerrilla activities expanded everywhere in South Korea and continued unabated throughout the whole of 1949. The South Korean government used strong punitive measures against them, such as forcefully moving families from guerrilla areas, thus creating desolate, uninhabited regions, and trying in many other ways to bottle up guerrilla actions. All the energies of the government were concentrated on maintaining order. The losses incurred through April 1950 were as follows: 36,000 persons killed; 11,000 persons wounded; 45,000 homes burned completely; 4,000 homes partly burned; 61,000 families, involving 316,000 persons, sustaining damages; and 78,000 families, comprising 432,000 persons, displaced.[35]

Cementing the Division

When the election itself took place on May 10, 1948, it was a complete farce, the proceedings marked by open fraud and police terror. The opposition showed its strength by paralyzing the country through a general strike. Under such conditions it was difficult to characterize this election as democratic and free. Yet the U.S. command and the South Korean Interim Government declared it a symbol of democracy and renunciation of communism. Not a few people, however, took a more balanced view of the situation: "Many unofficial reports were less favourable, some observers maintaining that the elections had been fraudulently conducted in an atmosphere of terrorism. A more moderate view was that the elections were not in fact a free expression of the Korea will."[36]

Nevertheless, this so-called "free election" was given international endorsement, a fact which goes far in demonstrating the power to manipulate world opinion which the United States possessed at the time. This was certainly the case at the United Nations, where Western nations had a confortable majority on most issues. UNTCOK itself included such well-known docile American satellites as the Philippines and El Salvador, two countries whose own political regimes are far from democratic. Other members were India and Syria, which were at the time compliant with American interests. Given this background it was of little significance that the commission declared the results to constitute "a valid expression of the free will of the electorate in those parts of Korea which were accessible to the Commission."[37]

Moreover, as pointed out by many students of Korean affairs, "those parts" could not have been large, since UNTCOK only had about thirty non-Korean observers for an area of 40,000 square miles and a population of twenty million. According to one estimate this corresponded to one observer for every 14,000 eligible voters. For purpose of comparison it may be noted that during the plebiscite in the Saar in 1935 and the Nicaraguan elections of 1930, there had been one neutral observer for every 500 voters.[38] The degree of intervention reached new heights when on December 7, 1948, the U.N. General Assembly adopted a resolution according to which the new government in Seoul was considered the *only* lawful government of Korea. Paradoxically, it was for the preservation of this regime, sanctioned by fraudulent elections, that the "free world" would soon thereafter go to war!

As a countermove to these elections and the proclamation of the Republic of Korea (ROK) in the American zone, the northern regime established itself as a political entity in the autumn of the same year, proclaiming itself to be the legitimate representative of the entire Korean people.

This claim was based on the results of elections held throughout the nation in August 1948, whose main purpose, of course, was to challenge the U.N.-sponsored "elections." According to North Korean sources the votes in the North were cast through direct, secret ballots, whereas in the South the difficult situation had made indirect voting (i.e., through elected representatives) necessary. Seventy-seven percent of eligible voters in the South are said to have participated. The elections produced 360 southern delegates (out of 572 members of the National Assembly) who met in Pyongyang in September 1948 and elected Kim Il Sung as head of the Democratic People's Republic of Korea (DPRK). Two months later the Soviet occupation troops were withdrawn. It goes without saying that Western sources never seriously dealt with the news of this countrywide election, which was dismissed as Communist propaganda. However, given the fact that in April 1948 a large number of well-known South Korean delegates actually *had* participated in the Pan-Korean Conference in Pyongyang to discuss the reunification question, the sending of elected delegates to Pyongyang five months later is not as improbable as it seems. Needless to say, the assertion that the Seoul government was the true representative of the entire people could not be taken seriously, since the mass terror during the election in the South had made any free expression of public opinion impossible.

What should be stressed, however, is the fact that the creation of the DPRK was a countermeasure following the American establishment of a separate regime in the South. As it claimed to represent the entire Korean people, the northern government never acknowledged the division of Korea into two sovereign states. Even in the 1970s the DPRK opposed double representation in the United Nations, suggesting instead the creation of a confederation which could share such membership.

In contrast to the instability which dominated the atmosphere below the 38th Parallel, the situation was rapidly stabilizing in the North. The main reasons for the lack of agitation in this part of the country were the economic and social measures taken to improve the general standard of living. As this important aspect will be dealt with in detail in the following chapter, it will suffice to mention here the land reform of spring 1946, which gained the support of the peasant population. Furthermore, all former Japanese property had been nationalized and a series of democratic reforms put into effect. In the words of George McCune:

> The mass of the Korean people in the North reacted favorably towards the Russian regime especially when it was accompanied by many of the revolutionary benefits of a socialist society. In South Korea, on the other hand, the so-called fundamental freedoms of democratic society were not much appreciated by the Korean people in view of the lack of social reform and because of the irregularity with which democracy was applied.[39]

As a matter of fact, the news about the reforms in the North penetrated into the South, thus contributing further to social unrest.

It is an interesting fact and an indication of the reactionary character of the Rhee regime that during the short occupation of the North by the United Nations forces—during the Korean War—an attempt was made to cancel all social reforms which had been introduced there. "During mid-October [1950] his [Rhee's] government repealed all Communist land reform laws and later announced that it would sell most nationalized industry to individuals."[40]

On the political level, the DPRK followed a careful line of People's Democracy, trying not to alienate nationalist capitalists or small traders. This policy was based on a broad united front, even including well-known conservatives from the South. Similarly, on the diplomatic front it pursued an active policy on the national question, making numerous proposals for the peaceful unification of the country and thereby gaining sympathy from nationalist circles in both North and South. The last such proposal was made only six days before the outbreak of the war.

In the South the regime was becoming increasingly dependent on U.S. military and economic aid. Symbolic of this dependency was the fact that in late 1949, 60 percent of the state budget was spent on the suppression of political opposition. In Washington, however, the confused situation in the Korean Peninsula was making a poor impression upon members of the legislative bodies. When the majority of U.S. troops was withdrawn late in 1949, it was done under the open assumption that Korea was "indefensible." In April 1950, impatience with the situation in South Korea had grown to such a point that the American Congress put pressure on Syngman Rhee by threatening to cut economic aid unless new elections took place before the end of May. The result was that on May 30, 1950, in the midst of extreme police terror and widespread fraud, Syngman Rhee suffered a disastrous electoral defeat: out of the 210 new assembly members, only 45 supported him. As an American conservative weekly magazine reported: "The regime was left tottering for lack of confidence, both in Korea and abroad" (*U.S. News & World Report*, July 7, 1950.) Under the circumstances, only events of an exceptional nature could save this "tottering" regime. Five days before the war, a Swiss paper echoed the prevailing climate of opinion when it wrote that in South Korea, "there is no shortage of people who see a solution for the serious economic problem in an armed attack on the North."[41]

The Immediate Prewar Period

If the Syngman Rhee regime seems to have had an obvious motive for starting the war, the same can hardly be said about the North. In fact, it is difficult to see what interest the DPRK could have had in starting a conventional war at a time when its own reunification plan was gaining wide support and the southern regime was so obviously crumbling from within. American experts on Korean affairs had the same opinion. Secretary of State Dean Acheson, on the basis of information from various official organizations—including the Far East Command, the Central Intelligence Agency, the department of the army, and the state department—later testified at the MacArthur hearings that a North Korean attack in the summer of 1950 had not been considered imminent, "since the Communists had far from exhausted the potentialities for obtaining their objectives through guerrilla and psychological warfare, political pressure and intimidation . . . ."[42]

As late as one week prior to the outbreak of the war, John Foster Dulles (who had been forced on the Democratic administration as a special Republican adviser to the state department as a result of the wave of McCarthyism which followed the "loss of China") went to South Korea to inspect the 38th Parallel. Addressing the Seoul National Assembly on June 19, he said that South Korea would "never be alone as long as it continued to play a worthy part in the fight for human freedom."[43] And indirectly answering the latest North Korean proposals for peaceful reunification, Dulles stated: "The eyes of the free world are upon you. Compromise with Communism would be a road to disaster." He further assured his audience of the "readiness of the U.S.A. to give all necessary moral and material support to South Korea, which is fighting against Communism." The South Korean leader also spoke on this occasion, warning: "Should we not be able to protect democracy in the cold war, we will achieve victory in a hot war."[44]

Coming at a time when Washington policy-makers had placed the peninsula outside the "defense perimeter" in Asia and had repeatedly threatened aid cuts if Syngman Rhee persisted in his oft-proclaimed intention of launching an attack on the North, this visit by the influential American politician could only be interpreted as an extremely provocative action. It implied that Seoul would now have the backing of certain circles in the United

States for any action it cared to undertake. The case could easily be made that these politicians wanted to use Rhee and the situation in Korea to fulfill a larger objective. In any event, upon arriving in Tokyo Dulles excitedly told journalists that he expected "positive results" from his talks at the Far East Command Headquarters. After one day of discussions he was quoted as predicting "positive action by the United States to preserve the peace in the Far East."[45]

Meanwhile, the change in the international situation in late 1949, the result of the Communist victory in China, had influenced the decision-making process in Washington. American ruling circles were split in their reactions to this event. Some influential elements had drawn the logical conclusion that having "lost" China, it would be irrational for the United States to get involved in yet another distant conflict on the Asian mainland. On May 2, 1950, the chairman of the Senate Foreign Relations Committee, Senator Tom Connally, gave an interview to *U.S. News & World Report* in which he stated flatly that South Korea would probably have to be abandoned, just as the Communists would probably overrun Formosa: "It has been testified before us that Japan, Okinawa, and the Philippines make the chain of defense which is absolutely necessary." However, according to the same senator, many important people had a different opinion: "They believe that events will transpire which will maneuver around and present an incident which will make us fight. That's what a lot of them are saying: 'We've got to battle some time, why not now?'" How much closer could one come to saying that important people in Washington were trying to create the pretext for a war?

This interview, widely published in the Japanese press, was also discussed at MacArthur's headquarters in Tokyo, where a top-level conference was held between John Foster Dulles, Defense Secretary Louis Johnson, General Omar Bradley, head of the joint chiefs of staff, and General Douglas MacArthur. During their meetings this influential group reached an agreement that the United States should maintain military bases in Japan, Formosa, and Korea to be used in the containment of China and Russia. In order to secure these bases it would be necessary to:

(1) Exclude China and Russia from the negotiations for a peace treaty with Japan (this was in violation of the 1942 agreement not to make a separate peace with any of the enemy countries);
(2) Cordon off Formosa and supply military aid to Chiang Kai-shek, who had fled the mainland in 1949 (Formosa had until then been considered by all parties to be a province of China);
(3) Supply military aid to Syngman Rhee in South Korea (in spite of the severity of his recent political setbacks).[46]

This plan in effect implied a total reversal of the previous American Far East policy—stated in no uncertain terms by both President Truman and Secretary of State Acheson—which had left Korea and Formosa outside the "defense perimeter." A few days after the Tokyo meeting (June 23), Acheson saw fit to issue a statement in Washington to the effect that the discussions in the Japanese capital had not altered the policy of the United States as formulated by the president in January of the same year. Because of this resistance at the highest level a reversal of the official policy could only be achieved through drastic action. Furthermore, time was of vital importance. First of all, Syngman Rhee's political demise seemed imminent, whereas the unification plan launched by North Korea was gaining momentum. Secondly, and not least important, it was expected that Chiang Kai-shek would be driven out of Formosa in a matter of weeks.

Rhee seems to have appreciated the opportunities offered him by the disagreement in Washington and the new international situation. In his New Year message he made his intentions quite plain: "Up to now, in view of the international situation, we have pursued a peaceful policy. . . . We must remember, however, that in the New Year in accordance with the changed international situation, it is our duty to unify Southern and Northern Korea by our own strength."[47] Time and again he had repeated his conviction that Korea ought to be united by force under his leadership; during his August 1948 visit to Washington he had made it his theme song: "The march on the North is the most important task." And in October of the following year, in a speech delivered on an American flagship of the Seventh Fleet anchored in a South Korean port, he spoke about the "unification of Korea with the help of armed force." "If we have to settle this thing by war," he said "we will do all the fighting that is needed." And he added, "I would wage war—but for this American help is needed." He probably would not have talked like that if he had not felt secure in the approval of his American protectors.

One interesting piece of evidence concerning Syngman Rhee's policy in the spring of 1950 is provided by a *New York Times* (March 14, 1950) report of the prison sentences imposed on thirteen deputies of the National Assembly in Seoul. Among the five charges leveled against them, number four read: "Opposing the invasion of North Korea by the South Korean forces." On April 27, 1950, a *New York Times* journalist, Richard Johnson, who had spent several years in South Korea, told a Press Club audience in New York that "there is a very real desire on the part of South Koreans to attack North Korea, restrained only by the fact that the U.S. authorities allow them only enough ammunition at a time for three days' fighting."[48] In his interesting chapter, "The Crucifixion of Korea," D. F. Fleming reaches the following conclusions about the intentions of the South Korean politician:

> We do not know that Rhee began the war, but we do know that he had ample reason to do so, from his personal standpoint, and that he was totally capable of touching off the conflict. Everything that we have learned about Rhee and his secretive, despotic methods since mid-1950 amply justifies the belief that he would have started the Korean War to advance the personal and patriotic ends which he has

since been openly willing to further by any and all means, including the world catastrophe of a hydrogen war. He has fully demonstrated that if he did not begin the Korean War it was only because the Reds beat him to it.[49]

The Many Facets of the Conflict

Now, whether the "Reds" actually did "beat him to it" is precisely the question which has to be determined. When large-scale hostilities began between North and South Korea on June 25, 1950, public opinion in the West was immediately presented with the picture of Soviet or Chinese aggression. Yet all the evidence seems to indicate that the war came as an equal surprise to both these powers. In this respect it should be pointed out that when the conflict broke out, the Soviet Union had just started a boycott of the Security Council at the United Nations, as a protest against the nonadmittance of the People's Republic of China to the world body. In view of the presence in the South of the pro-American U.N. Temporary Commission, it would seem rather shortsighted for Pyongyang to have begun hostilities without advising its main ally, who also had a permanent seat on the Security Council. Further, had the war been planned by the Communist side, as Western accounts would have it, some logical explanation would have to be offered for the strange fact that although the Soviet U.N. delegate was in New York at the time, he did not attend the crucial meeting of the Security Council at which the Western military intervention in Korea was given the backing of the world organization. With his veto right, the Soviet delegate could have prevented or postponed such a resolution by his mere presence. As one American commentator observed at the time, this was "one of the more intriguing mysteries in the history of the Politbureau's operations."[50] But it certainly was not the only "intriguing mystery" blemishing the Western version of those events.

Actually, the Western mass media made few attempts to

analyze reasons or motives, not to mention the general situation leading up to the conflict. Initially, this was certainly a *civil war,* one which should not normally have been the concern of the United Nations. The U.S. government, however, according to a prearranged plan,[51] treated it as an international conflict and convened an urgent session of the Security Council. At this session, the American delegate referred to a report from the U.N. Commission in Korea, as well as to a telegram sent by the American ambassador in Seoul six hours after the fighting began, asserting that northern aggression had taken place. These two documents—the texts of which were not made available until a month later, after all important decisions had been taken—contained *no evidence whatsoever* of how the conflict actually began, but only stated that each side accused the other of starting it. As a matter of fact, no U.N. eyewitness account existed and there was no investigation. Judgment was passed simply on the basis of what South Korean authorities had said (without confirmation by U.N. observers) and on circumstantial evidence of the "actual progress of operations" once the fighting had started.

When, on June 27, the Security Council was convened for the second time (still without having seen the report from the U.N. observers in Korea) the United States got what it wanted—full powers to carry out military intervention in the name of the United Nations. Besides being in violation of the U.N. Charter—since two of the permanent members of the Council (the USSR and China) were absent—the decision was made without regard for the normal procedure of mediation and without hearing the other side of the case. Still, there is no reason to believe that the United States would have acted differently had the U.N. refused its backing. Already prior to the Security Council vote President Truman had ordered "United States air and sea forces to give the Korean government troops cover and support." In the same statement the president said: "The attack upon Korea makes it plain beyond all doubt that

Communism has passed beyond the use of subversion to conquer independent nations, and will now use armed invasion and war. . . . "[52] The president went on to say that he had ordered the Seventh Fleet to prevent any "attack" upon Formosa and that he had decided to strengthen U.S. forces in the (nominally independent) Philippines and give added support to the suppression of the HUK guerrilla movement there. Simultaneously, military aid to the French in Indochina was increased. Thus, the United States, on the pretext of an alleged aggression by North Korea of which no evidence was offered, actually declared war on every socialist movement in Asia!

Apart from the question of how it started, the conflict was—until the intervention of American forces—obviously a civil war. The U.N. Charter explicitly prohibits intervention in the internal affairs of any state. Besides, it was the right of Korean people to free themselves from a dictatorship imposed from without, just as it had been the right of the American people to fight their own civil war. In his radio address to the entire Korean people on June 26, Kim Il Sung interpreted the war in precisely this light: "The war we are fighting against this traitorous clique, *a civil war* which it started, is a just one for the country's unification, independence, freedom and democracy."[53]

But this does not mean that the question of the start of the war is irrelevant. When on June 25, a North Korean radio broadcast alleged that South Korea had attacked the city of Haeju north of the demarcation line, the U.N. observers did not find it worth an investigation. Instead they accepted the South Korean version of an unprovoked aggression from the North. According to Indian expert Karunakar Gupta, however, "a close study of the military situation along the 38th Parallel on 25 June, 1950 on the basis of official communiqués, radio broadcasts, press agency and newspaper reports and U.N. documents should convince any detached scholar that *a prima facie case for the South's invasion of the North does exist.*"[54]

From the U.N. report—which was confirmed by press

releases—it appears that the North Korean army invaded South Korea on June 25, capturing the towns of Ongjin and Kaesong as well as all territory west or northwest of the Imjin River. But that is only one side of the picture—the other side received very little attention at the time. The aforementioned North Korean radio broadcast on the same day had claimed that South Korea, having rejected the latest northern proposal for peaceful reunification, had attacked several localities north of the parallel in the section of Haeju, thus *precipitating* the North Korean *counterattack*. Various press reports tend to corroborate this version. On June 26, 1950, the *Manchester Guardian* carried the following item (dateline Seoul, June 25): "The American officials confirmed that the South Korean troops had captured Haeju, five miles inside North Korea, near the West coast."

The capture of Haeju by South Korean units on the very day of the start of the war is much more interesting than would appear at first glance. First of all, this locality is situated just north of an area in South Korea which had been described by American military experts as indefensible in case of war. With its population of 82,000 people (in 1942) the town was a significant industrial, commercial, and mining center. Aside from its economic importance, Haeju was a key strategic area: the only railway junction just above the demarcation line which led directly to Pyongyang (sixty-five miles away) was located there, and there was also a road linking it to the capital of the DPRK. Under these conditions, in the words of Karunakar Gupta, an assault on June 25 on this locality "might reasonably be regarded by the North Koreans as an attempt by Syngman Rhee to fulfil his oft-repeated proclamation about capturing Pyongyang within three days, especially as it occurred immediately after Rhee had a personal assurance from Mr. J.F. Dulles the week before about American backing for South Korea."[55]

Disregarding the North Korean accusations, Seoul later

disclosed that on June 25, ROK troops had indeed launched a "successful counteroffensive" in the Haeju area. However, a serious examination of this version tends rather to confirm the North Korean charge of a southern military initiative: "The attack on Haeju would either have meant a heavy South Korean concentration of forces in this sector immediately below the 38th Parallel, which would have been physically impossible *after* the North Korean offensive, covering as it did, all the territory west and northwest of the Imjin River—or it would have implied a strong element of surprise—equally difficult to imagine *after* a North Korean attack." Consequently, from a strictly military viewpoint, as the Indian scholar points out, a logical explanation for the ROK weakness on the other fronts was that "the large concentration of Southern forces deployed in the surprise offensive on Haeju on 25 June, 1950, must have weakened the defense potential of the South Koreans on the other sectors of the 38th Parallel against a better-armed North Korean counter-offensive."[56]

The reason many observers came to the conclusion that North Korea had started the fighting, was the rapidity with which the People's Army (KPA) was able to advance, which was interpreted as a sign of better preparedness. In this connection two not necessarily contradictory explanations may be offered. In testimony to Congress on May 6, 1951, General MacArthur explained that important southern logistical supplies brought up near the 38th Parallel had been captured by the KPA, thereby enabling it to advance still faster. This would corroborate information emanating from Pyongyang before the war. On May 29, 1950, Peking's *People's Daily* had reported unusual South Korean concentrations below the 38th Parallel. The general's Congressional testimony, suggesting a forward deployment of ROK forces in an offensive position—without which an attack on Haeju obviously could not have taken place—in fact contradicted his own previous assertion, in a report to the United Nations, that the southern army had been "organized entirely for defense."

Another important asset in the KPA's speedy advance was of course the existence of guerrilla units in the South. Moreover, some of the Syngman Rhee forces actually joined the People's Army during the offensive. The *New York Times* of July 2, 1950, quoted an American reporter freshly returned from South Korea who estimated that a high percentage of the South Korean army had disappeared—"some of them wounded, some killed but most of them just plain deserters." Concerning the question of preparedness, a U.S. intelligence officer at MacArthur's headquarters disclosed one month later, during a briefing for journalists on July 30, 1950, that the North Korean Army had not carried out the mobilization plan at the time the war began, June 25; "only six full divisions had been ready for combat when the invasion started, although the North Korean war plans called for thirteen to fifteen."[57]

Even at the time, a more political interpretation of the early phases of the war had been suggested by the editors of the American publication *Monthly Review* (August 1951). According to this theory, the retreat of the South Korean forces had been part of a general strategy for creating an atmosphere of crisis which could serve as a pretext for embroiling the United States in a larger Asian conflict. If this holds true, it may be concluded that by continuing their advance, the North Koreans were lured into a trap. It should be pointed out, however, that the population in the South may have had expectations of the northern regime which would have led them to consider any other course of action as a betrayal. Much information indicates that at least a large proportion of South Koreans at the time considered the (North) Korean People's Army as a liberation army and that consequently the collapse of southern defense was genuine. Furthermore, once a certain point had been reached, the situation probably evolved according to its own inner logic.

Consequences of the War

The war itself went through several phases. The first, lasting about a week, ended with the almost total collapse of Syngman Rhee's forces and the complete victory of the KPA in the Korean civil war. Then came the American intervention which, after a month of fighting, brought the military situation more or less back to the status quo ante. At this point the war could have ended and the U.S. intervention's credibility as a "police action" might still have been preserved. But again, if peace had been made, the internal balance of political forces in Korea would have signified an American defeat. Discussing a Russian proposal for a ceasefire and the possibility of holding general elections in the entire country, the *New York Times* (August 25, 1950) described the situation as follows:

> The difficulty is that there is a strong probability of an overall Communist majority if the elections were held before the communization of North Korea had been undone, and before a U.N. reconstruction program had assuaged the bitterness of North and South Korea against the destruction of their homes during their liberation by U.N. forces. In that case communism would win by an election what it failed to obtain by an invasion.[58]

In the meantime, without waiting for a U.N. decision, General MacArthur ordered the invasion of North Korea with a rapid advance toward the Chinese border and bombardments of the area around the Yalu River. Indeed, the proposed ceasefire was not even seriously discussed. Had the purpose of the intervention been to "stop aggression," then the war could have been over in a month. Instead it dragged on for three more years in a vain attempt to "undo" communism in the North, provoking the entry into the war of half a million Chinese volunteers.

Many more examples of misinformation about this conflict, which had such deep and tragic consequences for Korea and which changed the global priorities of U.S. policies, could easily be produced. Besides the deliberate manipulations and the extreme ambiguity of the first Western documents about the outbreak of the war, world public opinion was "spared" the first "erroneous" U.S. news of the event, as overheard by John Gunther in Tokyo. While he was lunching with some officials of the U.S. occupation forces in Japan, John Gunther reports, "one of the important members of the occupation" was "called unexpectedly to the telephone. He came back and whispered: 'A big story has just broken. The South Koreans have attacked North Korea!' "[59] The story was later dismissed as a slip due to overexcitement. The falsification and withholding of news by the Anglo-Saxon mass media and press have been richly documented by the American political journalist I.F. Stone in his book *The Hidden History of the Korean War*. When the first article of this American newsman was printed in the French weekly *l'Observateur* (February 2, 1951) the editor, Claude Bourdet, accompanied it with the following comment: "If Stone's thesis corresponds to reality, we are in the presence of the greatest swindle in the whole of military history." Everything that has since been learned about the conflict tends to confirm this judgment.

Another shocking implication of the course of events in Korea relates to the decision-making process in Washington and its international repercussions. In the 1950s the split in the American political elite over policies in Asia, together with the extreme power of the military, almost led the world to a general conflagration. Completely blind to consequences of such an action, General MacArthur was clearly aiming at a major war against China. This attitude eventually led to his dismissal from office on April 11, 1951, by President Truman. But by that time the damage had already been done. Had the Chinese government remained passive and not, together with the Koreans, defeated the U.N.-sponsored invasion, the effects would have been felt in U.S. domestic politics as well as in international affairs. That General MacArthur had presidential ambitions was a well-known fact and had the American adventure in Korea been successful, his chances would have been correspondingly high. The consequences of such an eventuality would have been enormous, bringing about a dramatic change in U.S. global priorities.[60]

That the war itself did not evolve toward a major conflict with China (including the use of nuclear weapons) was due, among other things, to the anxieties of the European allies of the United States. "Throughout November the British and French had watched the events in Korea with mounting alarm, fearful that the Americans would withdraw their attention from Europe, and Prime Minister Clement Attlee was under strong pressure from both parties, but especially the Bevan faction of Labour, to bring the Americans to their senses."[61] That Britain exercised great diplomatic pressure on Washington did in fact help to strengthen that faction within the U.S. political elite which feared the consequences of a global conflict in Asia.

However, one should not push this line of thought too far, for the conflict did have beneficial effects for the so-called "free world." Economically, the war served as an important stimulus to the West, which had entered an ominous period of stagnation following the post-World War II reconstruction boom. This was especially true for both the West German and Japanese economic "miracles," which were able to profit from American military expenditures, while themselves remaining aloof from the conflict. "For the West German economy, the Korean War proved to be a remarkable stimulant: while the big industrial powers had to step up the production of armaments Germany, still subject to the restrictions of the Potsdam Agreement, was able to increase her entire industrial output, thanks to the orders that poured in from all sides."[62] This was to an even greater degree the case for Japan, which became the largest beneficiary of the U.S. adventures in both Korea and, later, Vietnam—so much so that the economies of Japan and the United States, which seemed compatible during the earlier postwar period, were to come into sharp conflict in the 1970s! The American war also served to strengthen traditional class relations in these two countries. Concerning Japan, Edgar Snow writes:

> Ironically, the Korean War solved the *zaibatsu* (monopolist capitalist) problem. Suddenly, America spent billions in army procurement orders in Japan. Under the exigencies of war, laws were "re-reformed" to the benefit of the old owning families, new credits and capital became available, and restrictions against monopoly control were so relaxed as to permit production to be restored under the *zaibatsu*—much as happened to the Krupps in Germany. Japan's industrial economy has now resumed much of its prewar ownership pattern. . . . [63]

Ideologically, the outcome of the conflict provided the peoples in the colonial world with concrete evidence that the most highly developed capitalist power could be held in check in its attempt to subjugate a small nation. On the other hand, while having a mobilizing effect for those peoples under the direct threat of imperialist aggression, it was used demagogically by the Western bourgeoisie against an entire generation of the European and American left during the "McCarthy era." Further, in the years that followed it was used as one of the pretexts for a major military buildup and a vast defense budget—a program which provided the economic stimulus needed to alleviate the internal difficulties faced by the imperialist camp at the time.

Politically, the conflict resolved many vital questions for U.S. Asian policy: within two days of the outbreak of the war, American military protection was extended to Chiang Kai-shek on Formosa; meanwhile, 700 million Chinese were refused representation at the United Nations. Furthermore, the conflict postponed the signing of a peace treaty with Japan, a step which might otherwise have meant the evacuation of military bases and withdrawal of U.S. troops from the Japanese islands. As far as the South Korean situation was concerned, the outbreak of the conflict gave Syngman Rhee international backing from the pro-American governments in the world at precisely the moment when he had become utterly isolated in his own country. As a matter of fact he did everything he could to prevent a truce. Even after the stalemate in the conflict had become clear to everyone else, he visited the United States and went so far as to request Congress to wage an atomic war in order to win him control of North Korea! D.F. Fleming draws the obvious conclusions concerning Rhee's personality:

> Since nothing . . . could change Rhee's objective, and since he urged the suicide of the human race, certainly of the West, in an effort to achieve it, it is quite clear that he would not have boggled at starting a civil war in Korea in June 1950, either in the vainglorious expectation of carrying it through himself or of being bailed out by his American friends, including John Foster Dulles . . . .[64]

For the Korean people, the price was very high. At the time of writing, nearly 40,000 American soldiers are still in South Korea, and the nation is still divided. But the defeat of the American venture did serve to set a limit to the ambitions of the American ruling class on the Asian mainland, while strengthening the military and political capabilities of the Asian peoples in the face of Western encroachment. The entire course of the Vietnam war was influenced by this experience.

Notes

1. Cornelius Osgood, *The Koreans and their Culture* (New York: Ronald Press, 1951), p. 285 ff.
2. Dae-Sook Suh, *The Korean Communist Movement 1918-1948* (Princeton, N. J.: Princeton Univ. Press, 1967), p. 132.
3. *Korea Must Be Free,* prepared by the Korean Commission to

America and Europe, 1930, p. 26 [quoted in Andrew J. Grajdanzev, *Modern Korea* (New York: John Day, 1944), p. 66].
4. Grajdanzev, *Modern Korea,* p. 64.
5. Organ of the Japanese Communist Party, *Jaka Hata,* August 20, 1932, describes the development of mass struggles in Korea as being inspired by the armed struggle in the border areas.
6. Prior to the Japanese capitulation this part of the world experienced the dropping of American atomic bombs on Hiroshima (August 6) and Nagasaki (August 9), not to mention the protracted anti-imperialist struggle in the Japanese-occupied parts of the Asian mainland, including China. Today, some historians have come to see the dropping of atomic bombs not so much as a necessary evil to defeat the Japanese, but rather as an attempt to prevent Russia from becoming an equal partner in the postwar negotiations in the Far East and thus influencing world events from a position of strength. Cf. Gar Alperovitz, *Atomic Diplomacy, Hiroshima and Postdam* (London, 1966), esp. chap. IV.
7. The role played by Korean partisans in the liberation has often been overlooked, but it is a fact that great parts of the country, including some of the more strategically important areas, were liberated before the Red Army had reached the spot.
8. D.F. Fleming, *The Cold War and Its Origins 1950-1960,* vol. II (New York: Doubleday, 1961), p. 589. This explanation nonetheless does not resolve entirely the enigma of why the Soviet Union did not take full advantage of its apparent position of strength in Korea. Other plausible explanations may be that Stalin hoped to acquire some geopolitical advantages in return for Soviet moderation, or that the strength of the Soviet army in the Far East was not as great as it seemed. [Such speculations are elaborated by Soon Sung Cho, *Korea in World Politics 1940-1950, An Evaluation of American Responsibility* (Berkeley, Cal: Univ. of California Press, 1967), pp. 55-56.]
9. This, as we said, is a source of disagreement between different investigators. Wilfred Burchett in a lecture in the spring of 1974 to the "Utrikespolitiska Föreningen" (Foreign Affairs Association) of Sweden declared that is was decided at the Potsdam Conference in July-August 1945 "that the Soviet and American forces should enter Korea to round up the Japanese forces and evacuate them back to Japan. The Soviet forces would take care of this north of the 38th Parallel up to the frontiers of China and the Soviet Union. American forces would carry out this south of the 38th Parallel." (*The People's Korea,* Tokyo, June 19, 1974.) This interpretation concurs with the information given by Soon Sung Cho, who writes that agreement between the Soviet and American chiefs of staff had been reached at Potsdam whereby some division into zones of military operation was needed but that "these would not necessarily be zones of mili-

tary occupation." (Cho, *Korea in World Politics,* p. 51.) In contrast, President Truman gave the gist of American policy in declaring that the dividing line "was proposed as a practical solution when the sudden collapse of the Japanese war machine created a vacuum in Korea," and that this line of partition "in Korea was never the subject of international discussions." [Harry S. Truman, *Year of Trial and Hope* (London, 1956), p. 334.]

10. Cho, *Korea in World Politics,* p. 31 [quoting from *The Conferences at Malta and Yalta: 1945* (Washington, 1955), p. 770].
11. See Walter Millis, ed., *The Forrestal Diaries* (New York: Viking, 1951), p. 56 (quoted by Cho, *Korea in World Politics, p. 31).*
12. Wilfred Burchett, *Again Korea* (New York: International Publishers, 1968), p. 110. The Moscow agreement had political repercussions, as it was at first opposed by all political organizations in Korea. But in January 1946 the leftists and Communists in the South pronounced themselves for it. This need not have been a result of Russian pressures, as many would have it. Dae-Sook Suh writes:

> For the Communists, therefore, the five years of trusteeship would be an opportue period to strengthen themselves. Their motives in agreeing to the trusteeship seem to have arisen primarily from their political position vis-à-vis the Nationalists, who enjoyed the support of the American military government (*Korean Communist Movement,* p. 306).

13. Gabriel Kolko, *The Politics of War* (New York: Random House 1968), p. 600.
14. Jon Halliday, "The Korean Revolution," *Three Articles on the Korean Revolution 1945-1953* (London: Association for Radical East Asian Studies, 1972, mimeo), p. 3.
15. Kolko, *Politics of War,* p. 601.
16. Harold Isaacs, *No Peace for Asia* (Cambridge, Mass.: MIT Press, 1947), p.94 (quoted by Kolko, *Politics of War,* p. 602).
17. Ibid.
18. George McCune, *Korea Today* (Cambridge, Mass: Harvard Univ. Press, 1950), p. 45. The testimony of this scholar has additional value since at the time of Korean liberation he was the chief of the Korean desk of the American state department.
19. Ibid., pp. 52-53.
20. This is the version of Baik Bong, *Kim Il Sung Biography,* vol. II (Beirut, 1973), p. 101.
21. Grant Meade, *American Military Government in Korea* (New York: Columbia Univ. Press, King's Crown Press, 1951), p. 55 (quoted by Fleming *The Cold War,* p. 590). Fleming terms it an excellent account of the events preceding the Korean war as told by a member of the U.S. military government in Korea.

22. Bruce Cumings, "American Policy and Korean Liberation," in Frank Baldwin, ed., *Without Parallel, The American-Korean Relationship Since 1945* (New York: Pantheon, 1973), p. 55.
23. William J. Lederer, *A Nation of Sheep* (New York: Fawcett World, 1961), p. 57.
24. Cho, *Korea in World Politics*, p. 72.
25. Takashi Hatada, *A History of Korea* (Santa Barbara, Cal.: American Bibliographic Center-Clio Press, 1969), p. 138.
26. October 1946 [quoted in Mark Gayn, *Japan Diary* (New York: W. Sloane, 1948), p. 388].
27. Cf. McCune, *Korea Today*, p. 100.
28. Alfred Crofts, "The Case of Korea: Our Falling Ramparts," *The Nation* 190, no. 26 (June 25, 1960): 546.
29. McCune, *Korea Today*, p. 105.
30. Ibid., p. 112.
31. The scepticism toward balloting at this time was due to the experiences related to the setting up of the Korean Interim Legislative Assembly (KILA), an American initiative in October 1946. In the words of a student of Korean affairs:

    > When the Bureau of Information of USAMGIK's Public Relations Office was asked by the high command in February about plans for an assembly, it had indicated that if there was universal suffrage, there was every indication that the left would triumph. Democratic suffrage was therefore avoided. Each hamlet, village, and district "elected" (or appointed) two representatives of the province by secret ballot. No rules specified who would vote in the initial election, however. The Japanese legislation restricting suffrage to taxpayers remained on the books. In some cases, the township heads, many of whom were holdovers from the Japanese period, simply appointed the elector or assumed the post themselves. No steps were taken to see that a democratic or even fair election was held. "You know," an American officer serving as chief of a provincial Home Affairs Division remarked to an American correspondent in explanation, "strategically, this is the proper time for the rightists."

    [Gregory Henderson, *Korea: The Politics of the Vortex* (Cambridge, Mass.: Harvard Univ. Press., 1968), pp.153-154. For these observations Henderson bases himself on: *USAMGIK Summation*, no. 13, October 1946, p. 3; Richard D. Robinson, "Korea: The Betrayal of a Nation" (unpub. ms, 1947), p. 174; and Gayn, *Japan Diary*, p. 395.]
32. Kai Moltke, *Korea Kæmper* (Skive, 1950). This Danish writer collected material from available Korean and international sources about the entire period. See also George McCune, *Korea Today*, pp.

262-264. Among the most distinguished southern political leaders participating in the conference were a Dr. Kimm, liberal chairman of the Korean Interim Legislative Assembly and leader of the Nationalist Independence Federation; Kim Koo, rightist polititian, former president of the Korean Provisional Government in Chungking and head of the Korean Independence Party; Choi Tongo, rightist vice-chairman of the Interim Assembly; Hong Myungki, liberal head of the Democratic Independence Party; Lyuh Woonhong, liberal chief of the Socialist Democratic Party and brother of the patriot Lyuh Woonhyung, who had been assassinated the year before.

33. Cf. Cho, *Korea in World Politics,* p. 231.
34. Ibid., p. 232.
35. Hatada, *History of Korea,* p. 140.
36. McCune, *Korea Today,* p. 229.
37. Fleming, *The Cold War,* p. 592. According to official South Korean sources, 589 persons were killed and about 10,000 "rioters" processed in police stations in the days prior to the election. (Cf. McCune *Korea Today,* p. 229.)
38. This comparison was suggested by Brig. Gen. Wickerling, U.S. liaison officer with the commission (quoted by McCune, *Korea Today,* p. 229, note 30).
39. Ibid., p. 181.
40. Joyce and Gabriel Kolko, *The Limits of Power. The World and United States Foreign Policy, 1945-1954* (New York: Harper & Row, 1972), p. 599.
41. *Neue Zürcher Zeitung,* June 20, 1950.
42. *Hearings Before the Committee on Armed Services and the Committee on Foreign Relations, United States Senate,* 82nd Congr., 1st Sess., Pt. 3, pp. 1990-1991 (quoted by Fleming, *The Cold War,* p. 599).
43. *The Times,* London, June 20, 1950.
44. Quoted by D. N. Pritt, K.C., *Light On Korea,* a Labor Monthly Publication (London, 1950), p. 7.
45. The *New York Times,* June 21 and 22, 1950.
46. Sir John T. Pratt, *Korea, The Lie that Led to War?* (London: Britain China Friendship Association, 1951), p. 2. (This account is based on detailed reports in American press.) See also Fleming, *The Cold War,* p. 596.
47. Quoted by Burchett, *People's Korea,* p. 125.
48. Quoted by Pritt, *Light on Korea,* p. 4.
49. Fleming, *The Cold War,* p. 655.
50. Richard P. Stebbins, *The United States in World Affairs, 1950* (New York: Harper & Row, 1951), p. 217 (quoted by Fleming, *The Cold War,* p. 602).
51. In a routine hearing by the Senate Appropriations Committee on June 5, 1951, John D. Hickerson revealed that the resolution to be

presented to the United Nations existed prior to the outbreak of hostilities "in very rough outline form." [Quoted by I.F. Stone, *The Hidden History of the Korean War* (New York: Monthly Review Press, 1970), p. 56.]

52. Reported in the *New York Herald Tribune*, June 28, 1950.
53. Kim Il Sung, "Every Effort for Victory in War," in *Selected Works*, vol. I (Pyongyang, 1965), p. 126. (Emphasis added)
54. Karunakar Gupta, "How did the Korean War Begin?" in *The China Quarterly* 52 (October-December, 1972): 700.
55. Karunakar Gupta, "Origin of the Korean War and India's Stand On Korea," in *The Calcutta Review* 139 (June 1956): 288.
56. Ibid., p. 289.
57. Walter Sullivan in the *New York Times*, July 31, 1950.
58. Quoted by Stone, *Hidden History*, p. 118.
59. John Gunther, *The Riddle of MacArthur* (New York: Harper & Row, 1951), p. 165.
60. This perspective is discussed by the Kolkos in *The Limits of Power*, p. 610.
61. Ibid., p. 604.
62. Heinz Abosch, *The Menace of the Miracle* (New York: Monthly Review Press, 1963), p. 79.
63. Edgar Snow, *The Other Side of the River* (New York: Random House, 1962), p. 675.
64. Fleming, *The Cold War*, pp. 654-655.

Part II
Building an Independent National Economy

Chapter 4
The Genesis of Korean Socialism

The liberation of Korea from the yoke of Japanese colonialism and the subsequent division of the country created a situation without precedent in the nation's history. The aim of the anti-Japanese struggle had been to liberate all of Korea. But since circumstances made it part of an international fight against German and Japanese imperialism during World War II, the Korean movement was not allowed to follow its course unhampered. As far as Japan was concerned, the defeat of the one-million-strong Kwantung Army—involving the concentration of all its main forces—meant the breakdown of Japanese imperialism. On the other hand, Takashi Hatada makes the interesting point that due to the international situation, "Japan's leaders surrendered before internal collapse occurred."[1] For Japan this meant that certain social reforms could be undertaken after the war—but without internal upheavals or thoroughgoing changes, since the United States intervened to prevent just such a process. This was surely a determining factor in keeping Japan within the capitalist sphere. For Korea, occupation by two foreign powers with opposing goals, at a time when the struggle against Japan was reaching its climax, deeply affected subsequent developments.

Establishment of Authority in the North

While the aim of the American intervention in the South, as we saw in the preceding chapter, had been to keep this part of Korea within the capitalist sphere, the Soviet occupation was of an entirely different nature. This was obvious from the beginning in the occupying powers' respective attitudes toward the question of authority. The Russians did not create a military government; the Americans, however, "not only established a military government, they insisted that it be the only governing body in Korea. The effect of this was to refuse the Koreans any share in administrative responsibility and to emphasize the strictly military character of American control."[2] The Americans' reliance on military rule in South Korea meant the country was being treated as a defeated enemy, rather than—as was the case—a friendly nation newly liberated from a vanquished foe! In contrast, the Russians operated through the people's committees and the local Korean administration.

When just after liberation the Koreans formed people's committees all over the country, Western propaganda portrayed them as simple tools of Soviet policy. But some people's committees had already been established by Korean liberation forces before the arrival of the Russians.[3] Furthermore, it must be borne in mind that during the years of Japanese domination, nationalist aspirations had become anti-imperialist in nature and what happened after 1945 was merely a continuation of this development. This state of affairs, highly disadvantageous to American aims, could hardly be admitted by Cold War ideologists.

The people's committees were actually the expression of a broad united front. Of course there were a few Communists on nearly every committee and their party had the advantage of being the only one with members everywhere. On the basis of an account by a member of the U.S. military government, who had opportunities to observe events in Korea first-hand, D.F. Fleming concludes, "In a revolutionary time the committees naturally leaned somewhat toward the left, yet they contained representatives of all groups, including the conservatives." This American historian cites the example of the important province of Cholla Nam Do, where the committee was headed by a pro-American Christian pastor and had a conservative executive council.[4]

According to Dae-Sook Suh, the Russians had scant knowledge of Korea prior to the occupation, and to a large degree let the Koreans themselves organize their society. That does not mean, however, that the Russians were completely prepared for the surprises the future had in store, nor that they always reacted in accordance with the interests of Korean nationalism. It has been argued by leftists in the West that had the Russians shown more genuine concern for the realization of the Korean revolution, the division of the country might have been avoided. This criticism, raised some twenty years after the event, may, however, underestimate the consequences of a more forceful position by the Soviet Union in the then-prevailing international situation. There was debate even at the time over the precise nature of the balance of forces. We do not mean to imply that the Soviet Union did not commit errors in its dealings with the Americans over Korea, but only that the situation was extremely complex and will need a good deal of study before any sound conclusions can be reached. Even among the Communist forces within Korea there was disagreement concerning the future path of development.

At the beginning, of course, no separate administration of North Korea had been foreseen. But as America's plans for the peninsula became increasingly clear, the regions above the 38th Parallel soon responded by organizing themselves into the North Korea Five Provinces Ten Administrative Bureaus. As far as Party affairs were concerned, from the beginning the Communist elements who, together with Soviet troops, had liberated the northern part of the country, worked to create a unified Communist

Party to lead the country's struggle. Differences of opinion emerged during that time: various groups in the South wanted to make Seoul the leading center for national activities, while Kim Il Sung, and the tendency he represented, insisted that under existing circumstances, with American forces in South Korea, the central organ of the Party should be located in the North, where conditions were deemed more favorable. Despite some initial resistance, a Central Organizing Committee of the North Korean Communists was set up to guide all political activities of the northern Party organizations. After a period of internal struggles, a conference was held on October 10, 1945, for the purpose of founding the Party. Here the political program and organizational principles worked out by Kim Il Sung were adopted.

Uniting and Organizing the People

Much has been written about the background of the Korean leader, and in the political climate at the time even the wildest speculations were given credibility as long as they were antisocialist. As mentioned above, many different groups had been carrying out anti-Japanese activities both inside and outside of Korea. But it does seem to be a fact—corroborated by Japanese sources—that the most important one, and the one with the greatest influence on political developments in the peninsula, was the guerrilla army led by Kim Il Sung, operating in the northern border regions. Nearly one million people, the vast majority of Koreans living in exile, could be found in Chien-tao, Manchuria. Among this population, which included political dissenters dating back to precolonial days, political consciousness had traditionally been high. In the 1920s Korean socialists became known all over Asia for their militancy, and it is no accident that quite a few of them had spent some time in that area. The border region became the base for ceaseless anti-Japanese activity; it was considered by the Japanese to be the main center of resistance. The Korean leader, originally called Kim Song Ju, became known as Kim Il Sung (The Sun of the Nation) in the early 1930s, when he organized the Koreans living across the Chinese border, armed them, and waged an armed struggle against the far superior forces, both numerically and technically, of the Japanese army. At a time when resistance in Korea itself was severely suppressed, this guerrilla army was an important source of inspiration; exploits of almost legendary proportions were attributed to it and to its leader, with his symbolic name. According to Kenichirō Sawada in *Chōsen chinwa* (*New Stories of Korea*), during World War II, when students at primary and middle schools in southern Korea were asked for the name of the figure they most respected under the assurance that their replies would be kept secret, as many as two-thirds of them selected Kim Il Sung.[5] Documents from the time provide evidence that Kim Il Sung was the leader the Japanese were most eager to eliminate, for the activities he led in the North were not limited to armed struggle, but included political organization and agitation which stretched deep into the peninsula. In 1945 Kim Il Sung thus emerged out of the anti-Japanese struggle as a hero, with great prestige and experience.

This of course does not mean that no other potential leaders existed. Yet when Kim Il Sung, only 32 years old, succeeded in taking over the leadership of the nation, it was, even according to as biased a writer as Dae-Sook Suh, mainly due to a combination of his own political abilities and the inadequacy of other Communist leaders.[6]

The situation at the time was extremely complex, requiring great political talents. This was to a large extent due to the tradition for splittism which had existed in the Korean Communist movement since its beginning. As Kim Il Sung states, "If the Communist Party which was organized in 1925 had not been destroyed owing to the manoeuvres of factionalists and saboteurs but had continued its existence, our Party would have greeted the August 15 liberation as an organized body and formed a solid leading core from the first day of the liberation."[7] The years of colonialism had furthered the above-mentioned tendency. It should be recalled that due to Japanese terror, many Korean revolutionaries had been forced to shift their activities to such places as China, Japan, and the Soviet Union. Returning after 1945, each group brought with it certain preconceived ideas and sympathies, corresponding to its particular background. This led to a high degree of factionalism at a time when unity was a prime necessity. Firm, prompt action was required in order to prevent a loss of initiative, which would have been fatal to the progressive development of the country. The question at the heart of political life at the time was the determination of a line which would take proper account both of the special conditions of the entire Korean nation and of the international situation. The occupation of the country by two competing powers, together with the fact that the Party was still not very strong, made this task very difficult.

Thus, to the problems created by the many different factions, further complications were added. It was during this entire process that Kim Il Sung showed his leadership qualities, his ability not only to unify the people but also to provide answers to the numerous problems involved. Dae-Sook Suh unwillingly confirms the fact that in the extremely urgent job of organizing the people's committees and the new administration as well as consolidating the Communist Party, Kim Il Sung showed every desire to work with the disparate groups involved—groups which had hardly had time to get acquainted and were thus having difficulty forging a new organizational unity. Between February and July 1946, he "worked tirelessly to unite the North Korean Branch Bureau of the Korean Communist Party and the Yenan Group."[8] Historically fragmented, the Korean movement had to await this immediate post-liberation period before a reintegration could take place. During the following years dissension had to be overcome, a task that was made all the more difficult by the division of the country. It was not until 1949 that the North Korean Workers Party and the South Korean Workers Party were merged into the Korean Workers Party, headed by Kim Il Sung.

Among the immediate problems to be tackled after the disarming of the Japanese and the dismantling of the colonial administrative apparatus was the setting up of instruments of people's power. It is more than probable that, due to its experience, the group led by Kim Il Sung had certain advantages which made it a more cohesive and determined core during this period. Even before liberation, in the 1940s, when Japanese capitulation could realistically be anticipated, this group had put great emphasis on the ideological and political preparation of its cadres: "To study is the first and foremost task of revolutionaries!" was the remarkable political slogan of these years. But not only theoretical preparations were made. In 1943 a military academy for Korean revolutionaries had been functioning in China, and from bases in the border areas attempts were made to multiply the underground revolutionary organizations in the homeland. As pointed out by the Korean leader at the time:

> We have already trained our own leading cadres to liberate the country. We have not only the commanding officers with combat skills and rich experiences in military and political activities obtained during the fierce battles and in different circumstances for ten-odd years, but we have also political workers possessed with the excellent art of leadership and revolutionary work method whereby they are united as one with the people, to organize and lead them.[9]

This effort was pursued in the period immediately following liberation, when schools for training security cadres were set up in all the provinces. There, advanced elements from among the workers and peasants were given political and military training. Weapons taken from the Japanese were used to arm them, as a measure to keep order and prevent counter-revolutionary activities. This endeavor to place all organs of state power under the control of the people no doubt contributed to the smooth implementation of the many reforms undertaken during the first twelve months after liberation.

The most important question in this immediate post-liberation period, however, was the formulation of a political line capable of uniting the majority of the people and mobilizing their efforts to carry out the huge tasks before them. During the previous years of anti-Japanese struggle, Korea had been analyzed as a colonial country with remnants of feudal landownership; accordingly, the tasks faced by Korean society were seen as related to the anti-imperialist, antifeudal, democratic revolution as well as to the creation of a Democratic People's Republic. This political line became the strategic point of departure, serving to unite all democratic forces and to isolate the minority of pro-Japanese and feudal elements.

> In order to oppose the remnant forces of imperialism and the feudal forces and complete the democratic revolution, a Democratic People's Republic, a people's power led by the working class, must be built by forming a democratic united front of which the working class is the core, and which embraces the broad sections of the peasantry and patriotic intellectuals, and even the nationalist capitalists who have a national conscience.[10]

This line showed itself successful in uniting the masses, thus setting in motion potent social forces which were to change the entire Korean situation in the years to come.

The Economic Point of Departure

Apart from the special conditions created by the division of the country, the situation in North Korea at the time of liberation resembled the state of affairs many former colonies have had to face upon independence. Just like these countries, Korea had been dominated by a structural deformation: for over thirty-five years, all major economic activities had been directed toward satisfying Japanese requirements (in 1944, for example, Japan absorbed 99 percent of Korean exports). Besides, Japanese ambitions and bellicosity in Asia had intensified the oppression and exploitation of Korea to a point almost without parallel.

In this state of complete destitution and misery, Koreans had to calculate their assets and liabilities. What could be called an asset was the rather highly developed infrastructure which, although destroyed by the Japanese, could be reconstructed. A school system had existed—albeit a very deficient one—and a tiny minority of Koreans had benefited from higher education. Some of these individuals proved valuable at a crucial point, when Korean intellectuals from both Japan and South Korea came to the North to help organize the educational system. Because of the colonial division of labor during Japanese domination, when Japanese civilians departed they took with them nearly all the technical and managerial skills necessary for the running of the economy. This created huge problems in the initial phases, although we do not mean to suggest that all Koreans were entirely without experience in management or organizational work. As pointed out by Grajdanzev at the beginning of World War II, when the Western powers were beginning to spread doubts as to the Korean people's ability to govern themselves: "There are in Korea people with ability to organize, with education, with some experience in handling public affairs . . ."[11]

On the industrial level, hydroelectric power had been developed and mineral resources exploited. During the later stages of the colonial period some industrialization had taken place: the Hwanghae Iron Works and the Kangson Steel Mill, for example, had produced semifinished goods. Today, having been rebuilt, they constitute part of the backbone of Korean heavy industry. There was also a sizeable chemical industry, a cement industry, and some factories specializing in the production of wooden pulp. But apart from these few and—in the case of the chemical factory—modern industrial activities, the majority were either geared to war production or of medium or small size, with many operating on the artisanal or repair-shop level. Under war conditions the upkeep of equipment had been neglected. During the later phases of the Pacific war much of the railway system became inoperative and factories were unable to sustain output because of lack of spare parts. Commercial relations, too, had to be established, but in a way that bypassed traditional markets and sources of supply. These complications caused the Korean economy added problems in the immediate post-liberation years:

> A resumption of production would require extensive repair and replacement, but Korea was dependent upon Japan as a source of parts and equipment because of its integration with the Japanese economy. Moreover, to get the Korean economy back into operation required not simply resumption of production, but redirection from Japanese military to Korean peacetime objectives. It would not be a Korean economy but rather the vestigial remains of a segment of the Japanese economy until such a redirection could be accomplished.[12]

Apart from the difficulties which arose from the wear and tear of wartime and the necessary reorientation of the economy toward Korea's internal needs, Japanese sabotage in August 1945 aggravated the situation. This was much more widespread in the North than in the South, where Japanese expected their property rights to be maintained after the arrival of the Americans. The American journalist Anna Louise Strong visited the North in 1947 and described the extent of this economic sabotage. Simply by letting the furnaces cool, the largest iron and steel plants were reduced to uselessness. Sixty-four mines were completely flooded while 178 others suffered the same fate to a lesser degree. Nineteen plants were knocked completely out of operation, including six of the most important ones: two iron and steel plants at Chongjin, two electric steel furnaces in Songjin, and two airplane factories in Pyongyang. Damage to forty-seven other factories was severe. Anna Louise Strong tells further of a struggle between the departing Japanese—who wanted to blow up the Hungnam Chemical Works with the plant's own explosives—and the Korean workers, with the latter succeeding in driving the Japanese out and saving the plant.[13]

In this immediate post-liberation period Westerners voiced many speculations with regard to possible Soviet stripping of Korean means of production. This is described as a complete fabrication by North Korean sources, and more objective Western investigations at the time seem to agree that nothing of the sort took place.[14]

In terms of the Korean nation as a whole, the North and the South could be characterized as two complementary economies. The political division of the country, therefore, could not fail to have severe economic repercussions. Most of the light industry and manufacturing industry (74 percent) were concentrated in the South, whereas North Korea possessed most of the heavy industry (86 percent). Because the industries which processed the raw materials extracted in the North were situated in the South, the North would have been at a disadvantage even if production had continued unhindered. "There were no manufacturing plants in North Korea to use the raw pig iron, the steel, aluminum, magnesium, copper, lead and zinc ingots, or the tons of acids, carbide, glycerine, absolute alcohol or rayon pulp which had previously been produced and exported to Japan or sent to South Korea for processing."[15] In heavy industrial production such as chemicals, metals, ceramics, cement, gas, and electricity, North Korea held the lead. But light industries such as textiles, machines, lumber, food, printing, etc., were found mainly in the South.

North Korea has been endowed by nature with a substantial hydroelectric potential. In fact 92 percent of all electric power was generated in the North, and the division thus created difficulties for the South. In mining, too, North Korea had a natural advantage, though the South did produce some of the more essential raw materials. The North possesses a wide range of important mineral resources (iron, coal, anthracite, copper, chrome, nickel, graphite, manganese, molybdenum, tungsten, gold, and silver), although none of them are found in great quantity. On the other hand, the North was put at a great disadvantage in the agricultural sector, since a large proportion of its territory (about 80 percent) consists of nonarable mountainous terrain. In the South, geographical as well as climatic conditions make higher productivity possible: "In the north, the dry fields prevail, while the south contains irrigated lands, the yields of which are almost double the yields of dry fields. Moreover, a substantial proportion of fields in the south bring two crops and, in some cases, even three crops a year."[16] The South thus accounted for about 75 percent of the country's paddy. For North Korea, therefore, the division of the country had tragic consequences for the survival needs of its people, since the unavailability of southern rice left the area with even less than the meager supply under the Japanese. In her article, Anna Louise Strong mentions a food crisis in 1946 which reduced rice rations in North Korea to 500 grams a day. This situation no doubt lent impetus to the sweeping land reform carried out so soon after liberation. Moreover, because of the scarcity prevailing on an international scale just after the World War II, no substantial relief from any external source could be expected. At a meeting of the North Korean Provisional People's Committee on November 25, 1946, Kim Il Sung indicated that under these circumstances the problem would have to be resolved through the Korean people's own efforts.

> The food shortage is not limited to Korea. Instead, because the whole world has only been freed from the sufferings of the war for a year, and also because of drought and floods, the people of the whole world are suffering from a food shortage. For this reason, we are not in a position to receive foreign aid in food. Therefore, with our utmost endeavor, we

must sustain ourselves with our own North Korean supply of food.[17]

Western sources at the time made much of the flow of refugees who moved to the South during this period. Among them were both former Japanese collaborators—people whose vested interests were in conflict with the reforms—and people who simply feared the food shortage. Another factor in the migration was the not inconsiderable number of people returning from exile in neighboring countries, many of whom had originally come from the southern part of Korea. Moreover, due to industrialization a significant population shift from South to North had taken place during the last six years of Japanese occupation. Part of the migration after the war could thus be explained by the fact that many people who had worked in the North wanted to rejoin the families and relatives they had left behind in the South.[18]

The Subjective Factors

To these material aspects of North Korea's point of departure must be added certain subjective factors. Although playing an important role, their precise influence is difficult to evaluate and is a source of controversy—not infrequently marked by certain ideological preconceptions—among experts. First of all, although this was hardly the Japanese intention, colonial occupation had brought about a social evolution: ". . . landlessness, more rural schools, expanding communications, and a greater exchange economy all made farmers less self-sufficient, hence less isolated within the economy," according to Gregory Henderson, with the result that "farmers came closer to political consciousness at the same time that they were losing or were increasingly alienated from the hierarchical structure through which they might express such consciousness."[19] In other words, what might be called a potential political consciousness existed. In the

North it could be funneled into constructive action, the introduction of social reforms; in the South however the confrontation between precisely this new awareness and the lack of any reforms—as well as people's general outrage at seeing the nation robbed of its newly acquired independence—led to chronic social instability.

On the political and organizational level an anti-Japanese resistance movement had, as we have seen, grown up over decades of extremely varied struggles. At the time of liberation the resistance consisted not only of a guerrilla movement with experience of protracted struggle, but of a whole range of illegal groups and associations. In 1932-1935, land reforms and democratic legislation had been enacted in the base areas around the Tumen River just across the Manchurian border—a kind of rehearsal for the measures later extended to the entire North. In the 1930s armed struggle was waged in these regions. After 1935 Mount Baikdu became the focal point of the resistance and from this center political activists and agitators were dispatched to all the provinces of Korea.[20] In these pre-liberation years the Association for the Restoration of the Fatherland, which emerged out of this center, played an important role. Its Ten Point Program, drawn up in 1936, survived liberation, becoming the guideline not only for anti-Japanese agitation but for the reforms introduced after 1945.

According to the North Koreans, this important organization was originally set up by Kim Il Sung and its Ten Point Program worked out personally by him. Western-oriented writers, however, deny this version of the Association's origins. Dae-Sook Suh, for instance, believes that neither the program nor the Association could have been initiated by Communists, since "throughout the Ten Point Program, not a word of Marxism is mentioned".[21] Neither did the program advocate the necessity of forming a Communist Party; moreover, only the property of Japanese nationals and Korean collaborators was to be confiscated.[22] The weakness in this line of reasoning is its failure to understand the national liberation struggle as a *stage* in a revolutionary process.

This program, the text of which is included in the appendix, formulated the necessary line for the formation of a broad anti-Japanese united front. All enterprises, railways, banks, ships, farms, and irrigation facilities belonging to Japanese or pro-Japanese elements were to be confiscated to obtain funds for the independence movement and to relieve the poor. Freedom of speech, press, assembly, and association were to be guaranteed, inequalities between nobility and common people eliminated, and equality of sex, nationality, and religion ensured. "Slave labor" and "slavish education" were to be abolished and compulsory free education introduced. The program advocated an eight-hour workday, as well as labor legislation, increased wages, and relief for the unemployed.

This manifesto is celebrated in the DPRK today as a revolutionary program which laid the foundation for a national united front. In a discussion on the occasion of the thirty-sixth aniversary of the foundation of the Association for the Restoration of the Fatherland, a Korean commentator stressed the basic principle for combining a revolutionary struggle with the requirements of an anti-imperialist movement: "It is essential for the victory of the revolution to bind together into a powerful political force all those who are interested in the revolution. This is a key issue decisive for the victory of the revolution, an indispensable demand of the revolutionary struggle. In particular in colonies, the formation of a united front and the development of its movement decide the success of the anti-imperialist national liberation struggle."[23]

Especially in the years 1936-1938, this program was used in illegal propaganda, forming the basis for the establishment of groups and organizations throughout the country. How much of this influence remained in 1945 is difficult to say—but the establishment of people's committees just after liberation and the efficiency and rapidity with which they functioned seem to indicate that a certain amount of political preparation had taken place. Indeed, there is a striking continuity between the line and slogans put forth by this Association during the anti-Japanese struggle and the political line followed in the North after 1945. In this respect the Ten Point Program of 1936 was clearly a draft version of the anti-imperialist and antifeudal reforms which ten years later were to form the basis of a kind of New Democracy in Korea, as in the case of China a few years later.

The Unique Postcolonial Situation

Immediately following liberation the North found itself in a situation calling for rapid and efficient measures, and there was a particularly urgent need for large-scale capital outlays. Because of the international political situation, however, it could expect little external assistance in this matter. As a result of the Cold War confrontation it was out of the question that Washington would extend any credits even if North Koreans had so desired. On the other hand, the Soviet Union was itself in urgent need of capital for postwar reconstruction. Discussing this issue, George McCune predicted the only viable policy:

> As a matter of principle it cannot encourage non-Soviet capital development, and as a matter of practice it could not attract such capital. Also as a matter of practice the North Korea regime cannot expect much assistance from areas friendly to it. Its orientation towards the Soviet Union, Manchuria, and perhaps eventually China draws it into an association whose other members are also in urgent need of capital. Therefore, whatever the costs in terms of retarded development and low living standards, North Korea will probably be obliged to pay its way to a much greater extent than South Korea.[24]

This initial handicap, intended to weaken North Korea

further, strengthened the country's determination to develop an independent national economy, a fact which later became its source of strength. The significance of this Korean experience, when capital literally had to be "made at home," becomes clear when comparing it to the usual situation in other Third World countries, including South Korea. There, access to foreign capital cemented the existing structures of dependence, obstructing any attempts at a self-centered process of accumulation.

The possibility of generating capital internally, however, derived not only from a conscious political choice, but from the special situation in which North Korea found itself. Unlike most Third World countries which upon acquiring independence are confronted with the enormous commercial and economic power of the developed world, North Korea was isolated from the capitalist bloc from the very start of the post-liberation period. And this applied especially to Japan, which, as a result of its defeat in World War II, was deprived of any influence whatsoever in the development of the northern half of its former colony. Moreover, the Soviet occupation prevented any of the victorious powers (especially the United States) from stepping into the so-called "vacuum" left by Japan. All this helped to give Korean independence some assurance of survival, especially in the first crucial years.

On the other hand, the Soviet Union's tasks of reconstruction at home, and the demands on its attention made by events in Europe, did not leave much room for directing developments in North Korea, even had it so wished. Similarly, internal developments in China—in the form of a civil war—kept that country from interfering in Korean affairs. The United States in those years had its hands full controlling the situation in the South, as well as on other continents, thus sparing North Korea (until 1950) direct intervention on a larger scale. Of course, many *indirect* attempts were made to influence the situation in the North.

Facing the Agricultural Question

Because of the pressure exerted by this situation and by the many urgent problems the North confronted, a series of campaigns and reforms were launched right after liberation. Immediate steps were taken to develop the administrative and political organization of the country, campaigns against illiteracy were undertaken in the very first months, and in an upsurge of patriotic energy the workers were mobilized to repair and reconstruct the means of production.

In March 1946, a complete Twenty Point Program was introduced which was to form the basis for the creation of a democratic state and government. Most of these twenty points, included in full in the appendix, were directed against Japanese property and colonial and feudal laws, beginning with the complete liquidation of "all the remnants of Japanese imperialist rule [in] the political and economic life of Korea." They also outlined a series of social reforms similar to those of the Ten Point Program of 1936, enumerating the main tasks of the anti-imperialist, antifeudal stage of the revolution. But since everything could not be done at once, the order of priority was very important. If any step had been undertaken in an incorrect manner, it might have endangered the unity of the progressive forces and given reactionary elements possibilities for action. As Kim Il Sung once put it, although in a different context, to weaken the counter-revolutionary forces is just as important as to strengthen the revolutionary forces.[25] This line of thinking was no doubt the strategic guide to the way these first reforms were carried out.

Apart from the food question, agriculture constituted an important sector of the national economy, employing the majority of the population. A correct solution of the land question was therefore not only a precondition for democratization but also an important political factor in the internal mobilization process.

According to Kim Il Sung, "The feudal relations of landownership prevailing in our rural areas had not only shackled millions of peasants to feudal exploitation and slavery and restricted the development of the productive forces of agriculture but also had impeded overall social progress. Therefore the solution of the land problem was the basic content of the anti-imperialist, anti-feudal democratic revolution."[26] At the time (1945), there were deep class divisions in the countryside, with landlords constituting no more than 4 percent of all households but owning nearly 60 percent of the land, whereas poor peasants, accounting for about 56.7 percent of all farm households, owned only 5.6 percent of total arable land. Rents on land often exceeded 60 percent and this, combined with many additional burdens, forced the peasants to live in complete destitution.

Viewed in a broader, more political context, the feudal landowner system constituted a bastion of reaction which could be used by foreign imperialist forces. As we have seen, Japanese imperialism maintained and strengthened feudal production relations, while enforcing private land ownership to serve its own ends. This is hardly something unique to Japanese colonialism. In a book published in 1957, Gunnar Myrdal describes how such policies serve the political objectives of the various imperialist powers in the colonial world:

> A main interest of a metropolitan country was order and social stability. By an almost automatic logic it therefore regularly came to ally itself with the privileged classes in the dependent country; sometimes such classes were created for this purpose. These favoured groups were, by and large, primarily interested in preserving the social and economic status quo under which they were privileged, and they would not normally press either for a national integration policy aimed at greater equality within the country, or for the progressive economic development in the main subsistence sector of the economy.[27]

Besides breaking the power of socially backward elements, the transformation of property rights to land had a special significance in Korea, having to do with traditional sociological attitudes, past and present, toward the soil:

> ... every peasant yearned for land he could call his own, especially if it were land associated with his ancestors. For him, the land was everything: his link with the past and the future, his source of livelihood, the central point in his value system. It involved the spiritual and the material, the immediate and the eternal. Thus, in promising the peasant that he who tilled the land could own it, the government touched some of the most profound emotions of the rural population, and that population constituted at the time more than two-thirds of the North Korean people.[28]

Under the circumstances, it was not surprising that news about such reforms also had political repercussions in the South, where the agrarian population was motivated by similar ties to their environment. As a matter of fact, rumors about land distribution in the North did indirectly result in peasant uprisings and demonstrations in several provinces of South Korea.

Land Reform

As the experiences of many different countries have shown, the realization of agrarian reform is a most delicate matter. Its preparation, implementation, and consolidation involve the accomplishment of a multitude of tasks. From the beginning, political work among peasants had been given high priority and efforts were made to gradually begin preparing them for the coming reform. The first step in this direction was the movement for the introduction of the so-called "three-seven system." Previously, peasants had been deprived of 50 to 80 percent of their harvest by landlords. The new system meant that the tenant farmer now gave 30 percent of his harvest to the proprietor, while retaining the remaining 70 percent. This measure not only immediately alleviated the economic situation of the peasantry, but gave them concrete proof that new winds were blowing over Korea. Organizationally, numerous rural committees were now formed with poor peasants and farm hands playing a leading role. Everywhere meetings were held where poor peasants were encouraged to denounce the crimes of the landlords, while easily understandable slogans gradually prepared the peasants for further steps. Finally, on the occasion of the twenty-seventh anniversary of the March 1st Movement—i.e., March 1, 1946—three million or so peasants held demonstrations and meetings under the slogans "Land to the tillers!" and "We want an agrarian reform!"

On March 5, 1946, the agrarian reform was officially announced in a decree radically affecting rural life. Because its first three articles set out the purpose and scope of the program, it is worth quoting them in full:

Article I. The land reform in North Korea arises from historical and economic necessity. The mission of land reform lies in the abolition of Japanese land ownership, land ownership by Korean landlords, and of land tenancy, and bestowing the right to exploit the land on those who cultivate. The agricultural system in North Korea shall be founded on individual ownership by farmers who are not shackled to landlords, and in the management of land.

Article II. The land coming into the following categories shall be confiscated and transferred to ownership by farmers: (1) land owned by the Japanese state, Japanese individuals and organizations; (2) land owned by traitors to the Korean people, those who have damaged the interests of the Korean people, and who actively participated in the political machinery of Japanese imperialism, and also land owned by those who fled from their own districts at the time of Korean liberation from Japanese oppression.

Article III. The land in the following categories shall be confiscated and distributed freely for ownership by farmers: (1) land owned by Korean landlords in excess of 5 *cho* per family; (2) land owned by those who did not cultivate but rented land solely for tenancy; (3) all land, regardless of acreage, which is continuously in tenancy; (4) land owned by shrines, temples, and other religious sects in excess of 5 *cho*.[29]

The 11,500 rural committees were given the task of registering the land, farm implements, draft animals, seed grains, buildings, irrigation facilities, orchards, and forests liable to confiscation. At the same time, plans for the free distribution were worked out. This procedure took into consideration the size of each family as well as the quality of the land. From the material quoted above it is clear that the confiscation comprised all lands owned by Japanese nationals or their Korean collaborators as well as absentee landlords, some of whom had fled during liberation. "Landlords" were defined as all those who owned more than five *chongbo* of land. The limit of five *chongbo* per farm (about five hectares) was chosen because it represented the bounds within which cultivation by a single individual farmer could efficiently take place. In addition, farmers who held less than five *chongbos* but who leased some of it out, had this leased land confiscated. According to Article IV of the decree, however, land and property belonging to schools, hospitals, and scientific institutions was not to be seized, even if the land had formerly been rented for continuous tenancy. Future tenancy, though, became prohibited. Schools, it was declared, "should cultivate such land with the labor of their own students and their families, and utilize the crops for school projects." In this manner all land held in permanent tenancy was expropriated, thus eliminating this system of land tenure while isolating a small group of conservative landlords. There was one more exception: forests and orchards were not divided, but turned over to local or state administrations. Moreover, several state farms were established for the specific purpose of animal husbandry. Often they were located in the regions where firefield cultivation had been practiced, with the aim of gradually drawing this population into a more modern type of agricultural production.

As a result of these measures, within a period of about twenty days some one million *chongbo* changed hands,

Table 5
Disposition of the Confiscated Land

Recipients	Number of families	Area (chongbo)
Farm laborers	17,137	22,387
Tenants without land	442,973	603,407
Farmers with little land	260,501	345,974
Landlords wishing to farm in new localities	3,911	9,622
Total	724,522	981,390

most of the land redistributed free to about 724,000 poor and landless peasants.[30]

Confiscation was made without compensation, since the land was regarded as originally having belonged to the peasantry. The landlords were accorded equal rights to five *chongbo* of land each, with the provision that they move to another province where they were not known by the local population. This latter measure was intended to break the ageold relationship between the feudal masters and their almost serflike former laborers. The strength of this traditional tie can be gauged by the fact that in some cases peasants, not understanding the new situation, had elected their landlords to be heads of rural committees! Through the relocation of the former landlords the counter-revolutionary forces among them were deprived of an economic foothold while possibilities for a new life were opened to those who did not want to resist. In this way the enemies of the agrarian reform were weakened. "During the agrarian reform some 44,000 landlords were expropriated from their lands. Their number was not inconsiderable. We did not hang or shoot the landlords, but only deprived them of their lands and moved them to other localities to let them live a life."[31] At this stage, capitalist trade and industry were left untouched; the main thrust of the social reform was against a minority of landlords.

An interesting aspect of this movement was that the new system of land ownership was still based on individual property. Article V of the decree stipulated that land was to be distributed gratis for "permanent ownership." And article VIII provided that lands given to farmers in this manner were to be "exempt from debts and liabilities in general." A further step to eliminate feudal relations was the prohibition of all sale, mortgage, or tenancy of land. Some critics of this reform have maintained that peasants who received land did not really obtain ownership in terms of the right to dispose fully of their land. It is highly doubtful, however, that such limitations on ownership were regarded as negative by the beneficiaries. It will be recalled that prior to Japanese colonialism private landownership in the capitalist sense had not developed very far. Moreover, as pointed out by McCune, "Under the Japanese, usurious interest rates and depressed crop prices operated like a pincers to squeeze thousands of Korean farm families into tenancy, wage labor, or even out of agriculture altogether."[32] By putting an end to the buying and selling of land, mortgages, and tenancy, the reform checked the trend toward speculation in land and also made future relations of exploitation based on land ownership impossible. In this manner the beginning of a new vicious circle of impoverishment and deprivation was prevented. In a somewhat broader context, when land is no longer considered a commodity, the development of capitalism in the countryside is discouraged, while the way to further preparatory steps toward a later socialist reorganization is left open.

In view of the complexities involved in such a gigantic undertaking, mistakes could hardly be avoided. Errors due to subjectivism in classification and confiscation procedures were committed and in many instances readjustments had to be made. The Party organization itself was not yet fully prepared politically and certain right and left errors were made. Nevertheless, a wide variety of observers agree that compared to other such experiments, it was a most successful affair. Anna Louise Strong, who had witnessed similar reforms in the Soviet Union and Eastern Europe, wrote after her visit to North Korea that "probably no land reform in history was carried out so rapidly with so little disturbances."[33] Even a nonsympathetic Korean writing about the land reform had to admit that "unlike that of neighboring China, it was accompanied by little bloodshed."[34]

The fact that a number of absentee landlords had been living in Seoul, the former capital, may have played a role in minimizing strife in the North Korean countryside. Furthermore, the division of the country into two zones gave the most reactionary elements the option of moving south. Writing six months *before* the announcement of the land reform, Grajdanzev made the following observation:

> Many of the Korean landlords were absentee-owners, and as the capital city of Korea is in the American hands, there is no doubt that many of the landlords from the Russian zone live also in Seoul. In all probability a number of the landlords from the Russian zone, as a measure of precaution, fled (or will flee) to the American zone. Thus the number of the landlords in the north would be smaller than in the south.[35]

While there can be no question of the decisive importance of the political lines followed during the implementation of the reforms in the North, the evidence does seem to indicate that similar measures—all other things being equal—would probably have met stronger resistance in the South: the Korean Interim Legislative Assembly, organized in December 1946, was "preponderantly representative of landlords and thus understandingly reluctant to initiate programs which might jeopardize the position of the propertied class. Even a measure to distribute the former Japanese holdings among the tenants would endanger their position."[36] As a point of interest it may be added that this Japanese-held property represented about one quarter of the entire cultivated area of Korea. In some counties in the South the Japanese controlled about half of the cultivated area, including some of the country's best agricultural soil.[37]

When finally, a full two years later, a kind of "land reform" was put into effect in South Korea, it was neither as comprehensive nor as efficient as the one in the North. In fact the mounting pressure by the peasantry, who were also influenced by the land reform in the North, made pacifying measures necessary. According to a U.S. military government decree (dated March 22, 1948) 686,965 acres of former Japanese property were sold—after compensation—to 587,974 tenant families. Such enthusiasm greeted these measures that South Korean politicians became aware of the benefits they could derive from the sentiment for land ownership. "The obvious popularity of land reform made it politic for office-seekers participating in the May 10, 1948, National Assembly elections to go on record as favoring the distribution of privately-owned lands as well."[38] Rhee opposed this movement and did his best to sabotage it, even dismissing his minister of agriculture and forestry for favoring strong agrarian changes. Many landlords took advantage of this unstable situation by selling land at high prices: "Meanwhile landlords, in the expectation that some sort of land distribution law would eventually be enacted, were compelling their tenants to buy land on very unfavorable terms or be evicted."[39]

The northern reform put most antisocialist observers of Korean affairs on the defensive. The free distribution of land, affecting about 76 percent of the rural population, was obviously a very popular measure. Nevertheless, by stretching his imagination to the fullest, one such observer managed to paint a picture of reluctant and embarrassed tenant farmers being forced to accept this land: "The peasants' consciences were clear; they did not initiate the land reform programme, and in fact, they loathed it. They were as helpless as the landlords."⁴⁰

Without claiming any such insight into the Korean peasant's frame of mind, the authors of the present study would suggest that this judgment is dictated more by ideological bias than by common sense. This does not mean that some peasants, or even the majority of them, may not have been surprised by these great transformations in their way of life. Yet the history of the Korean countryside has been marked not by a fatalistic attitude but by continuous peasant uprisings. Evidence also suggests that the Japanese occupation had turned many traditional ways of thought upside down. Writing in 1940—i.e., at a time when the possibility of land reform still seemed quite remote—W. J. Ladejinsky had the following impression of the Korean peasant mentality:

> The Korean tenants were never satisfied with their lot, but until the early twenties customs and traditions regulating the landlord-tenant relations were sufficient to prevent open conflict and insure relative peace in the village. In the past two decades, however, the life and work of Korean tenants has become increasingly conducive to discontents. The growing agricultural distress has brought about a sharp change in the attitude towards landlords. . . . The causes underlying them were numerous, but the principal ones in order of importance were termination of leases, excessive rents, and attempts to raise rents still higher.⁴¹

Consolidating the Reform

Cold War fantasies aside, it can be stated with a fair amount of certainty that it was precisely the opportunity it gave peasants to improve their lot that made the North Korean measure so popular. That the principle of private ownership—although modified—had not been abandoned, contributed to the favorable outcome. This represented a departure from its historical forerunner, the Bolshevik land reform, which had been more radical, but prevented by circumstances from following a consistent line. "The decree of February 1918 on the 'socialization of the land' pronounced 'all forms of individual utilization of land' to be 'transitory and obsolete.' . . . "[42] This step was later revoked—during the period of the New Economic Policy— providing an example of the way the policies adopted toward the peasantry in the Soviet Union had been prone to error, causing confusion and disorder. This was not the case in the Asian socialist experiments. First in Korea, then in China, the initial steps taken showed a prudent concern with the limits of the existing situation. The purpose was clearly to arouse the enthusiasm of the majority without causing any interruption of production. "First, the initial 'land reform' program, both in China and North Korea, which aimed at winning mass support in the rural areas and, at the same time, abetting, not disrupting, agrarian production, was relatively moderate. So far as the great majority of peasants were concerned, the reform was beneficial."[43]

The explanation may be connected to basic differences between these nations. In imperialist Tsarist Russia the question of national liberation did not arise. But for the victims of imperialism and feudalism this struggle was an important component of the emancipation process. As it was, the abolition of colonial and feudal remnants in Korea simultaneously deprived imperialism of a most important potential ally in the countryside and strengthened the socialist forces. The gradual manner in which the reform was conducted made it possible to win over large masses of peasants. One political result was that while the reform was being implemented, the Party was admitting numerous new members from among the peasants who had been most active. Thus, Party cells could be organized in every village and through political education it became possible to build up organizational discipline, promoting the development of a unitary political line. The Koreans explain how their method was at variance with the classical socialist approach: "The land problem had till then been regarded as a component part of the socialist revolution which liquidates the whole of the old relations of production based on private ownership. Accordingly, the nationalization of land had been considered as the supreme principle to be followed in the solution of the land problem." However, since in colonial and semicolonial countries the land question is raised not as part of a socialist revolution but as a "principal task of the anti-imperialist, antifeudal democratic revolution" the methods had to be different. An agrarian reform would have to take into consideration the balance of power of the different classes in the countryside as well as the peasants' ageold desire for land. It was the greatest desire of the peasants to till their own soil, an attitude fostered by the commercialization of land. And the Koreans argue that had they raised the demand for nationalization as the first step, it would have been impossible to win over the peasants and to awaken them politically. Consequently, it would have been impossible "to strengthen the worker-peasant alliance and build up the motive power of the revolution solidly." Economically, it would have paralyzed the "zeal of the peasants for production." The redistribution of land permitted it to be utilized more rationally. At the same time the peasants—making up the majority of the population—were firmly won over to the side of the revolution, and their enthusiasm for increasing production could be aroused.[44]

Instituting this type of land ownership, and the corresponding small peasant economy on which it was founded, did away with feudalism and created a more democratic base. But this diminutive, individual peasant economy was far from being the final goal. It was felt that developments outside agriculture would influence the countryside. In an economy where industry and other sectors were in the process of being nationalized and were developing in a socialist direction, it was considered possible to prevent the introduction of small peasant ownership from opening the way to capitalism. In order to ensure that this would not occur, such measures as the abolition of tenancy or of the buying and selling of land were not enough; conscious guidance of the working class by the Party and the state would also be necessary. This entire process will be discussed in more detail later on.

Meanwhile, the agrarian reform is not merely a question of politics but also an economic matter. Once agriculture was freed from its feudal fetters, new possibilities were opened for increased production. However, this would not occur automatically; certain measures had to be taken. How could it benefit the peasants to be masters of the land if they were short of the seed grains, draft animals, fertilizers, and farm implements needed for cultivating the fields?

In the production drive, as in land reform, little seems to have been left to chance. "Greet the first spring of liberated Korea with increased production, don't let even an inch of land lie idle." Such was the slogan in the first spring after the land distribution. At the same time, the Provisional People's Committee of North Korea had taken steps to overcome the shortage in agricultural means of production. First, all such property seized from the landlords was distributed to the poor peasants. In addition, more draft cattle were bought by the state from the mountain areas and sold at low prices to the peasants in the plains. Financial problems were tackled through the establishment of a "farmers' bank" where peasants could get loans on reasonable terms and thus be freed from exploitation by usurers. In the crucial one-and-a-half months after the reform, this farmers' bank loaned out 150 million *won* to finance the first spring farming (official rate: 1 *won* = dollars 0.403). Furthermore, propaganda was conducted to induce the middle peasants to share means of production with the poor peasants; mutual aid and oxen-sharing teams were formed. Another innovation was the setting up of consumers' cooperatives where farmers could buy farm implements and daily necessities at low prices. The production of farm tools was stepped up, in some cases by converting former Japanese repair shops; similarly, fertilizer could be produced in the existing chemical works. In the distribution of tools, fertilizers, etc., preference was given to poor farmers who had just received land. Those who could not pay received supplies on the condition of repayment in the autumn.

In fact, no material and political efforts were spared to consolidate the land reform. In response to a call for forming "assistance brigades for rice transplanting," tens of thousands of young workers from factories, mines, enterprises, offices, and schools all over the country took part in this struggle to raise agricultural output. This was accompanied by political agitation which, among other things, resulted in the formation of about 70,000 "rural production teams" and more than 16,000 "shock brigades for increased agricultural production." As a consequence of this campaign a larger crop area was sown than during any previous year and numerous dry fields were transformed into paddy fields through the many irrigation projects. These projects were organized as a mass movement right from the beginning; subsequently, the state invested some 155 million *won* in such endeavors, with the result that 55 new projects were completed, irrigating an area of more than 20,000 *chongbo* of paddy fields. One consequence of this social effort and of the conscious promotion of improved farming methods was an increased yield per land unit. In 1947 the grain output was 170,000 tons larger than the previous year and agricultural production continued to increase until, at the time of the outbreak of the war, basic self-sufficiency in food had become possible.[45]

On other levels, as well, a new life was beginning for the peasantry. Thousands of new peasant houses were built. Growing numbers of peasant children obtained access to regular schooling and adult education courses were systematically organized. Koreans today emphasize the establishment of closer ties between town and country, as well as between industry and agriculture, as the major sociological accomplishment of this period. As we shall see later on, a key problem in founding an independent national economy is how to break the satellitization of agriculture and integrate it into an all-embracing national economic process.

The Industrial Question

Compared to the usual Western development theories, the methods used in North Korea seemed to turn everything upside down! According to the former, main emphasis must be put on encouraging private initiative. Various methods may be used, including tax exemptions, good credit possibilities, and other financial inducements, as well as the extension of privileges, which tends to augment internal inequalities and limit the purchasing power of the majority. Although this theory of economic development regards economic inequality as a necessary investment incentive, it makes little attempt to deal with the problems created by the resulting unequal development of the various sectors of the economy.

Opposing this analysis through practice, North Korea regarded inequality as a social fetter on development. First of all, according to the Koreans, only fundamental reforms granting greater social justice and security could call forth mass participation in the economic process. And secondly, from a purely economic point of view, only by planned and equal development of all sectors of the economy would it be possible to create an integrated economic process and thereby achieve a sustained, accelerated rate of growth. Thus the distribution of purchasing power was seen as a necessary step to activate the internal market and redirect the colonial production pattern toward domestic needs.

In the industrial sector an extensive labor law was promulgated in June 1946. This legislative measure decreed a general eight-hour workday—reduced to seven hours for those engaged in hazardous or unhealthful occupations, such as mining—and abolished child labor. A major portion of the labor law was devoted to the welfare and security of workers. Legally fixed holidays and a minimum of two weeks' vacation—one month for workers in harmful occupations—were prescribed, with payment during vacation to be based on the average of the past twelve months' wages. Pregnant women were to be accorded twenty-five days off before childbirth and forty-two days after, with pay. Special provisions were also made for giving lighter work to pregnant women and for time out for mothers nursing children of less than one year.

Article XVIII of this law included a comprehensive compulsory social insurance system which covered: (1) aid for temporarily disabled workers, (2) aid during the period of incapacitation due to pregnancy and childbirth, (3) aid for funeral expenses, (4) annuities for people disabled by work functions or occupational diseases.[46] According to Anna Louise Strong, as early as the summer of 1947 the social insurance system operated about 85 hostels with 1,400 beds, mostly former private Japanese summer residences. These were expected to provide free vacations to about 25,000 workers during the season.[47]

Wages were not to be influenced by sex or age but fixed in accordance with a codified system of rates, taking into account the occupation, position, and skill of the wage earner. In privately owned enterprises, wages were to be determined by collective or labor contracts, and in cases of dispute the final decision would be made by the people's courts. In a country where labor unions had not previously existed, the post-liberation labor movement was of course related to state policies, which actively encouraged the organization of wage earners. In the South, in contrast, the American occupation forces suppressed labor unions. As a result of these differences, a structural separation between northern and southern labor organizations was unavoidable. In the North, by the end of 1947, 380,000 out of a total of 430,000 workers belonged to trade unions.[48]

These and other measures, including the law on the

equality of the sexes, put into effect in the northern zone of Korea were considered vital steps toward uniting all the patriotic forces in building a democratic state. The specific decision to undertake North Korea's transformation into a socialist system had not yet been taken at that stage. (It is interesting in this connection that the labor legislation was put through *before* the decree nationalizing industries.) As Kim Il Sung put it, "Economic construction in our country at the present time is not socialist, nor, of course, is it going in the direction of capitalism."[49] The intention was not, however, to keep the country eternally in a kind of no man's land between two social systems.

In concrete terms, this meant that the labor legislation was not "identical with the labor law of socialist society," but that it was, as Kim Il Sung put it, "fundamentally different from the labor law of a bourgeois country which defends capitalist exploitation. Ours is a democratic labor law conforming to the actual conditions in Korea."[50] Its explicit purpose was to protect the interests of the employed in both the private and state sector. But at the same time, in an attempt to gain the support of all who could be won to the new cause and out of concern with the requirements of economic development, the regime allowed and encouraged native capitalists to continue their business activities. This policy again was connected to the peculiar situation in which former colonies or semicolonies find themselves at the time of liberation—a situation which requires a different approach to the resolution of class contradictions:

> During their socialist revolutions other nations eliminated the capitalists and rich peasants as classes by means of expropriating them, but we had no need to do so. From the time immediately after liberation we had constantly pursued the policy of encouraging the economy of the small and medium entrepreneurs. The small and medium entrepreneurs can fight side by side with the workers and the peasants against imperialism.[51]

In a certain sense, Japanese imperialism itself had prepared the ground for an easier transition toward a noncapitalist society in Korea, weakening as it did the bourgeois classes. Moreover, the most conservative elements in the North had chosen to migrate to the American zone, creating a favorable climate for the process of transformation. The policy of a Democratic United Front that included the national bourgeoisie further weakened the resistance.

A measure nationalizing all enterprises that had belonged to Japanese capitalists or Korean collaborators was announced on August 10, 1945. Instead of meeting political resistance, this step on the contrary was gratifying to the people's nationalist sentiments, gaining support for the regime.

> It is important . . . to note that the nationalization of industry, transportation, communications, banking, commerce, and foreign trade was not only natural but also relatively simple. Few if any emerging states of that immediate postwar era had an indigenous "capitalist" class so weak and insignificant. Each of these economic areas (except for small-scale handicraft and commercial operations) had been mostly under Japanese control, either state or private. Nationalization was thus in its essense an act of nationalism as much as of socialism.[52]

However, as pointed out by Korean socialists, the aim of this period was not socialism. This was the democratic phase, and nationalization was seen as one of the tasks of the anti-imperialist struggle.

While a radical position was taken toward both Japanese property and that belonging to traitorous elements, the attitude toward national capitalists was in conformity with the Democratic National United Front policy: property of national capitalists and merchants was not to be touched. An example of this policy is provided by Decision No. 91 of the North Korean Interim People's Committee, dated October 4, 1946, the very title of which is noteworthy: "Decision Concerning the Protection of Private Ownership in Industrial and Commercial Activity and the Procedure for Encouraging the Development of Private Initiative."[53]

It is interesting to note that the nationalization program in the North was so popular among the people of the southern part of Korea that it called forth pronouncements no less radical on the part of the southern regime. In February 1948, a year and a half after the nationalizations above the 38th Parallel, in a radio broadcast Syngman Rhee proposed as part of a twenty point program not only to nationalize former Japanese property, but "to nationalize all heavy industry, mines, forests, public utilities, railways, water power, fisheries, communication and transportation systems. To inaugurate state supervision of all commercial and industrial enterprises to ensure fair treatment to consumers, traders, and producers alike."[54] But this pronouncement was merely a tactical manoeuver directed against the people's committees, it never received practical application.

Even though many of these reforms appear moderate when considered individually, they were broader in scope than contemporary legislation in most developed countries. The speed with which the measures were carried out —all within the first twelve months after liberation—was also quite amazing. It is true that in both China and Vietnam reform programs of similar content had been promulgated during the years of anti-Japanese struggle. Similar measures were put into effect in the liberated areas of China as well as by the Korean minority in Manchuria. Nevertheless, the program in North Korea was the first democratic reform legislation introduced on a national scale in the entire colonial world.

Unlike the nationalization process undertaken in many Third World countries in the period following political decolonization, the measures in North Korea were carried out without financial compensation. In this respect, the country was fortunate, since the military defeat made Japanese intervention inconceivable. Besides, there was no World Bank or other international financial organization which could threaten to cut off funds or credits in retaliation. In most states of Asia, Africa, or Latin America this question of taking over foreign investments poses great difficulties and is one of the main reasons for political confrontation with Western governments—a confrontation which not infrequently has led to military intervention.[55] Whatever problems North Korea faced after 1945, its isolation from the sphere of international capitalism did offer the possibility of reappropriating its own resources without at the same time acquiring enormous debts.

Accumulation Through Internal Mobilization of Resources

Western theories very often ascribe the problem of underdevelopment to the lack of capital and/or a shortage of technical knowledge. The usual conclusion drawn is that only foreign capital investments from the industrial centers (combined with their technical knowhow) can break the vicious circle. The case of Korea directly contradicts these assumptions. It will be recalled that the country had no possibility of obtaining foreign capital in any substantial amounts. Even though Korean speeches from that period are full of expressions of gratitude to the Soviet Union, it seems probable that besides delivering limited, but highly valuable technical assistance and granting certain limited loans the comrade country was rather passive as far as direct economic assistance was concerned. Under these conditions, the funds for financing the development of the economy had to be raised internally. As a matter of fact, the Korean example shows that once social reforms have been carried out and the main branches of the economy nationalized, the economic surplus—formerly appropriated by the colonial power—may be mobilized for national development.

Previously, Japan had absorbed huge amounts of Korean raw materials with little benefit accruing to the Korean economy. Now some of these could be exported to the Soviet Union and other countries in exchange for machines, tools, construction materials, etc. Equally detrimental had been the former shipments of excessive amounts of agricultural produce to the "motherland," leaving the Korean peasantry in a state of deprivation. Now the state could channel resources from agriculture (in the form of the 25 percent tax in kind) into the financing of industry without imposing an overly oppressive burden on the peasants.[56] Still another source of capital was the encouragement given to the construction of various kinds of light-industrial enterprises by mobilizing local resources and labor power. The significance of such a measure consisted in the fact that it took next to no initial investment on the part of the state. Industries, often in the form of producers' cooperatives, could thus be created on the basis of handicraft traditions and potential reserves in the countryside. Light industry with its quick turnover could become an important source of accumulation.

But by far the most important "source of capital" was probably found in the people's enthusiasm, initially roused by liberation and further promoted by the many reforms which concretely ameliorated their way of life. In many instances, as has already been shown, this improvement did not involve any large expenditures on the part of the state. Projects such as the campaign against illiteracy cost almost nothing. Draining and irrigation, as well as construction of dikes and certain industrial and cultural buildings and institutions, were often carried out with the help of voluntary, cost-free labor power. The money thus saved enabled the state to spend relatively more on technicians and material. During the colonial period, Koreans had often been forced to furnish unpaid labor for the construction of the military fortifications, roads, etc., demanded by the Japanese war machine. How different it must have been to be able to help voluntarily with the completion of projects resulting in direct improvements to their own livelihood! And this, furthermore, in the atmosphere of a newly liberated nation. Korean traditions, in the form of musical and artistic performances, were reborn and revitalized as the country regained its national identity and pride.

In this connection it should be recalled that all over Africa and Asia decolonization and the formal declaration of independence gave rise to enormous popular enthusiasm accompanied by what has often been described as the "revolution of rising expectations." In most of these former colonies, however, the economic system remained more or less intact after independence, resulting in widespread disillusionment after a few years. In North Korea, these expectations were far more likely to be fulfilled, thus maintaining a psychological climate conducive to mass participation in economic construction. As a result of this "give-and-take" system, many extra efforts were made. In the wake of the agrarian reform, for example, a campaign of voluntary contribution of so-called "patriotic rice" (probably stimulated by the Party) was carried out. The rice thus accumulated did not "disappear" but was used to build the first university in North Korea, the Kim Il Sung University. This step had particular symbolic value in this country where traditional respect for formal learning has been so profound, and at a time when the nation was just lifting its head after decades of cultural oppression. The political leadership seems to have shown great skill in formulating inspiring and easily understood campaigns and slogans which could mobilize the people's initiative and ingenuity.

Ideological and Organizational Efforts

The mass movements in the economic sphere were accompanied by efforts on the organizational level to mobilize people further. Besides the NKW Party, which by March 1948 had increased its membership to 700,000—374,000 of whom were of poor peasant origin—other organizations such as peasants' federations, the Democratic Youth League, and the Women's League were active in the countryside, where over 70 percent of the population lived at that time. In urban areas the workers' leagues and the youth and women's organizations carried on similar activities.[57]

On the ideological front, educational campaigns and organizational activities were used to encourage the population to show initiative and reject all conservatism, passivity, and mysticism. Two liberal observers of Korea were not far wrong when they wrote: "The immediate objective of the North Korean regime during this early period of social reconstruction (1945-1950) was to transform through re-education and reorientation a backward and previously subjugated society into a highly regimentated and energetic society."[58]

This task was all the more necessary in a country where Confucian attitudes were deeply rooted. According to this tradition, formal, abstract scholarship was exalted and officials accorded exaggerated respect, whereas manual labor was viewed with contempt. Such attitudes were a handicap to the creation of a modern economy, and they had to be fought in a systematic manner. Furthermore, with the departure of the Japanese the scarcity of trained Koreans to succeed them in various fields of economic and educational activity created a good deal of confusion. Little if anything had been done to establish adequate schools for the training of Korean scientists, engineers, administrators, etc. There was even a scarcity of skilled workers to carry on the economic activities of the country, as we have seen. Grajdanzev mentions the situation which arose in 1939 when Japan's plans for expansion were adversely affected by its own failure to educate Koreans:

> The plan of turning Korea into a military base of supplies ran into difficulties because of the extreme shortage of trained labor. In order to meet this crisis the Government started various types of short-term professional schools in 1939 (machine, electric, and mining courses); but it ran into

another difficulty—shortage of teaching personnel, textbooks, and equipment. Japan's educational policy in Korea thus proved to be a boomerang: the failure to provide advanced training for Koreans became an obstacle in the realization of Japanese plans of aggression.[59]

At the time of liberation perhaps 90 percent of the adult population had not received any formal schooling. Public schools were short on qualified personnel to take over the teaching duties.

This situation was, of course, common to both zones of the peninsula, but in the North an all-embracing effort was made right from the beginning to overcome this legacy from the past. All vestiges of Japanese culture and influence in the educational system were purged, while at the same time steps were taken to rehabilitate the national culture and modernize education. Korean was again made the exclusive national language and by 1949 all textbooks were printed in the Korean *Hangul* alphabet, eliminating the ageold use of Chinese characters and Japanese expressions. This simple phonetic Korean alphabet facilitated the literacy campaigns which were carried out as part of mass movements. Just after liberation a campaign was initiated requiring anyone with reading ability to teach five to ten illiterates so that a certain general level could be reached in a relatively short time. Children educated their parents at home, while study groups were formed at all workplaces. The movement was organized and supervised at all levels and the results widely publicized in a nationwide emulation campaign to eliminate illiteracy in record time. For the younger generation it usually took four to six months to learn to read a newspaper, write a little, and acquire a rudimentary knowledge of arithmetic and history. For adults over fifty the task was more difficult, as they often felt they were too old to start learning. Prior to liberation North Korea had had 2.3 million illiterates. By 1947 about 50 percent of these were classified as literate, while by 1949 all illiteracy was said to have been eliminated.

In the meantime a new educational system was being organized for both adults and youth. From the beginning an effort was made to base education as much as possible on national cadres, but some Koreans did of course study abroad. All who could be mobilized to perform teaching tasks were called upon to contribute: in 1946, some 2,000 teachers were assembled, some of them having come from South Korea and others having returned home from Japan.

On the cultural level an immense effort was made to erase from the minds of Koreans the concept of themselves as an inferior and subjugated people. A systematic study of Korea's history and cultural heritage was undertaken in order to provide the people with a historical past on which to build their national identity. These efforts were especially popular in a period of resurging Korean nationalism.

The combination of economic policies and political guidance had almost immediate socioeconomic results. The concerted efforts to conserve and fully utilize all resources and capacities, accompanied by ideological mobilization and measures which improved the people's livelihood, seem to have encouraged the masses to unite behind the political leadership. It must be understood that considering the original point of departure, learning to read and write, being allocated a plot of land, and obtaining some security of employment and protection against overexploitation, represented unprecedented progress for the majority of people. Moreover, adequate fulfillment of such daily requirements as basic food and clothing constituted a tremendous improvement. This intelligent mixture of ideological and material incentives played a fundamental role in economic development and seems to have become a characteristic feature of the "Korean model."

What the Korean experience of those years tends to show is that a process of overcoming underdevelopment can be achieved by activating the population, but that in return such a social mobilization can hardly take place unless the concrete interests of the masses are taken seriously. Such a theoretical observation was made in a different context by Professor Charles Bettelheim, who pointed out that *"particularly in countries of weak economic development . . . the population constitutes the principal productive force."*[60] This explains why, no matter how technically correct its concepts of economic development, a bureaucratic apparatus would never be able to carry through a policy of sustained rapid development. Administrative miracles in themselves would not motivate people to make a maximum effort. In this light, political work becomes not just an abstract theoretical question, as one might be inclined to believe, but rather the major precondition for efficient economic construction.

Despite difficuties of adjustment in the early years, the introduction of reforms had great socioeconomic impact, increasing production and encouraging independent initiatives. This was the first mass experience of the Marxist principle of self-reliance. The Korean idea of *Juche*—translated as "relying on one's own forces," "thinking with one's own head," "applying Marxism-Leninism to one's own realities"—is often given as the political explanation for all economic successes in the DPRK. In fact, this principle had deep roots in Korean nationalism, and early on developed in reaction to the elite—and harmful—tradition of *sadae* ("rely on the great"). Furthermore, during the years of the anti-Japanese struggle, in the remote and desolate areas of partisan activities, self-reliance had been a matter of survival. Today the idea of *Juche* seems to encompass self-identify in ideology, self-determination in politics, self-sufficiency in economic matters, and self-defense in the protection of the nation. In a broader perspective it is related to the Marxist vision of making the masses masters of their society and the conscious creators of history. Finally, the principle no doubt acts as a strong socio-psychological method of revitalization, releasing new energies among a previously subjugated people.

While inspiring the necessary frame of mind for the huge tasks of reconstruction, it simultaneously provides a way to prepare the road for self-sustained and self-centered development.

Planning Begins

Having identified the potential human and material resources, which, following the implementation of certain structural reforms, could be mobilized for internal accumulation, the next question must be: how is this capital to be used? As has been so convincingly demonstrated by Paul A. Baran, what determines a country's development is not so much the size of the invested capital as its utilization.[61] This implies a certain system of priorities. In Korea, the preconditions for a rational planning system had already been created by the fundamental transformation of social relations. By 1947 the nationalization program had brought 80.2 percent of industrial output under state control, while only 19.8 percent remained in private hands. In mining the state sector accounted for 100 percent of total output. Railway transportation, communications, foreign trade, and banking were also under state control. All this made economic planning possible; as a matter of fact, the first plan was introduced in that year.

Not much is known about this plan, the first in the country's history. Its emphasis seems to have been on rehabilitating and reorganizing existing assets as well as promoting rural development. A year later, however, in a public address Kim Il Sung reviewed the accomplishments made during the previous period, as well as future tasks and the strategy they would involve: "When the Japanese imperialists were chased out of Korea, they laughed and said that without them all industries and transports would be completely paralyzed."[62] Domestic reactionary elements too had ridiculed the plan, calling it a dream. However, the results achieved were substantial. Apart from the many socioeconomic reforms put into effect, many factories were put back into production rather rapidly. The Hungnam Fertilizer Plant, the nonferrous smeltery of Nampo, the Hwanghae Iron Works, the steel mill of Songjin, and the power center of Supung, as well as other industrial establishments, were rehabilitated and put into regular service, thus facilitating the fulfillment of the first economic plan. Similarly, the first electrical pumps were produced, while repair shops formerly serving Japanese needs were reconstructed and used to produce simple farm implements or other necessary instruments for agriculture. As far as transportation is concerned, railroads were again in operation, with trains being run by conductors only seventeen or eighteen years old, young men previously employed as coal shovellers. These formerly unskilled laborers had now become mechanicians capable of operating the railroad system. The method followed seems to have been to go from rather simple tasks to more complicated ones. First the existing means of production were rebuilt and put into use, then others were added. This process was carried through by relying mainly on the country's own resources, although Soviet technicians were of valuable assistance.

In the speech of 1948 Kim Il Sung set forth for the first time the outline of what was to become an original strategy of development: "It goes without saying that it is important to develop heavy industry. It is only by developing it that the foundations of an independent national economy can be laid and likewise create the material conditions for improving the living standard of the people." Under existing conditions, he maintained, it would be necessary for some time to put a great deal of emphasis on the development of raw materials, rehabilitating existing heavy industry, creating a new light-industrial sector, and rapidly developing agricultural production. Only through such a line of all embracing economic growth would it be possible to "stabilize and ameliorate quickly the living standard of the people and exalt still more the enthusiasm and creative spirit of the popular masses in the economic construction." Since the economic situation required the balanced development of all social sectors, the strategy was to consider heavy industry the priority, while simultaneously stressing the development of agriculture, light industry, and mining. Any other course would have been wrong.

> . . . it is erroneous to neglect the rehabilitation of heavy industry and the reenforcement of the country's economic base; but it is no less erroneous not to establish a light industry which is called for to ameliorate the people's living standard, by only putting emphasis on heavy industry. To improve the people's livelihood it is necessary to increase rapidly the production in its totality, increase production of necessity goods and systematically lower the prices.[63]

Another important point stressed in this speech was the necessity to make *fully integrated plans* which were at the same time *progressive* and *active*. Passive plans, which take account simply of things as they are, only serve to maintain the status quo. Giving some concrete examples, Kim Il Sung mentioned that while the area around Kanggye had an abundance of timber, no plans had yet been made for producing more wood and fabricating containers, furniture, or the like. More generally, in order to increase consumption the consumers' cooperatives as well as other enterprises were expected to try to pool their efforts and start producing various common necessities and articles on the basis of the resources immediately available, as well as taking care to develop new resources such as silk-worm cultivation, raising of pigs and cows, etc. "If one produces a lot and sells it at reasonable prices, it will be excellent! Then the people's needs will be satisfied. The rentability of the enterprises and the revenue of the workers will be increased at the same time!"[64]

The Importance of Political Guidance

Because the technical and political aspects of the development process are so complex, they require both correct theories and conscious leadership. This is where the importance of a party comes in. Not only must it offer political guidelines to keep mass mobilization alive, but it is also responsible for the fulfillment of the plan. Now, what kind of human material is needed to fulfill these tasks? The American sociologist C. Wright Mills made some interesting comparisons between the "private entrepreneurs" as agents of capitalist industrialization and what he termed "the political man" who, with his dedication to collective work and his discipline, was becoming a history-making agent for socialist industrialization.[65] According to Charles Bettelheim, the political cadres involved in the task must have "a clear view of the objectives and priorities of the struggle against underdevelopment. That is an essentially ideological necessity." Furthermore, the men and women in question must be of a certain type: "A second human and subjective demand of the struggle against underdevelopment is the total devotion of the political cadres to the national interest."[66]

In the case of Korea, these cadres had not really had time to acquire adequate knowledge of economic construction and experience in the field of management. These skills had to be acquired in the course of the process of transformation. This was a source of difficulties during this period. As Kim Il Sung pointed out in 1948: "In some industrial establishments, labor discipline is slack, the turnover of labor is excessive, expenditure for non-productive purposes and waste are tolerated and worse still, the bad practice of embezzling state property still persists."[67] Some Party members even failed to grasp the Party's economic polity of emphasizing the state sector of the economy. This attitude led in some cases to a paradoxical situation where leading cadres collaborated with private entrepreneurs instead of protecting the interests of the state sector.

Other shortcomings manifested themselves on the political level. Some Party members lacked "a genuinely popular style of work"; because they were not sufficiently concerned for the interest of the masses, sometimes they were guilty of deviations in implementing Party policies. In the longer run this weakness might result in decreased popular enthusiasm, a demobilization detrimental to the political climate required to build the economy. If not corrected in time, it might eventually lead to the creation of a political movement directed against the leading organs. In the present case, because of the division of the nation, an eventuality of this nature could have dangerous implications. Consequently, ideological vigilance and campaigns against wrong attitudes among the cadres were necessary. On the other hand, the strengthening of the political institutions and of state power was recognized as the only way to assure the continuation of the social process under conditions of inherited economic weakness and external threat.

> As the history of mankind shows, no class and no people can victoriously build a new society and defend their national independence in the absence of their own strong political power. Particularly under the present conditions, when our country is still divided and South Korea is being converted into a colony of U.S. imperialism, it is necessary to strengthen the people's organs and state power in every way in order to expedite national unification and assure the complete independence of all Korea.[68]

Regardless of the difficulties encountered, economic progress was registered throughout the period prior to the Korean War. According to a Korean economist living in Japan, "Industrial production jumped 70 percent, and labor productivity 51 percent, in fiscal 1947, in comparison with the previous year."[69] As is the case for most socialist countries, few absolute figures and statistics from North Korea are available. But the following comparative figures from official North Korean sources have been fairly well corroborated by non-Korean sources from the same period. According to these, industrial output increased 3.4

times from 1946 to 1949. The state industrial sector increased 4.2 times, exceeding the total 1944 production level by 20 percent. National income in 1949 was double that of 1946, and salaries for factory and office employees had increased by 83 percent. Gross agricultural output increased 1.4 times between 1944 and 1949.[70]

What all this amounts to is that in fact only a few years after liberation North Korea had already surpassed production of the last years of Japanese rule. The plan for 1950 set a goal for overall national production which was 230 percent above the equivalent figure for 1944. The greater purchasing power of both peasants and workers had created an internal market which was stimulating production in all sectors. On the cultural level all the existing Japanese schools, schools run by religious institutions, and private boys' and girls' schools had been amalgamated into a government-controlled educational system. Thousands of new schools had been established for both children and adults, while new cadres were in the process of being trained in several higher educational institutions, as well as in the Kim Il Sung University. A plan for four years of universal, free, compulsory education was drafted and expected to be put into force in 1950. On the political level the line of New Democracy was continued. Free play—within limits—was given to national capitalists, private trades people, and middle peasants, with the purpose of uniting as many people as possible behind the huge task of rapidly rebuilding the country.

One can only speculate on how things would have developed had this process been allowed to continue. As we have seen, the outbreak of war in June 1950 rudely interrupted this socioeconomic experiment and reduced most material advances to ashes. Yet it may unequivocally be stated that even before the war, the DPRK had reached the qualitative "takeoff" stage so familiar to us from development theories, and had entered upon a process of rapid independent economic development.

Notes

1. Takashi Hatada, *A History of Korea* (Santa Barbara, Cal.: American Bibliographic Center-Clio Press, 1969), p. 131.
2. Soon Sung Cho, *Korea in World Politics 1940-1950, An Evaluation of American Responsiblity* (Berkeley, Cal.: Univ. of Cal. Lomia Press, 1967), p. 88.
3. Koon Woo Nam, *The North Korean Communist Leadership (1945-1965)* (University, Ala.: Univ. Alabama Press, 1974), p. 15.
4. D. F. Fleming, *The Cold War and Its Origins 1950-1960*, vol. II (New York: Doubleday, 1961), pp. 589-590 [quoting E. Grant Meade, *American Military Government in Korea* (New York: Columbia Univ. Press, King's Crown Press, 1951)].
5. Kentaro Yamabe, "A Note on The Korean Communist Movement by Dae-Sook Suh," *Developing Economies* 5, no. 2 (June 1967): 411. The official North Korean biography does not deal with the many different versions of Kim Il Sung's life, according to which he was at one time a member of the Chinese Communist Party or fought in the Russian Red Army. As Japan was the common enemy, there was a natural tendency to cooperate among all progressive groups in that area of the world. According to Yamabe (pp. 405-412) any objective analysis of Kim Il Sung's entire career in the anti-Japanese movement shows a personal pattern of independence more pronouced than that of any other Nationalist or Communist leader. The main problem for Koreans was to ensure unified leadership of the highly fragmented *Korean* movement, and this seems to have been the persistent endeavor of Kim Il Sung during and immediately following the anti-Japanese struggle.
6. Dae-Sook Suh, *The Korean Communist Movement 1918-1948* (Princeton N. J.: Princeton Univ. Press, 1967), p. 238. The theory that Kim Il Sung was pushed into power by the Russians is contradicted by the fact that in the beginning Seoul was recognized as the political and administrative center.
7. Kim Il Sung, "On Some Questions Concerning Party and State Work in the Present State of the Socialist Revolution," speech on April 4, 1955, in *Selected Works*, vol. 1 (Pyongyang, 1965), pp. 295-296.
8. Suh, *Korean Communist Movement*, p. 321. The result of this effort was the merger in August 1946 between the Communist Party and the New Democratic Party, with its influence in the rural areas, thus further strengthening the alliance of the proletariat and the peasantry. This new Workers' Party of Korea has endured to the present day. Similar attempts were made in the South, but here the Party was soon proclaimed illegal.
9. Kim Il Sung, *The Korean Revolutionaries Must Know Korea Well*, speech addressed to political cadres of the Korean People's Revolutionary Army, September 15, 1943 (Pyongyang, 1973), p. 28.

10. Kim Il Sung, "The Building of New Korea and the National United Front," speech addressed to the responsible functionaries of the provincial Party Committee, October 13, 1945, in *Selected Works*, vol. I, p. 7.
11. Andrew J. Grajdanzev, *Modern Korea* (New York: John Day, 1944), p. 279.
12. George M. McCune, *Korea Today* (Cambridge, Mass.: Harvard Univ. Press, 1950), p. 39.
13. Anna Louise Strong, "Industrial Workers in North Korea," *Soviet Russia Today*, February 1948.
14. On the basis of extremely subjective testimony by refugees, Robert A. Scalapino and Chong-Sik Lee in a recent work renewed this old allegation. [*Communism in Korea*, vol. II (Berkeley, Cal.: Univ. of California Press, 1972), p. 1198.] Strangely enough, they overlook the fact that a U.S. special envoy at the time visited both Manchuria and North Korea in order to investigate these reports without finding any circumstantial evidence. Actually, upon his return, U.S. Reparation Commissioner Edwin W. Pauley reported that he had seen "little" sign of despoliation in North Korea, adding that "only on two or three occasions did we view anything that would indicate that such removals had taken place, and those only to minor extent . . ." [*USAMGIK Summation*, June 1946, pp. 17-18, quoted by Cho, *Korea in World Politics*, p. 87. See also Edwin W. Pauley, *Report on Japanese Assets in Soviet Occupied Korea to the President of the United States* (Washington, D.C.: Gov't. Printing office, 1946).]
15. McCune, *Korea Today*, p. 55.
16. Andrew J. Grajdanzev, "Korea Divided," in *Far Eastern Survey* 14, no. 20 (October 10, 1945): 282. Since the South is more densely populated, the acreage per capita may be slightly bigger in the North. According to S.J. Park, however, no less than 75 percent of the country's paddies were situated in the south. [*Die Wirtschaftsbeziehungen zwischen Japan und Korea 1910-1968* (Wiesbaden, 1969), p.46.]
17. *Kin Nichisei sensha*, vol. I (quoted by Scalapino and Lee, *Communism in Korea*, p. 1032). The Korean situation of complete destitution was very unlike the point of departure in Cuba in 1958 after the revolutionary takeover and may explain some basic differences in the economic policies of the two countries:

> . . . something that struck us again and again during our stay in Cuba, namely the extent to which rapid and important results could be obtained merely by eliminating some of the worst abuses and wastes of the old order. To put the point in different terms, there was a very large unused (or abused) potential in the Cuban economy and society, and this circumstance has enabled the new regime to accomplish quickly and relatively easily certain things which in less favorable conditions might have taken

years. [Leo Huberman and Paul M. Sweezy, *Cuba: Anatomy of a Revolution* (New York: Monthly Review Press, 1960), p. 95.]

18. "The American zone includes almost two thirds of Korea's population. This data, however, is for the year 1939. During the last six years there has taken place a significant shift of population from the south to the north because of industrialization." (Grajdanzev, *Modern Korea*, p. 281.)
19. Gregory Henderson, *Korea: The Politics of the Vortex* (Cambridge, Mass.: Harvard Univ. Press, 1968), p. 77.
20. Mount Baikdu (or Baikdu-san) is Korea's highest mountain (2,750 m). Even in the history and legends of old Korea it had a special significance. In modern times it has become the symbol of the Korean revolution.
21. Suh, *Korean Communist Movement*, pp. 269-270.
22. Ibid.
23. Li Chang Gol, "The Association for the Restoration of the Fatherland and Its Immortal Achievements," *The Pyongyang Times*, May 13, 1972.
24. McCune, *Korea Today*, p. 259-260.
25. Cf. Kim Il Sung, "Let Us Strengthen The Revolutionary Forces in Every Way to Achieve the Cause of Reunification of the Country," February 27, 1964, in *Selected Works*, vol. IV (Pyongyang, 1971), p. 100.
26. Kim Il Sung, "Victory of Socialist Agricultural Co-operativization," Janurary 5, 1959, in *Selected Works*, vol. II (Pyongyang, 1971 ed.) p. 284.
27. Gunnar Myrdal, *Economic Theory and Under-Developed Regions* (Mystic, Conn.: Verry, 1957), p. 59.
28. Scalapino and Lee, *Communism in Korea*, p. 1025.
29. Hankun Tralim, "Land Reform in North Korea," *Amerasia* (February 1947): 56-57 (quoted by McCune *Korea Today*, p. 202. McCune points out that this text is a more literal translation of the original decree than the two other versions published in Japan and South Korea).
30. *Choson Chungang Nyongam (Korean Central Almanach)*, 1949, pp. 71-72 [quoted by Chong-Sik Lee, "Land Reform, Collectivisation, and the Peasants in North Korea," *The China Quarterly* 14 (April-June 1963): 68].
31. Kim Il Sung, "The Organizational and Ideological Work of the Party," March 8, 1962, in *Selected Works*, vol. III (Pyongyang, 1971), p. 312 (the wording is slightly different from the original text which we are quoting).
32. McCune, *Korea Today*, p. 205.
33. Anna Louise Strong, *Inside North Korea* (Montrose, Cal.: A.L.

Strong, 1951), p. 29 [quoted by Jan Lönn, *Nordkorea* (Stockholm, 1972), p. 35].
34. Chong-Sik Lee, "Land Reform," p. 68. (Actually the agrarian reform in China is generally recognized as having been relatively bloodless considering the size of the country.)
35. Grajdanzev, "Korea Divided," p. 282.
36. McCune, *Korea Today*, p. 130.
37. Grajdanzev, *Modern Korea*, pp. 284 and 106.
38. McCune, *Korea Today*, pp. 133-134.
39. Ibid.
40. Chong-Sik Lee, "Land Reform," p. 68.
41. W.J. Ladejinsky, "Korean Agricultural Problems," *Foreign Agriculture* (February 1940): 114 (quoted by McCune, *Korea Today*, p. 206).
42. E.H. Carr, *Socialism in One Country*, vol. I (London, 1958), p. 212.
43. Scalapino and Lee, *Communism in Korea*, p. 1044.
44. Cf. *The Pyongyang Times*, August 21, 1971. (This was the first of a series of articles under the title, "Agrarian Reform Enforced in Our Country Under the Leadership of Comrade Kim Il Sung, The Great Leader of Revolution.")
45. Hatada, *History of Korea*, p. 139.
46. McCune, *Korea Today*, p. 210.
47. Anna Louise Strong, "Industrial Workers in North Korea," p. 17.
48. Cf. ibid., p. 26.
49. Kim Il Sung, "On the Draft Labour Law," June 20, 1946, in *Selected Works*, vol. I (Pyongyang, 1965), p. 31.
50. Ibid.
51. Kim Il Sung, interview with the Japanese newspaper *Mainichi Shimbun*, in *The Pyongyang Times*, September 23, 1972.
52. Scalapino and Lee, *Communism in Korea*, p. 1196.
53. McCune, *Korea Today*, p. 187.
54. Henry Chung, *The Russians Came to Korea* (Seoul: Korea Pacific Press, 1947), pp. 207-210 (quoted by McCune, *Korea Today*, p. 189).
55. Conscious of the necessity for Third World countries to control their own economic activities and the antagonism to such measures on the part of industrial countries, President Boumedienne of Algeria at the U.N. General Assembly's Special Session on Raw Materials made the following appeal: "This assembly should condemn all those, be they governments or enterprises, who use force or economic power in order to perpetuate this new form of economic aggression which consists in trying to destroy, curtail or discourage the effective exercise of the sovereign right to nationalize." [Quoted in *Peking Review* 16 (April 19, 1974):13.]
56. In the political climate of the period, even the wildest speculations were awarded serious attention. Thus some Western sources maintained that in 1947 a so-called "special contribution" was imposed

upon the peasantry. Neither the kind or the size of this contribution was ever made clear. Some observers estimated the tax in kind together with the special levy to amount to about 30 percent; others arrived at an estimate of 72 percent of the total crop. These allegations are denounced as complete fabrications by Korean socialists.

57. Chong-Sik Lee, "Land Reform," p. 70.
58. Key P. Yang and Chang-Boh Chee, "North Korean Educational System: 1945 to Present," *The China Quarterly* 14 (April-June 1963): 126.
59. Grajdanzev, *Modern Korea*, p. 263.
60. Charles Bettelheim, *Planification et croissance accélérée* (Paris; Maspero, 1965), p. 50. (Emphasis added)
61. Paul A. Baran, *The Political Economy of Growth* (New York: Monthly Review Press, 1962).
62. Kim Il Sung, "Que ferons-nous cette année et comment travaillerons-nous ?" January 12, 1948, in *Oeuvres Choisies,* vol. I (Pyongyang, 1971), p. 167. (This contribution is absent in the 1965 English edition.)
63. Ibid., pp. 176-177.
64. Ibid., p. 178.
65. Cf. C. Wright Mills, "The Problem of Industrial Development," in *Power, Politics and People* (New York: Oxford Univ. Press, 1963), p. 153.
66. Bettelheim, *Planification,* pp. 49-50.
67. Kim Il Sung, "Report to the Second Party Congress," March 28, 1948, in *Selected Works,* vol.I (Pyongyang, 1965), p. 98.
68. Ibid., p. 99.
69. Kim Byong Sik, *Modern Korea* (New York: International Publishers, 1970), p. 33.
70. Yoon T. Kuark, "North Korea's Industrial Development During the Post-War Peroid," *The China Quarterly* 14 (April-June 1963): 52.

Chapter 5
Priorities in Postwar Reconstruction

A completely new chapter in North Korea's socioeconomic development was opened by the Korean War. First of all the process of economic construction was dramatically interrupted. Taking advantage of its air superiority, the U.S. airforce dropped an average of eighteen bombs per square kilometer. Considering that large, thinly populated forest areas in the northern regions were relatively infrequent targets, one can imagine the tonnage of bombs dropped on towns and economic installations. As an eyewitness with experience as a World War II correspondent wrote, "No country in history suffered so much material destruction, except some small states in the direct path of the Mongol invaders."[1]

Measuring the Havoc of War

According to official North Korean estimates, industrial facilities amounting to more than 8,700 factories and enterprises were destroyed. Had it not been for the enormous effort made to keep underground production of military and other material in operation during the conflict, the economic base of the country would have been entirely shattered. Due to the destruction, there was a leveling off of industrial production in 1953 at about 64 percent of the

164 *Socialist Korea*

1949 output. For the most important sectors production had fallen to the following percentages of the last prewar year: electrical power, 26 percent; fuel, 11 percent; metallurgical production, 10 percent; and chemical production, 22 percent. The facilities for the production of iron ore, pig iron, crude copper, crude lead, motors' transformers, coke, sulphuric acid, chemical fertilizers, carbide, caustic soda, cement, etc., were completely destroyed.

The situation was similar in the rural sector, which had been particularly hard hit by the destruction of dikes and irrigation systems. More than 370,000 *chongbo* of farmland were damaged, with the result that total food production decreased considerably. About 250,000 cows and 380,000 pigs were killed. All this, together with the human losses, created havoc in the economic situation. In financial terms, North Korean sources estimated material destruction at 420 million (old) *won* (about $3,000 million)—equivalent to six times the country's national income of 1949.[2] Western sources indicate that about 2.1 million persons were killed or dislocated. These circumstances could not but affect the basic requirements of the population in the period immediately following the end of hostilities:

> It is not difficult to understand why food production declined in this period. In addition to wartime destruction itself, the basic factors were a massive labor shortage (women, children, and old men constituted the bulk of the available manpower); the extensive destruction of animals, including work animals, and farm implements; the damage to irrigation systems and reservoirs . . . ; and the drastic reductions in available fertilizer, insecticides, and even seeds.[3]

Besides the lack of food, there was a desperate need for clothes and shelter. In the city of Pyongyang, only one house was left standing. Overall, about 600,000 of the country's dwellings had been destroyed. Thousands of schools and hospitals as well as cultural and welfare institutions had been leveled to the ground.[4]

The tasks confronting the political leadership after the

armistice in 1953 were therefore both urgent and of enormous scope. Nevertheless, when talking about those days, Koreans often point out that the postwar reconstruction was relatively easy compared with the reorganization of society after 1945. The main reasons for this apparent paradox lie in the experience and institutions for rebuilding and administering the national economy which had been acquired during the five years of prewar construction following the Japanese-inflicted destruction. With regard to technical skills, too, the situation was better than in the immediate post-liberation period. In 1950, there were about fifteen higher educational institutions and a large number of specialized schools training technical and economic experts. This educational effort had been pursued in remote areas and underground shelters during the war. Moreover, in the middle of the hostilities, the order had been issued to withdraw some of the most capable men and cadres from combat duty in order to educate and train them for the huge tasks of reconstruction. In general, the population was better educated and organized in 1953 than they had been in 1945. Politically, their consciousness had reached a higher level. Besides, the people were solidly mobilized around a widely recognized and respected political leadership which had both the will and the concrete ideas necessary to solve the many problems of the ruined economy.

Still another factor contributing toward rapid restoration was the aid North Korea received from socialist countries. After liberation from colonial rule this type of help had been rather limited, as these countries were themselves engaged in either revolutionary struggle or recovery after World War II. Now, the situation was different. In addition to the Chinese volunteers—who stayed in the country until 1958 and helped with the reconstruction of bridges and railways—both direct aid and loans in the form of technical assistance, machinery, and consumer goods were made available to the country by the united socialist camp.[5] This foreign assistance was concentrated in the first years after the war, decreasing thereafter, and since 1960 hardly playing any role. According to North Korean computations direct aid received in the postwar period amounted to about $550 million.[6] There is no doubt that this aid, coming at a very decisive time, was both valuable and put to highly efficient use.

Rehabilitation of the national economy was further aided by the country's own natural resources, which, through the rapid restoration of extractive industries, could be traded for equipment from foreign sources. However, while the significance of these combined factors should not be minimized, there can be no doubt that the principal element in bringing the country out of this very difficult postwar situation was the political system's ability to mobilize the people. If—as has been argued—the majority of the population did not actively participate in the anti-Japanese struggle,[7] the situation was the complete opposite during the Korean War. Had the people been hostile to the regime, the outcome of the war would certainly have been different. That does not mean that every single individual was happy with the political system. Reliable statistics on the flow of refugees from South to North or North to South are hardly available, but a factor which must be taken into consideration was the fact that in order to escape the intensive U.S. bombings not a few people probably sought refuge south of the demarcation line, where they may also have had family. However, it can be established that the overwhelming majority did support the regime. The very strategy used by the Americans contributed to the creation of an unprecedented degree of mass mobilization, a fact that was fully recognized in Korea:

> The Fatherland Liberation War strengthened decisively the subjective revolutionary capacity of our country. As a result of severe trials during the war, the people were awakened more and tempered more, and the People's Army developed into an invincible revolutionary army, well trained politically, ideologically and in military technique, and equipped

with rich combat experience. At the same time, several hundreds of thousands of revolutionary cadres were trained in the blazing flames of war. They were to be the precious foundations for the victory of the revolution.[8]

As a consequence, anti-imperialist sentiment, together with a new sense of national identity and urgency, became a strong motivating force in the following years—a force that could be directed toward material achievements. But the commitment of the people, though important, is not a sufficient guarantee for successful economic construction. As the English economist Joan Robinson points out, "the credit must go to well conceived economic strategy and to patriotic rage and devotion expressing itself in enthusiasm for hard work."[9] Experience shows the existence of a dialectical relationship between these two elements, with popular enthusiasm tending to lose its vitality if progress is too slow.

The Politics of Recovery

In postwar Korea a precondition for the intensive work of reconstruction was the clarification at the decision-making level of some political problems. As the conflict had resulted in an inconclusive armistice, a mood of uncertainly prevailed among some cadres. Because of the possibility of a reopening of hostilities, some were of the opinion that it would be futile to start reconstruction. At the other extreme, some were under the impression that all risks had evaporated and felt that vigilance was no longer needed.[10] As a matter of fact, the strengthening of the country's defense potential has been a constant concern of the leadership of the DPRK. Since the level of any country's defense potential depends in the last instance on its economic foundation, the discussion revealed that in fact no contradiction need exist between defense preparations and peaceful reconstruction of the economy.

Once a consensus was reached on the necessity of rebuilding the country, many important issues involving the strategy of economic development remained to be tackled. Some of these were of such fundamental importance that they later became subjects of dispute within the socialist camp. Even though there are certain universal laws of economic development, they do not operate in a vacuum but are dependent on concrete conditions. In the case of Korea, the particular postwar situation made necessary a new and orginal model of development. The Korean strategy, with its main emphasis on heavy industry, in a way resembled the earlier orthodox Soviet version of economic development; it differentiated itself from this model, however, by *simultaneously* paying the utmost attention to the development of light industry and agriculture.[11]

This line was a logical consequence of Korea's specific situation as well as the embodiment of the leadership's thinking on this question, as already expressed in prewar formulations on economic development. However, this policy of parallel construction did encounter opposition, both from Party members in Korea and from fraternal parties abroad. These elements complained that too much emphasis was being put on the building of heavy industry at a time when the population was confronted with serious shortages of food and other commodities. Kim Yong Ju and Sin Joe Hoe of the Pyongyang Institute of Economic Science explained the essence of the dispute in a discussion with us:

> When the Party had set out this line [of building heavy industry simultaneously with light industry and agriculture] factionalists within the Party were against it. Some foreign friends also interfered into the policies of our Party. The factionalists said we were putting too much emphasis on heavy industry: "How can machines produce rice?" they asked. In other words, they wanted us to "eat" all resources and foreign aid, living well for a short period and then have nothing. Our Party rejected this line because without giving priority to heavy industry, we would have been unable to stabilize the people's livelihood, our defense power would

have suffered, and we would have been unable to lay the foundation of an independent national economy. As a matter of fact, machines can also produce rice! Heavy industry is the foundation for agricultural and light industrial development. When we make more agricultural machines, we produce more rice; when we make building equipment, we produce many more houses; and with vessels we catch more fish.

The counterargument was based on the reasoning that the DPRK should, on the one hand, increase imports of consumer commodities instead of machinery and equipment, while on the other hand, concentrate on exports of raw materials and depend on fraternal nations for machinery. "Our foreign friends when giving us assistance asked: 'Why are you not taking textiles and some consumer goods but only asking for machines?'" Fortunately, this rather inconsistent "advice" was rejected. Indeed, had it been followed it would certainly have slowed down the economic development of the country. In the longer run, moreover, Korea's independent political line might have been affected by the establishment of relations of dependency not unlike those existing between the industrial centers and the periphery of the capitalist world. The two Korean economists quoted above seem to have understood this danger:

> If we had exploited our natural resources for export purposes alone, then our wealth would have benefited other countries. If we had not developed manufacturing industries we would have been forced to continue selling mineral ores and in exchange buy finished goods at high prices resulting in a true economical loss. This type of relationship explains why backward countries are forced to cling to mining industries and have to buy expensive manufactured goods. This is a process which keeps them in their backward state.

Thus, as Koreans see it, for a country like theirs the way to overcome an unfavorable balance of trade in international commerce is through building an independent national economy. If this line of reasoning applies to a member of the socialist camp, it must be doubly relevant for other Third World countries.

On the other hand, the prevailing conditions in the DPRK after 1953 did not allow a one-sided, exclusive emphasis on building heavy industry. The rapid development of agricultural production and the furthering of a multitude of light-industrial enterprises were essential in order to provide food, clothing, and other daily necessities to a population made destitute by war and subjected to constant antisocialist propaganda from the South.

Plans and Priorities

The economic theories of the leadership could not just remain on the drawing board, but had to be put into immediate practice in order to set the economy in motion again. Only one week after the signing of the armistice, on August 5, 1953, the main line of postwar strategy was established in a speech by Premier Kim Il Sung to the Central Committee of the Workers' Party of Korea. Since all problems could not be tackled at once, a certain order of priority was devised, with reconstruction envisioned as a process consisting of three stages: (1) a six-month to one-year period for the preparation of the overall reconstruction; (2) a three year plan for complete rehabilitation and economic development with the goal of restoring prewar production levels in all sectors; (3) a five year plan laying the foundation for general industrialization. Thus, even while theoretical discussions were going on at the highest level over the order of importance of the various sectors, the country as a whole was from the earliest possible moment engaged in the process of reconstruction.

First priority was generally given to rebuilding important factories and enterprises, for this was the basic link which would facilitate the overall rehabilitation of the economy. As a result, the Hwanghae and Kim Chaek Iron Works, as well as the Songjin and Kangson Steel Works, resumed production in 1954 and reached prewar levels by 1956. Great stress was put on the development of a mechanized industry, and while much machinery still had to be imported, as many machines as possible were produced domestically. Precedence was given to machinery necessary to set up new factories, but there was considerable emphasis also on the manufacture of equipment for transportation, mining, and farming, as well as irrigation pumps and motors for fishing boats. The exploitation of mineral resources required special attention too, not only in order to supply the home industries with raw materials but also to acquire foreign exchange that could pay for imported machinery. Other important tasks were the reconstruction of railways, the restoration of the irrigation system, power production, the manufacture of building materials, and so on.

In the reconstruction of towns and cities it was decided to give preferential treatment to factories, schools, and hospitals with public buildings and dwellings having a somewhat lower priority. Meanwhile, temporary housing also had to be rapidly built. But urban centers were not to be rebuilt in the old, Japanese-influenced way. Instead, there were to be proper waterworks and sewage, plenty of grassy, open-air recreation grounds, and a good lighting and heating system. The plans for cities and towns included all the necessary cultural and welfare facilities—schools, clubhouses, cultural institutions, theaters, cinemas, hospitals, and bathhouses. Whereas the state was to finance the building of higher educational institutions, common schools were to be built rapidly through a nationwide mass movement. Campaigns to improve sanitary conditons and anti-epidemic measures were to be carried out and the production of medicines stepped up through the collection of medicinal herbs all over the country.

This important speech by Kim Il Sung, which dealt with every aspect of postwar Korean society, further emphasized the need to find methods of conserving and rationally utilizing material and labor, since there was a shortage of both. Simplifying administration, doing away with unnecessary, unproductive jobs everywhere, was one proposed measure. Actively drawing women into productive work was another. Since much labor was performed with primitive, manual methods, productivity could be raised through the introduction of simple implements such as wheelbarrows, or through a more intelligent organization of work. Further, certain tasks could be simplified. The labor shortage was a particular problem in the construction of certain key enterprises, those necessary for the overall development of the economy. Once constructed, these enterprises would require relatively little labor power for their operation, but in the short run, their erection demanded tremendous amounts of labor. In such cases all technical and material resources were concentrated on the job and mass mobilization of workers, peasants, functionaries, and army personnel delivered the hard work. This method was utilized in the reconstruction of a whole succession of large factories, roads, dikes, and so on.

In addition, the problem of technical knowhow had to be solved. As has already been mentioned, a fairly significant number of intellectuals and technicians had been trained since liberation in 1945. These could serve as the backbone of cadres and teachers during the reconstruction process. But this was far from enough. In order to alleviate the shortage of qualified personnel, students were asked to shorten their terms of study or move their "classrooms" to construction sites, thus contributing to the solution of many problems while learning at the same time. To make the fullest possibe use of cadres, the method of collective consultation between workers and technicians was encouraged; the "summing up of experiences, using collective wisdom and intelligence and learning from each other" had to become a habit. A factor which is downplayed by the Koreans today was the presence of foreign technical cadres from the Soviet Union and other socialist countries, who had been invited to assist in the reconstruc-

Priorities in Postwar Reconstruction 173

tion. At the time this was seen as a unique opportunity to acquire advanced technique and knowhow. The translation and publication of Soviet books was therefore intensified: "The road of learning is open to us; we are provided with every condition to do so. We must learn humbly and modestly, and with an open mind, from Soviet scholars, specialists and technicians."[12]

Perhaps unavoidably, Koreans tended to become somewhat dogmatic in their attachment to this great ally. In the next few years, Soviet influence in the Korean educational system actually became rather extreme: sometimes pictures of Mayakovsky and Pushkin would look down on Korean children from the classroom walls instead of pictures of their own artists or heros. Intellectuals got into the habit of using Russian terms. Such trends of reliance on foreign culture were later opposed. It must be remembered that prior to its subjugation by the Japanese, Korea had experienced a wave of foreign influence so pervasive that it undermined national culture and the will to resist external dominance. In his famous speech, "On Establishing *Juche*" (self-reliance), Kim Il Sung cited the cases described above; he went on to remind his audience of the negative controversy on the method of political work in the army which had taken place during the war between people who had studied in China and those who had studied in the USSR, and of the consequent need to develop an independent Korean stand:

> If we ignore the history of our country and the traditions of our people and take no account of our realities and the level of awareness of our people, and mechanically copy from foreign experience, it will lead to dogmatic errors and will do much harm to the revolutionary cause. Such practice cannot be considered an expression of faithfulness to Marxism–Leninism or to internationalism; it runs counter to them.[13]

This did not mean that the country should not learn from

others, but the aim was first and foremost to further the Korean revolution.

As far as the economic phase of the rehabilitation program was concerned, the tasks of the first stage were fulfilled within a period of nine months. With Chinese members of the voluntary corps of the People's Liberation Army lending a useful hand, the main railway lines had been restored and made temporarily useable only one month after the armistice had been signed. Thousands of temporary houses had been built in both rural and urban areas. Production facilities in the countryside, as well as bombed-out cities and factories, were being restored or rebuilt from ruins; as a consequence, a number of mines as well as industrial and agricultural enterprises were once again partially or entirely in production. At the same time light-industrial enterprises were preparing to go into full production. For the planners this meant the fulfillment of the preconditions for the launching of a general rehabilitation and development of the economy.

The Three Year Plan—Expanding the Socialist Sector

Following these initial successes, the Three Year Plan was introduced. This second stage had the basic aim of raising production for the years 1954-1956 to prewar levels and improving the general standard of living of the people, as well as developing science, culture, and the arts. At the same time, the plan called for rectification of some basic colonial deformations of the economy. As we have seen, under the Japanese all economic activities had been incorporated into the sphere of colonial relations. Thus, most industrial establishments had been built on the east or west coasts, far removed from the sources of raw materials. For the colonial power such an arrangement had been convenient for shipping products out of the country. However, during the Korean War, the location of these installations had made them easy targets for American naval bombardments. All these factors were taken into consideration in the task of building a new economic base, and criteria different from those existing in colonial days were applied. Thus, while some industries could be restored in their previous locations, others were moved to places where transport facilities and raw materials were more accessible. Similar relocations took place later on when modern cooperative farms were established. Many agricultural establishments, formerly located in the middle of plains, taking up valuable arable land, were set up instead on foothills or mountain slopes, thus adding charm and efficiency to the rural sector.

Another prerequisite for rectifying the lopsidedness inherited from colonialism was an increase in productivity. According to the plan, this was to be increased by 76 percent in industry and 74 percent in construction during the three-year period. The means employed to achieve these results were educational, technical, and socioeconomic. The progressive organization of Korean society along socialist lines was seen as a means to more rational utilization of both human and material resources.

This socialist evolution could be observed in the ever-decreasing role of the private sector. Following liberation, three basic economic forms had emerged as a consequence of the various reforms carried out in the prewar period: (1) a socialist or semisocialist form based on the state and cooperative economy; (2) a small commodity production by individual farmers and handicrafts people; (3) a capitalist form practiced by merchants, industrialists, and rich farmers. Due to the nationalizations of property belonging to Japanese and comprador capitalists, including transport and communication facilities, banks, etc., the state had soon come to play a dominant role. Following the war, this tendency was further accentuated.

> Under these [war-created] circumstances, the capitalist traders and industrialists found it impossible to restore their ruined economy unless they relied on the assistance of the state and the socialist economy, and unless they pooled their means of production, funds and efforts. Moreover, as

agriculture and handicrafts were being transformed on cooperative lines, they could no longer obtain raw and other materials on the private market.[14]

The postwar years were consequently characterized by the growing cooperativization of private small trade and industry as well as the collectivization of agriculture, bringing about remarkable transformations in the country's socioeconomic structure.

As a result of this process the share of total industrial output represented by state-run and cooperative industries increased from 90.7 percent in 1949 to 98 percent in 1956. Meanwhile, in the rural sector the cooperatives, which were introduced gradually, from 1953 on, began to increase their share of total agricultural production from 8 percent at the beginning to 73.9 percent in 1956. A similar trend could be seen in the field of commerce: private trade had decreased to 12.7 percent of the total by the end of the Three Year Plan. Table 6 shows the movement from small private production and capitalist enterprise toward a growing socialist sector.

Table 6
National Income According to Different Economic Sector
(in percent)

	1946	1949	1953	1954	1955	1956
Socialist economy	14.8	44.5	45.6	55.5	77.0	81.8
State-owned	14.6	40.3	39.4	48.4	53.4	49.5
Cooperative	0.2	4.2	6.2	7.1	23.6	32.3
Small commodity production	64.2	46.6	51.2	41.4	20.7	15.5
Private capitalist economy	21.0	8.9	3.2	3.1	2.3	2.7
Total :	100.0	100.0	100.0	100.0	100.0	100.0

Source: *Postwar Rehabilitation and Development of the National Economy of DPRK* (Pyongyang, 1957), p. 59.

Another important aspect of Korean postwar reconstruction was the judicious balance maintained between the need for huge quantities of capital investment and the need for steady improvement of the material and cultural living conditions of the population. Overstressing either aspect could have had equally negative results. The difficulty resides in the fact that while consumption meets immediate demand, accumulation is necessary for later improvement of the standard of living.

> We must lay aside more for our future welfare. Yet we must guard against putting too much stress on accumulation, only on future welfare, and neglecting the present life of the people. It is, therefore, of great importance to solve rationally the problems of economic construction and the people's livelihood by keeping a proper balance between accumulation and consumption as we have done up to now.[15]

Concern for current living conditions was manifested from the very start. For example, there were price reductions averaging 10.3 percent on 550 consumer items between 1954-1956, and seven more such reductions followed later on. There were also wage increases: 25 percent in April 1954, 35 percent in November 1956, 10 percent in January 1958, and 40 percent twelve months later. "As a result, the average real wage level at the end of 1956 was said to have reached the prewar level of 1949, and the index (using 1949 as the base year) showed 136 in 1957, and 159 by 1958."[16] At the same time large sums were allocated to the improvement of social welfare, including social security and social insurance allowances, paid summer camps and vacations, free medical treatment, and (from 1959) free education. All these measures, together with tax reductions for workers and office employees, further raised the average standard of living. This of course does not mean that there was a movement toward consumerism. But the material needs of the people were taken seriously and more equal distribution achieved.

Politically speaking, any course resulting in the introduction of luxury items and superfluous commodities would have created differences among the people, as the supply of such items would necessarily have been limited. Economically speaking, such a policy would also have meant less efficient resource utilization. All other things being equal, "each reduction in useless consumption corresponds to an increase in the investment surplus, or . . . can allow an augmentation in useful consumption."[17] This raises some fundamental points. Since for historical reasons the transition to a new social system has been undertaken primarily by countries which had been unable to develop under capitalism, the process has been characterized by the urgent need to develop the productive forces. It should not be forgotten, however, that the project of socialism cannot be reduced to a "simple" method of industrialization and development. Historical experience, moreover, seems to indicate that the priorities dictated by the socialist aim promote economic construction:

> In real political practice, it is clearly possible to distinguish between a proletarian practice and a non-proletarian practice. The former is constantly preoccupied with "financial strictness," stable and declining prices, with raising the standard of living of the masses by lowering the prices of widely used consumer goods. This was one of the concerns of Soviet policy until the Twentieth Congress. This is the constant concern of Chinese policy. Such concern is not "fetishism"; it stems from respect for the labor furnished by the masses, and for their rights.[18]

Without such a policy, the alienation of the masses from the political system would soon threaten to reduce the influence of the Party as well as the ideological and political appeal of socialism. In the Korean case the opposite took place. The gradual betterment of the people's livelihood was accompanied by the swelling of the Party's ranks. Most of these new members were drawn from among the many new activists who had emerged in the process of cooperativization, thus broadening the base of the Party and further enhancing its prestige. This convergence between economic improvements and political enthusiasm greatly strengthened the political line of the Party leadership under Kim Il Sung, while correspondingly weakening whatever other tendencies existed within the Party. Subsequently this aspect was to acquire additional significance for the country's independent course as serious disagreements surfaced within the socialist camp.

The Five Year Plan

With the return to prewar levels of industrial and agricultural output ahead of schedule, the postwar economic rehabilitation was achieved in the relatively short period of three years, making possible the introduction of the longer range Five Year Plan in April 1956. This new plan was unprecedented not only from the point of view of its time span but also with regard to its aims. The main goal was to lay the foundation for the creation of an independent socialist industrial state, not at the expense of the material needs of the people, but in a way that simultaneously resolved all the basic problems of food, clothing, and housing. This involved tackling a whole set of theoretical and practical problems with regard to economic development. The basic line put forth was to give priority to the development of heavy industry, while simultaneously developing light industry and agriculture in a coordinated manner. Under existing conditions it was felt that the only way such a project could be launched was through a radical transformation of production relations. Only by developing a socialist economy would it be possible to eliminate all sources of exploitation and thereby mobilize fully all human and material resources for the rapid and planned development of the country's productive forces.

Notwithstanding the fact that the socialist transformation of the economy had been an important implicit objective from the start, the policy of "People's Democracy"— i.e., uniting broad sections of the population—had prevailed up to 1950. The reason for this apparent moderation had not been principally the division of the country, but the fact that in those years the majority of the people were ideologically unprepared for socialism. On the theoretical level this is in accordance with the concept of socialist construction as a process composed of different phases.

As is the case in most Third World countries, the political consciousness of Koreans during the colonial period had been influenced against socialism by the foreign occupant. This was a factor the socialist forces had to take into account during the political process following independence. Nevertheless, when in 1955 socialist transformation became the order of the day, some people criticized the Party for not having propagandized more actively for socialism before. In response to this criticism, Kim Il Sung pointed out that at the time subjective conditions had not been ripe: "If we had advocated building socialism in Korea immediately after the liberation, who would have listened to us? People would never have come near us, because the Japanese imperialists had conducted malignant propaganda, even alleging that under socialism many share one bed and eat meals from one common pot."[19] A gradual, step-by-step process of "uniting the many and defeating the few" was clearly necessary. However, as mentioned before, the effects of the war accelerated and facilitated the socialist transformation of agriculture and the remnants of private industry and handicrafts.

The Great Socialist Dispute in the Korean Context

Other critics at that time—among them some of Korea's foreign friends—took the attitude that the country was embarking on too ambitious a program of development and that the socialist transformation was advancing too rapidly, while proper attention was not given to improving living standards. The fact, however, that China was advancing along similar lines probably helped the DPRK to maintain an independent position.

The points of disagreement revolved around general economic policies. It seems more than probable that the new Five Year Plan, with its emphasis on the importance of heavy industry and machine-building, had been worked out by the Koreans independently of Soviet assistance or approval. Thus, at the Third Party Congress of the Workers' Party of Korea in 1956, the Soviet delegate not only hinted at criticisms of the Five Year Plan, but made it clear that the Soviet Union expected a certain type of interdependence between the two countries: "As we see from the report, the Party and the Government are contemplating a stupendous plan for the development in the near future of the economy and culture of the country . . . In carrying out the future Five Year Plan for the development of the national economy . . . you will probably meet with no few difficulties. . . . " The Soviet delegate recommended a different order of priorities, pointing out that the results of the Three Year Plan make it "possible to discuss at this time the question of more rapidly restoring and further enhancing agriculture . . . [and of raising] considerably the living standard of the workers, peasants, and intellectuals."[20] In this disagreement once again we encounter the questions of accumulation or consumption, heavy or light industries and, ultimately, dependence or independence. Years later, during a state visit to Indonesia, Kim Il Sung referred to these differences:

> The anti-Party elements lurking within the Party, and the revisionists and dogmatists both at home and abroad loudly protested against the line of ensuring the priority growth of heavy industry while simultaneously developing light industry and agriculture. According to their arguments, everything should have been directed to the daily need of consumption, leaving the future out of account. *Their purpose,* in the final analysis, *was to prevent our country from building its economic foundations.*[21]

The strong language used would indicate that this was not just a matter of friendly disagreement over tactics, but of deep strategic differences. The Korean emphasis on self-reliance, the so-called *Juche* principle, based on political mass mobilization, was obviously not to the taste of the Soviet delegate, who instead stressed the fact that in its endeavors to create a better life, Korea "*leans upon* the cooperation and fraternal, mutual assistance of the socialist states."[22]

The Soviet comments at the Third Party Congress in Pyongyang might still have been interpreted as sincere advice by one fraternal party to another, had it not been for a certain part of the speech which seemed to criticize Kim Il Sung's dominance and appealed to the Party to introduce the "Leninist principle of collective leadership."[23] It must be remembered that this was only three months after the famous Twentieth Congress of the CPSU where Nikita Khrushchev, in his co-called "secret report," had pronounced his condemnation of Stalin (who had died in 1953) and the "cult of personality." As will be recalled, none of the fraternal parties had been given advance warning of the accusations contained in the speech. This caused a general ideological crisis in many Communist parties, especially in Europe. As far as most Asian Communist parties were concerned, their attitude was that although errors had been committed by Stalin, it was necessary to have a less onesided conception of the role of the former Soviet leader than the one indicated by his successors. Thus, while accepting the principle of criticism of Stalin as an internal problem for the Soviet Union, they were not prepared to acquiesce in Soviet intervention in their own affairs, especially with regard to the question of leadership. The Soviet delegate's use of the post-Stalin experience in his own country in order to intervene in Korea's internal party affairs could only be interpreted by the Koreans as an intolerable attempt at interference.

The Koreans are very discreet in their treatment of these differences. Although references to them are frequent, they never use names and when asked more directly they often dismiss the dispute as a "family quarrel" which should only be discussed in the closed circle of family members! From the later speeches by Kim Il Sung it may be deduced, though, that the aforementioned Soviet intervention at the Third Party Congress precipitated an internal crisis endangering the very foundation of the Korean Workers' Party. An opposition tendency within the KWP used the same arguments put forward by the Soviet representative against the Five Year Plan and against the "cult of personality" in an attempt to weaken the leadership of the Party. These dissidents, however, were in the minority and disappeared from all important posts during the following two years. Recalling these events on the twentieth anniversary of the Workers' Party, October 10, 1965, Kim Il Sung made the following points:

> The modern revisionists . . . opposed the socialist revolution in our country prattling that it was as yet premature; they opposed our Party's line of socialist industrialization, the line of construction of an independent national economy in particular; and *they even brought economic pressure to bear upon us inflicting tremendous losses upon our socialist construction.* . . .
>
> The attack of the opportunists on our Party became most glaring between 1956 and 1957. At that time the handful of anti-Party factionalists and die-hard dogmatists lurking within our Party challenged the Party, in conspiracy with one another on the basis of revisionism and *with the backing of outside forces.* They not only calumniated the lines and policies of our Party, but also *plotted* together *to subvert the leadership of the Party.*[24]

In the same year, during his visit to Indonesia, he officially stated:

> As is known, the years 1956-1957 were those when modern revisionism emerged on a wide scale. . . . The anti-Party elements within the Party *and their supporters abroad,* revisionists-big-power chauvinists, lined up as one in oppo-

sition to our Party and resorted to subversive activities in an *attempt to overthrow the leadership of our Party and Government.*[25]

Lacking proper evidence, we cannot be sure of what actually happened. But from what we do know, it seems likely that the Soviet leadership was heavily involved in the internal Party strife of 1956 and 1957.[26]

The Koreans' insistence on a course of self-reliance and their rejection of attempts to create an international division of labor within the socialist camp may have been the main factor behind the further deterioration of relations with Moscow. This culminated in 1962 in the withholding of essential material, spare parts, and other important elements of Soviet-Korean economic cooperation. As the country was not yet entirely self-sufficient but relied on such deliveries from the Soviet bloc, the repercussions could not fail to be extremely severe. In an important article in the official party organ, *Rodong Sinmun,* in the fall of 1963, under the title "Let Us Defend the Socialist Camp," the use of economic intimidation against fraternal countries was condemned in unequivocal terms:

> Today some people . . . have unilaterally repealed their agreements with fraternal countries and have virtually cut off the relations of economic and technical cooperation. They brand the construction of an independent national economy a "nationalistic tendency" . . . Those who oppose the building of an independent economy advocate, instead, the establishment of an "integrated economy" of the socialist countries. . . . Under the signboard of "integrated economy" they want to stamp out the economic independence of fraternal countries . . . and make them subordinate to others. . . . It goes without saying that the loss of independence in economy will make it impossible for any country to maintain its genuine independence and sovereignty. . . . "Aid" with strings attached or "aid" given as a precondition for interference in others' internal affairs, as practiced among capitalist countries, cannot exist and must not exist among socialist countries.[27]

It is a sign of the intensity of the dispute within the socialist camp that even military deliveries seem to have been used as a means of pressure. For the DPRK the withholding of material in the sphere of military cooperation (until 1965, according to some Western sources) was particuliarly dangerous because of its special situation with regard to the South. The increased defense expenditures imposed upon the country during the late sixties were probably partly due to this factor. Moreover, deep disagreements seem to have arisen during these years over the question of war and peace and the relative importance of strategic arms compared to other factors. The rationalization that all members of the socialist camp were protected by its leading member was, for obvious reasons, unacceptable to the Korean leadership. The above-quoted article contained a passage reflecting dissatisfaction with this state of affairs:

> ... certain persons propagandize as though a certain individual country's armed forces alone were safeguarding the entire socialist camp, as though the latest military technique of a certain individual country alone were maintaining the security of the socialist camp and world peace. They make light of the role of the other fraternal countries in the defense of the socialist camp, and neglect the cooperation necessary to the strengthening of the defenses of these countries. ... This does not mean that the defense of the socialist camp can be left entirely with the military power of any one country ... it should not rest solely on a certain weapon of the latest type, but should rest first and foremost on the strength of the people. ... [28]

In any event, there is no doubt that the Korean leadership in the second half of the fifties and the early sixties did feel threatened, and this serves to explain many subsequent attitudes on the question of leadership as well as the persistent emphasis on the principles of independence and self-reliance.

The Chollima Movement

When Koreans today refer to the situation in 1956 as extremely serious, it is no exaggeration. Three years had hardly passed since the end of one of the most devastating wars in history. Moreover, the threat of renewed hostilities from the South was far from eliminated. The people were suffering from the aftereffects of the war, including a very low living standard. Economic difficulties, combined with the internal and external pressures concerning the strategy to be followed in the coming years of unprecedented socioeconomic transformations, added to the crisis which was to become a turning point in the country's development.

This was the background for a campaign which started after the Plenum of the Central Committee of the KWP in December 1956. Political Committee members were sent to major factories and villages throughout the country to explain the difficult situation of the country, and Kim Il Sung himself went to the Kangson Steel Plant for this purpose. At a meeting at the plant, the Korean leader openly described the state of affairs created by "factionalists" inside the Party and by the "big-power chauvinists" at a time when the danger of a new "march north" by the "U.S. imperialists and the Syngman Rhee puppet clique" persisted. At this time of hardship, he asked, to whom should the Party turn for support? "We trust only you, the working class, the main force of our revolution, and we have no one else but you to rely on. Therefore, to tide over these grave difficulties facing our Party, you must be in high spirits and work hard to produce plenty and construct well, and thus push economic construction more vigorously."[29] At the same time the slogan, "Let us advance at the speed of Chollima!" was promoted to accelerate the building of socialism.

According to a Korean legend, Chol-li-ma (literally, the ten-thousand-li steed) is a winged horse capable of carrying those fortunate enough to mount it at great speed to-

Priorities in Postwar Reconstruction 187

ward the land of happiness. Shortly after the visit to the Kangson Steel Plant, the premier paid similar visits to a number of other key production centers, explaining the situation. The response on the part of the workers to these personal pleas was overwhelming. Thus a movement started which was to fundamentally transform the economic situation of the country—a movement little known to the outside world.

Because of the almost simultaneous launching of the Chinese Great Leap Forward (1957) speculations have been voiced as to the extent of Chinese influence upon events in Korea. There can be no doubt that policies in the two countries exercised a certain mutual influence. But as we have seen, in Korea the movement started as early as December 1956 because of specific conditions in the country, and both its form and content were different from the Chinese movement. In China, the movement was definitely a result of Chinese policies and became closely associated with the creation of people's communes. Although the cooperativization of Korean agriculture reached mass movement proportions in the years 1956-1958, the Chollima Movement itself seems to have been most pronounced in the industrial sector. Nor did this campaign seem to imitate the Soviet example of mobilization. Unlike the Stakhanovite movement of the 1930s, with its emphasis on individual performance, the Korean campaign of emulation encouraged collective innovations and the mastering of new techniques.

As a result of the Chollima Movement old production records were broken, and innovations and accomplishments were made on the scale of a mass movement. Kim Byong Sik enumerates some of the exploits of the workers in this movement:

> They built a blast furnace with an annual capacity of 360,000 to 400,000 tons in less than a year, laid over 80 kilometers of wide-gauge railway in 75 days, and built a large-scale vinylon factory in a little more than one year on a broad expanse of wasteland. They developed a "machine-

tool-to-beget-machine-tools" movement and produced some 13,000 machine tools in excess of the state plan; they constructed over 1,000 local enterprises, utilizing idle local materials and labor, and they carried out a large-scale reclamation project to irrigate 370,000 hectares of farmland in only six months.[30]

And Kim Byong Sik adds that "countless other examples could be cited."

During the upsurge of patriotic enthusiasm generated by the Chollima Movement, reports were published stating that the targets of the Five Year Plan in the main fields of industry had been reached in the record time of two-and-a-half years, while all quotas for major industrial products were fulfilled or overfulfilled within four years. The following period was used to readjust the resulting imbalances in the economy and prepare for the even more ambitious Seven Year Plan which was to be started in 1961, one year ahead of schedule. It was this period which made the few informed experts talk about the "Korean miracle." In the years 1953-1960 the average annual rate of industrial growth is said to have been 39 percent (36.6 percent from 1957 to 1960). Although agricultural production, predictably, increased more slowly, the country was said to have achieved basic self-sufficiency in food by around the beginning of the 1960s. Even more important than any figures were the socioeconomic transformations which took place: cooperativization of small trade and industry as well as of agriculture had been completed; in the industrial field a firm foundation for further development of heavy and light industries had been laid. At the same time the people's living standard had been stabilized, eliminating worries about basic food, clothes, and housing.

Meanwhile, the policy of political mobilization was not abandonned—on the contrary. During a later visit by Kim Il Sung to the Kangson Steel Works in February 1959, the Chollima Work Team Movement was initiated as an attempt to develop the Chollima Movement in a more organized direction. This campaign continued in subsequent years and even today visitors to Korean cooperative farms and industrial plants may be able to see decorations displayed at the entrance of workshops whose work teams have excelled in innovations or production. Sometimes machines will be decorated as a sign that there innovations were made to ensure faster or cheaper production.

Today, the term "Chollima" has almost as much significance as the word *"Juche"* in the political vocabulary, and it is considered an expression of the "general line of the Korean Workers' Party." As such, Chollima is now seen essentially as a method to educate the working people in Communist ideas and rally them firmly around the Party thus enabling the masses to give full play to their revolutionary initiative and to take "the attitude of a master" toward their environment in the spirit of *"Juche."* In the wake of the continuous efforts by the Party to develop the mass line, *priority* was to be given *to politics in combination with technical and economic activities*. It was the experience gained in the Chollima Movement which later gave rise to innovations in the general administration of society, with an attempt to institutionalize the mass line within a general planning and management system. This will be taken up again in the sections on socialist agriculture and industrial management.

Notes

1. Wilfred G. Burchett, *Again Korea* (New York: International Publishers, 1968), p. 65. Apart from the southern capital, Seoul, which changed its occupants four times and was heavily destroyed, the damage inflicted to the South was less devastating that that to the North, which was submitted to onesided U.S. bombings.
2. Jan Lönn, *Nordkorea* (Stockholm, 1972), p. 79.
3. Robert A. Scalapino and Chong-Sik Lee, *Communism in Korea,* vol. II (Berkeley, Cal.: Univ. of California Press, 1972), pp. 1054-1057.

190   *Socialist Korea*

4. *Postwar Rehabilitation and Development of the National Economy of the DPRK* (Pyongyang, 1957), p. 8.
5. In the above-quoted booklet from 1957 this aid is eloquently described:

   ... the economic assistance, both material and technical, which was rendered by the Soviet Union, the People's Republic of China and other brotherly countries of the socialist camp contributed much to the successful reconstruction of the postwar national economy.... They sent us machinery needed in heavy and light industries, fuel, construction machines, electric appliances, farm implements, various kinds of transport and communication facilities, asphalt, oil, insecticides, various daily necessaries, chemicals, public health facilities, materials for cultural need, scientific research instruments, technical documents and books, medicines, cattle and food, cotton fabrics, underwear, shoes and so forth. And they gave us immense technical assistance in the reconstruction of the national economy. (*Postwar Rehabilitation*, p. 63.)

6. *Pukham Ch'onggam (Comprehensive Book of North Korea)*, published in Seoul in 1968, indicates (p. 374) that until the Soviet Union cut off its economic aid in 1962 North Korea had received an estimated $1.4 billion in economic assistance (of which $719 million were in the form of loans). Of this total, 48.8 percent had been granted by the Soviet Union, 30.9 percent had come from China, and the rest from Eastern Europe. [Taken from Joungwon Alexander Kim, "Soviet Policy in North Korea," *World Politics* 22, no. 2 (January 1970): 249.] The figure mentioned by the DPRK of course does not include repayable loans or trade exchanges, but only direct grants.
7. "A small part of society, perhaps under five percent, had committed itself to the nationalist movement, hence active opposition to Japan." [Gregory Henderson, *Korea: The Politics of the Vortex* (Cambridge, Mass: Harvard Univ. Press, 1968), p. 110.]
8. Kim Byong Sik, *Modern Korea* (New York: International Publishers, 1970), p. 40. (This Korean economist living in Japan is vice-chairman of the General Association of Korean Residents in Japan. As representative of the official North Korean way of thinking he is quoted rather extensively in the following.)
9. Joan Robinson, "Korean Miracle," *Monthly Review* 16, no. 9 (January 1965): 543.
10. Cf. Kim Il Sung, "Everything for the Postwar Rehabilitation and Development of the National Economy," August 5, 1953, in *Selected Works*, vol. I (Pyongyang, 1965), p. 164.
11. Critics of the regime have claimed that this version of Korean postwar politics is a rationalization after the fact and that actually,

Priorities in Postwar Reconstruction 191

priority was given to heavy industry in a way similar to what had been the case in the Soviet Union. At the same time one of the latest of such critical analyses points out the important fact that progress in consumer production was made rather early. (Cf. Scalapino and Lee, *Communism in Korea,* p. 1213.) What these authors unwillingly reaffirm is that attention was given to light industry even though heavy industry was considered the fundamental sector.

12. Kim Il Sung, "Everything for Postwar Rehabilitation," p. 203.
13. Kim Il Sung, "On Eliminating Dogmatism and Formalism and Establishing Juche in Ideological Work," December 28, 1955, in *Selected Works,* vol. I, p. 325.
14. Kim Il Sung, "Report to the Fourth Party Congress," September 11, 1961, in *Selected Works,* vol. II (Pyongyang, 1965), p. 137.
15. Kim Il Sung, "For the Fulfilment of the First Five-Year Plan," March 6, 1958, in *Selected Works,* vol. I, p. 347.
16. Yoon T. Kuark, "North Korea's Industrial Development During the Post-War Period," *The China Quarterly* 14 (April-June 1963): 60.
17. Charles Bettelheim, *Planification et croissance accélérée* (Paris: Maspero, 1965), pp. 137-138.
18. Charles Bettelheim, "On the Transition Between Capitalism and Socialism," *Monthly Review* 20, no. 10 (March 1969): 9.
19. Kim Il Sung, "Some Questions Concerning Party and State Work," April 4, 1955, in *Selected Works,* vol. I, p. 291.
20. Third Congress Documents, p. 348 (quoted by Kim, "Soviet Policy in North Korea," pp. 245-246). In contrast, the Chinese delegate expressed his confidence that the plan would be carried out "without fail."
21. Kim Il Sung, "On the Socialist Construction in the DPRK and the Revolution in South Korea," lecture in Indonesia, April 14, 1965, in *Selected Works,* vol. II, pp. 513-514. (Emphasis added)
22. Third Congress Documents, p. 349. (Emphasis added)
23. Here is the crucial passage of the speech by the Soviet delegate who, by the way, was none other than Leonid I. Brezhnev:

> The Twentieth Congress has pointed out with great satisfaction the special significance of the work done recently by the Central Committee of the Communist Party of the Soviet Union to restore the all-important Leninist principle, the principle of collective leadership.
> The principle of collective leadership—this is the only correct way of improving the Party leadership from top to bottom. . . .
> The Third Congress and the whole Workers' Party of Korea attach great importance to the resolutions of the Twentieth Congress of the Communist Party of the Soviet Union and the

members of the Workers' Party of Korea are widely studying them.

By creatively utilizing the experiences of the Communist Party of the Soviet Union and other fraternal parties and by setting the scientific theory of Marxism-Leninism as its guide the Workers' Party of Korea will be further strengthened.

The Congress will *help to fully establish in the Party organizations from top to bottom the Leninist principle of collective leadership,* the enforcement of which lends a powerful force to each Marxist Party and keeps it from making mistakes related to the cult of personality.

(Third Congress Documents, 350. Emphasis added.)

24. Kim Il Sung, "On the Occasion of the 20th Anniversary of the Workers' Party of Korea," October 10, 1965, in *Selected Works,* vol. II, pp. 579 and 580. (Emphasis added)
25. Kim Il Sung, "On the Socialist Construction," pp. 515-516. (Emphasis added)
26. At this time the Chinese were still present in Korea, but there is no evidence that they played any role in this quarrel and it is known that Chinese loans continued through 1964. In fact China itself, because of its own domestic policies and the international situation, became even more involved than Korea in ideological confrontations with the USSR and was subjected to severe economic pressures.

    Another type of Chinese interference in Korean internal affairs is said to have occurred after a showdown in the Korean Workers' Party in 1956, when some highly placed individuals from the so-called "Yenan group" had fled to China to present their case to Defense Minister P'eng Teh-huai. Prior to the Eighth Party Congress of the Chinese Communist Party, P'eng traveled to Pyongyang with the Soviet delegate to the Chinese Congress, Anastas Mikoyan, and held discussions with Kim Il Sung about this matter. (Kim, "Soviet Policy," p. 248.) This is said to have infuriated Kim Il Sung, who complained about interference in Korea's internal affairs. According to one version, Mao Tse-tung later expressed apologies to Kim Il Sung. (Scalapino and Lee, *Communism in Korea,* p. 515.) It may be recalled that policy differences existed at the time within the Chinese leadership. P'eng Teh-huai himself belonged to the pro-Soviet and anti-Mao elements of the CCP. He was purged from his position in 1959.
27. Slightly different excerpts of this article are quoted in Kim, "Soviet Policy," p. 249-250, and by Scalapino and Lee, *Communism in Korea,* p. 630-633. It is also published in the paper *The People's Korea,* Tokyo, October 28, 1963.

28. Ibid.
29. *Short Biography of Kim Il Sung,* vol. II (Pyongyang, 1972), p. 138.
30. Kim Byong Sik, *Modern Korea,* p. 156.

Chapter 6
Socialist Methods of Economic Development

Following this brief survey of the main priorities in the postwar reconstruction period as well as the external and internal political disputes which influenced decision-making, we can attempt to extract from the Korean experience, in a more general sense, the main mechanisms of its economic development—agricultural, educational, and industrial.

A. AGRICULTURE

The Limitations of Land Reform

Because of the social relations and the form of production in the rural sector, the socialization of agriculture has always been the most complex problem for socialist experiments. In the case of Korea, the agrarian reform of 1946 was a necessary step toward the abolition of the previous system of land ownership based on a semifeudal or feudal relationship.[1] But this could not remain an end in itself. Seven years later, there were—as we have seen—compelling economic and political reasons for further initiatives in the reorganization of agriculture. As will be recalled, while the socialization of industry had, for all practical purposes, been completed shortly after liberation, a private commodity economy still prevailed in agriculture, making it difficult to improve the productive capacity of this sector. The survival of small-scale, scattered private farms complicated the planning as well as the achievement of expanded reproduction. Had it not been remedied, this state of affairs could eventually have led to a clash of interests between the different sectors of the economy. As Koreans saw it, "If the contradiction between socialist industry and private farms had been left as it was, not only would the development of agriculture have been hampered, but also the balance between industry and agriculture would have been destroyed, and the problem of foodstuffs would not have been solved."[2] In the longer run, differences between town and countryside would also have been deepened.[3]

The rural question thus has a wide range of political implications, especially in preindustrial societies. The introduction of an agrarian reform through the distribution of land to private individuals, in order to break down the old order and win over the peasantry, strengthens the principle of private property. If this is not handled correctly, in the longer run it can be dangerous, opening the way for a reversion to capitalist agriculture. From a theoretical viewpoint socialists had very early been aware of the strength and weakness of reforms based on distribution of land. According to Lenin, the policy and slogan of such distribution had "a progressive and revolutionary significance in the bourgeois-democratic revolution." But for socialists it was accepted only as a necessary measure in a political process: "We Bolsheviks shall help the peasantry to outlive petty bourgeois slogans, to make the transition as rapidly and easily as possible to socialist slogans."[4]

In this area of agrarian reform we find one of the key differences between the main currents of Eastern European and Asian socialism after 1945. According to an expert on Central Europe, Lynn Turgeon, the policies adopted there were decidedly *away* from collectivization: "In agriculture, in contrast to industry, the initial postwar emphasis was on land reform rather than on collectivization or socialization."[5] This led to political decisions which in some cases could not but spread confusion. In Poland, for example, the general secretary of the Workers' Party, Wladyslaw Gomulka, went so far as to declare, in late 1946: "Ours is not a country with a socialist system. . . . We have rejected completely the collectivization of agriculture. . . . "[6] Following the defection of Yugoslavia from the socialist camp, however, Gomulka was removed from his post and collectivization was implemented both in Poland and Czechoslovakia with a speed and suddenness comparable to the Soviet experience. Nevertheless, after the Posnan revolt in 1956, Gomulka was returned to power and a decollectivization of Polish agriculture took place on the same model as post-1948 Yugoslavia.[7]

In Korea, it was recognized—on the basis of the country's own experience and in line with the aforementioned Leninist principle—that the distribution of land could not remain an objective in itself. "As a result of the land reform, small-scale commodity production in the form of private farms became dominant in the countryside. As is well known, this situation breeds capitalism and a bourgeoisie."[8] Besides being contrary to the socialist path, such a development can be politically dangerous, since the new proprietors are apt to be more vulnerable to antisocialist propaganda. In the case of a divided Korea, this could have had broad implications, as Kim Il Sung recognized at the time: "We . . . cannot close our eyes to the fact that rich peasants are continually emerging in the countryside. . . . Though they benefited from the land reform, those newly-emerging rich peasants, as their farming assumes a capitalist character, gradually are liable to be influenced by South Korean reactionary circles."[9]

A similar tendency toward the development of "kulakism" following distributions of land to the peasantry could

Socialist Methods of Economic Development 197

be observed at approximately the same time in both China and Vietnam. As far as China was concerned, Mao Tse-tung brought up the issue a year after the above warning by Kim Il Sung:

> As is clear to everyone, the spontaneous forces of capitalism have been steadily growing in the countryside in recent years, with new rich peasants springing up everywhere, and many well-to-do middle peasants striving to become rich peasants. On the other hand, many poor peasants are still living in poverty for lack of sufficient means of production, with some in debt and others selling or renting out their land.[10]

In the Democratic Republic of Vietnam, after the land reform of 1957, with its principle of "land to the tillers," "a spontaneous tendency appeared among a certain number of peasants to constitute themselves as a small-scale agrarian bourgeoisie. This bourgeoisie originated from the principle of individual property, which in turn stemmed from the disintegration of semi-feudal property."[11] The buying and selling of land had not been prohibited in Vietnam, so when a series of natural calamities and epidemics struck, a number of poor peasants were forced to sell part of their newly acquired land and cattle. This tendency, if allowed to continue, might have led to renewed concentration of land ownership.[12]

In Korea, because of the way the land reform had been carried out, the risk was probably not as great. Besides, the hardships of the war had led to the spontaneous formation of various forms of collaboration. The existence from ancient times of traditional types of labor exchange likewise contributed to making the notion of cooperatives less objectionable to Koreans (or other Asian peoples) than one would imagine. A Western writer who observed daily life in a South Korean village as late as in 1947 described the traditional heritage of mutual aid in this anything-but-socialist environment: "Since the transplanting of the rice, as well as its cultivation and harvesting, is a cooperative affair, something should be said on the latter subject. Men who work cooperatively in the rice fields vary the size of their groups from two to fifteen, but six is most common. Men usually enter into this relationship on the basis of village friendships and work for each other year after year."[13] According to the same author, in the very old days such common labor groups frequently included a musical group which played in the morning and often continued with music and dancing in the evening. The wife of the farmer whose fields were being worked was expected to bring out a basket with food three times a day. Even though the Japanese destroyed much of this gay tradition, it has since been partly resurrected in the northern part of the country, where today singing and dancing are common features of peasant life.

It is true that similar cooperative traditions have existed in many parts of the globe. Nevertheless, these may have been more widespread in Asia because of the region's specific conditions. The French anthropologist J. Suret-Canale points out that the requirements of agriculture in this area would tend to favor collectivization:

> Traditional agriculture in the Far Eastern countries, especially in regions of irrigated rice cultivation, with extreme parcellization of individual plots because of rural overpopulation, has known the necessity to organize the struggle against floods, the maintenance of draining and irrigation. All these geographical, historical and social features may be found in Korea effectively facilitating the transition to a socialist organization of agriculture.[14]

In Korea, this combination of cooperative traditions and war-created conditions proved conducive to revolutionary changes in the rural sector.

The Question of Cooperativization

Of all their achievements in the sphere of socioeconomic relations the Koreans' treatment of the rural question is without doubt the most remarkable, a performance worthy of the attention of students and specialists in problems of economic development.

As far as can be ascertained, the Korean Workers' Party envisaged the development of the agrarian system as a process consisting of several stages. The land reform in the stage of democratic revolution gave the land to the tillers, instituting a modified form of private land ownership. The second stage, cooperativization, was meant as a step from the individual economy to a socialist form of ownership in the rural sector. The third and present stage seems to be based on a policy of strengthening and developing the foundation of the socialist economy, while narrowing the differences between town and country, industry and agriculture; its ultimate goal, after a long period of ideological remolding and the introduction of a modern mechanized agriculture directed by industrial-like management, is the transition to "all people's ownership." No definite timetable seems to have been set up; the implementation of the separate phases will depend upon the maturation of the objective and subjective conditions. In the case of the DPRK it seems probable that the war influenced the decision to move into the second stage of the process earlier than might otherwise have been the case. As we have seen, the war-inflicted destruction placed enormous demands on Korean agriculture, both during the conflict itself and in the subsequent rehabilitation and industrialization process.

During the war nearly all able-bodied men were either at the front or engaged in underground manufacturing activities, leaving mostly old people, women, and children to till the soil. This situation continued after the armistice, bringing more flexible forms of organization as a means of overcoming difficulties and paving the way for the creation of cooperatives. Not surprisingly, war widows were often the most active element. Shortage of labor power, the destruction of irrigation works, the loss of draft animals, as well as the physical elimination of a great number of villages, all seemed to point in the direction of a new social organization in the countryside. Under these circumstances, even though Korea may not in the orthodox "technical" sense have been "prepared" for collectivization, the political leadership had no choice but to give further and more conscious stimulus to a movement which had already started almost spontaneously at the grass-roots level.

Before the war a number of state farms had been set up, especially in the field of livestock raising. But the "socialist economy" still accounted for only slightly more than 3 percent of total agricultural production. The socialization of agriculture was undertaken first on an experimental basis, starting as a gradual process in 1953. To begin with, a few coöperatives were tentatively established in every district in order to acquire experience in dealing with the existing conditions throughout the country. This period was characterized by the coexistence of several different types of organization. In time, three basic forms became dominant. The first and least developed was based on permanent mutual-aid teams. These could be of two kinds, the *sogyori* (cow exchange) and the *p'umasi* (labor exchange) units, comprising up to ten families. Farm work was done collectively but property and harvests were not shared. The second, considered a semisocialist form, involved the disribution of harvests according to the amount of labor and land invested; lands were consolidated and farm management carried out jointly. The third form—today the only one remaining in the DPRK—is a socialist organization, with remuneration made solely on the principle of labor input, and all resources—land, farm implements, draft animals, etc.—integrated within each unit. Each farm household was allowed to retain individual ownership of a small plot of land (its precise size depending on the quality of the soil and the size of the family) as well as to keep a few chickens and raise pigs or sheep.

Although this third type of structure was preponderant from the beginning, a campaign was conducted in order to enlist the peasantry in these three kinds of cooperative organizations. Table 7, which is in the Industrial Museum in Pyongyang and reproduced in numerous sources, indicates the gradual transformation of the rural structure.

Toward the end of 1954, approximately one-third of all private households belonged to cooperatives. The program was accelerated in the years 1955-1956 and was said to have been completed by 1958. In promoting cooperativization, the policy was to rely on the poor peasantry (constituting about 40 percent of the rural population at the end of the war) and strengthen their alliance with the middle peasants. The crucial question, of course, was how to treat the rich peasants. In order to influence their decisions in the desired direction, the power and options of rich peasants were gradually limited, while the cooperatives were given preferential treatment. In spite of the lack of modern means of production, the cooperatives—with efficient assistance by the state—very early showed their superiority to individual farming, eventually convincing formerly reluctant farmers into participating in the movement.

Table 7
Cooperative Organizations

	Percent of peasant households organized in cooperatives	Percent of cooperative acreage
1953	1.2	0.6
1954	31.8	30.9
1955	49.0	48.6
1956	80.9	77.9
1957	95.6	93.7
1958 (August)	100.0	100.0

It goes without saying that certain errors were committed, as for instance when some political cadres—eager to show good results—took liberties with the principle of voluntary participation and started pushing farmers too rapidly into cooperative organizations. Such methods were severely criticized. It is characteristic of Korean methods that though the process was based for the most part on the principle of free choice, it was not left to develop spontaneously. Of great importance on the political level were the intensive courses given once or twice a year —beginning in 1955—to several thousand leading members of both central and local rural organs. Here the guidelines worked out by the Party were discussed and a unified perspective developed—a significant factor in the political and economic consolidation of the agricultural cooperatives. Measures were taken to prevent the formation of cooperative units composed exclusively of "rich" peasants, while the poorest units were granted tax reductions and additional help by the state. However, a certain difference in standards between cooperatives was unavoidable and even today differences persist in the prosperity and maintenance levels of the various cooperative farms.

Another significant point needs to be mentioned: at no time during cooperativization did the agricultural output decrease; on the contrary, the process was accompanied by a steady increase in production. As one student of Korean affairs has pointed out, this may be the first historical example of successful collectivization without a temporary diminution of agricultural production. The same expert cites statistics showing that food production increased from 2,873,000 tons in 1956 to 3,803,000 tons in 1960.[15]

Following collectivization, the proper size for agricultural units had to be chosen. This reorganization took place in October 1958—that is, two months after the official announcement of the completion of the first stage. Cooperative farms were comparatively small at first, covering about 40 to 100 households each. Their reduced size made them easier to organize, but in order to facilitate more advanced methods of production and carry out bigger projects (soil improvement, draining, irrigation, regulation of rivers, terracing of hills, etc.) larger units seemed more rational. Gradually their size increased so that in the end they included an average of 275 households (3,843 cooperatives for 1,055,000 peasant households in 1958),[16] i.e., still a much smaller unit than the Chinese people's communes. At the same time they became fully integrated with the local authorities and the already existing cooperative enterprises (consumers' cooperatives and credit cooperatives). This administrative setup was later changed.

A great stride had thereby been taken, not least because —as most observers agree—the process had been rather gradual and devoid of serious excesses. Socially, this meant that the main sources of exploitation had now been eliminated from the countryside. The peasants were on their way toward becoming socialist worker-farmers, leading a different kind of life in surroundings which could gradually be transformed into advanced modern villages.

Raising Productivity Through Collectivization

During the period under consideration there were heavy demands made on North Korean agriculture: the countryside not only had to provide the necessary food for a population with increasing purchasing power, but also deliver industrial crops and place a percentage of its labor force at the disposal of other expanding sectors. In this respect a great population movement from agriculture to the industrial, administrative, and service sectors took place in a relatively short period of time. Official statistics show a constant decrease of the population engaged in farming to the point where in 1958 less than half of the work force remained in agriculture. The scope of this shift could be seen in the fact that "between 1953 and 1967, the urban

Table 8
The Shift in Occupation Division from 1946 to 1960
(in percent)

	1946	1949	1953	1958	1960
Workers and office employees	18.7	26.0	29.7	40.9	52.0
Farmers	74.1	69.3	66.4	56.6	44.0
Others	5.0	2.9	2.4	2.0	3.3
Total	100.0	100.0	100.0	100.0	100.0

Source: *Facts About Korea* (Pyongyang: Foreign Languages Publishing House, 1961), p.9.

population grew from 17.7 percent to 47.5 percent of the total."[17]

Obviously, in order to adjust to such demands the productivity of the rural sector had to increase. It should be kept in mind, however, that in an agrarian society collectivization is more than "simply" an attempt to make up for the shortage of labor power, as was the case in Korea. In this respect one of the main differences between the Chinese and Korean rationales for collectivization lies in their different situations with regard to population reserves. In China, rural surplus labor could be absorbed by the new system, reducing idleness in the slack seasons through labor-intensive projects. In Korea, no such problem of surplus population existed, although there too the question of more effective use of labor was a factor in the strategy of economic development. Collectivization thus seems equally applicable to very different conditions.

The traditional attitude toward the rural question is that a rise in labor productivity can only be attained through the modernization of this sector, demanding huge investments with rather slow returns. Another less accepted option is the transformation of forms of organization combined with gradual improvement of the means and methods of cultivation. At the time various arguments against collectivization were raised within the Workers' Party of Korea. Because of the division of the country, some opponents argued that such a step would further increase the differences between North and South.[18] Against this line of thought the Party leadership maintained that only by building socialism could the northern part of the country consolidate itself economically and politically, and that only a strong North could eventually promote the unification of the country.

Another major argument against agricultural cooperatives was that the country did not yet possess sufficient technical means to reorganize the rural sector. In general, this problem acquires particular significance when socialist construction takes place in preindustrial societies. A solution had to be devised by all Asian socialist states because their agrarian economies provided them with limited access to the benefits of the industrial revolution. The political leadership of these countries, characterized by very different situations, each arrived at the conclusion that the social reorganization of the rural sector had to be undertaken not only in order to strengthen socialism in the countryside but *precisely in order to raise productivity,* thus supplying a surplus which could be channeled into the industrialization process. To orthodox critics it was unthinkable that such a transformation might be achieved in nonmechanized agrarian environments, as this was a departure from the Soviet model of "tractors first, then collectivization."[19] But the theory of raising productivity through social reorganization of agriculture, thereby pushing socialism one step further, is actually in complete agreement with classical Marxism-Leninism.

Karl Marx seems to have been conscious of the advantages labor collaboration and organization can have on productivity as compared with individual labor:

> ... co-operation allows the work to be carried on over an extended space; it is consequently imperatively called for in

certain undertakings, such as draining, constructing dykes, irrigation works, and the making of canals, roads and railways. On the other hand, while extending the scale of production, it renders possible a relative contraction of the arena. This contraction of arena simultaneous with, and arising from, the extension of scale, whereby a number of useless expenses are cut down, is due to the conglomeration of laborers, to the aggregation of various processes, and to the concentration of the means of production. The combined working-day produces, relative to an equal sum of isolated working-days, a greater quantity of use-values, and, consequently, diminishes the labor-time necessary for the production of a given useful effect.[20]

As far as the political aspect is concerned, Lenin pointed out that the act of grouping people together was in itself conducive to socialism: "When the population is organized in cooperative societies to the utmost . . . socialism . . . achieves its aims." And on the importance of the peasantry's participation in socialist transformation, Lenin added: "It is one thing to draw up fantastic plans for building Socialism by means of all sorts of workers' associations, but it is quite another thing to learn to build it practically, in such a way that *every* small peasant may take part in the work of construction."[21] Koreans seem to have been aware of the classical Marxist teachings on this question: "Lenin pointed out that even a collective economy that merely pooled the peasants' land and farm implements could achieve an economic improvement that was impossible in the individual small peasant economy, and could double or treble the productivity of labour. We were guided by this theory in our agricultural co-operative movement."[22]

The Relationship Between Industry and Agriculture

The implication is that the social reorganization of labor in the rural sector not only favors the political project

Socialist Methods of Economic Development   207

of socialism but contributes to a better utilization of human resources in the struggle against underdevelopment. One specialist on Korean affairs seems to underrate seriously the scope of the issues involved: "The land reform in 1945-47 and the cooperativization immediately following the Korean War were typically Communist attempts to increase agricultural production through rigid control, and to siphon off as much of that output as possible to pay for industrialization."[23] In today's world, however, for most underdeveloped countries the generation of a surplus in order to finance an industrialization process is an imperative, not a matter of free political choice. The question is rather how to achieve a rapid accumulation sufficient for industrialization without causing harm to other sectors. Since philanthropy in international relations is the exception rather than the rule, no country in the underprivileged category can expect adequate amounts of foreign funds to finance its development. Preindustrial societies—not having had access to the "fruits" of imperialism; having in fact, been victimized by such ties—do not in the last instance have any viable alternative but to transform their production relations in order to promote their internal accumulation. The social reorganization of the rural sector and the resulting increase in productivity serve precisely this purpose.

If history up to now has known few examples of a rapid and efficient solution to this complex problem, experience has shown many cases where development is hampered by the inability to achieve a correct relationship between industry and agriculture, often resulting in political tensions. The well-known Brazilian sociologist, Josué de Castro, put his finger on the basic weakness behind Latin America's dilemma:

> The archaic and unproductive agriculture prevents progress; its feeble productivity and the resulting high costs of food is a handicap for industry. The prices for subsistence goods are such that industry tends to establish salaries at a level which condemns the workers to hunger. Nevertheless,

thanks to labor unions, workers are no longer willing to die from hunger. This puts industry in a difficult situation. There are hardly any raw materials available at a competitive price. There is no national market for the industrial products: between 50 and 80 percent of the population lives in the countryside in a subsistence economy. Those products which are not competitive on the world market find no internal absorption [market].[24]

This structural mechanism, connected to backward agriculture, is to a large degree responsible for creating a position of dependence vis-à-vis the world market, resulting in the so-called "development of underdevelopment." In order to fulfill its role in economic growth, agriculture (under any system) should be able to release new labor power for industry and other services, cultivate low-priced industrial crops for that sector, and guarantee an abundant food supply in order to keep prices and wages low and prevent inflation. Finally, on account of the high proportion of the population involved in the rural sector and its increased purchasing power for both farm implements and consumer goods, the peasantry becomes the backbone of the national internal market. In other words, unless agriculture is developed, industry will also be handicapped and sustained economic growth obstructed.

A case in which a stagnant agriculture has constituted an insurmountable barrier to progress is India.[25] It is that country's failure to solve the rural question and develop a means of financing its own industrial development which explains to a large extent its retarded position despite the amount of foreign aid it has received from both the United States and the USSR when compared to its initial possibilities.

The importance for economic development of a correct resolution of the agrarian question may further be illustrated by the difficulties experienced by the first socialist state at the beginning of its industrialization:

> The latter [industrialization] was slowed down as long as agricultural surplus was insufficient. It became necessary to

adopt institutional methods such as compulsory deliveries to assure the supply of a large enough agrarian surplus to satisfy the demands of industrialization. The example of the Soviet Union of the late twenties and the beginning thirties shows furthermore, how technical changes may be indispensable in agriculture in order to make it capable of furnishing the labor force to industry without diminishing the agrarian surplus.[26]

In the case of Korea, had the solution of the agricultural problem been postponed until the means of modernization were available, the country's later development and industrialization process would have been negatively affected.

Socialist versus Capitalist Accumulation

Recognizing the feasibility of raising productivity in agriculture *before* the means for modernizing that sector have been developed opens a wide range of perspectives. By developing agriculture side by side with light and heavy industry, Korea avoided the pattern of concentrating all resources on the development of a highly centralized industry. Such a concentration of modern means of production in the hands of a small minority of skilled workers, leaving the rest of the population with a largely inefficient production apparatus, would amount almost to a reproduction of the capitalist mode of development.

It often goes unrecognized that from an economic point of view the increased productivity of a minority of the population, though it seems logical, can hardly compensate for a backwardness of production on the part of the majority. On the other hand, even a mediocre improvement in the productivity of the majority has a greater overall impact. On the political level the pattern of highly centralized investment tends to perpetuate a lopsided social structure and foster elitism. The discrepancies between town and country may grow bigger, while the passivity of the huge peasant masses continues, preventing them from gradually making themselves masters of their work conditions. Symptoms of such a development might include a growth of centralized bureaucratism, a mystification of technology on the part of the masses, and a lack of rapid improvement of living conditions—in other words, a course which would alienate the masses from the Party and from political life as a whole.

In Korea, special attention was given to this entire problematic. The negative political and economic implications of a policy of exploitation toward the peasantry were fully realized:

> Should rural work be neglected, should the rural areas be left without aid or, worse still, should there be industrial development alone at the expense of agriculture and urban construction alone at the sacrifice of the countryside, then the discrepancy between town and country, far from disappearing, will grow even greater. This will make it impossible to give full play to the activeness of the peasants, develop agriculture or improve the peasants' living standards. It will, in the long run, hinder the development of industry itself, as well as that of the whole national economy, and cause severe damage to the building of socialism and communism.[27]

In Korea, industrialization based on a form of exploitation of the rural areas by the center was consequently considered an inherently capitalistic mode of accumulation. The political leadership would therefore disagree with the theory advocated by the opposition in the Soviet Union in the 1920s, as formulated by Preobrazhensky, according to which the exploitation of agriculture was a necessity for socialization:

> The idea that a socialist economy can develop by itself without touching the resources of the petty bourgeois economy, and particularly the peasant economy, is beyond doubt a reactionary, petty bourgeois utopia. The task of the socialist state consists not in taking from the petty bourgeois producers less than was taken by capitalism, but to take more out of the even greater income which will be assured to the

small producer by the rationalization of everything, in particular the small production of the country.[28]

It is well known that in the Soviet Union enormous difficulties arose in the handling of the rural question and that it became a principal point of controversy within the Communist Party. In the end, a solution not very different from the one proposed by Preobrazhensky was implemented, with a "tribute" paid by the peasantry to provide capital for the building of heavy industry. In this way one may say that for what may have been historically predetermined reasons, the Soviet Union adopted a method which was in some respects similar to the capitalist mode of accumulation and failed to bring into full play what the Koreans call the inherent superiority of the socialist system (i.e., the harmonious development of all sectors combined with the political mobilization of the masses). This may have played an important role in subsequent developments, including the further alienation of the peasant masses from the Party and the failure to overcome differences between various strata in terms of material conditions, technical expertise, and the wielding of political power.

It is interesting to note that some Eastern European socialist countries, no doubt influenced by the difficulties experienced by the Soviet Union, have followed quite a different pattern and achieved quite different results. As pointed out by Lynn Turgeon, in the German Democratic Republic, Czechoslovakia, and particularly Poland, the peasantries were the chief beneficiaries of the method of accumulation. The peasants' "economic position in these countries is somewhat analogous to that of capitalist farmers in their wartime seller's market. Relatively equal income distribution and over-full employment have thus maintained a vigorous demand for the produce of the agricultural sector, similar to that found in the West only under wartime conditions."[29] This tendency was most apparent in the case of Poland where, according to another expert, in contrast to the method utilized in the Soviet

Union, "the brunt of intensive forced saving has been carried by industrial workers rather than by the peasantry: this has been so because of the preservation of individual farming stiffened the peasants' resistance to the pressure for centralized capital accumulation."[30] The question may even legitimately be raised of whether the socialization of agriculture has not been abandoned in Poland, at least for some years to come. Since the Polish peasants' fierce rejection of collectivization in 1956, cooperative production has gradually decreased, constituting no more than 1 percent of the cultivated area in 1973. At the same time, the state farms—former latifundia—which cover about 14 percent of the area have not shown very positive results, in spite of some technical progress. It is family farming, prevailing over 84 percent of the cultivated area and furnishing 87 percent of agricultural production, which ensures an annual growth rate of 3 percent—one, which compares favorably with French agriculture.[31] The result of this favoritism toward agriculture has been rather high prices for necessary consumer goods such as food—representing about 50 percent of a worker's budget —and clothes. It was price increases which in 1971 triggered large-scale workers' demonstrations and violent confrontations in various Polish cities. The mechanisms which operate in a country like Poland, therefore, are not unlike those of capitalist systems. The basic difference is a certain degree of state intervention which gives preferential treatment to private agriculture at the expense of socialist industry!

Industry Helps Agriculture

In Korea, even though agriculture at first supplied a surplus for industry and the urban sector, at the same time the relationship between these two sectors was a kind of two-way street. The rural population never had to suffer a deterioration of living conditions for the sake of industrial growth. Accordingly, support for agriculture in the early postwar years took the form of financial and technical assistance and managerial and administrative guidance, as well as direct labor power help. During the Three Year Plan (1954-1956) much progress was achieved through mass participation in land reclamation, irrigation projects, and the building and repairing of reservoirs and pumping stations. In this period state investments totaled 7.4 billion old *won*, with over half that amount, 4.2 billion, going to irrigation and river dike projects.[32] This was a decisive factor in opening up 123,000 additional *chongbo* or arable land and constructing dikes for the protection of another 160,000 *chongbo*. Again in 1957, 1,400 million old *won* were spent by the government on rural construction. In the years 1954-1957 the irrigated area increased from 227,000 *chongbo* to 384,000 *chongbo*, while the proportion of irrigated paddies increased from 39 percent to 77 percent of the total paddy area.[33] Total capital expenditures for increasing agricultural output during 1954-1959 amounted to about 23,900 million *won*.[34] In the same period the supply of simple but efficient farm implements increased, while farm machinery leasing stations multiplied threefold, thereby increasing the productive capacity of the rural economy.

Because of the need for labor in the rural sector, tens of thousands of demobilized men and many junior and senior graduates as well as middle school pupils went to the countryside in the busy seasons and rendered assistance amounting to millions of days of work. During the process of collectivization, cooperatives had been given priority for receiving such help. This factor, combined with the technical aid, greatly contributed to making the initial phases a success. Everybody took part in this work: militiamen, office workers, students, and children. Similar mass movements were used to carry out forestation of hills and mountain slopes to prevent erosion following the destruction brought about first by ruthless Japanese exploitation and later by the Korean War. This tradition is still alive, and at harvest or seeding time travelers to Korea will often see youths or soldiers working in the fields side by side with work team members from cooperatives.

Moreover, the fact that the shift of rural population to urban centers was of relatively recent origin made assistance to the countryside not only politically acceptable but almost a necessity in that many industrial workers were of peasant origin with family ties to the countryside. For this reason an attitude of neglect toward the peasantry could very well have created tensions in industry.

Reorganization of Small Trade and Industry

As all socioeconomic activities are closely interconnected, the reorganization of social relations in the countryside permitted important transformations in the society as a whole. Even before the war the cooperativization of handicrafts had been stimulated through loans on favorable terms and the provision of raw materials, with the aim of increasing production and overcoming the weaknesses inherited from colonialism. In 1950, the Federation of Producers' Cooperatives was formed and material and technical aid was given to help impoverished handicrafts workers. During and immediately after the war, the cooperativization of handicrafts was further developed, and was completed only a few years later.

Private trade and industry were treated differently. In the period up to the war use was made of their "positive aspects"—i.e., their ability to provide various necessities—and to this end assistance was granted. At the same time their "negative aspects" were controlled through the labor law or by drawing private enterprises into organizations so that they had to carry on their business through the "people's market," thereby preventing the buying up or hoarding of goods. Until the outbreak of the war the existence of private commerce and industry was dependent on the role they played in the countryside, acting as middlemen between rural and urban populations. According to Kim Il Sung: "Private trade and industry in our country were negligible from the start, and were kept going mainly on the strength of small commodity production in the countryside."[35] Socially, this constituted a surviving form of exploitation, based as it was on the possibility of buying farm produce cheaply from the peasants and selling it, with a substantial profit margin, to workers and office employees. The collectivization of agriculture was consequently bound to have a profound influence on the fate of this inherently weak sector. As will be recalled, because of Japanese domination the role of indigenous capitalism had been rather insignificant from the beginning. With the nationalization of Japanese property and the possessions of Korean collaborators following liberation, the private sector no longer represented an independent economic force. The war further aggravated the plight of the remaining private handicrafts industries and other small commodity-producing enterprises, forcing them into a closer relationship with the state sector. This situation actualized the need for socialist transformation of commerce and small-scale industry.

In order to encourage merchants and private industrialists to try cooperation on a voluntary basis, it was necessary to introduce types of cooperatives in which their means of production could be merged without harm to their interests. The Korean Workers' Party proposed three forms. In the first, the means of production of the various businesses were not yet integrated, but relations of mutual assistance were maintained and modest contributions made to common funds. This form disappeared, however, once the movement for cooperativization got into full swing. The second was a semisocialist type with collective management and pooling of production and funds, but with income distribution according to the volume of investment as well as to labor input. Finally, in the socialist type, the one which became dominant, the means of production and funds were placed under collective ownership and distribution was in accordance with work performed.

The reorganization of the nonagricultural private sector

and the political remolding of entrepreneurs depended on the possibility of offering them a viable means of economic integration. Various incentives were used to encourage them to produce more, and to sell through state agencies instead of on the market. At the same time, the state-run enterprises and consumers' cooperatives narrowed down the market, following the line that "private trade should be abolished by competition."[36] The cooperatives gradually increased the volume of their sales through the state wholesale agencies while private channels dried up, and in the end these cooperatives engaged in production only. As the Koreans see it, the fact that merchants and entrepreneurs were allowed to produce material wealth by their own labor had a radical effect on their ideological development. "In this manner a change in class relations took place and the former merchants, industrialists or handicraftmen became working people, cooperative workers or working intellectuals."[37]

Against the background of a virtually ruined private sector whose remaining material foundation was disappearing because of the policy of cooperativization of handicrafts and agriculture, to have chosen a different course would have meant bypassing a golden opportunity. Such passivity would have complicated any later attempts at socialist reorganization of this sector. Reviewing this period, Kim Il Sung observed, "If our Party had missed this chance when conditions were favorable for the socialist transformation of private trade and industry, and had not carried it out until they accumulated some assets, we would have taken a long time and have faced a lot of problems."[38]

Another important factor that needs to be taken into consideration is that commerce is not only a form of intercourse between different sectors, but an important element in the accumulation of capital. Consequently, the stimulation of producers' cooperatives, handicrafts, and various other light consumer industries should not be underestimated, as such production is the basis of commercial activities. The relatively limited investment required, considering the quick turnover, in light industry and trade (compared to investments in heavy industry and agriculture) gives this field of economic activity added significance. This was clearly kept in mind from an early date: "We must make every effort not only to ensure the smooth supply of commodities required by the working people but also to secure funds for the state, by expanding and developing the circulation of commodities between town and country."[39] In fact, the organization of trade and circulation became the object of very careful attention.

Technical Revolution in the Countryside

The social reorganization of the rural sector in Korea did not, however, mean that modernization of agriculture should or could be postponed. As pointed out by Kim Il Sung, ". . . once the foundation of socialist industry has been laid, the emphasis should be switched so that industry may come to the aid of agriculture. From that time on, agriculture should be given ever more powerful and all-round assistance."[40] Indeed, only by revolutionizing the methods of farming can this sector show progress in the longer run, once the initial gains brought about by collectivization have been consolidated.

The organization of the peasantry into cooperatives actually facilitated the technical revolution in the countryside, which would have been incomparably more difficult and costly (not to say impossible) if individual, small-unit farming had been allowed to dominate. In his interesting "Theses on the Socialist Rural Question in our Country" Kim Il Sung summed up the fundamental aspects of the technical revolution:

> Irrigation, mechanization, electrification and chemicalization are the four fundamental components of the technical revolution in the countryside. The steady increase of crop yields is impossible if irrigation and chemicalization are neglected while mechanization and electrification are one-

sidedly emphasized. If, on the contrary, efforts are concentrated only on irrigation and chemicalization while mechanization and electrification are neglected, labour efficiency cannot be raised, nor can the peasants be relieved of their onerous toil.[41]

Again, this was in line with the policy of bringing industry to the assistance of agriculture, since these transformations would have been impossible without a heavy industrial base.

The order of priority of these four elements of modernization may differ according to the level of industrial development or specific regional conditions. In Korea it was logical to give irrigation priority from the beginning. In the words of Kim Il Sung:

> Unlike industry, agriculture is largely influenced by natural and geographical factors, and particularly by climate. It is the duty of the Communists to lay the solid foundations for a situation in which production will be unaffected by climatic changes or other chance factors by conquering and remaking nature, and to provide the people with stable conditions of life.[42]

Especially during the cooperativization period, mass campaigns involving huge numbers of people carried out irrigation works and forest and water conservation projects. While minor irrigation and draining schemes were undertaken by the cooperatives themselves, larger projects were usually taken in charge by the state.

By the end of 1960, the task of irrigation was basically completed. Between 1946 and 1960, the area of irrigated rice paddies had increased from 387,000 to 509,698 *chongbo*—and in 1970 it reached 700,000 *chongbo*. Today, North Korea's extensive irrigation system, comprising about 40,000 kilometers of canals, about 11,200 electrical pumping stations, and 1,234 reservoirs, makes it one of the world's most advanced countries in this field. This permits a widespread use of chemical fertilizers, which are dependent on water supplies during their application. Fur-

Table 9
Development of Irrigation

	1953	1956	1960	1967	1970 compared to 1960
Number of reservoirs	203	897	1234	1234	capacity increased 1.5 times
Number of pumping stations	1792	3862	7797	9584	capacity increased 3.2 times

Source: J. Suret-Canale, J. E. Vidal, *La Corée populaire vers les matins calmes* (Paris, 1973), p. 48.

ther, irrigation serves the socioeconomic function of making agriculture less dependent on climatic conditions, thus minimizing one of the main differences between industrial and agricultural production. One even more important effect of this elaborate water system has been the prevention of the chronic floods which formerly plagued the country.

Mechanization, probably the most difficult problem in the technical revolutionization of a backward agriculture, is nevertheless imperative for increasing productivity and lightening the burden of farm work. In the beginning (1953) the major emphasis was placed on perfecting simple farm implements. Also in that year 15 machine-service stations operating 500 tractors (15 horsepower) were established, covering an area of 95,000 *chongbo.* By 1957, with the assistance of the Academy of Science's Agricultural Research Institute and of various agricultural colleges, about 50 machine-service stations operating 2,092 tractors were tilling about 19 percent of the total arable land. At this juncture Korea did not yet produce tractors but had to import them. During these early stages of mechanization, what claimed priority was the elimination of time- and labor-consuming work such as ploughing, weeding, and transportation. By 1959 the number of machine-service stations had increased to 84 units with 8,050 tractors, and a variety of machines were doing 2.9 times the work they had done in 1953.[43] In the five-year period from 1956 to 1960 the number of factories specializing in the production of agricultural machinery doubled, while in 1960 the assembly-line production of tractors (including heavy, 75-horsepower tractors) gave further impetus to the mechanization of agriculture. Thus, according to one source the number of tractors (calculated in 15 horsepower units) had jumped to 12,500 in 1960 and by 1965, about 20,000 were operating in the country.[44] According to figures given in the late 1960s there were 1.46 tractors per 100 hectares of land, implying a total number of 30,000 tractors. By 1972 the Kyiang Tractor Factory had been expanded to include enlarged, automated workshops. The plant, renamed Kumsong, is supposed to be one of the world's biggest with an estimated annual capacity of 30,000 tractors. In his speech on July 27, 1974, Kim Il Sung reported that there were about 80,000 tractors operating in agriculture, which would seem to indicate that mechanization under the Six Year Plan is getting under way. Actually, even in 1971 the mechanization of Korean agriculture was clearly on the increase, with lorries and tractors seen everywhere in the busy seasons.

The third aspect of the technical revolution, electrification, is closely related to the first two. Without electricity in the countryside, irrigation and mechanization cannot be fully accomplished nor modern villages constructed. In colonial times, this source of energy had been exploited in a lopsided manner based exclusively on water power. After liberation an effort was made to overcome the seasonal differences in power production by reducing dependence on the level of rainfall through the construction of numerous thermal power plants. Another approach was to promote small- and medium-sized power stations built with local manpower and widely distributed over various sections of the country, while simultaneously constructing large power stations as well. This diversification made it possible to tap smaller streams; it also made power supplies less vulnerable in case of military conflict.

The scope of the effort can be grasped from the following statistics. By 1960, 62.1 percent of the country's smallest administrative units (*ri*) in rural areas had access to electricity, whereas the figure for households was 62 percent. By 1967, the figures were 98.2 percent for the *ri*s and 86.1 percent for farmers' dwellings. Today, electrification is said to have been completed: practically all households, even in remote hamlets, have access to the benefits of electrical power.

Overall priority for the utilization of electricity was given to productive operations such as water pumping, threshing and feed processing, milling, etc. But electrification also played a key role in raising the standard of living of the peasantry by giving them electric light as well as access to various cultural activities such as radio, cinema, and television. In this manner another difference between urban and rural life could be reduced. In 1970, the consumption of electricity in rural areas amounted to one billion kilowatts/hour per year, most of it for productive purposes. When traveling by night in North Korea lights can be seen everywhere in populated areas—not the millions of bright bulbs and neon lights of Western cities, but sufficient to serve its purpose. Waste is avoided.

Internationally, the DPRK ranks among the most advanced countries as far as economical utilization of electricity is concerned. This is partly due to the country's natural hydroelectrical potential which, once tapped in an efficient manner, could play a decisive role in the modernization of the country. In this connection it should not be forgotten that quite a few Third World countries have similar potentialities.

Chemicalization is the fourth cornerstone of modern agriculture. The application of modern techniques in an appropriate manner implies a knowledge of soil construction and composition, climatic variations, and a number of other complicated details involved in the science of agronomy. This is the major prerequisite for proper utilization of fertilizers to improve the soil and the application of various insecticides and herbicides to protect plants against insects or disease.

During the colonial occupation some fertilizer was produced in North Korea, but this was mainly exported to Japan. After the complete destruction of these fertilizer factories during the Korean War, priority was given to their reconstruction. This was no simple task. While production levels within most branches of the economy had by 1956 surpassed those of 1949, the fertilizer output had only reached 49 percent of that last prewar year. This imbalance was corrected during the Five Year Plan and production was further developed under the Seven Year Plan. Today, the country possesses the biggest factories of this kind on the east coast of the Asian mainland, even exporting some of its products. Similarly—according to official figures—the average use of chemical fertilizer increased from 131 kilograms per hectare in 1949 to 160 kilograms in 1960, 300 kilograms in 1965, and 510 kilograms in 1970 (700 kilograms of chemical fertilizers were applied to each hectare of paddy, while in dry fields the average was 500 kilograms). Since liberation the production of chemical fertilizers has increased about tenfold and it is expected that it will reach 2.8 to 3 million tons by 1976 and 5 million tons by 1980.

A question which has been on the minds of many foreign visitors to the DPRK, especially in recent years, is how the problem of pollution is dealt with. We discussed the subject with the chief engineer of a chemical factory, several teachers, professors at the Marine College at Wonsan, and others. The responses varied: some knew little of the problem; others showed a keen awareness of it. It should be pointed out that industrial pollution is a problem the authorities were aware of rather early; during the reconstruction period, for example, industries were relocated outside of residential areas. Recognition of the full scope of the question is a relatively recent phenomenon, but with increasing worldwide understanding of its seriousness, the DPRK too will surely give priority to the struggle against all forms of pollution. It is obvious that the context of the problem is different in the newly industrialized, planned economy of Korea than in the industrialized capitalist world.

It is interesting to note that in order to increase the supply of fertilizer and protect land fertility, which cannot be maintained with chemicals alone, the use of manure has been encouraged. Consequently it is recommended that every farm household raise two pigs a year, in addition to other livestock; the manure, mixed with limestone and apatite can be turned into good organic fertilizer in the form of compost. Not only does this improve the soil and thereby increase the harvest, but it yields a larger quantity of meat. To provide the necessary animal fodder, every strip of land is used—on river dikes, between trees in orchards, along roads. Only in certain areas of Holland have the authors seen such intensive utilization of land.

Besides the different technical aspects of agricultural modernization, much attention was paid from the very beginning to the introduction of more scientific farming methods—rice seeding on cold beds or dry fields, wide-row and crisscross sowing, use of quality seeds, etc. While priority was given to the production of grain, constituting about 82 percent of all agricultural produce in 1960, industrial crops, vegetables, fruit, and fodder were also developed. The extensive irrigation of rice fields generaly permits two crops per year—the second being a dry field winter crop in the spring before rice planting takes place (although in certain areas winter crops do not have sufficient time to ripen and have to be green-harvested and used as fodder). In addition, the polder reclamation program on the coast of the West Sea has extended the land area.[45] As rice fields in terraces are labor-intensive and difficult to adapt to mechanization, a movement to plant fruit trees in terraces on hills and mountainslopes was started in 1958. Today more than 300,000 *chongbo* are taken up by fruits trees. Besides making the country an exporter of good quality apples, the many orchards growing on the red-colored soil in all the hilly areas have added a special touch of beauty to the countryside.

Animal production also increased, although at a relatively slower pace. By 1960, 672,000 head of cattle were being raised, still below the 1949 total of 788,000—with the important difference, however, that the decreased need for draft animals resulted in a higher proportion of cows, permitting dairy farming to increase. Pig production was expected to reach 3.5 million in the years 1967-1970. As it is both a time-consuming and relatively expensive task to develop pig- and cow-raising, the greatest and most rapid progress was made with the introduction of state farms specializing in chicken, ducks, and rabbits, and managed in an almost industrial manner. In 1970, egg production reached 700 million, probably including the household supply. The present Six Year Plan foresees a yearly production of about 3 billion eggs, half from modern chicken farms, and the other half from the cooperatives.

Other important protein sources are soybeans and fish. The fishing industry seems to be extremely diversified, yielding an ample supply of food—not only fish but various shellfish, seaweed, etc., which are important ingredients in a variety of Korean dishes. Fishing is developed actively not only along the coasts and in lakes and streams, but in the water reservoirs. We were told that sometimes fish are even raised on the irrigated paddy fields. The fish seem to thrive in the low muddy waters, and their constant movement of the plant roots is said to stimulate the growth of rice. When the water is drained at harvest time, the mature fish may be caught. Flour can be made of fish as well as of soybeans and is widely used in various food products, including baby food. All kindergarten children receive not only a daily glass of milk but an additional supply of protein in the form of fish-flour or soybean products. In most Afro-Asian and Latin American countries today protein deficiency takes its annual toll among children in the form of crippling diseases. Youngsters growing up in the DPRK are safe from such risks for the first time in their country's history.

As far as industrial crops are concerned, agriculture was relieved of a burdensome task with the introduction of synthetic fibers. Since the climate is not very favorable to cotton, its cultivation could gradually be decreased—from 78,000 tons in 1949 to about 7,000 tons—without affecting textile production. At the same time the manufacturing of textiles from reed, corn cane, etc., was developed. According to Korean figures, even under their particularly unfavorable conditions, one hectare of reeds can yield the same amount of fabric as twenty hectares of cotton. Viscose is made of wood and woven into blankets, while the production of vinalon is based on flax and limestone. All this has meant that a larger area of arable land could be devoted to other useful crops, better suited to local climatic conditions. A rather large sericulture also exists. Some of the silk is meant for export, but some is also consumed at home, since silk is used extensively in traditional women's costumes as well as for bed covers. In order to save wood, paper is made locally from pulp made of rice straw, in what seems to be a consistent policy of economizing on the country's resources.

Other nonessential crops were also reduced. Tobacco production, 10,000 tons in 1949, had decreased to 8,000 tons by 1969, but this seems sufficient both to cover the domestic demand and to allow for some exports.

The economic course implemented through the reform policies after liberation, the establishment of cooperative farms in the immediate postwar period, and the gradual technical transformation of the farming process, have enabled North Korea to practically resolve its agrarian problem. According to Joseph S. Chung, the average annual rate of growth for the DPRK's Gross Agricultural Product was 10 percent for 1954-1960 and 6.3 percent for 1961-1970.[46] These were very high growth rates for a rural economy, which generally has much less growth potential than the industrial sectors. In 1960 the achievement of self-sufficiency in food was announced. Considering the complexities involved, this was no small achievement, especially when it is recalled that originally 75-78 percent of the country's paddy was situated in the South and only about 20 percent of the area in the North was accessible arable land. The yield of 42.3 hundredweight of rice per hectare claimed in 1960, compared to 30 hundredweight in 1949, makes one realize the rapidity with which progress has been made. Following the early sixties, when the low level of technology and management techniques resulted in rather slow increases in productivity, agricultural production took great leaps in the Seventies. By 1974 average per-*chongbo* rice yield was as high as 5.9 tons; this compares favorably with the advanced agriculture of such countries as Japan and Australia, making the North Korean yield the highest on the Asian mainland.[47] The corresponding maize yield for the same year was claimed to be about 5 tons, also very impressive.

Based on what are admitted to be unreliable U.N. figures for North Korean exports and imports, some critics of the regime have questioned the date for the achievement of self-sufficiency in food, maintaining that it occurred somewhat later. Ironically enough, these same writers, upon investigation, have had to acknowledge that this crucial goal actually has been achieved "partly by virtue of the increased production of other agricultural and marine commodities, supplementing the grain output, and also the continuance of a rigorous grain rationing and distribution system."[48] The rationing of rice, however, has another explanation, one related to the policy of subsidizing grain production. The cooperative farmers are allowed to keep enough grain for their own consumption, while the rest is bought by the state at a price of 0.60 *won* per kilogram, and resold in shops to workers and office employees for only 0.08 *won* per kilogram. If the rice was not rationed, it would simply be too tempting to try to resell rice bought cheaply. This example of consciously promoting agricultural production has a political explanation:

> Why then does the state buy rice from the co-operative farmers at such a high price? It is to improve their living standards and, at the same time, to encourage them to be more earnest in running the collective economy .... If the state procurement price is too low for the grain the farmers have grown collectively, their cash income will be small. If they get a small income from the collective economy, they will be inclined to get more from the private sideline economy. Our farmers now have little interest in private sidelines, because it is more profitable for them to work on the co-operative farm than in sidelines.[49]

B. REVOLUTIONIZING THE EDUCATION SYSTEM

Ideological Revolution in the Countryside

On the sociopolitical level the modernization of agriculture is directly linked to an ideological transformation of the people involved. Without such a process, the mentality of the peasantry remains attached to former social relations and ancient methods of production. A kind of cultural revolution is necessary, with special emphasis on ideological remolding and on raising the level of general knowledge and technical knowhow. According to Korean socialists, only by paying close attention to these elements can the gap between the rural and urban sectors, together with the existing distinctions between the working class and the peasantry, eventually be eliminated.

228 *Socialist Korea*

The attitude of the socialist forces in an agrarian environment is dictated by a dialectical understanding of the peasant's role in the political process. Despite their rhetoric, the following observation by two pro-Western specialists on Asian affairs may not be completely off the mark:

> To the Communists, and particularly to the Asian Communists, the peasant has represented a hope and a challenge. Deeply cognizant of the need to capture and use this class, alternately optimistic and pessimistic about its revolutionary potentials, ambivalent over the mixture of coercion and persuasion to be used in soliciting rural cooperation, the North Korean Communists never come closer to revealing the essence of their movement than when confronting the peasant "problem."[50]

This problem, however, is only one aspect of overall social change and must be considered within that context.

Since the very essence of their strategy is the understanding of the necessity for change, Koreans view the solution to the question of the transformation of the rural sector within the general framework of constructing a new type of society. Several elements are involved. First, following the abolition of the old production relations, priority is given to ideological work, while at the same time technical and cultural education is carried out. Second, the working class has to assist the peasantry; the city must help the countryside, and industry must come to the aid of agriculture. The third point is the necessity of institutional changes, replacing cooperative ownership with all-people ownership, developing the principle of collective management instead of one-person management, and bringing methods of rural management to a level equaling that of industry.

The strategy of ideological transformation in Korea is based on the concept that class struggle continues under socialism, although assuming a somewhat different form than under the former social order. In practice this means not only that the people have to be politically mobilized against subversive elements from the outside and remnants of the old exploiting classes, but that their own surviving obsolete ideas have to be overcome. The outcome of such a struggle depends largely on the very recognition that there is a problem. Socialists previously tended to believe that ideological problems would disappear by themselves once production relations were transformed. Kim Il Sung's position is precisely the opposite:

> The remolding of the peasants' thought and consciousness does not come of itself with the establishment of the socialist system and improvement of the livelihood. It goes without saying that with the triumph of the socialist system, the economic foundation generating obsolete ideas disappears and the social and material conditions for equipping the peasants with new ideology are created. But, under socialism too, the residue of the obsolete ideas, and particularly petty-proprietor inclinations, persist for a long time in the minds of the peasants, and may revive and even grow when the ideological work is slackened.[51]

In the course of this political struggle, members of agricultural cooperatives were shown that one should respect public property and subordinate one's own petty interests and inclinations to those of the community and the state. At the same time a positive attitude toward labor was encouraged, with work considered an honorable endeavor; leading an idle life, depending on the work of others for one's livelihood, as the old exploiting classes had done, was frowned upon and morally condemned. Similar strictures existed against waste of material or labor; there was great emphasis on valuing and protecting the wealth created by the working masses. This remolding process was not based entirely on moral appeals, however. It was accompanied by concrete measures (such as the previously noted rationing of rice), which made negative attitudes difficult to maintain. Thus, the struggle against egoism and indolence was strengthened through the principle of socialist distribution, i.e., material remuneration in accordance with labor performed. Ideological/political incentives were combined with material benefits that increased the general standard of living. Another aspect of the revolutionization of consciousness was the promotion of a spirit of "opposing the old and aspiring for the new," and of "loving the future and being armed with revolutionary optimism." Passive, conservative, and mystical attitudes toward the solution of actual problems were to be opposed. Furthermore, the peasantry was to be educated in the policies of the Party and its revolutionary traditions.[52]

Presenting positive examples, patiently persuading and influencing people into a new mentality—these were the principal methods employed in this educational process. Another recommended approach was to conduct ideological work through practical activities and collective labor at the very site of production. This emphasis on practice, so characteristic of the Korean perspective, is probably designed to prevent errors of idealism and the creation of false issues, which would divide the people. When political work is combined with practical everyday tasks, knowledge becomes generalized and a deeper understanding is achieved. As Kim Il Sung explains, "We should vigorously carry on the ideological revolution in the rural areas so as to equip peasants with working-class ideas and eliminate gradually the differences in the level of thoughts and consciousness between workers and peasants."[53]

On a more material level, this ideological endeavor was followed up by efforts to develop more advanced forms of property relations through promotion of the principle of "ownership by the whole people." In the rural economy, state farms of various kinds and state-owned machine stations coexisted with the cooperatives, serving as examples of higher forms of ownership. But changes in property relations came slowly; by 1960, cooperative farms accounted for 83.9 percent of the total area under cultivation as against 16.1 percent for state farms.[54] These figures have not altered substantially since, but surmounting this state of affairs is considered a precondition for the future evolution of the countryside: "For successfully building socialism, we must consolidate and further develop collective ownership, i.e., socialist ownership, in the countryside. And for building communism in the future, collective ownership should be turned into ownership by the whole people. Without eliminating selfishness, the process of all this development cannot be accelerated."[55]

It should be clear that the development of the countryside was not left to chance nor to the working of spontaneous forces. In the same vein, new and improved methods of administration and management were introduced. Against the background of a technical and cultural revolution, the mentality of the rural population seems to have changed almost as rapidly as their surroundings. The methods involved in this transformation of the Korean countryside may be considered a contribution to the theory and practice of the transition to socialism in agrarian societies.

In the urban sector, when the industrialization process began it suffered from many material and cultural limitations comparable to those affecting agriculture. Here too a technical and cultural revolution was of paramount importance in modernizing the composition and mentality of the labor force.

Creating an Advanced Industrial Labor Force

Because of the low level of their means of production, in former colonies and semicolonies the modernization of the labor force is a more pronounced problem than it is in highly industrialized nations. In the event of a transition from developed capitalism to socialism, the new regimes would not inherit this kind of difficulties (although no doubt radical ideological remolding would certainly be called for). The lack of a trained and disciplined labor force would not be a factor of any significance. Modern liberal theoreticians of development often devote much of their attention to the lack of managerial ability in Third World countries but fail to realize the full implications of the weakness of these countries' working classes in both the technical and sociological sense of the word. Overcoming this handicap may very well be a precondition for industrial development. Writing some years ago on the problems of the Chinese economy in the years after liberation, the economist Solomon Adler made the following important point:

> *Given an adequate supply of food,* the creation of a skilled labour force is the crux of the process of industrialization. With it the problems of capital formation and capital maintenance can be solved; without it, the best machinery in the world will rust unused. The speed of reconstruction in devastated industrial countries is proof enough of its overriding importance. But the creation, or at any rate, the rapid expansion of a supply of skilled workers amenable to factory discipline is a problem of a very different order from that of mobilizing a trained labour force already in being. The discipline needed for the smooth and continuing operation of a factory system is at least as hard to acquire as modern industrial skill. . . . [56]

In Korea this problem was particularly severe. During colonial domination very few Koreans had worked at skilled jobs; technology, and the privileges it conferred, were monopolized by Japanese nationals. At the time of liberation, there was thus a serious lack of technical cadres, although this problem—as seen above—was on the way to being remedied. However, with the war many of the country's ablest workers were lost. In the immediate postwar period, with the emphasis on reconstruction, the needs of the industrial sector were probably relatively uncomplicated; as the rehabilitation process progressed, however, the demand for both more qualified cadres and skilled workers increased. Similarly, due to the peasants' lower ideological and cultural levels, the transfer of workers from agriculture to industry could hardly alleviate this fundamental weakness in the short run. This problem was recognized by Kim Il Sung, who stated at the time that ". . . at present there are no small number of workers at our factories who are not yet armed with working-class consciousness. They lack discipline and organization and fail to understand correctly their class stand as masters of the state."[57]

As in the rural sector, the method chosen to overcome this weakness was the elimination of the old customs and ideas harbored by members of the new industrial labor force both through ideological education, raising their political and cultural level, and through the improvement of their technical skills and standard of living. The resolution of this problem was considered to be of prime importance: "No great results can be expected in the postwar rehabilitation and development of the national economy, unless the ideological, cultural and technical levels of the working-class are raised."[58]

Although ideological remolding is a long-term project that continues throughout the entire period of socialist transition, the elevation of the cultural and technical level of the people also demands immediate measures, including the establishment of institutions. Under the prevailing conditions, education had to fulfill two principal functions: in the short run it had to provide the cultural and technical training required for the development of all sectors of the economy, while in the longer run it was to pave the way for the socialist objective of reducing the contrast between town and country, the distinctions between intellectual and manual labor, and the differences between various kinds of work. The way a country tackles the educational problem can serve as an indicator both of its ability to solve the problem of underdevelopment and of the seriousness of its intention to introduce socialism.

The Failure of Traditional Education

To understand the highly strategic significance of education in the socioeconomic development of nonindustrial nations, it may be useful to examine this problem more generally, with reference to the Korean context. Even though Korea may in some ways have been in an exceptional situation upon acquiring independence from colonialism, it nevertheless originally suffered from many of the same symptoms observable in most of the former colonial world.

An important feature of the Korean cultural background after liberation was the relative nonexistence of a traditional indigenous educational system adaptable to modernization. As a matter of fact, much had been done during the colonial occupation to eradicate Korean cultural identity. In this and in other respects, Japan had followed the usual colonialist pattern of restricting education to what would serve its own interests. The original purpose of any colonial education has always been the formation of a minority of civil servants and trades people to serve as middlemen between the foreign power and the indigenous population.

In most newly independent former colonies the problem of education is principally rooted in the survival of such a system—introduced from the outside, often out of touch with the realities of the country, and at cross-purposes with the objective of development. Under colonialism even the teaching used to be done in the language of the colonialist and in many countries this practice, with all its adverse implications for the sociopsychological climate, still persists. But even when teaching is done in the mother tongue the entire setup usually remains divorced from the needs of the native environment. One financial byproduct of this situation is that because of the tradition of paying higher wages to teachers (who used to be mainly foreigners) instruction in such countries tends to be both uneconomical and inefficient. As a matter of fact, some African nations devote about one third of their national budgets to education, yet are unable to reach more than about one out of ten children! Even in those cases where literacy campaigns among the masses have been carried out, the results are often limited, as the effort is seldom accompanied by corresponding socioeconomic changes. People have a tendency to forget their acquired knowledge, since it seems of little practical use. The result is that a process of "re-analphabetization" sets in. Most experience with literacy campaigns seems to indicate that the ability to learn is strongly related to the degree to which education is integrated with the immediate everyday problems of the group in question.[59] As such integration is usually lacking, the results remain correspondingly poor.

The sociological problems resulting from nonintegrated education are particularly acute in rural areas. Where children of peasant origin do receive some kind of instruction, they have a tendency to become utterly alienated from their native environment. They speak a foreign language, or at least express themselves quite differently from their original friends and their families. They usually show contempt for manual labor and consider it a personal failure should they have to return to work in their native villages. It is, nonetheless, precisely in rural areas that the need is greatest for doctors, teachers, and technical experts. In many such countries highly educated people in their most productive years are concentrated in the cities, where they are unemployed or underemployed; the possibilities of absorbing them on a level commensurate with their qualifications are nearly nonexistent, as their training has in no way been attuned to national needs.

South Korea, which adopted Western educational standards, offers a contemporary example of profound cleavages between the educated minority and the masses. The main motivation for instruction has remained the competitive struggle for individual advancement. Writing on this question, the director of the Central Education Research Institute in Seoul concludes:

Consequently education has been made a tool for the advancement of personal expectations, that is, for rising in the world, and thus it has been made to neglect the more important function of preparing the rising generation to become public-minded citizens by teaching them social cooperation and the ideal of social service. The polarization of the rich and the poor in Korean society, and evils rising from this structural bifurcation, constitute the major challenge for Korean education.[60]

Because of the inability of these societies to fulfill such expectations many highly educated individuals often simply emigrate to industrial countries, where prospects for employment and higher wages seem brighter. The cultural barrier is greatly reduced, as their education has often involved not only learning the foreign language, but imitating the ideals and way of life of Western Europe or the United States. This tendency is further accentuated by the spread of films and music of Western origin. This complex set of relations, which encompasses an almost systematic neglect of the cultural traditions and historical past of the former colonial world, on the one hand, and an emphasis on the exploits of the industrially developed societies, on the other, has been described as "cultural imperialism."

According to a seminar of French educational experts held in the spring of 1973, conventional (usually Western) educational systems fail to solve the actual problems of the former colonial world. In fact, what these systems *do* produce is a small elite of so-called educated people, whose social behavior and world outlook usually have more in common with their colleagues abroad than with their fellow citizens and whose knowledge is ill adapted to the requirements of their own country.[61]

Meanwhile, of course, this situation is far from static. Present limitations on the capacity to absorb newly educated generations will represent a future political challenge in these countries—especially as the situation in Western capitalist nations tends to deteriorate, reducing the outlet provided by the so-called brain drain from the

Socialist Methods of Economic Development 237

Third World. As a matter of fact, students and intellectuals are already at the forefront of the political opposition in many countries, including South Korea.

To return to North Korea, the fact that Japan had belonged to the losing side during World War II offered the country different opportunities than those open to most Third World countries upon acquiring their independence from Western imperialism (or to South Korea, which remained under such external influence). Thus, the new system which evolved in the DPRK was less a revision and remodeling of traditional education than it has been in most Third World countries (even compared to most European socialist countries, education in Korea constitutes a more radical break with previous educational practice). Following liberation, all Japanese cultural and educational influence was purged and an effective literacy campaign carried out. At this juncture the Korean educational system might still have evolved along the more conventional lines typical of most socialist European countries. The war-inflicted devastation of the DPRK, however, dictated an untraditional course. For obvious reasons, the educational program had to become closely associated with the overall effort of reconstruction.

In other words, what the new postwar situation did *not* permit was the slow and expensive training of a small elite of highly specialized technicians and intellectuals. In order to be effective, instruction had to be oriented toward the solution of immediate tasks as well as based on a mass line. Furthermore, the war had given North Koreans a stronger sense of national identity and purpose, thus helping to involve the population in all spheres of social activity.

To overcome the lack of cadres, teachers, and skilled workers during reconstruction, a system of cooperation between students, workers, and technicians was established. Students were called upon to move their educational activities to construction sites in order to "learn while building." In this manner a remarkable system combining theory and practice was instituted during the earliest period. This, together with ideological mobilization, became an important lever for development not only immediately, but in the longer run as well.

Learning While Building

With the coming of liberation, because of the need to educate the entire population, instruction had not been limited to adolescents but had been organized at factories and places of work in order to give all age groups some minimum amount of education. As early as April 1950, a system of "workers' schools" had been established to dispense short-term instruction on a middle-school level and to prepare peasants and workers for regular college education. Because of the war, the true advantages of that approach did not become clear until the postwar reconstruction period, which intensified the demand for skilled adults with practical experience. The establishment in this period of a new type of technical school, specializing in the training of what might be called medium-level technicians or skilled workers, was a step in the same direction as the prewar attempts to accelerate training of industrial cadres and qualified personnel.

However, the country could not simply "relax" and await the results of these efforts before creating and running industrial enterprises. Thus a course was devised for solving the problem of the shortage of cadres and skilled workers while simultaneously engaging in industrial development. The most important innovation in the field of adult education was institutionalized in 1960 with the setting up of "factory colleges" at all major plants. In this way higher theoretical education was made available to advanced workers right at their place of work. (Similar opportunities were offered to the rural population with the establishment of colleges in all provinces.)

This represented a great departure from conventional methods of spreading technical instruction. The example of attacking two major aspects of underdevelopment at the same time may in fact be of general interest for other countries faced with a similar dilemma. In his address to the Second Asian Economic Seminar held in Pyongyang in 1964, the Korean delegate discussed the lack of technical cadres faced by former colonies in the development of an independent national economy and summed up the essence of his country's solution to the problem:

> In order to solve the question of national technical cadres in a short time and advance faster in economic construction, we did not wait till we had mastered technique so as to undertake industrial construction, but adopted the positive measure of acquiring advanced technique in the course of building a modern industry, and turned all the production sites throughout the country into schools for learning techniques. Now our country has established extensively the study-while-work educational system such as factory college side by side with the regular educational system.[62]

In 1961, this line was further promoted when a comprehensive program for adult education, including the smallest units in the countryside, was presented at the Fourth Party Congress. Adults were encouraged to participate in free-time programs such as evening schools or correspondence courses in order to develop their technical level and cultural background. New nationwide organs were also set up to promote the "technical and intellectual revolution." The Federation for Scientific Knowledge Dissemination established educational centers on all levels: provinces, cities, counties, and cooperative farms. Democratic Propaganda Class Rooms were opened in libraries, factories, farms, and residential areas. It is estimated that about 15 percent of the country's workers and peasants are currently engaged in study at various institutions of learning. Some workers study in the evening, others take part-time courses, and others still are full-time students. Under this procedure, the economically active population can improve its educational level *without leaving production*.

The advantages of the systems are many and operate on

a variety of levels. With the alternation between production and education, it becomes almost inevitable that studies be directed toward the solution of concrete, immediate problems. On the socioeconomic level people's technical and theoretical knowledge is enhanced through practical experience, while on the political level a large number of people of proletarian background are incorporated into the educated stratum of the population. On the personal level individuals are given an opportunity to acquire additional skills and knowledge at almost any stage in their life, regardless of their original level. As far as the state is concerned, this system trains technicians and specialists at a great saving of expense while relieving it of the administrative burden of supplying cadres to all production units.

Further, through this system the role and responsibility of local organs are increased, although they remain under Party supervision. At present, every province has enough colleges for its all-around functioning and development. Through technical, medical, agricultural, and teachers' colleges, as well as institutes for national economy, the provinces meet their own demands for cadres and specialists.

The near self-sufficiency of provinces with regard to technicians extends also to the formation of political cadres. In 1960 "communist colleges" replaced the old cadre schools. These political institutions are attended by model workers, farmers, and Party cadres, as well as by members of various governmental, industrial, and agrarian agencies. The colleges have an average enrollment of 2,000, and they are also equipped to handle night-school and correspondence courses. The primary function of these colleges is to train Party and governmental cadres for the districts and provinces as well as for industrial enterprises and cooperative farms. Further up the ladder is the "people's college of economics," a higher institution of management and administrative education which in 1954 replaced the "central cadres' school." There, higher economic and administrative cadres are either trained or given refresher courses in such subjects as economic planning, accounting, finance, banking, labor administration, and economic management. The highest institution of this kind, however, is the "Kim Il Sung higher party school" where important officials and functionaries are given courses in ideology as well as in political functions.

While political and administrative training is centrally organized, the smaller institutions for popular adult education are managed locally. The "factory colleges" themselves operate with a certain autonomy, being self-reliant with respect to funds and teaching personnel. "Thus the factory manager becomes the 'dean of the college' and the factory scientists, engineers, and specialists constitute 'the faculty.' "[63] The students are selected from among the graduates of correspondence courses or senior technical schools and are recommended by the factory Party committee. At the college they receive instruction in mechanical engineering, chemistry, electrical engineering, mining engineering, etc. It takes about three years to train a competent technician and five years to qualify as an engineer.[64] As the workers both learn and apply their knowledge immediately at their places of work, factories are no longer simply economic production units, but simultaneously educational and technical centers. In this manner an efficient method has been found for mass formation of cadres and for raising the cultural level of the working class without putting any strain on the production process. Today, many managers of enterprises or chief engineers are graduates of such educational institutions.

In his report to the Fourth Party Congress in 1961, Kim Il Sung summarized the benefits of this system:

> Experience gained in the year following the establishment of factory colleges and communist colleges reveals that a factory is capable of managing a college, and that in many respects such colleges have advantages. These colleges make it possible to train intellectuals of a new type en masse

from among the working class and to provide the possibility of combining education very closely with production and theory with practice. Because large numbers of advanced workers are receiving a higher education without being separated from production, the development of production and technique is accelerated.[65]

It goes without saying that this type of autonomy does not prevent the state from switching qualified personnel from one production unit to another if necessary.

Achievements in adult education came quickly. More than 400,000 technicians were trained during the Seven Year Plan alone, bringing the total number to 600,000. In 1960 technicians constituted 7.7 percent of the entire industrial labor force; by 1965 the figure had increased to 15.8 percent. Over the same period a similar process took place in agriculture, with the number of technicians in cooperatives growing from 1.2 percent to 17.5 percent of all agricultural workers. Today the country is totally self-reliant with regard to the national demand for technical cadres.

Given the innovative nature of this experiment, it is no exaggeration to call it a revolution in education. The DPRK's pioneering efforts in this area compare favorably with similar attempts at adult education in the People's Republic of China. Although differences between these two countries exist, the aims behind their experiments are very similar, probably as a result of their comparable situations. Both societies are not only raising the technical and cultural level of their peoples, but are also attempting to evolve a system for creating an entirely new type of intelligentsia.

A great number of intellectuals in the West are now beginning to ask fundamental questions about their role in the societies in which they live. The experiences of both these Asian socialist countries may thus capture the interest and imagination not only of activist Third World intellectuals but of their counterparts in the industrialized West. The following conclusion, reached by two of the

Socialist Methods of Economic Development 243

staunchest critics of the Korean and Chinese regimes, may serve to illustrate the point. In both societies the following broad goals may be observed:

> to overturn traditional intellectualism, with its elitist, humanistic, antiwork ethic; to emphasize knowledge for use, placing the highest premium upon technical and scientific training; to put politics in command, at least in terms of blending political principles into every training program; to provide cradle-to-grave educational opportunities via the work-study concept, at least for the modernized (nonagrarian) sector of the society.[66]

The Regular School System

Parallel to and fully integrated with adult education, a general school system has been established which reflects the same principles and ideals. It was as part of the mobilization and enthusiasm generated after the war that schools were rebuilt as a mass movement, with pupils and teachers participating side by side with peasants, workers, and soldiers. By the end of 1955 there were as many schools as there had been before the war. Over two million young people were attending a total of 5,455 schools distributed equally throughout the country, with two elementary schools in every *ri* (the smallest rural unit, comprising 2,000-2,500 people). The total enrollment in 1956 was thus 170,000 more than in 1949 and 320,000 more than in 1953. At the same time, 25,000 persons were participating in correspondence and evening courses. During the Three Year Plan, 26,000 technicians, specialists, and engineers graduated from institutions of higher learning.[67]

The return of about 7,000 Korean students from special training courses in various socialist countries in the years 1955-1957 also helped alleviate the shortage of both teachers and technicians. Although few foreign teachers seem to have been used, a spirit of shared learning between

Koreans and foreign experts was consciously stimulated at the many work sites during reconstruction.

The nationwide accessibility of educational establishments made possible the introduction of four-year primary compulsory education in the autumn of 1956, coinciding with the launching of the first Five Year Plan. Since the Five Year Plan gave priority to the building of heavy industry a special effort was made to meet the demand for technicians. This was the background for the establishment of a kind of technical high school or college which over a course of two or three years offered instruction up to the level of medium technician. Several new universities for the training of engineers and managers were also established. By the end of 1956 there were 22,458 students at nineteen specialized institutions.

During the Five Year Plan the entire school system was administratively reorganized as well. In 1958 a system of secondary compulsory education was established, but in 1959 new changes were proclaimed in a government decision of March 2, 1959 entitled "Reorganization of the Educational System." Most important was the abolition of the previous senior secondary school system and the technical colleges. These were replaced with two years each for both technical school (formerly senior secondary school) and senior technical school (formerly college level). According to two Korean specialists this scheme was unique, differing from the systems of both China and the Soviet Union.

In 1960 the first system of compulsory seven-year tuition-free education in Asia was introduced in the DPRK and by 1961, 97,000 students were studying at seventy-eight institutions of higher learning, of whom 65 percent were technical or engineering students. North Korea thereby attained a percentage of technical school or university students comparable to that in several "advanced" countries: 90 students per 10,000 inhabitants as compared to 180 for the United States, 107 for the Soviet Union, 73 for Japan, and 57 for South Korea.[68] It is significant that about half of the total number of new students at these institutes were workers who had gone through the adult education program at their place of work.

An important feature of the entire Korean educational system is its flexibility and its amalgamation of theory and practice. The general educational system is fully integrated with a structure of adult education. From the earliest possible moment the aim obviously seems to have been to provide every person with at least one specialized skill and to elevate the educational level of the entire population. In 1967, a nine-year compulsory cost-free technical education including two years of special technical instruction, was put into effect. Since the early seventies North Korea has been in the process of introducing a ten-year school system.[69]

During visits to the DPRK in 1969 and 1971 the authors visited close to two dozen ordinary and specialized schools and each visit was a singular experience. Whether in town or country, schools have their own small workshops or laboratories, machinery, lorries, and tractors which serve educational purposes. While learning how to operate a machine or drive a tractor, adolescents also learn how it functions and how to repair it. The schools often have small plots of land where pupils experiment with various cultivation methods, learn about the composition of soil, etc. Live chickens or rabbits are brought into classrooms to be examined for various animal diseases, and the pupils learn how to take care of them. Besides learning the usual textbook theories in biology, the children are educated in first aid as well as basic hygiene. They also take turns doing outside agitation work in their neighborhood or village, spreading knowledge of sanitary measures, nutrition, baby care, etc., or assisting the school doctor in daily work. In physics, the curriculum may include learning how to make rudimentary explosives and mines (a rare example of confidence in the people!); the children do not just read about radios and telegraphs in books, but learn how to operate and repair them. Music and art seem to be cultivated from kindergarten level on up—for example, every child is taught to play at least one musical instrument. It would take us too far afield to elaborate on the functioning of such a mixture of theory and practice at this level of education. But one point is obvious, namely that youth is being prepared for the future by becoming integrated within their surroundings and by learning to deal with precisely those problems which occupy the adult world. As a matter of fact, they also receive military training! The result, as far as we can judge, is a highly motivated youth, as well as a great interest on the part of the parents and adults of the neighborhood in what the children are learning.

If one adds to this the fact that on finishing school most teenagers (apart from those attending specialized schools) work for a couple of years before starting their higher education, it seems clear that there is less risk of creating a new elite that sets itself above the majority of people. It should further be pointed out that candidates for higher education are selected not only on the basis of personal wishes but have to be recommended by their fellow workers and the Party committee at the enterprise where they are working. As a result, very few educated people emerge who have not had experience with practical work.

The present compulsory ten-year system of technical education is free of charge. Students at higher institutions receive wages, while workers at factory colleges continue to draw salaries from their enterprises. Theory and practice thus imply some form of participation in productive labor. School children under the age of sixteen are not directly involved, but this does not mean that they are not taught to respect work and make themselves useful. Their contribution may include planting flowers on roadsides, growing cucumbers, feeding rabbits, collecting scrap iron and waste, cleaning their classrooms, and doing propaganda work. After the eighth school year, they take part in an annual one-month stint of light productive labor in nearby factories or cooperatives. On the political level this contact familiarizes the pupils with the conditions of the working people. Educationally it provides an additional opportunity for closing the gap between theory and practice. The system of compulsory ten-year education has the further advantage of reducing the contradictions between town and country, as all children everywhere are offered similar educational opportunities.

The long-range sociological implications of this method of education (which may still undergo further transformations) are various, but in general they seem perfectly suited to the present and future requirements of the country. In a study of the North Korean approach to this problem two Korean scholars conclude, "The school system incorporates a theory–practice concept of education in which the theories of the classroom are translated into active participation in government-directed labour units designed to consolidate the student's learning and also to assist the government in its efforts to industrialise the country." And they point out the important fact that had education been based principally on purely abstract ideological concepts the results would not have been so productive:

> The educational system's life-oriented, purposeful theories of learning are supported basically by the Marxist ideology of the dignity of labor as the origin of all value and wealth, it is true; but these educational theories are enhanced and become particularly potent motivational devices when an emotional appeal to national pride and national identity becomes a stimulation force within a society.[70]

Mobilization of Science—
Against Technological Mysticism

Given the concrete demands imposed by the rapid development of the country, it was important that the intelligentsia join in contributing toward the common goal. Thus, the amalgamation of theory and practice had far-reaching implications for the concept of science. Official policy emphasized that science could not remain aloof from the main social current:

> ... scientists should not waste their time and energy in research on useless, fantastic subjects, but they should concentrate on the problems vital to our national economy today, the solution of which brooks no delay. This must become their primary task. Our country does not have many scientists. It is important for them to solve burning questions, rather than going in for "grand plans."[71]

While the country was being mobilized at all levels, a certain reliance on intellectuals trained under the old system was necessary in order to expand the number of technicians and improve the general educational level. This sometimes caused problems within the ranks of this small but important scientific intellectual group. Because of their background, many of these intellectuals possessed advanced academic knowledge but a somewhat retarded ideological and political consciousness. Often the shortcomings of the intellectual stratum were similar to those displayed by rural elements that had recently joined the ranks of the industrial working class. Even within the highest institutions, such as the Academy of Science (established in 1952), leading members showed a reluctance to adapt to the special situation of the country and the objectives it had formulated. The main source of difficulty was the policy whereby new intellectuals, technicians, and specialists were produced through rapid training of people with no intellectual background. Some of the scientists maintained that the creation of a large force of technical cadres and a widespread spirit of innovation could not be achieved in so short a period of time. Perhaps, from a conventional point of view, such doubts were not unnatural, but insofar as they proved an obstacle to the intended process, they were criticized: "Conservatives insist on mystification in industry, in science, in technology and in all matters concerning machinery. According to them, everything is mysterious and only 'God' understands it.

This means that they, and only they, understand science, industry and technology like 'God,' and ordinary people cannot understand such matters."[72] Only through a conscious collaboration between intellectuals and workers could innovations and progress take place rapidly in industry. Such a spirit of mutual aid would be beneficial from an ideological viewpoint too, as it would require a certain reciprocity on the part of both social groups. While the educated personnel were not to show contempt for workers, an equally responsible attitude was required of the workers themselves: "If scientists, technicians and directors of factories and enterprises stifle the initiative of the workers and do not help them but hinder their positive endeavours, that is wrong. All this is the tendency of conservatism. If, on the contrary, the workers do not want to learn from technicians and scientists or co-operate with them, that is also wrong. This is a tendency to ignore science."[73]

This meant that the Party, as "the general staff of the revolution," had to wage an ideological struggle against conservatism and passivity in order to mobilize all talents that could be of use in economic growth. The Party had already had some experience in dealing with this question; it had developed a certain flexibility of policy, enabling it from time to time to make successful appeals to old-line intellectuals living abroad to return and help in the reconstruction. Patriotic intellectuals returning from Japan had already contributed to the national cause during the post-liberation period. In this fashion a new group of "old intellectuals"—including some southern professors who moved north during the Korean War—was added to the North Korean scene.[74] These intellectuals were an important concern to the Party. Since all of them had received their educations either in foreign countries or under the old system in Korea, they had to be ideologically remolded if they were to become an effective force in overcoming the country's cultural and technical backwardness.

The policy adopted toward these old-line intellectuals (i.e., intellectuals from rich families, educated in the pre-liberation period) proved most productive. In "some countries," Koreans tell their visitors, intellectuals are bought with money. But such a method, besides being very expensive, makes it impossible to move them in the direction of communism. The Party therefore followed a different course, turning the "old-line" intellectuals into "red" intellectuals. According to the Koreans, intellectuals in colonial countries often take a revolutionary stand, both because they are discriminated against by the exploiter society, even though they are also its servants, and because, being educated, they understand scientific arguments and laws of development. Therefore they may be brought to the side of the revolution.[75]

In this connection it will be recalled that any individual antagonistic to socialism had had the option of fleeing south. Since little propaganda on this point has been made by opponents of the regime it may be assumed that the southward migration by northern intellectuals was limited. Scalapino and Lee, for example, speak only of "two-way" migration. Most intellectuals, however, apart from a handful of reactionaries, seem to have been touched by the great emotions brought forth by the liberation and reconstruction of the nation. It is true that in the initial phases of the Korean War some northern intellectuals went south to do political work, but most of them returned clandestinely during the period of the so-called "strategic retreat."

In the DPRK today, the role once played by old-line intellectuals has to a great extent been taken over by a new generation coming from previously uneducated sections of the population. This tendency has been most pronounced in the field of education: by early 1966, "the 'new intellectuals' constituted approximately 95 percent of the some 80,000 teachers."[76] In view of the importance the regime attaches to the younger generation it is not surprising that it is the teaching functions in particular which

Socialist Methods of Economic Development 251

have been assumed by people trained under the new system. In a speech to educational workers Kim Il Sung elaborated on this question: "You are Red educators engaged in the education and training of people of a new type in a new society. In doing so, we must follow a new policy and apply a new method, different from those of education in the old society."[77] Yet there is continuity, too. The new intellectuals are brought up under the slogan of "learning from the old intellectuals," whose uniquely valuable experiences and contributions earn them great esteem.

In many respects the new generation of intellectuals is probably the very opposite of what intellectuals were like in traditional Korean society. Their orientation is toward problem-solving; hence, in all fields research is directed at finding answers to practical questions. This new intelligentsia forms a rather homogeneous group which, because of its origins among the common people, constitutes a solid source of support for the regime. These intellectuals' recollections of conditions in the old days provide a very concrete reminder of what the present regime has meant for themselves and their families. Writing on the attitude of intellectuals toward the regime, Scalapino and Lee grudgingly confirm this point:

> Our respondents indicate that one of the most powerful benefits derived from the system lies in the fact that, under Communism, life has a purpose and a meaning. Every individual knows precisely where the society is heading, what is expected of him, and what priorities are to be held. Hence, he is prepared to work hard and sacrifice unstintingly for the regime and for a top leader whom he admires. It is generally estimated that fully 80 to 90 percent of the intellectuals now active in North Korea are loyal to the regime, in striking contrast to the situation in South Korea or any politically open society.[78]

(Anyone who reads newspapers will probably be more than surprised at finding South Korea classified as a "politically open society!")

The Objectives of Socialist Education

The cultural policies carried out on all fronts in Korea seem to be in full accord not only with the laws of economic growth but also with the political project of socialism. Only by increasing the productive forces of a country can sustained development toward a modern industrial society be achieved. One prerequisite for such a goal is the broad dissemination of science and technique—in other words, the desegregation of theory and practice or the demonopolization of theoretical knowledge. As pointed out by Charles Bettelheim, "One of the effects of the separation between the sciences and techniques and the practice of production, contrary to what one might think, is the conservative character of techniques."[79] Simply developing a small but highly modern technological sector, while leaving the majority of people in a state of cultural backwardness, cannot defeat the inheritance of underdevelopment. Consequently, the political system must not only stimulate the people to activity but also arm them with the weapons they need to emerge from their retarded condition. "The labor zeal and creative initiative of the masses can display their real power only when they are combined with science and technique. With the enthusiasm of the masses alone, devoid of advanced science and technique, we cannot go ahead far, nor can we make continuous innovations."[80]

This conversion of enthusiasm into a material force could only be accomplished through intervention on three levels: the ideological, the economic, and the cultural. These three levels, obviously interconnected, would be subject to a changing order of priority and emphasis, depending on the circumstances. While the economic improvement of the people's living standards plays a determining role in their ideological and cultural development, the latter in turn affect the rapidity with which material advances can be made. "In promoting a high degree of labor enthusiasm and creative activeness among the masses for socialist construction, it is very important to incessantly enhance their political and ideological consciousness, adequately combining it with the principle of material incentive."[81] This type of motivation can only be effective, however, in a society where a certain degree of equality of opportunity exists. The promotion of this principle was a major feature of North Korean cultural policies.

In a more general context, the Korean *Juche* system of education seems to fulfill many of the economic and political criteria of a workers' state, since it serves production while also tending to reduce differences between social groups. As explained by officials of the ministry of education, the aim of bourgeois education is lopsidedness, i.e., specialization and the cementing of class differences. As the aim in Korea is completely the opposite, the method too must be radically different. As a result of close coordination between adult education programs and the objectives of the general educational system, by the early 1960s more than half of the university students of the country were from the ranks of the adult working population. On the economic level, this principle of disseminating technical knowledge to as many people as possible, rather than investing in the development of a small, highly educated elite, has already proven its superiority. Politically, it serves the socialist project of diminishing distinctions between peasants, workers, and intellectuals, and helps to prevent future contradictions among the people. Such contradictions are an objective fact during a transitional period, but they are strengthened if knowledge is monopolized by an elite; the spread of culture and practical expertise, on the other hand, may serve to consolidate the system of "people's power."

Looking back over more than fifty years of socialist experimentation, the importance of breaking the traditional bourgeois educational system becomes increasingly clear. At the point of departure in most socialist countries, the revolutionary regime has had to contend with a shortage of technical cadres and a huge burden of illiteracy. To solve these immediate problems, it has been forced to a great extent to rely on people, usually from the upper classes, who had received their education under the old regime. In order to obtain their cooperation, it has often been necessary to give them special privileges. This in itself serves to institutionalize a certain inequality, something quite opposed to the socialist project. Moreover, the children of these people are apt to be better educated too, since because of their background they have greater opportunities for learning and become better students than the children of peasants and workers. This tendency may be further accentuated if the educational system continues to operate according to the old norms, i.e., competition and an emphasis on highly abstract and theoretical knowledge divorced from the realities of practical life. Experience has demonstrated how such tendencies in some socialist countries have led to the creation of power groups consisting of technocrats and bureaucrats who enjoy certain privileges and are alienated from the majority of the people. In this way such an educational system reproduces bourgeois norms even within a society which is said to be in transition toward socialism. In bourgeois society the power of the capitalist class is not derived exclusively from the ownership of means of production; its monopoly on science and technology also serves to consolidate class domination, condemning workers and peasants to a state of mystification and impotence vis-à-vis the decision-making process. Thus, the transformation of the Korean educational structure into a working-class system that serves the people and fulfills immediate social needs, bears a significance which should not be underestimated. In the final analysis it may well be a determining factor both in economic development and in the building of socialism.

In an interview in 1973, conducted by the managing editor of the Japanese paper *Sekai,* Kim Il Sung mentioned some current problems and future perspectives:

In our country today approximately six million members of the rising generation are receiving education at state expense at kindergartens, primary schools, senior middle schools and higher specialized schools. This imposes a considerable burden on the state. The burden is heavy now, but the prospects are bright. It will bear fruit ten years later. In the old society the intelligentsia was regarded as a social stratum. Of course, it is still in capitalist society, but the intelligentsia may disappear in the future. When all people become intellectuals, then there will be no intelligentsia.[82]

Were it not for the North Koreans' past record of achievements, such a prediction might be considered utopian. Yet even in an earlier period two Korean scholars, whose study of North Korean education is cited above, appeared convinced that Korea could obtain rather advanced results in this field under the leadership of Kim Il Sung. Based on our own observations the authors of the present study feel that the following statement by these scholars is probably equally applicable to North Korea's current goals: "He [Kim Il Sung] has daringly initiated an inclusive system of free compulsory education that totally surpasses that of either Russia or Red China. The smallness of his country and the unswerving discipline of his regime, plus his past record of accomplishment in the face of great social and economic odds, make his future objectives reasonable possibilities."[83]

Whether or not the ultimate objective envisioned by Kim Il Sung—the disappearance of the intelligentsia as such—is realized, it will be of the greatest interest to see how this question, which has affected all class society throughout history, is resolved in Korea. Historically, it will be recalled, traditional Korean society was itself organized around a highly elitist system of learning. All officials had to pass a rigorous examination procedure, and since Confucianism had inspired an exaggerated awe for "learned men" among the common people, the result was that in their minds "men of merit" became identified with official authority. In this light the transformations in the educational system in the DPRK and the political thinking governing them necessarily involved a dramatic rupture with previous social practice in this part of the world.

C. SOCIALIST INDUSTRIAL CONSTRUCTION

In the twentieth century no social modernization can take place without industrialization. While the bulk of liberal economic theory stresses consumer-oriented industries in its prescription for most "developing countries," socialist models of development have been known for their emphasis on heavy industry. The latter approach, however, should not mechanically lead to the conclusion that light industry is less important.

Aspects of Light Industry

First of all, in order to improve the standard of living of the people a certain amount of goods and services must be made accessible to them. Without this there could be no policy of material incentives, as practiced during socialist construction, thus robbing the regime of an important stimulus to active popular involvement in the production process. Even if the main stress is on political, non-material incentives, it goes without saying that as the economy develops, so does the demand for consumer goods.

An equally important argument for giving immediate attention to the development of light industry is that it can play a significant role in the accumulation of funds for the building of a heavy industrial base. In other words, on purely economic grounds—even if we disregard the people's needs, which should not be the case under socialism—in order to give priority to heavy industry it is, paradoxically, necessary to promote light industry and agriculture. Both these sectors are sources of capital for the industrial branch and both represent important markets. The dialectical relationship between all economic sectors must be grasped in order to chart an effective strategy of growth which mobilizes all the potential resources of a country.

While there had been some industry in North Korea during the Japanese era, light industry was almost nonexistent since this sector—such as it was—was concentrated in the southern part of the colony. Accordingly, immediately following liberation it became a matter of policy to stimulate small industries and local handicrafts by encouraging the formation of production cooperatives, especially in food processing and other light-industrial activities. But light industry, like the rest of the country's economic structure, was destroyed during the war. The general destitution of the people in the years following the conflict influenced the course charted for light-industrial development; as a matter of fact, these industries engaged in consumer production showed the most rapid advance and seemed to have reached a rather satisfactory level even prior to the introduction of the Five Year Plan.

In order to mobilize the resources of the economy, small and medium-sized local factories were developed along with large-scale central industries. Such smaller en-

Table 10
Indices for Gross Values of Industrial Production
in Terms of Means of Production
and Consumer Goods, 1949-1958
(1949 = 100)

	1949	1951	1953	1956	1957	1958
Means of production	100	33	42	171	250	337
Consumption goods	100	65	99	208	297	414

Source: *Choson chungang nyongam,* 1958, p. 176, quoted in Scalapino and Lee, *Communism in Korea,* p. 1213.

terprises had the advantage of requiring relatively modest initial outlays of funds, materials, and labor power on the part of the state. Besides, the quick turnover characterizing this sector, as compared to agriculture or heavy industry, makes it an important accumulator of capital, permitting further investments both in bigger consumer-goods factories and in heavy industry. In practice this course not only proved highly efficient in stimulating the overall growth of industry but helped to develop the economy in a more independent and many-sided way without imposing too heavy a burden on either the state or the people. Korean economists consider this line a basic method for former colonies to achieve rapid and balanced economic development.

Following the completion of the Three Year Plan, the rehabilitation and stimulation of light-industrial production was further promoted through an important mass movement. At a Central Committee Plenum meeting of the Workers' Party of Korea in June 1958, it was decided to launch a nationwide campaign for the general increase of consumer production by tapping available local resources in all geographical regions. In order to reach this objective every district was to establish at least one local factory in each of its townships or countries.

These were the years of the Chollima Movement, with the result that more than a thousand local factories were built throughout the country within a few months.[84] This was done with complete reliance on locally available materials and marginal labor, so that little government financing was required. Although the means of production thus manufactured were often rudimentary, they nevertheless managed to turn out relatively large quantities of different goods. At later stages these first rather primitive means of production, buildings, etc., were gradually modernized and improved. In 1970 there was another nationwide campaign for the creation of more local industries during which 1,760 new light-industrial enterprises were established in the countryside. Whereas in 1958 local factories had been crude, with low technical standards, often of a semihandicraft nature, and in many cases needed to be rebuilt, this latest generation of local industries were modern enterprises. One reason for this was that in the interim a powerful machine-building industry had been created which was able to furnish modern equipment; another was the general improvement in the technical skill of the labor force.

The emphasis on the development of local light-industrial production had many advantages. In its foreign trade the country's dependence on external supplies was reduced; by 1967, in fact, the DPRK had reached a level of near self-sufficiency with regard to consumer goods. Within the national economy, the small and medium-sized local factories play an important role, delivering about half the total output of consumer goods and thereby contributing greatly to the general development of the country. Table 11 gives a picture of the importance of local industry as early as 1961.

Establishing local industries has meant a more equalized regional development; furthermore, many transportation and distribution costs are eliminated when such goods are produced close to the consumers: during the postwar period of reconstruction, for example, industrial centers were formed "on a basis of maintaining close connection between localities of production and consumption, of accelerating comprehensive development of industries, of effecting rational utilization of local raw materials and of keeping organic relations among industry, agriculture and transport."[85]

This course also gave rise to a certain administrative "decentralization" as the supervision of local enterprises became the responsibility of political organs operating on the town and county levels. The system of local industries has an additional advantage from a military point of view, since if war should break out the destruction of the entire

Table 11
Proportion of Main Consumer Goods Production Represented by Local Industrial Production, 1961

Product	Percent
Textiles	19.4
Underwear	65.6
Socks	58.5
Shoes	34.0
Confections	85.0
Processed alcohol beverages	86.2
Soy sauce	100.0
Bean paste	100.0
Vegetable oil	66.8
Processed vegetables	98.5

Source: Pak Yong-song, "The Formation of a Firm Foundation of Local Industry and Its New Stage of Development," *Kulloja*, no. 15 (September 20, 1962), p. 19, quoted in Scalapino and Lee, *Communism in Korea*, p. 1227.

production apparatus through strategic bombing would be more difficult than if industries were located in a few highly concentrated complexes.

It may be difficult for present-day visitors to local industries to trace the tortuous path the people involved have had to follow. The Koreans are certainly proud of their achievements but find it somewhat hard to understand that foreigners might be more interested in the means employed in reaching the goals than in admiring the results. For instance, in a local knitwear factory the authors saw what seemed to be a modern and complicated machinery complex, looking rather out of place in these otherwise modest surroundings. Upon being told that the machines had been manufactured by the local workers themselves it was difficult not to believe that the interpreter had made a translation error. This gave rise to additional questions. Our curiosity was further aroused when during our tour of the enterprise the manager reluctantly pointed to a barely visible chimney behind a nearby hill, saying that this was the workshop where the machines had been made. In response to our request to see it, the answer was that this would be inconvenient, since the workers of the shop were unfortunately just having their lunch break! Refusing to accept what could be considered a "good excuse," and forgetting all about etiquette, we nevertheless insisted on disturbing them. After a somewhat agitated discussion our request was honored. As this kind of workshop has a special significance which goes beyond purely economic considerations, the sight of it was of course even more interesting than the factory itself. Here one could actually examine the homemade oven where the metal was smelted as well as the casts for the machines we had just seen operating inside. The workers themselves took pleasure and pride in showing visitors the place where machines are manufactured and repairs done. The development of this type of machine-building required not only skill and knowhow, but above all a spirit of self-reliance. In some cases the local skilled workers spent a certain period in another factory in order to learn the functioning of the machinery involved. But in most cases, especially in the beginning, the workers had to rely very much on their own ability to solve construction problems.

Sociological Effects of the Spread of Local Industry

According to conventional criteria such a degree of "do-it-yourself" self-reliance may seem uneconomical as it probably initially involves a certain waste of time and material. However, in the longer run this broad dissemination of industrial experience may have a wide range of positive implications. One byproduct of this entire movement is that many people with no previous contact with industry become familiar with industrial procedures, thus ridding themselves of their traditional attitudes of awe toward modern technology. Such effects cannot be measured statistically, but definitely represent an important educational aspect of modernization.

On the sociopolitical level this strategy had the further advantage of incorporating a greater part of the rural population into the proletariat—what the Koreans call the process of "working-classizing" nonproletarian elements. This was especially the case for the many housewives who took jobs in such enterprises, thereby developing workers' consciousness while at the same time increasing their family income. Further, this policy contributes toward the goal of diminishing differences between town and country: "To build factories extensively in the provinces means bringing industry closer to agriculture. This is of tremendous importance for the strengthening of the ties between industry and agriculture, the acceleration of the construction of a socialist countryside and the elimination of the distinctions between town and country."[86] With the ever-increasing mechanization of farming it can be foreseen that a greater number of people will be released from agricultural occupations. This is where the local-industry movement may prove to be of special significance, since former agricultural laborers will be able to find jobs locally instead of being drawn to the larger cities in search of a livelihood.

> When Koreans talk about liquidating the differences between the working and peasant classes and abolishing the peasantry as a class, they do not mean an exodus from the villages or the disappearance of these bustling communities. Instead it is the intention to give these the same possibilities as the cities, and give the peasants similar working conditions as the workers, while at the same time through urban planning make the cities look more like villages by the creation of huge green recreation areas.[87]

Even though a certain emphasis has been put on the development of small-scale local industries in the rural areas, this does not mean that large-scale, centrally controlled, modern light-industrial enterprises do not exist. In fact, two to three such factories may be found in every province, thus contributing to the development of the region and of industry itself. The most famous example of large-scale light industry is the big modern Vinalon textile factory in the Hamhung area, which produces about 85 million meters of cloth annually. The Koreans are extremely proud of this plant and its history. It is an enormous, almost entirely automated factory employing about 3,000 workers, many of whom are exclusively engaged in construction and maintenance. The main raw material used by the factory is limestone, of which the DPRK possesses rich deposits. The process itself was invented by a South Korean chemist who had studied in Japan, Dr. Le Sung Gi. After having tried in vain to complete his work in Seoul, he went north when the Korean War broke out. Here he was given all the assistance necessary to continue his research—some of it in underground laboratories at the height of the war. After the armistice the experiments were completed and the concrete work could begin. In a little more than a year's time the first plant was built. The production of Vinalon, based on Korean raw materials and developed by Korean specialists, is considered an outstanding example of the *Juche* principle. Today Vinalon factories based on Korean patents are built in Japan and in various socialist countries and a number of foreign technicians study at the Vinalon plant. Such big enterprises, together with the many small and medium-sized textile mills, give the DPRK a large and diversified textile output—a total of 500 million meters in 1970. As a consequence most people today appear to be "equally welldressed."

The establishment of big central light industries side by side with small and medium-sized local light industries contributes to a harmonious relationship between the center and the regions. The large-scale enterprises constitute a guarantee that the policies of the central organs of power will be carried out, thus checking possible tendencies toward regionalism. The existing "decentralization" thus operates within a highly centralized sociopolitical framework which performs planning functions and oversees capital and labor allocation.

At the local level close cooperation between the cooperative farms and industrial plants in a region has been encouraged. Cooperatives find local markets for their produce, supplying vegetables and animal products to those who work in industry. This collaboration may also take the form of mutual labor assistance—as, for instance, when workers help out in the fields during the busy farming season or when farmers during their slack season take a hand in industrial production. The very large enterprises often have their own farms and stockbreeding facilities in order to ensure adequate supplies of fresh vegetables and other food for their workers. In coastal areas a similar type of cooperation may be found between fishermen and workers, with the former delivering fresh fish and the latter helping out during especially busy fishing seasons. A further implementation of this policy is found in the Hamhung Woollen Textile Factory, where the agricultural cooperatives in the vicinity have each household raise one sheep yearly in order to supply the factory with some of the needed raw material.

Heavy Industry—the Backbone of the Economy

As mentioned above, one of the many important socioeconomic functions of light industry and agriculture was the accumulation of capital in order to meet the highest priority—the development of heavy industry. If production figures from the 1950s seem to indicate a different order of priority, it is due to the fact that "many light industries were much easier to rehabilitate than heavy industries, requiring limited capital and technique."[88] Yet the construction of a heavy industrial base, although time and capital-consuming, was never relinquished; it was, in fact, considered the key problem. Only through a large and

Socialist Methods of Economic Development 265

stable output of coal, iron, steel, and machinery could enlarged reproduction be secured and a firm foundation laid for the economy as a whole.

Consequently, when liberal economists portray an emphasis on heavy industry as detrimental to all-around economic growth, they miss a vital point. What would indeed be harmful would be an over-reliance on either of two extremes: underrating the importance of heavy industry and failing to give it priority, or putting too exclusive an emphasis on heavy industry at the expense of other branches. With regard to this problem, the Koreans have understood the relationship of heavy industry to other sectors, considering it "most important . . . to develop heavy industry not for its own sake but in a manner that would serve directly and most effectively the development of light industry and agriculture."[89]

In retrospect it seems clear that without heavy industry light industry would to a large degree have had to rely on foreign sources of machinery and on external markets for its products, given the lack of internal purchasing power. Such a course would have meant dependence and lopsidedness in the national economy and a slower rate of development. By promoting all sectors at the same time, with priority going to heavy industry, overall production and development was stimulated by an ever increasing domestic demand.

Moreover, although assistance from socialist bloc countries may have been substantial at the beginning of the rehabilitation period, a few years later—after the record year of 1954—this foreign aid began to decrease and North Korea gradually had to become self-supporting. Thus by 1957-1958, self-sufficiency had become a prominent theme. "The era of large-scale bloc assistance was coming to a close and would probably have ended in any case. The Soviet Union was facing its own developmental problems. China, moreover, had just launched the Great Leap with its extremely heavy demands upon the domestic economy. Thus, in one sense 'self-sufficiency' was a necessity."[90]

However, to describe the policy of self-reliance as a necessary evil means missing one of the basic elements of all Korean economic policies. As Gordon White has remarked: "It is important to note, moreover, that the initial large amounts of external aid were used to minimize future reliance on aid, i.e., to finance imports of capital goods intended to create the material basis for an autarkic industrial complex . . . ."[91]

Although there had been some heavy-industrial activity in the country during the era of Japanese occupation, industry had been unequally developed, concentrating mainly on the production of raw materials and semifinished goods. For finished goods and machine-building Korea had been completely dependent on supplies from the metropolis. Consequently, the reconstruction of the economy also offered an opportunity to eliminate the lopsidedness which had been the foundation of Japanese imperialist domination.

In the beginning the method was to rebuild the old enterprises destroyed during the war, while at the same time expanding them through the introduction of new techniques. In addition, entirely new industrial facilities were built. This was considered the best way to make use of the existing industrial base and resources. In the field of external commercial relations the emphasis during the same period was put on the import of machinery and equipment. Thus, through the concentration of all resources and energies—mass mobilization for the construction of one plant after another, capital investments, technical skill, and the country's not insubstantial natural resources —it was possible to lay the foundation of a heavy industry in a relatively short period of time. The goal was to make power, equipment, and material available to an expanding light industry and to contribute to the modernization of agriculture; accordingly, the first plants to be put into operation after the war were big steel works, cement factories, power plants, and mines.

It must be pointed out that the DPRK did have favorable

natural conditions for such a process. But the dominant factor was the line put forward by the Party to create a heavy industry which used new techniques, relied on *domestic* resources, and was able to *meet the demands of the national economy*. In other words, it was to be an independent heavy industry founded on the *Juche* principle, not one catering to foreign markets and based on foreign equipment and raw materials.

At the same time, the building of machines was pushed ahead. We have already seen how light industries recovered relatively rapidly compared to the heavy-industrial sector, which was particularly hard hit in 1953. Nevertheless, from this low point the output of means of production had increased 51.7 percent by 1955, while output of consumer goods was up 48.3 percent[92] (illustrating that while priority was given to heavy industry, light industry and agriculture were not neglected). Today, a firm base in the form of a large production of steel and coal has made it possible to develop both machine-building and light industry.

The Importance of Machine-Building

Machine-building is considered the core of heavy industry and as such received special attention in Korea. Such an industry had hardly existed before liberation; moreover, whatever had been achieved in this field prior to 1950 was destroyed in the war. "The machine-building industry, which made great progress during the postwar Three Year Plan period, is new to Korea. Never before were produced mining, electric, farming, and textile machines and tools. However, for the first time in Korea, a machine-building industry has been established."[93] The problems caused by this lack of experience with machine-building were intensified by the opposition to the ambitious Korean postwar plans voiced by socialist industrial countries. They considered it uneconomical for the DPRK to develop a machine-building industry under existing conditions, and had their own ideas about the international division of labor.

An example of how the difficulties encountered in the building of advanced machinery were overcome despite adverse internal and external conditions is the Kim Jung Tae Electrical Locomotive Factory near Pyongyang. Under the Japanese, the plant had been a repair workshop for locomotives and railroad cars. In spite of a serious lack of technicians after liberation—since Korean nationals had had little access to technical training—attempts had been made between 1946 and 1950 to build a locomotive factory. Destruction during the war interrupted the process. As its reconstruction did not receive top priority it was not completed until 1959, when, during a visit by Kim Il Sung to the plant, it was decided that the factory should now concentrate on producing electric locomotives. This was done in the face of considerable discouragement from abroad. As Vice-director Kim Jong explained to a Scandinavian visitor: "The foreign revisionists didn't want us to construct the locomotive factory. They tried to make us buy from their country and clamored that we Koreans would never succeed in building our own electrical locomotives."[94] But in August 1961, the first "Red Flag" electric locomotive was produced and since then production has reached a yearly output of forty-five to fifty 120-ton engines. However, had it not been for the fact that some Korean technicians had studied in socialist countries, this achievement would not have been possible, since most workers had never even seen an electric locomotive.

Another classic example of machine-building on the *Juche* principle is the Kyiang Tractor Factory, originally a small light-industrial enterprise serving the Japanese. After 1945 the plant had been converted into a chemical factory making soap and different types of acids, but it was completely destroyed during the war. Once it was rebuilt, due to the great need for assisting agriculture in the immediate postwar period it began to produce simple farm implements. When the collectivization of agriculture led to a growing demand for means of mechanizing the rural economy, this direction was further accentuated, with the factory now called on to produce trucks and tractors.

At this point the factory was small and lacked equipment, experience, and technicians. As it had been impossible to obtain blueprints from foreign sources, an imported tractor was disassembled in order to draw the plans. The workers actually remade every part one by one, copying the original. Many difficulties had to be overcome. Officials at the plant enjoy telling the story of how, at the ceremony celebrating the assembly of the very first Korean-made tractor, the machine was only able to move backward! Fortunately, this proved to be a minor technical problem, but the embarassment must have been great. By 1960, the factory had a yearly production of 3,000 28-horsepower "Chollima tractors" and 75-horsepower "bumper harvest tractors." Functionaries at the plant explained to us how conditions had been in those early years: "At the time the equipment was short and we had no technicians. Therefore 'other countries' said we wouldn't be able to produce tractors. Since the technical standard of Korea was low and Korea is a small country, they claimed that it would be wiser to import them. But they misunderstood the Korean people. Under the wise leadership of Kim Il Sung and with the power in their own hands the people quickly produced tractors." Only later did this plant begin an exchange program with technicians from other socialist countries.

The fact that Korea embarked upon the establishment of domestic mechanical industries speeded up the mechanization of agriculture. According to a French expert, this "enabled Korea to acquire in three years an equipment which import would have taken at least 10 years to furnish, and moreover, it has enabled Korea to acquire autonomy in this field."[95]

Even though the content of the policy on establishing a modern machine-building industry was revolutionary—as illustrated by the above examples—the process itself followed a kind of evolutionary principle. As this is one of the most important problems in most of the Third World, it may be of interest to mention some of the main aspects of the line pursued. The basic point of departure was the recognition that this industry usually demands high standards of technique and large capital investment. Because of the lack of both, the initial targets were set rather low, with a gradual progression toward higher goals. Often spare parts were produced first, then small and simple machines. After the ability to produce such machines was confirmed in practice, bigger and more complicated machinery was produced. Next came the production of precision machinery, and finally, the manufacture of complete sets of machines. The abovementioned tractor factory, for example, produced farm implements before going on to specialize in tractors. And the huge Rakwan Machine-Building Plant, which began by making average-size cranes, soon went on to produce larger cranes and later, excavators.

In this context, our visit to the Chollima Ryongsong Machine-Building Factory proved highly instructive. Called a "mother-factory," this enterprise is equipped with such machinery as a 3000-ton press, an 8-meter turning lathe, and a 200-mm boring machine. (The other "mother-factory" is the Huichon Machine Tool Plant.) The reason for the special name is that these factories produce and supply complete sets of equipment whenever new metal, chemical, and power plants are built. This kind of plant is truly an "industrializing industry," for it breeds new industrial enterprises through its delivery of whole aggregates of machinery. Before liberation this Ryongsong factory was a small repair shop with only two or three lathes, producing small accessories for the Japanese-controlled Hungnam Fertilizer Plant. After liberation, production followed a sort of evolutionary pattern: first manufacturing small, less complicated machines, then producing larger machinery with more advanced technical requirements, while gradually training new technicians. Like most other industrial installations, the factory was completely destroyed during the war. In the course of the rehabilitation period Kim Il Sung paid a special visit to the place and in speaking to the workers emphasized the idea that from then on, the machine-building industry was to become the vanguard of the economy. Such visits were repeated during the Five Year Plan, and construction of the new plant was carried out under the slogan, "Iron and Machines Are the Kings of Industry." For the celebration of the Fifth Congress of the Workers' Party in 1970, this factory produced a 400-mm boring machine and a 6,000-ton press, thus making it possible to undertake the manufacturing of almost any needed machinery. Today this plant is concentrating on heavy machinery, specialized machine sections, and the mass production of heavy compressors.

At the beginning of this evolutionary process there was some overlapping of production, since there was little specialization: the few factories in existence had to produce many kinds of machines. But with industrial development, a certain division of labor has come into being, with the main factories concentrating on producing finished products and the smaller satellite factories delivering spare parts. For example, tractors and trucks are produced at large plants while several small factories specialize in spare parts and cooperate with the main plant in the manufacture of the final product. It was in this context that in 1959 the above-mentioned campaign to promote machine-building was launched under the motto: "Every machine tool should beget another machine tool." During this campaign 13,000 new machine tools were produced in excess of the plan. At present the country is capable of making 6,000-ton presses, heavy trucks, big tractors, large excavators (3 and 4 m^3), bulldozers, buses, electric and diesel locomotives, ships in the 15,000-ton class (in 1973), precision machines, and equipment for modern factories.

During the period of the Seven Year Plan the machine industry has produced and supplied complete sets of equipment for over 100 modern factories, including power stations, metallurgical factories, and chemical plants. These accomplishments can be assessed in their proper proportions when it is recalled that before liberation this industry for all practical purposes did not even exist. By 1948 it represented 1.6 percent of the national product, while it had reached 31.4 percent in 1967. This is a rather high percentage which compares favorably even with such countries as Great Britain, the Soviet Union, France, the German Democratic Republic, and Czechoslovakia. By 1968 the self-sufficiency rate in machinery was 98.1 percent, which means that nearly all machines needed in the DPRK can be made domestically.

On the basis of his country's experience, the Korean delegate to the Second Asian Seminar pointed out the importance of developing both heavy industry and machine tools:

> To carry out industrialization in the Asian, African and Latin American countries which did not have any independent national economy in the past, it will be indispensable, in the final analysis, for them to build heavy industry with the machine-building industry as its backbone. The construction of heavy industry with the machine-building industry as its core ensures the technical reconstruction of the national economy and the rapid development of the national economy as a whole. One of the important problems in building heavy industry is closely to link it with the development of light industry and agriculture.[96]

In many Third World countries today, however, the weakest link is still the lack of an independent machine-building industry serving the national industrialization process.

Socialist Methods of Economic Development 273

Notes

1. Korean socialists describe the pre-1945 land ownership system as feudal.
2. Kim Byong Sik, *Modern Korea* (New York: International Publishers, 1970), p. 50.
3. Developments in South Korea illustrate the adverse consequences of a different policy:

   First of all, the land reform was carried out in such a mild and smooth atmosphere that there was no detectable tension at all, and this might have made farmers unable to evolve autonomous activities through organizations aimed at the promotion of their self-interests. Second, the reform resulted in the formation of a thick populace of independent farmers. Therefore farmers became more homogeneous in terms of economic standards and self-reliant. Nevertheless, the conditions following the reform being unfavorable for farmers in some sense, the pauperization of farmers has been accelerated ever since. It would be still hard to expect the emergence of progressive farmers willing to dedicate themselves to the cultivation of an enlarged production process and a renovated form of agricultural administration.

   [Quoted from Lee Man-gap, "Rural People and Their Modernization," in C. I. Eugene Kim and Ch'angboh Chee, eds., *Aspects of Social Change in Korea* (Kalamazoo, Mich.: Korea Research and Publications, 1969), p. V-74].
4. *Sobranie Uzakonenii, 1917-1918*, vol. 23, p. 398 [quoted by E. H. Carr, *The Bolshevik Revolution, 1917-1923*, vol. II (London: Penguin, 1953), p. 45].
5. Lynn Turgeon, introductory essay, in Dorothy W. Douglas, *Transitional Economic Systems. The Polish-Czech Example* (New York: Monthly Review Press, 1972), p. xiii.
6. W. Gomulka address on November 29, 1946, reprinted in *Political Affairs,* April 1947 (quoted by Douglas, *Transitional Economic Systems,* p. 49).
7. Cf. Turgeon, Introduction to Douglas, p. xiii.
8. Kim Byong Sik, *Modern Korea,* p. 49.
9. Kim Il Sung, "On Our Party's Policy for the Further Development of Agriculture," November 3, 1954, in *Selected Works,* vol. I (Pyongyang, 1965), p. 219.
10. Mao Tse-tung, "On the Question of Agricultural Co-operation," July 31, 1955, *Selected Readings from the Works of Mao Tse-tung* (Peking: Foreign Languages Press, 1971), pp. 411-412.
11. Le Chau, *Le Viet Nam socialiste: une économie de transition* (Paris: Maspero, 1966), p. 166.

12. According to a high-ranking member of the Vietnamese political leadership, the situation was as follows:

> Rich peasants and even higher middle peasants continued to exploit the poor and lower middle peasants. The latter struck by natural calamities or illness had become indigent and were forced to sell part of their lands and animals thus no longer being able to retain for themselves the fruits of the agrarian reform, whereas a small number was succeeding in enriching themselves by acquiring the means which were for sale and by exploiting wage labor. The condition in the countryside during these later years (1957 and 1958) has proven that if individual exploitation was continued then the paddy fields would progressively be concentrated in the hands of a minority, while classes would once again become differenciated in a pronounced manner. [Truong Chinh, *La coopération agricole au Nord Viet Nam* (Hanoi, 1959), p. 26.]

13. Cornelius Osgood, *The Koreans and Their Culture* (New York: Ronald Press, 1951), pp. 65-66.
14. J. Suret-Canale and J.E. Vidal, *La Corée populaire vers les matins calmes* (Paris: Editions sociales, 1973), pp. 41-42.
15. M.Y. Cho, *Die Entwicklung der Beziehungen Zwischen Peking und Pyongyang 1949-1967,* Analyse und Dokumente. Eine Studie über die Auswirkungen des sowjetisch-chinesischen Konfliktes. Band 20 der Schriften des Instituts für Asienkunde in Hamburg (Wiesbaden, 1967), p. 30.
16. Cf. Suret-Canale and Vidal, *La Corée populaire,* p. 40.
17. Joungwon A. Kim, "North Korea's New Offensive, *Foreign Affairs,* October 1969, p. 175.
18. The discussion indirectly resembled the debate in the 1920s around the question of constructing "socialism in one country"—the Soviet Union—or awaiting the revolution in Europe.
19. Foreign revisionists . . . were critical of our Party's policy on agricultural co-operativization, too. They alleged that agricultural co-operativization was impossible when socialist industrialization had not been realized and modern farm machines were not available, and alleged that the co-operativization of agriculture in our country was proceeding too quickly.

 [Kim Il Sung, "On the Socialist Construction in the DPRK and the Revolution in South Korea," lecture in Indonesia, April 14, 1965, in *Selected Works,* vol. II (Pyongyang, 1965), p. 522.]
20. Karl Marx, *Capital,* vol. I, part 4 (Moscow: Progress Publishers, 1961), p. 328-329. (Translation revised by authors.)
21. V. I. Lenin, "On Cooperation," in *Selected Works in Two Volumes,* vol. II, part 2 (Moscow: Progress Publishers, 1952), pp. 715, 716, 717.

22. Kim Il Sung, *On Some Experiences of the Democratic and Socialist Revolutions in our Country,* October 11, 1969 (Pyongyang, 1973), p. 18.
23. Yoon T. Kuark, "North Korea's Agricultural Development during the Post-War Period," *The China Quarterly* 14 (April-June 1963): 85.
24. Josué de Castro, "A la recherche de l'Amérique," *Esprit,* nos. 7-8 (July-August 1965): 75.
25. This too slow growth of the agrarian surplus has in the course of the Second Indian Five-Year Plan been responsible for rising agricultural prices and, partly, for the deficit in the commercial balance, which characterized the period of rapid industrial expansion. Both elements have been an obstacle to an industrialization policy of greater scope.
    [Bettelheim, *Planification et croissance accélérée* (Paris: Maspero, 1965), p. 93.]
26. Ibid.
27. Kim Il Sung, "On the Socialist Construction," p. 523 (wording slightly different).
28. Eugene Preobrajensky, *Novaia ekonomiikaya,* French translation in *La Nouvelle Economique.* Paris: E.D.I., 1966, p. 140.
29. Cf. Turgeon, Introduction to Douglas, p. xxv.
30. Alfred Zauberman, *Industrial Progress in Poland, Czechoslovakia, and East Germany 1937-1962* (New York: Oxford Univ. Press, 1964), p. 93.
31. Cf. J. Chombart de Lauwe, "La socialization de l'agriculture polonaise est-elle definitivement écartée?" *Le Monde,* July 17, 1973.
32. Kuark, "North Korea's Agricultural Development," p. 83.
33. Ibid.
34. Ibid., p. 84. (The figure usually cited in North Korean statistics for the same period is 12,000 million *won,* i.e., about $5 billion at the official rate of 1 *won* = $0.403.)
35. Kim Il Sung, "Victory of the Socialist Co-Operation of Agriculture," January 5, 1959, in *Selected Works,* vol. I, p. 444.
36. Kim Il Sung, "For the Fulfilment of the First Five-Year Plan," March 6, 1958, in *Selected Works,* vol. I, p. 361.
37. "Socialist Transformation of Production Relations," *The Pyongyang Times,* June 2, 1973.
38. Kim Il Sung, *On Some Experiences,* p. 30.
39. Kim Il Sung, "Everything for the Postwar Rehabilitation and Development of the National Economy," August 5, 1953, in *Selected Works,* vol. 1, p. 199.
40. Kim Il Sung, "Theses on the Socialist Rural Question in Our Country," February 25, 1964, in *Selected Works,* vol. II (Pyongyang, 1965), p. 426.
41. Ibid., p. 436.

42. Ibid., p. 433.
43. Official figures taken from *North Korea's Economic Development Since Liberation* (Pyongyang, 1960), Japanese edit., pp. 25-26 (quoted by Kuark, "North Korea's Agricultural Development," p. 84).
44. Cf. Suret-Canale and Vidal, *La Corée populaire*, p. 49.
45. According to Suret-Canale, problems caused by soil erosion in this area make it unlikely that this reclamation will continue much after the completion of the Six Year Plan (ibid., p. 46).
46. Joseph Sang-hoon Chung, *The North Korean Economy: Structure and Development* (Doct. Diss. Series No. 65-7720, Wayne State University, 1964), p. 248.
47. According to some observers, however, North Korean rice data refer to unhusked rice, which may inflate the figure somewhat compared to FAO figures based on polished rice.
48. Robert A. Scalapino and Chong-Sik Lee, *Communism in Korea* (Berkeley, Cal.: Univ. of California Press, 1972), pp. 1125 and 1158.
49. Kim Il Sung, *On Some Experiences*, pp. 27-28.
50. Scalapino and Lee, *Communism in Korea*, p. 1011.
51. Kim Il Sung, "Theses on the Socialist Rural Question," pp. 423-424.
52. Ibid., p. 441 ff.
53. Ibid., p. 443.
54. Suret-Canale and Vidal, *La Corée populaire*, p. 52.
55. Kim Il Sung, "Victory of the Socialist Co-operation," p. 475.
56. Solomon Adler, *The Chinese Economy* (New York: Monthly Review Press, 1957), p. 59.
57. Kim Il Sung, "Everything for the Postwar Rehabilitation," p. 206.
58. Ibid., p. 207.
59. This has been demonstrated by the methods of Paulo R. N. Freire in *Pedagogy of the Oppressed* (New York: Seabury Press, 1970), and *Cultural Action for Freedom* (Cambridge, Mass.: Harvard Education Review, 1970). In recent years sharp criticism of traditional school systems has been raised by Ivan D. Illich in *Celebration of Awareness—a Call for Institutional Revolution* (New York: Doubleday, 1971) and *Deschooling Society* (New York: Harper & Row, 1972).
60. Paik Hyung-ki, "The Korean Social Structure and its Implications for Education," *Aspects of Social Change in Korea*, p. I-9.
61. Cf. paper from French seminar on *"Coopération et systèmes d'éducation dans le tiers-monde—crises et perspectives,"* May 12-13, 1973 (SID, 49, rue de la Glaciere, 75013 Paris).
62. Nam Choon Hwa, "The Building of an Independent National Economy," speech by the head of the Korean delegation at the Second Asian Economic Seminar in Pyongyang, June 16-23, 1964 [reprinted in *Revolution* 2, no. 1 (September-October 1964): 36].

63. Scalapino and Lee, *Communism in Korea,* p. 913.
64. Cf. Jan Lönn, *Nordkorea* (Stockholm, 1972), pp. 131-132.
65. Kim Il Sung, "Report to the Fourth Party Congress," September 11, 1961, in *Selected Works,* vol. II, pp. 156-157.
66. Scalapino and Lee, *Communism in Korea,* p. 906.
67. *Postwar Rehabilitation and Development of the National Economy of the DPRK* (Pyongyang, 1957), p. 55.
68. Key P. Yang and Chang-Boh Chee, "North Korean Educational System: 1945 to the Present," *The China Quarterly* 14 (April-June 1963): 136. John Kuark arrived at the figure of 176 North Korean students per 10,000 inhabitants for 1961, probably on the basis of a broader definition of students (Cf. *A Comparative Study of Economic Development in North and South Korea During the Post-Korean War Period* (Minneapolis, Minn.: Univ. of Minnesota Press, 1966), pp. 130-131).
69. Since 1971 the ten-year school system has been extended every year by 20 percent, thus gradually including all schools. The changes are effected through a lowering of the school age by one year. Simultaneously, one year of kindergarten has been made compulsory. In reality the system thus comprises eleven years of compulsory free education.
70. Yang and Chee, "North Korean Educational System," p. 129.
71. Kim Il Sung, "For the Successful Fulfilment of the First Five-Year Plan," March 6, 1958, in *Selected Works,* vol. I, p. 361.
72. Kim Il Sung, "Against Passivism and Conservatism in Socialist Construction," September 16, 1958, in *Selected Works,* vol. I, pp. 398-399.
73. Ibid., p. 401.
74. Cf. Scalapino and Lee, *Communism in Korea,* p. 878, who mention a figure of 200 professors, which is probably greatly exaggerated.
75. Cf. lecture given us in Pyongyang by Kim Yong Ju assisted by Sin Joe Hoe, both from the Institute of Economic Science.
76. Scalapino and Lee, *Communism in Korea,* p. 912.
77. Kim Il Sung, "On the Duty of Educational Workers in Rearing the Children and the Youth," *Selected Works,* vol. II, p. 109.
78. Scalapino and Lee, *Communism in Korea,* p. 888.
79. Charles Bettelheim, *Cultural Revolution and Industrial Organization in China* (New York: Monthly Review Press, 1974), p. 81.
80. Kim Il Sung, "Report to the Fourth Party Congress," in *Selected Works,* vol. II, p. 166.
81. Ibid., p. 165.
82. Kim Il Sung, *Talk With the Managing Editor of the Japanese Politic-Theoretical Magazine "Sekai"* (Pyongyang, 1972), pp. 15-16.
83. Yang and Chee, "North Korean Educational System," p. 140.
84. In addition to these 1,000 factories and 5,600 light-industrial facilities were set in operation, together with the further activation of

nearly 32,000 previously inactive facilities. (Cf. Pak Yong-song, "The Formation of a Firm Foundation of Local Industry and Its New Stage of Development," *Kulloja,* no. 15 (September 20, 1962): 17, quoted by Scalapino and Lee, *Communism in Korea,* p. 1226.)
85. *Postwar Rehabilitation and Development,* p. 30.
86. Kim Il Sung, "Theses on the Socialist Rural Question," p. 455.
87. Lönn, *Nordkorea,* p. 114.
88. Scalapino and Lee, *Communism in Korea,* p. 1213.
89. Kim Byong Sik, *Modern Korea,* p. 42. In China a similar understanding was developing: " . . . if you have a strong desire to develop heavy industry, then you will pay attention to the development of light industry and agriculture. This will result in more daily necessities, which in turn will mean more accumulation, and after a few years still more funds will be invested in heavy industry. So this is a question of whether your desire to develop heavy industry is genuine or only a pretence." See "On the Ten Great Relationships" (April 25, 1956), in Stuart Schram, ed., *Mao Tse-tung Unrehearsed* (Harmondsworth: Penguin, 1974), p. 63. (The Chinese never published this text.)
90. Scalapino and Lee, *Communism in Korea,* p. 1219.
91. Gordon White, "North Korea's Chuch'e: The Political Economy of Independence," *Bulletin of Concerned Asian Scholars,* April-June 1975, p. 50
92. Kim Byong Sik, *Modern Korea,* p. 46.
93. *Postwar Rehabilitation and Development,* p. 20.
94. Lönn, *Nordkorea,* pp. 98-99.
95. Suret-Canale and Vidal, *La Corée populaire,* p. 44.
96. Nam Choon Hwa, "The Building of An Independent National Economy," pp. 34-35.

Chapter 7
Economic and Social Achievements

Although the solution of the agricultural question is very significant, since it constitutes one of the most difficult and complex problems in preindustrial countries, it is the overall transformation of relations of dependence into independence which constitutes the essence of North Korea's economic success. Industrial development has been based mainly on Korea's own natural resources and made to serve the internal accumulation process. A good example has been the development of Korea's hydroelectric potential, which had been used only in a limited way under the colonial regime. With a firm base in heavy industry, in the form of a rather large output of steel and coal as well as machines, it has been possible to develop light industry and agriculture. It was precisely this emphasis on heavy industry which made possible the technical revolution in the countryside: irrigation, electricification, chemicalization, and mechanization. This in turn increased agricultural productivity, released labor power for other sectors, and provided not only raw materials for industry, but also the food and daily necessities necessary to increase the people's standard of living. The increased purchasing power of the peasantry stimulated industrial production, which found a ready market in the countryside for both light-industrial goods and agricultural machinery. This integrated process has been a key factor in the dynamics of Korean development.

Present Results and Future Perspectives

The use of statistics as a measure of economic development can often be tricky, but in the case of the DPRK certain indices do reveal the scope of the economic revolution which changed a predominantly agrarian society into a socialist industrial state, as Koreans today consider their country to be. In 1946, the primary sector, agriculture and fishing, accounted for 72 percent of the national product while industry contributed only 28 percent. Today the pattern has been reversed, with industry accounting for about 74 percent of the gross national product. These figures also reveal an increase in labor productivity—for example, while agriculture now employs somewhat less than half the active population, its production has doubled three times since 1946.[1] Most of all, perhaps, such statistics bear witness to the balanced nature of the DPRK's economic development—the result of efficient planning—as well as to the tremendous effort involved in carrying out its technical and cultural revolutions.

A factor affecting the DPRK's economic growth in a negative manner was the worsening of the international situation in the early 1960s. In the midst of its Seven Year Plan, the country was unexpectedly forced to allocate additional resources to national defense. This shift was prompted in part by the military coup in South Korea in 1961 and by the aggressive U.S. policies during the Cuban crisis in 1962. And with the advent of the Sino-Soviet conflict—at a time when the United States was expanding its war in Indochina, while the Soviet Union was carrying out a policy of rapprochement with Washington—an independent defense policy seemed all the more indispensable. This necessarily affected overall economic planning. Defense expenditures were increased from 1 percent of the national budget to 6 percent in 1962, while by 1967 they

Table 12
Change in the Relation Between Industry and Agriculture in Total Production, 1946-1970

	1946	1949	1953	1956	1960	1970
Industry	28	47	42	60	71	74
Agriculture	72	53	58	40	29	27

Percentage of the active population:						
Peasants	74.1				44.4	
Workers and employees	18.7				52	
Individual handicraft	5				0	
Cooperative handicraft	0				3.3	

Source: Robert A. Scalapino and Chong-Sik Lee, *Communism in Korea* (Berkeley, Cal.: Univ. of California Press, 1972), p. 1225. See also J. Suret-Canale and J. E. Vidal, *La Corée populaire vers les matins calmes* (Paris, 1973), p. 60.

had reached over 30 percent, the level at which they have since remained.[2] The vigilance of North Korean defense became apparent with the capture of the American spy ship *Pueblo* in January 1968; since then, there have also been a number of cases in which American intelligence planes were shot down.

But the result of this effort, together with an unknown amount of Soviet pressure, was that the Seven Year Plan had to be extended to ten years, reflecting the new line of economic construction combined with the building up of defense. Another factor influencing planning in this period may have been a tendency to overestimate output (whether deliberately or not) on the basis of the high growth rates achieved in the 1950s. Whereas during the Five Year Plan, industrial development showed an average annual increase of 36.6 percent, the yearly increase in industrial growth in the entire period from 1957 to 1970 has been given as 19.1 percent. This means that the current output of twelve days' production is equivalent to the result of a whole year of productive activity in 1944.[3] If one leaves aside the years of war and reconstruction, the main industrialization process of the DPRK was accomplished in about fourteen years. Moreover, if the country had not been forced to spend one third of its budget on national defense and had been able to concentrate all its resources on economic development, with no outside pressure or interference, its rate of development would have been even greater.

By 1970 the Seven Year Plan was considered completed. Although in some sectors the plan had not quite been fulfilled, in others it had been surpassed. This was probably due to the changes made in the plan after it had already begun. In 1971 a new Six Year Plan was started with a planned annual rate of industrial growth of 14 percent. In this plan, to be completed in 1976, the emphasis is on furthering the technological revolution in both industry and agriculture with a view to narrowing the differences between hard and light labor, between industrial and agricultural labor, as well as lightening the burden of household work. Raising productivity is a constant concern, since labor shortage may eventually become a problem for the country.

In several areas North Korean production had by 1970 reached a level comparable to highly industrialized countries, as Table 13 shows. These figures, of course, should not be directly compared to production figures of capitalist industrial countries, as the *utilization* of the material has to be taken into consideration. The DPRK is no "consumer society": people do not drive about in private automobiles, the cities are not bathed in multicolored neon advertisements, and production is not directed toward a system of

Table 13
Annual Per Capita Output in 1970

Electricity	1,184 kilowatts
Coal	1,975 kilograms
Steel	158 kilograms
Chemical fertilizer	108 kilograms
Cement	287 kilograms

Source: Kim Il Sung, *Report on the Work of the Central Committee to the Fifth Congress of the Workers' Party of Korea* (Pyongyang, 1970), p. 11.

institutionalized waste. In other words, while the North Korean figures reflect a real capacity for dynamic expansion in the coming decade, the same probably cannot be said for most other industrial countries. Furthermore, as far as can be ascertained, present-day progress in production is not being made at the expense of future gains but is part of a plan which takes the country's material resources and long-term needs into consideration.

In its economic development the DPRK has made impressive progress in comparison not only to nonsocialist countries but to other socialist societies as well. According to a French Asian expert, it is a recognized fact "that the North Korean agricultural and industrial expansion is probably the most remarkable one in the entire socialist camp."[4] Many observers believe the country is currently on its way to becoming a rather highly developed industrial state. After the fulfillment of the Six Year Plan (1970-1976), it will certainly be interesting to compare the country's production with that of other nations. Table 14 provides one measure of past progress and future prospects.

Avoiding Unequal Exchange in Foreign Trade

The *Juche* principle by no means implies a closed economic system, although major self-sufficiency is at-

Table 14
Volume of Main Production

	1944	1946	1961 (all Korea)	1964	1970	1976[a]
Electricity (million kw/h)	8.1	3.9	9.7	12.5	16.5	28-30
Coal (million tons)	5.7	1.2	12	14.4	27.5	50-53
Castings (million tons)	0.481	?	1	1.34		
Steel (million tons)	0.1655	0.005	0.79	1.13	2.2	3.8-4
Chemical fertilizer (million tons)	0.5	0.156	0.7	0.75	1.5	2.8-3
Cement (million tons)	0.89	0.103	2.4	2.6	4	7.5-8

Source: Suret-Canale and Vidal, *La Corée populaire*, p. 61.
[a] Six Year Plan targets.

tempted: from the beginning Korean imports were made to serve a growing economic independence. By narrowing the range of imported goods and diversifying the number of exportable industrial goods the DPRK was increasingly able to break the relationship of unequal exhange in foreign trade. Thus, the visitor to Korean factories should not be surprised to find West German, Dutch, or other foreign machinery and equipment which would probably be too uneconomical to produce at home. The principle seems to be that while items needed in large numbers are manufactured domestically, it is preferable to import complicated, special machines for which the demand is smaller, and which are costly and time-consuming to produce. With regard to highly developed technology the

DPRK is still somewhat behind. Other considerations may also intervene and exceptions be made.

From both the economic and political points of view commercial exchanges are regarded as a positive thing. The fact that relations with the West have hitherto been relatively limited has not been primarily the result of a political decision on the part of the government in Pyongyang. Rather, the responsability rests with the different administrations in Washington which, through the United Nations, have imposed extremely extensive embargoes against both Korea and China since the Korean War.[5]

Although economic boycott has been used as a weapon against the entire socialist camp, the measures directed against the Asian socialist countries were much more severe:

> While the embargo actions against Eastern Europe were usually presented as purely strategic actions, directed at the military and adjacent sectors of the economies, it is noteworthy that the embargo against China was openly proclaimed to have more far-reaching aims. It was designed partly to punish an aggressor by inflicting as much damage as possible to its economy and partly to affect the internal policy in China.[6]

What could be said of China was even more the case for the DPRK. Here the embargo started back in 1945, when the excuse of "punishment against an aggressor" could hardly have been applied. In fact, the United States has consistently carried on aggressive policies against the DPRK.

When it is considered that one of the most acute problems in the industrial development of nations with a low starting point is created by the competition of the "advanced" nations, one can grasp the shortsightedness of such an embargo policy. As a matter of fact, in the historical development of industrial capitalism, many countries followed protectionist policies vis-à-vis the industrial production of more advanced countries. This was the case for

France, Germany, and even the United States with respect to English industry in the nineteenth century. Great Britain's own initial industrialization period was also based on protectionism; it was only later that it became the chief advocate of the philosophy of free trade: "British industry succeeded in dominating the world market only by carrying on an extreme protectionist policy."[7] Thus, strange as it may appear, the effects of the Western embargo against the Asian socialist countries may have been far different than those intended.

But at the same time there is an important difference in conceptions of development. Whereas most Western development specialists look upon foreign markets and imports as factors which encourage growth, North Korean strategy stresses production principally for domestic demand. This means that even if international conditions had been different, and the country not subjected to such economic discrimination, the DPRK would still have done its utmost to avoid the "unequal exchange" characteristic of world commerce. "An end has been put to the one-sidedness in industry which in the past produced mainly raw materials and semifinished goods and was almost entirely dependent upon foreign countries for the supply of machinery, equipment and consumer goods."[8]

Thus, as a result both of Western policies and the DPRK's own political choice, most of the nation's foreign trade was conducted with socialist countries. In 1962, statistics show that 50 percent of the country's export–import trade was with the Soviet Union and 30 percent with China. The role of commercial relations with the Soviet Union, already decreasing by the end of the 1960s, will probably be further affected as more nonsocialist countries establish diplomatic and trading relations with the DPRK. Even the trade with the Soviet Union has undergone a fundamental transformation over the past ten years. While Korean imports from the Soviet Union increased from 39.7 to 73.9 million roubles between 1955 and

1964, exports for the same years went up from 36.7 to 79.3 million roubles. Thus, what was initially a deficit has since 1962 been transformed into a surplus.[9] This development is probably a result of Korean industrial expansion, since a growing part of that country's exports—even to socialist industrial countries—consists of finished products, machinery, and equipment. A look at commercial agreements signed with Poland, Rumania, Hungary, and Bulgaria in the autumn of 1971 and with the Soviet Union in 1968 reveals that the DPRK supplies these countries with machine tools, transformers, different kinds of tools, magnesium clinker, talcum powder, porcelain ware, glass products, light-industrial goods, electrical motors, insulators, steel alloy, chemicals, and other goods. Not exactly typical export items for an underdeveloped country. This tendency toward exporting industrial products has been growing ever since.

Korea's only real external dependency is in the field of fuel energy. But with the establishment of long-term contracts with some of the oil-producing countries (Iraq, Iran, Algeria) and the development of oil production and export in China, at least the DPRK will no longer have to rely exclusively on the Soviet Union for this source of energy. Even though North Korea is interested in developing commerce with all countries, foreign trade, which played a far from neglegible role in its reconstruction period, is probably less important for the country today. On the other hand, with the trend toward economic nationalism in many Third World countries, trade between these countries and Korea will certainly increase. Developed capitalist nations, in their search for additional markets, might also provide Korea with new trading partners.

The country's strategy of economic self-reliance has found additional justification in light of the escalation of the Sino-Soviet dispute. Economic dependence on either one of these countries would have had its effect on the DPRK's political line. As it is, internal consumption is completely based on domestically produced finished goods, and it is doubtful that this will change in the immediate future. Although covering the people's needs, consumer goods are still somewhat crude. But from a socioeconomic viewpoint there is an advantage in not opening up a country's market to foreign-made consumer goods, as economist Joan Robinson points out:

> Certainly it is sensible for a developing country to make do with home-produced comsumer goods, for what the eye does not see the heart will not yearn for. But for machinery, the textbook prescription for a small country is to concentrate on a few lines and import the rest. Korea rejected this policy primarily on political grounds—they had no desire to remain a one-sided economy, dependent no matter on whom. But it turns out that their policy of self-reliance has some economic advantages also.[10]

Furthermore, it seems to have been recognized in Korea that the exclusive reliance on imported equipment and knowhow is not conducive to the eradication of traditional attitudes toward technology. A final advantage of self-reliance is that dependence on foreign deliveries may be disruptive to economic planning. The Koreans found that they sometimes had to wait a few years for essential equipment to arrive from some socialist countries—equipment which they could often produce more quickly and cheaply themselves, once initial difficulties had been overcome.

In 1973, the organ of foreign trade of the DPRK announced that the country had trade relations with eighty foreign countries and planned to expand light industrial exports six times by 1976. Because of the technicalities involved in world trade as well as the recession in the West, it was reported in 1975 that the DPRK was facing a short-term foreign currency crisis and had been unable to pay creditors on time. It can be assumed, however, that such problems will be overcome with no difficulties as the DPRK learns more about trade with capitalist countries.

Standard of Living

Considering the degree of destruction caused by the war and the immensity of the task of industrialization, the amount of what economists would call "unproductive investments" undertaken by the DPRK is truly amazing. Since 1953, the entire population has been given new housing, schools, hospitals, cultural centers, etc.—all built from ashes. A system of free medical care, beginning during the war and fully implemented in 1954, has been instituted—something which some of the world's wealthier nations are still "unable" to afford. One result has been a twenty-six-year increase in life expectancy since liberation.[11] The health system, based on preventive medicine, includes two annual checkups for every adult in the DPRK, whether sick or not. The number of doctors per 10,000 inhabitants is given as 17 (in comparison to 12 in Sweden and 25 in the Soviet Union). Through the so-called "section doctor system," the population is divided into sections of 500-700 people and one doctor is in charge of the health care of that section. This responsibility includes daily visits to homes, studying general health conditions, and mobilizing people to improve hygiene and promote other health measures. Thus, each person has his or her own doctor. Children in nurseries and kindergartens are given daily checkups. All schools, workplaces, and cooperatives have their own clinics or hospitals (in 1971, there was a drive for all the cooperative farms to convert their clinics into small hospitals with in-patient facilities). In addition to its humanitarian aspect, preventive medicine serves an economic function. When diseases are discovered early they are easier to cure, and keeping people healthy reduces the loss of workdays. When sick family members can be nursed at small local hospitals, which are equipped to handle less serious ailments, their relatives do not need to stay home to look after them.

The free educational system, starting with nurseries and kindergartens, is another amazing investment for this type of country. In 1971, about 80 percent of all babies and small children were cared for at such institutions. This is a rather high percentage compared to other countries, but quite sound economically since it releases more women for social labor (over 85 percent of all women under the retirement age of 55 work outside their homes). As far as education proper is concerned, it is anticipated that with the present compulsory ten-year technical training system it will be possible for every individual—if necessary through independent study—to reach university level. Not only does everybody learn at least one skill before leaving school, but she or he will also be able to play at least one musical instrument.

The social security system is all-embracing, with special care given to elderly people, workers employed in particularly strenuous jobs, and mothers.

It may be difficult to find concrete statistical criteria for evaluating the standard of living in North Korea. In December 1969 the correspondent for *Le Monde* made a few calculations which may serve as a tentative indication. With their double salary a married couple might earn about 150 *won* (i.e., about $60) monthly. This might not seem like much, but it should be remembered that lodging, heating, electricity, and transportation may amount to only about 3 *won* a month. Medical care and education are free, and sometimes housing as well. At the same time progress is constant. Thus the average size of apartments in cities has increased from 33 to 60 square meters in the period from 1958 to the early 1970s. School uniforms for all children are furnished at extremely low prices (the charge varies depending on the size of the family) just as work clothes are often provided by the factory at no cost to the worker. According to official figures (1969) it should (theoretically) be possible for an individual to live on about 20 *won* a month (about $8).

The biggest item of expenditure in an average budget seem to be high-quality clothes, which are relatively expensive compared to work clothes, everyday clothes, and

Economic and Social Achievements 291

other basic necessities. Another portion goes to cultural activities—the DPRK probably has the biggest per capita distribution of newspapers and magazines of any country in Asia. Many families have savings, and a surprising number own television sets, the production of which is heavily subsidized.

If all the widely used consumer goods and daily necessities are extremely cheap, any kind of luxury is expensive. In the latter category the purchasing power of the population in the North is probably somewhat lower than that of their compatriots in the South. Even though monetary comparisons have very little meaning when dealing with countries of different social systems, Gerhard Breidenstein, after making adjustments for certain exchange rates, inflationary factors in the case of South Korea, and the socialist definition of National Income, reached the conclusion that North Korea's 1970 per capita National Income of $375 corresponds to $110 for South Korea. In other words, Breidenstein writes, "in 1970 South Korean economic output per person was less than one third of North Korea's."[12]

But the concept of average is of little value as a measurement of living standard in a society characterized by great inequalities. Even South Korean social scientists admit that an increase in per capita income—which was calculated to amount to 180 percent between 1961 and 1967—does not mean that conditions for the masses of South Koreans have risen accordingly.

> For the majority there has been no visible improvement in living conditions. This is probably due to the inequitable distribution of wealth. The greater part of the national wealth is in the hands of the very rich few. Only five percent of the whole population can be called the upper class. Of the remaining 95 percents, only 25 percent can be said to maintain a level of living proper to the middle class, while 70 percent lead a miserable low-class life.[13]

In September 1970 wages for North Korean workers,

technicians, and office personnel were increased an average of 31.5 percent, with the lowest paid receiving the largest increases. It should further be kept in mind that the DPRK does not suffer from inflation but, on the contrary, follows a policy of price reductions. At the time of writing the most recent example of this was the February 1974 decision reducing prices on manufactured consumption goods from an average of 30 percent to a maximum of 50 percent on certain items.[14] This was followed on April 1 of the same year by the abolition of taxes. In a country where all means of production are state or cooperative property, the abolition of taxes is of course mainly a technical question, although political problems are also involved. Still, at the bottom of any taxation system lies a certain inequality of opportunity. The future goal in the DPRK is to abolish all income differences. However, since the system of socialist distribution is followed income disparities still exist (according to our own tabulations, on a scale of about 1 to 4). Income is not determined by the position one has, but by the work one is actually doing—thus, not infrequently a factory worker may earn more than the manager of the same factory.

Two Social Systems in One Nation

Compared with the DPRK, where the economic outlook is full of promise, developments in the South have been going in an opposite direction. Socioeconomic imbalances there may eventually reach serious proportions and if they do it will be the result of past policies. The main weakness of the South Korean economic strategy is that it is oriented neither toward reliance on its own forces, nor toward the mobilization of an internally generated surplus for national development.

In economic terms this is one of the main differences between the courses pursued by the two regimes. "Consumption in North and South appears to be about the same, but North Korea has, until recently, saved upward of one third of her GNP, investing most of this in industry, while South Korea has until recently saved and invested almost none of hers, allocating in 1963 only about 14 percent (most of which came from foreign aid) for industry."[15] We find the same difference in policy with regard to foreign trade and foreign assistance. While northern imports have always consisted of industrial machines and industrial raw materials, only 20 percent of imports to the South before 1962 was in the form of nonconsumable capital goods.

After a period of economic expansion beginning in the mid-1960s—based on foreign capital and stimulated, among other things by the escalation of the Vietnam war —South Korea is starting to experience the disadvantages of being closely connected to the world capitalist market, dependent as it is on the fluctuating demand for its export-oriented light-industrial products. In an article in *Le Monde* the French Asian expert quoted above, Alain Bouc, analyzed the prospects of the South Korean economy. The export problem of South Korea, he writes, "is related to the payment of foreign debts. The latter has been calculated for the third Five Year Plan of 1972-1976 to amount to about $1,580 million." In fact, the country's sole development strategy seems to consist of an appeal to foreign capital combined with an increase in exports. This explains why the industrial sector is so exclusively turned toward foreign markets, making a policy of self-reliance impossible. "South Korea owns numerous industries, but one cannot talk about it as industrialized. The relationship between the different branches in the secondary sector is limited. To develop without any basic industry, without trying to build one's own motors, tools and the fundamental industrial equipment is a dubious undertaking of which the world has until now seen few examples." And the French expert points out that "the industrial structure of South Korea reflects the country's foreign relations. The main part of new industries are turned towards export, because the country needs foreign currency to pay for previous loans or to finance the export of profits."[16] Despite a considerable growth in exports, imports have been increasing even more and the country's balance-of-payments deficit was expected to rise from $1.1 billion to $1.8 billion in 1974. For that same year the interest on foreign debts would absorb an estimated $500 million. In order to deal with this situation South Korea would have to appeal for even more foreign credits, which will, in turn, only augment its foreign debt.

Toward the end of 1975 the limitations of this strategy were becoming apparent. Thus the *New York Times* (November 21, 1975) reported that according to official estimates, South Korea's long-term debt will reach $6 billion, an increase of 35 percent from 1974. In the somewhat longer perspective it was expected that the country's outstanding debt would increase by $2 billion a year for the next five years, reaching $16 billion by 1981. Thus it can be foreseen that repayment and financing the debt will become a terrible burden for the economy. Not surprisingly, the article carried the title, "U.S. Banks Grow Cautious on Loans For South Korea as Its Debt Surges."

The appeal to foreign investment, however, implies that the internal social situation must be made and kept attractive to foreign capital. In other words, the wage level must be kept low. The efforts exerted in this direction explain the great interest of Japanese business in establishing enterprises in South Korea, where wages are three times lower than in their own country. The results for the working class are described by a recent visitor:

> Many workers, especially in the small and middle-sized enterprises, are affected by conditions which resemble those in existence in the West during the last century. People are working ten or more hours in deplorable hygienic conditions, without any holidays, withat social benefits. Burdened by poverty, they are without political consciousness, and if they dare make claims they are fired and forced to join the jobless army. Labor unions, when they exist, are instruments of the employers and the political power. Social

security is nearly nonexistent. The medical problem is particularly dramatic: the patient unable to pay in advance is not admitted to the hospital.[17]

No wonder, then, that social unrest is a permanent threat to the country's stability. Furthermore, the prospects of solving the economic problems are not particularly bright, as the two main foreign trade partners on which South Korea depends, namely Japan and the United States, are themselves having serious difficulties and are cutting down on their import quotas from South Korea.

Conditions are no better in agriculture, which still occupies about half the population. Since foreign capital has little interest in a sector where the turnover is slow, the rural economy has been passed over by domestic and foreign investments. Under these circumstances agriculture suffers from a shortage of funds, farm implements, and infrastructure (only 20 percent of the roads in the countryside are usable, while 40 percent of villages are still without electricity). Besides, the average size of farms—less than one hectare—is not very conducive to modernization. South Korean agriculture, once the breadbasket for the entire country as well as for Japan, today is unable even to cover its own national needs. "The public investments have remained three times smaller in agriculture than in industry: one of the weaknesses of the country being that of having launched itself in industry without yet having a subsistence agriculture."[18]

Many of the problems affecting this sector (and the country as a whole) are connected to external influences. On the advice of American economists and institutions, the Pak Chung Hi regime in the 1960s decided to put greater emphasis on commercial agriculture, as a source of foreign exchange, while disregarding the principle of self-sufficiency in food. As a matter of fact great quantities of mushrooms, asparagus, and other vegetables were exported during this decade. But Scalapino and Lee, who point out this aspect of South Korean agriculture, laconically inform their readers that this policy actually has become a great problem: "As the decade of the 1970s opened, however, importation of cereals from abroad began to drain South Korea's foreign currency (in 1970, 244 million dollars were spent for cereals); the political pressures to achieve food self-sufficiency mounted and pledges in that direction were made."[19] This is not surprising, as the demand for mushrooms and asparagus probably decreased with the termination of the U.S. military effort in Indochina.

Korean nationals in Japan, well-qualified to interpret developments in their homeland, have long been aware of material conditions on either side of the 38th Parallel. Although the North comprises only about 30 percent of the population of the peninsula, the Korean minority in Japan has to a large extent escaped the influence of the southern regime and chosen a North Korean passport. "The Chōsen Soren Association (in Korean: "Choung Ryun") which is without any doubt the most effective foreign service of Pyongyang, counts about 233,000 members, whereas Mindan—the pro-southern association—has about 80,000 to 90,000 members (about 260,000 persons remain aloof from the North-South confrontation)."[20] The same tendency was observed by a Harvard specialist, Edward W. Wagner, who noted as early as 1961 that many former native South Koreans living in Japan were emigrating to North Korea:

> It is this appeal of a better material life that has led Koreans in Japan to choose to go to North Korea. To be sure, there are special circumstances surrounding this movement. Koreans have had only a minority position in Japan, and this has meant a marginal existence for most of them; they also have had a position there of social inferiority and have been excluded from the rights of Japanese citizenship. Accordingly, Koreans in Japan have been peculiarly susceptible to manipulation by the Communist activists among them, and the task of these has been simplified by the poor advertisement for itself offered by South Korea. Yet all but a fraction of those accepting repatriation to the North originated in the

South. The choice they have made, therefore, in a very real sense reflects their judgement as to which half of the divided peninsula offers the better hope for the future.[21]

In its propaganda against the regime in the South, and in favor of increased national collaboration, North Korea has repeatedly offered jobs to any unemployed people who would like to move north. It is doubtful, though, that many southern compatriots ever heard about the invitation, as the most complete censorship is imposed on all news from the northern part of Korea.

It is also on account of the economic situation of the DPRK that loyalty to the regime—in contrast to that of the South—is so strong. This is acknowledged even by the fiercest critics of Korean socialism: "The fact that the average North Korean peasant is loyal to Kim Il-song and prepared at this point to follow the Party in whatever it commands, must be accounted a major success for North Korean communism, and places it in a strong position vis-à-vis a divided, loosely organized south." The same writers had to admit that a similar loyalty existed on the part of workers.[22]

Whereas the main thrust in the North was toward promoting an equal development of all economic sectors and eliminating all artificial divisions of the population, the South evolved in the opposite direction. Under Western tutelage South Korea has reached a point where it suffers from all the adverse symptoms of a deeply divided class society. Even though the setting is modern, South Korea displays many of the same lopsided structural deformations that were found under Japanese domination. Thus, signs of progress and modernization are everywhere accompanied by the miserable results of an anarchistic mode of development. No consideration is given to the standard of living of either the population in the countryside or the city dwellers. South Korea's largest daily newspaper, commenting on the rapid expansion of cities, writes that "Urbanization in its true sense does not mean an increase in the urban population alone but a change in the way of life from agricultural to urban. Urbanization in Korea reveals much confusion and many self-contradictions. The rural population points a finger at the cities for one-sided growth, arrogance, and luxury."[23] Not only is there growing inequality between urban and rural communities, but social problems are cropping up in the cities themselves. Such problems—including sanitation (water supply and sewage), traffic, housing, and heating—have been accentuated by the flow of people to towns. And relatively few jobs are available for the newcomers. According to a South Korean source:

> Most of them join the ranks of the unemployed, or the potentially unemployed, and lead a most poverty-stricken life. But there are in cities also the very rich who, though very limited in number, live a highly luxurious life. Thus we see the fatal duality again running in Korean city life. In fact, we can say a three-part partition is dividing Korean society—the whole nation is divided into city and country and the city is divided into upper class and lower class.[24]

Indeed, the chickens may come home to roost sooner than expected. Problems accumulate day by day, increasingly posing a threat to South Korean political authorities. Although a detailed comparative study of the two societies on the Korean Peninsula is beyond the scope of the present study, let it be said in conclusion that the Korean nation since World War II—much to the detriment of the Korean people—offers the most "clinical" example imaginable of two opposite socioeconomic systems.[25] The economic position of South Korea is basically one of dependent capitalism. In this modern setting neocolonial structures persist, preventing any attempt at authentic South Korean development. Only those sectors catering to foreign capital are developed, while such vital areas as the rural economy are neglected, with low productivity the result. The wealth created by the hard-working South Korean people does not benefit the national economy but enriches the foreign

Economic and Social Achievements 299

investors and a small local comprador class who control all the important means of production and other activities. And no amount of foreign aid or loans can in the long run replace the internal process of accumulation. This was recognized by the leadership in the North, and what applies to the DPRK may be doubly relevant for the South: "We must manage our affairs by our own efforts, not relying on the strength of others. We have received a great deal of aid from the peoples of the fraternal countries, but this has only constituted a condition for accelerating our development. What is decisive here is the struggle of our own peoples."[26] Here in a nutshell is the main difference between the two socioeconomic systems, and herein, too, lies their relevance not simply to the Korean Peninsula, but to all Third World countries.

Notes

1. The same tendency toward increased productivity also characterized other branches of the economy: whereas the labor supply had increased five times in the industrial sector between 1953 and 1963, total industrial production had increased fifteen times. [Robert A. Scalapino and Chong-Sik Lee, *Communism in Korea,* vol. II (Berkeley, Cal.: Univ. of California Press, 1972), p. 1265.]
2. Jan Lönn, *Nordkorea* (Stockholm, 1972), p. 94.
3. Kim Il Sung, *Report on the Work of the Central Committee to the Fifth Congress of the Workers' Party of Korea* (Pyongyang, 1970), p. 7. Gerhard Breidenstein regards the following data on annual growth rates for Gross Industrial Output as essentially correct: 49.9 percent for the years 1947-1949 (post-liberation reconstruction), 41.8 percent for 1954-1956 (postwar reconstruction), 36.6 percent for 1957-1960 (shortened Five Year Plan period), and 12.8 percent for 1961-1970 (extended Seven Year Plan period). "While the post-liberation and post-Korean War growth rates are extremely high probably due to exceptionally low and incomplete base figures, the average annual industrial growth for the entire period 1954-1970 was 23.5 percent, still very impressive." ["Economic Comparison of North and South Korea," *Internationales Asienforum* 5, no. 2 (April

1974): 217. His conclusions are based on J. S. Chung, *The North Korean Economy: Structure and Development* (Detroit, Mich.: Wayne State Univ. Diss., 1964), p. 248.]

4. Alain Bouc, "L'économie nord-coréenne compte parmi les plus dynamiques du monde communiste," *Le Monde,* December 9, 1969.
5. "Progress of Embargo Measures Against China and North Korea," *United Nations Bulletin* 11, no. 1 (July 1, 1951): 4-5.
6. Gunnar Adler-Karlsson, *Western Economic Warfare 1947-1967, A Case Study in Foreign Economic Policy* (Stockholm, 1968), p. 204.
7. Ernest Mandel, *Marxist Economic Theory,* vol. II (New York: Monthly Review Press, 1968), p. 446.
8. Kim Il Sung, "Report to the Fourth Party Congress," in *Selected Works,* vol. II (Pyongyang, 1965), p.148.
9. *Korea, North and South* (Moscow, 1965, quoted by Suret-Canale and Vidal, *la Corée populaire,* p. 69).
10. Joan Robinson, "Korean Miracle," *Monthly Review* 16, no. 9 (January 1965): 548.
11. At the present stage of industrialization a potential labor shortage exists and birth control does not seem to be an important issue. However, young people are encouraged to marry rather late: men at 29 and women at 24.
12. Breidenstein, "Economic Comparison," p. 216. (The article contains a section dealing with methodological considerations and discussing various ways of calculating comparable figures.) National Income is of course a different economic aggregation from Per Capita Consumption, but for purposes of comparison the former seems more appropriate.
13. Paik Hyun-ki, "The Korean Social Structure and Its Implications for Education," in C.I. Eugene Kim and Ch'angboh Chee, eds., *Aspects of Social Change in Korea* (Kalamazoo, Mich.: Korea Research and Publications, 1969), p. I-7 (figures taken from Yi Man-gap, "Structural Characteristics of Korean Society," in *Essays on Social Sciences,* p. 86).
14. *The Pyongyang Times,* March 2, 1974.
15. Gregory Henderson, *Korea: The Politics of the Vortex* (Cambridge, Mass.: Harvard Univ. Press, 1968), p. 329.
16. Alain Bouc, "Une expansion industrielle rapide," *Le Monde,* September 6-7, 1970.
17. Robert Guillain, "La Corée du Sud sous l'état d'urgence: La fin du 'boom' économique," *Le Monde,* January 12, 1974.
18. Ibid.
19. Scalapino and Lee, *Communism in Korea,* p. 1182.
20. Alain Bouc, "Tokyo veut renforcer son contrôle sur les émigrés coréens et chinois," *Le Monde,* July 16, 1969.

Economic and Social Achievements 301

21. Edward W. Wagner, "Failure in Korea," *Foreign Affairs* (October 1961): 132-133.
22. Scalapino and Lee, *Communism in Korea*, pp. 1176, 1294.
23. Editorial in South Korea's largest daily newspaper, *Dong-A Ilbo*, October 31, 1967 (quoted by Paik, "The Korean Social Structure," p. I-4).
24. Paik Hyun-ki, "The Korean Social Structure," p. I-4.
25. Breidenstein concludes:

    Notwithstanding possible inaccuracy of particular data from the DPRK or the ROK, the trend of this North–South comparison is evident. In all but one of the industrial output categories the DPRK has the lead over the ROK, even in absolute terms. If expressed in per capita data the North Korean energy production in 1970 was at least 2.8 times higher than the South Korean, steel production 4 times, pig iron more than 100 times, cement 1.5 times, chemical fertilizer 2.5 times, rice production about 1.2 times, and textile fabrics 2.5 times. . . . The comparison of per capita National Income, which in 1970 was 3.4 times higher in the DPRK than in the ROK, is confirmed by the trend of all other data collected.

    ("Economic Comparison," pp. 221-222.) Breidenstein draws attention to the fact that, even allowing for various inaccuracies, the foreign economic assistance given to the South between the end of the Korean War and 1970 was at least seven times higher than the aid received by the DPRK. In fact, since the late 1950s the North has received little if any outside assistance.
26. Kim Il Sung, "On Further Developing the Daean Work System," November 9, 1962, in *Selected Works*, vol. II, p. 389.

Part III
Problems of Socialist Transition

Chapter 8
The Need for a Socialist Political Economy

The scientific socialism of the nineteenth and early twentieth centuries was characterized above all by its critical analysis of *capitalism*. But up until the time of the October Revolution in the Soviet Union and the abortive revolutions in Central Europe, very few attempts had been made to visualize future *socialist* society. As pointed out by Oskar Lange, "The founders of scientific socialism, Marx and Engels, . . . made only a few highly generalized remarks about the socialist economy. As a matter of principle, they refused to enter into the problem in greater detail, out of fear of proving more utopian than scientific."[1]

With the victory of the Soviet Revolution came the material conditions and empirical data necessary for a discussion of the problems connected to the socialist transition—problems which took on an immediate importance. Viewed historically, it is therefore only over the short span of about fifty years that Marxism has tackled this problem. But this did not happen automatically. At the beginning the nature of political economy itself under the new conditions became a subject of controversy.

During the first ten years that followed the October Revolution of 1917, years which covered the periods of War Communism and the NEP, Soviet economists shared the belief that political economy, the traditional Marxist term for the science of economics, was to be applied to the capitalist order only. Indeed, during these years, the overwhelming majority of Soviet economists considered a political economy of socialism to be an obvious and unpardonable contradiction in terms.[2]

The view that political economy is restricted to capitalism and loses its role as a science under socialist construction was not limited to Soviet Marxists. Rosa Luxemburg, the Polish–German revolutionary, was probably the most articulate spokesperson for this school of thought among Western Marxists:

> Since political economy is the science about the specific laws of the capitalist mode of production, its existence and function is obviously tied to the existence of the latter and loses its basis as soon as that mode of production has ceased to exist. In other words: Political economy as a science has had its day as soon as the anarchical economy of capitalism is replaced by an economy that is planned, consciously organized, and directed by the whole of the laboring society. Therefore the victory of the modern working class and the realization of socialism signify the end of political economy as a science.[3]

Possibly it was the influence of such thinking, as well as the impact of the period of War Communism, which led the Soviet economist Nikolai Bukharin to expand on the same theme in his essay on the transition period. According to his line of reasoning, all the problems which exist under the capitalist system simply disappear following the proletarian revolution and its reorganization of the economy. "Indeed, as soon as we deal with an organized national economy, all the basic 'problems' of political economy such as value, price, profit, etc., disappear. In this case 'relations between men' are no longer expressed as 'relations between things;' for here the economy is regulated, not by the blind forces of the market and competition, but by a consciously carried out *plan*."[4] The opinion has been voiced that the means employed during the years of War Communism created the impression among some Bolsheviks that drastic political measures could by themselves actually pave the way to socialism, replacing economic methods.[5] However, at the Tenth Congress of the Soviets, while introducing the New Economic Policy (NEP), Lenin criticized himself and the Party for thinking that without a strategy, a frontal attack could be made on capitalism in backward Russia. "We went farther than was necessary, theoretically and politically. . . . " And in a speech reported by *Izvestia* (October 19, 1921) he stated that "War Communism was a 'mistake' and a 'jump' in complete contradiction to all we had written previously concerning the transition from capitalism to socialism."[6] Nevertheless, traces of the argument that economic laws and political economy are irrelevant under socialism survived among Soviet economists. Not until the 1950s did the first serious attempts at formulating principles of a socialist political economy emerge in the USSR. Shortly before his death, in his last book, *On Economic Problems of Socialism in the USSR,* Stalin rejected this tendency, emphasizing the existence of objective economic laws in socialist societies. But even in recent times remnants of voluntarism deriving from a similar conception of transitional politics could be observed in China during certain phases of the Cultural Revolution, and in Cuba as well.[7]

This insistence on identifying political economy with capitalism not only overrated the political possibilities of abolishing the inherited mechanisms of that system at one fell swoop, but inhibited an understanding of the tasks that must be undertaken after the seizure of power. As Baran and Sweezy emphasized:

> The tasks of Marxian political economy are different under different economic and social orders, in different countries, and in different historical periods. It is an error to believe, as some Marxist writers have, that political economy being the science of capitalism *par exellence,* becomes superfluous under socialism. While under socialism both the object

and objectives of political economy undergo a profound change, its responsibilities actually increase.[8]

The nature of these tasks has gradually been revealed through the practical experiences of more than half a century of socialist construction.

Complexities of Socialist Transition

It should be emphasized that all countries presently identifying themselves as socialist are at best *transitional* societies, with all the implications that involves. Their designation as socialist means only, at this point, an explicit determination to move in such a direction. The criterion for whether a country is proceeding toward socialism or not is consequently not so much a matter of the existence of market relations or other capitalist remnants— because all transitional societies contain elements of both the old and the new. As Oskar Lange saw it, "The essential difference in the operation of economic laws in a socialist society is that they do not operate there in an elemental way. Organized society shapes in a conscious, purposive way the circumstances which determine their operation."[9] In other words, the question is rather one of political power, and how such power is used.

The wielding of political power consciously to transform society in a certain direction presupposes a theory about the economic laws governing such a transformation. Whereas some economic laws are directly related to the capitalist form of production, others are more universal. According to historical materialism the fundamental motive force of social development depends upon the interaction of two basic contradictions: (1) between the development of the productive forces (machinery, technology, etc.) and the restrictive character of the relations of production; and (2) between the economic base (the relations established between producers in the course of their work) and the superstructure (institutions, management, political organization, ideology, customs, etc.). Such contradictions may also arise in a socialist society and be a moving force in its development. But whereas in the social formations based on capitalist domination, the contradictions are antagonistic, in the socialist society they may remain essentially nonantagonistic, since socialism *offers the possibility* of continuous adaptation and change, with the abolition of class differences as the final objective. Such an evolution, however, is not inevitable; it depends in the last instance on the political factor.

In other words, if under capitalism certain economic laws exist which influence the entire system, the same may be said of socialism. According to Marx these laws were fundamentally linked to the prevailing relations of production. Thus, under capitalism the private ownership of the means of production determines that production be motivated by the pursuit of profits. This same relationship also conditions the way human activities interact—i.e., under capitalism they take the form of competition and/or monopoly, and development proceeds in an anarchic manner, with thousands of decisions made more or less independently of each other on the basis of a market economy.

The socialization of most of the means of production tends to ameliorate the contradiction between the relations of production and the productive forces. Basically, the social ownership of the means of production makes it possible to coordinate productive activities according to a common plan directed toward the satisfaction of short-term and long-term human needs. Nevertheless, the sweeping away of former property relations does not in itself create a new social formation. In fact, when the productive forces, freed from outdated structural constraints, begin their rapid expansion, new strains emerge demanding superstructural transformations. New systems of organization, a new set of social values, a different order of priorities, new forms of incentives—all these have to be introduced in order to direct and control the operation of economic laws.

Thus, besides the purely practical economic solutions demanded of socialist countries, they also have to tackle questions of a more theoretical nature for which there are no guidelines in classical socialist texts. Furthermore, the fact that the practice of socialist construction initially took place in less advanced societies created additional difficulties, since this process was originally expected to occur first in industrialized countries. In the preceding chapters we have already seen how questions of economic priorities during socialist construction may have a positive or negative influence on the general direction of society. The urgent demand for rapid development of the productive forces at a time when the laws governing the "political economy of socialism" were still in the process of being discovered, in some cases had a negative impact on the course of development. Charles Bettelheim, who has studied the process in the first socialist state, writes that "in the Soviet Union the technical line followed (which was determined by a set of ideological and political conditions) has led to the realization of an onerous 'primitive socialist accumulation,' whose economic and political consequences have been so considerable that, in the final analysis, it is the socialist character of the accumulation that has been compromised."[10]

This led some Marxists to believe that the introduction of socialism in an underdeveloped country might lead almost automatically to a system incompatible with the socialist project. Writing before the full impact of the socialist experiences in Asia had been realized, even Paul A. Baran was inclined toward such a conclusion. Generalizing from the history of the Soviet experiment, he drew the lesson that "socialism in backward and underdeveloped countries has a powerful tendency to become a backward and underdeveloped socialism."[11] But time has shown that scientific socialism's capacity to adapt to different social situations and ability to learn from past ex-

The Need for a Socialist Political Economy 309

perience are greater than could originally have been anticipated. Besides, backwardness itself may hold certain advantages, as Mao Tse-tung has said:

> Apart from their other characteristics, the outstanding thing about China's 600 million people is that they are "poor and blank." This may seem a bad thing, but in reality it is a good thing. Poverty gives rise to the desire for change, the desire for action and the desire for revolution. On a blank sheet of paper free from any mark, the freshest and most beautiful pictures can be painted.[12]

Indeed, considering the complexities involved, what is striking about the international socialist experience is not that errors have been committed but that progress on all levels has been made. The necessity not only to expand productive capacities but consciously to replace old social relations with new ones make socialist construction an intricate process. Writing on the transformation of production relations, Charles Bettelheim makes the point that during previous historical transitions from one socioeconomic formation to another, interventions on the ideological and political level also took place: "Thus, the transition from the feudal mode of production to the capitalist mode of production brought to light a whole series of interventions ('reform' of religious ideology and corresponding ideological institutions, the emergence of new 'moral rules,' political revolutions) that had to accompany the emergence of capitalist relations of production and ensure their dominance and consolidation."[13] It is precisely by drawing an analogy with the process of transition from feudalism to capitalism that we may get some notion of the full range of difficulties involved in socialist transformation.

However, although feudalism was replaced by capitalism through the bourgeois revolution, the tasks involved in this process were less urgent that the present transition to socialism.

> Bourgeois revolution was confronted by only one task—to sweep away, to cast aside, to destroy all the fetters of the preceeding society. By fulfilling this task, every bourgeois revolution fulfills all that is required of it; it accelerates the growth of capitalism. The socialist revolution is in an altogether different position. The more backward the country which, owing to the zigzags of history, has proved to be the one to start the socialist revolution, the more difficult is it for her to pass from the old capitalist relations to socialist relations. To the tasks of destruction, are added new, incredibly difficult tasks, viz., organizational tasks.[14]

Another element differentiating the two transitional processes is the fact that feudalism was not so highly organized into an international system as is capitalism. Societies on the road to socialism thus must bear the full weight of capitalist antagonism, for the developed capitalist states, because of their economic power, have the means to influence these socialist experiments in a negative manner. Had the transition first taken place in the most advanced countries, the full advantages of the new system could have exerted an even greater influence on a world scale.[15]

How to Avoid Deviations

What this entire discussion really amounts to—and what historical experience seems to imply—is that the accession to power through the replacement of one political force by another, even with the socialist project specifically in mind, is no guarantee for a real revolutionization of the social system. This is the case even when such a political change is accompanied by the transformation of property relations. As pointed out by Oskar Lange, such changes certainly open up new opportunities for economic development and political guidance. "These opportunities, however, are only opportunities. They result from the abolition of obstacles (inherent in the capitalist system) which prevent the rational use of the means of production and a harmonious economic development."[16] Private vested interests no longer hamper the rational use of the means of production in the social interest. Today, surveying the evidence of a half century's worth of experiences, it seems reasonable to raise the question of whether a transitional society, while still professing its commitment to socialism, may not in fact be regressing toward some sort of nonsocialist formation. In discussing the situation following the initial revolutionary seizure of power, Charles Bettelheim justly remarks that "such a period does not lead to socialism; it may lead there, but it may also lead to renewed forms of capitalism, especially state capitalism."[17]

In the process of socialist transformation, therefore, how the regime views the establishment of the dictatorship of the proletariat is a matter of decisive importance: whether it is seen as a short-term measure related primarily to the change of property relations, or whether it is seen as only the initial step in a "long march." This distinction between the short-term measures connected to the introduction of the new system and the long-term struggle it involves has been a subject of controversy within the international socialist movement. In the DPRK, the construction of socialism is seen as a long-term process:

> Considering the issue on the basis of what the founders of Marxism-Leninism said or considering it in the light of the experiences we have gained in our actual struggles, we cannot say that a complete socialist society is already built just because the capitalist class has been overthrown and socialist revolution carried through after the working class seized power. We therefore, have never said that the establishment of the socialist system means the complete victory of socialism.[18]

During this transitional period certain distinctive traits inherited from capitalist society continue to survive. In the words of a Korean socialist, this period is consequently characterized by a real confrontation between elements of the two systems: "It is clear that the transitional period from capitalism to socialism must combine characteristic features of the two socio-economic systems. Hence sharp struggles are inevitable between the newly born socialism and capitalism, which was defeated but not yet completely eliminated."[19] Only this recognition permits the development of a concrete strategy.

While the strength of capitalism at this stage is to be found in the economic categories and institutions inherited from the past, as well as in such remnants of capitalist ideology as egoism and individualism, the strength of socialism lies in the political sphere. Under the direction of the political party the state is able to influence developments through the so-called "law of social regulation of the economy." As such the exercise of political control "constitutes the mode of appearance (specific for the transitional economy) of the action of the political on the economic level, under conditions in which the value-form exists. It is the specific law of the *reproduction* and *transformation* of relations of production of economies in transition between capitalism and socialism."[20]

The primary mechanism through which the regime exerts its dominance is the state plan, which controls the economy and guides it in the desired direction. It is through the inner workings of this planning system—allocating resources according to established priorities, thus avoiding waste—that political authority over capitalist remnants is maintained and the industrialization process carried out. In the beginning, when the ideological consciousness and technical level of the masses is comparatively low and the economy still relatively incomplete, a highly centralized system of administration is necessary for socialist economic construction. Oskar Lange, arguing that the extent to which such a centralization may be justified is to a certain degree determined by historical conditions, makes this interesting point:

The Need for a Socialist Political Economy 313

> Socialist industrialisation—and particularly very rapid industrialisation—which was necessary in the first socialist countries, particularly in the Soviet Union, as a political requirement of national defence and of the solution of all kinds of political and social problems due to backwardness, requires centralised disposal of resources. Thus the very process of transformation of the social system, and in addition, in the underdeveloped countries, the need for rapid industrialisation, impose the necessity of high centralisation of planning and management.[21]

There has been a tendency to ascribe most of the contemporary problems facing socialist countries to the extreme centralization of decision-making through the plan. It seems to be true that with the economic and political development of those societies, a system of overcentralization emerged which had a tendency to become too inflexible, ill prepared to adapt to the new and complex conditions. The transformation of this centralized system from a positive necessity into a negative hindrance, is aptly described by Oskar Lange: "The fate and history of these methods is a classical example of the dialectical character of the development of socialist society. Methods which are necessary and useful in the period of social revolution and of intensive industrialisation become an obstacle to further economic progress when they are perpetuated beyond their historic justification."[22] Thus, with the advent of a complex modern economy the nearly exclusive reliance on overcentralized planning resulted in what has been described as "bureaucratic centralism," while reducing mass participation to the minimum.

The symptoms of such a situation might include increasing apathy and apoliticization of the masses, as well as stagnant productivity and other economic disorders indicative of profound weaknesses in the handling of the economic, ideological, and political elements of the transitional period. Prior to the Soviet invasion of their country in 1969, Czechoslovakian economists had to a certain degree recognized the scope of the problem and based their entire reform program on it:

We have abolished capitalist property and thereby paralysed the former driving force of the economic self-movement. This negation, however, has not by itself created any higher stimuli, and forms of movement of the economic development, it has not brought into being a particular socialist system with a universal spirit of enterprise. The negation has merely transferred the direction of the whole economy to the centre which under these conditions had to succumb to bureaucratisation and subjectivism. Outside the centre this has led to a lack of interest and irresponsibility.[23]

Various Experiences

It is instructive to look at the ways the political leadership of various countries has responded to these difficulties, for such choices yield insight into how the transitional process is perceived. The method most in accord with the aims of socialism would be a return to the socialist ideals of the first, revolutionary period, raising the political consciousness of the masses and giving the producers themselves increased decision-making power and responsibility.

The other path, which increasingly seems to have been chosen in Soviet-bloc countries, was to respond with an economic answer. But to the extent that the transition period is characterized by "sharp struggles" between a newborn socialism and a moribund capitalism, any policies which tend to strengthen elements of one formation cannot fail to weaken the other. The so-called "liberalization" process—associated with Libermanism in the Soviet Union and the proposals of Ota Sik in Czechoslovakia, as well as with the actual methods used in many parts of Eastern Europe today—gives factory managers more independence and financial responsibility, relies on market mechanisms, makes profitability the main criterion of success for the individual enterprise, and tends increasingly to emphasize material incentives.

The English economist Joan Robinson discusses this attempt to surmount the problems of the rigid, overcentralized Soviet-style management and planning system, and points out some of the limitations of this type of reform:

> Breaking out of that system can no doubt produce striking immediate improvements, but "market socialism" seems to run into a fundamental objection, quite apart from the erosion of socialist morality that monetary incentives brings about. The difficulty is connected with the determination of prices. When the enterprise has the right to fix the prices of its own products, much of the waste and irrationality, such as is only too familiar to us in a market economy, is found to follow—monopolistic prices, advertisement, catering to tastes of the higher income families and neglecting the poorer ones. In Yugoslavia, giving the workers of each enterprise a direct interest in its profits worked wonders as far as the internal efficiency of management was concerned but it failed to give them an interest in providing employment for others or in evening up the level of development between regions.[24]

In other words, such a course is problematical not only from a political point of view but also from an economic one.

As a matter of fact difficulties can already be observed in those countries which have gone furthest in this direction. Under the headline "Hungary Acts Against Wealthy," the correspondent of a British daily writes, "The government has taken new measures to clamp down on the wealthy and pacify the working class which is now openly dissatisfied with the widening gulf between living standards. The measures were expected as part of a chain of restrictions against 'the undue accumulation of wealth.'" The article specifies that the new regulations "are aimed at people with large houses or weekend cottages, boat-owners and people buying expensive paintings and antiques."[25]

The important point about these reforms, which in substance cannot be considered anything but compromises with capitalist remnants within the transitional society, is not their introduction as such, but the way they are perceived. In the course of socialist construction it is quite conceivable that a temporary and reversible retreat may be a necessary tactic for progressing toward the desired strategic goal. This was the case with the Soviet Union in the 1920s, when comparable measures—in the form of the New Economic Policy—were introduced to relieve a desperate economic situation. "As Lenin saw it," writes Paul Sweezy, "NEP was precisely a move of this kind (i.e., temporary and reversible). But the increasing reliance on the market in the Soviet Union and Eastern Europe today is something entirely different. It is not regarded as a temporary retreat but rather as a socialist advance which receives ideological approval and legitimation."[26]

The recognition of the inherent weakness of the liberalization movement in the Soviet bloc leads to the question of whether a country in transition toward socialism can avoid the pitfalls of capitalist restoration, thus sparing itself a "revolution in the revolution" such as took place with the Cultural Revolution in China.

In that country, at the height of this revolutionary event there was a tendency to think that all socialist countries would have to go through the same process at a comparable stage in their development. Red Guard extremists went so far as to voice criticism of the DPRK and its leader for alleged revisionism. We now know that some critics themselves, with their ultra-leftist slogans and actions during the Cultural Revolution, were sabotaging and endangering the achievements of socialism in their own country. Besides causing a temporary dislocation of production, the struggle during the Cultural Revolution had certain political side effects, with symptoms of political apathy appearing as a consequence of ultra-left enthusiasm.[27] Following the Cultural Revolution, therefore, a period of stabilization was necessary before the launching of new campaigns for mass political activities.

These observations should not be interpreted to mean that the Cultural Revolution was a mistake or that it failed

The Need for a Socialist Political Economy 317

to reach its goal in terms of the Chinese "long march" to socialism. Had the old methods been allowed to continue unchallenged, socialist construction in China might have been compromised. Methods resembling those employed in the Soviet-bloc countries would eventually have led to similar difficulties—with all their grave implications for the future of socialism.

Pro-Soviet critics of the Chinese Cultural Revolution have often cited the disruption of production as proof of the antisocialist nature of the event. Such criticism, however, fails to make the distinction between tactics and strategy necessary in evaluating socialist policy—a distinction clearly made by Lenin: "For the sake of the success of this revolution, the proletariat has no right to shrink from a *temporary* decline in production, any more than the bourgeois enemies of slavery in North America shrank from a temporary decline in cotton production as a consequence of the Civil War of 1863-1865."[28] Any decrease in production during the Cultural Revolution, however, was absolutely unintentional and not the product of a deliberate policy, as some sympathetic, ecology-conscious Western intellectuals would have it. On the contrary the intention was to remove certain sociopolitical constraints in order to pave the way for long-term economic construction under the slogan, "Make Revolution, Grasp Production!" One of the best publicized results of the Cultural Revolution, in fact, has been precisely such an increase in production.

The Search for a Korean Solution

It might have been these two examples—the Chinese experience on the one hand, and the process of depoliticization which can be observed in most Eastern European countries on the other—that Premier Kim Il Sung had in mind when, in a talk with Japanese journalists in 1972, he discussed the problem of class struggle under socialism and its inherent pitfalls.

A person will commit a "Left" error if he emphasizes and overestimates the class struggle only, forgetting that the alliance of the working class, peasantry and intelligentsia constitutes the basis of social relations under socialism. In that case, one will tend to suspect people, treat guiltless persons like hostile elements and create an atmosphere of unrest in society.

On the other hand, one will commit a Right error if he sees only the political and ideological unity of the masses of the people and absolutizes it, oblivious of the fact that there exist hostile elements and ideological survivals from the past and a class struggle continues under socialism, too. In that case, vigilance against hostile elements could be dulled, the struggle against outdated ideas weakened and the capitalist way of life could become widespread in social life.[29]

Thus, at a time when the various international socialist experiments show signs of both strength and weakness, the DPRK is trying to avoid errors by learning from the failures and excesses of policies in what it considers fraternal countries. In this the country relies mostly on its own development of theory and practice in the country's socialist construction. Here, the idea of *Juche* assumes an added dimension. Students of Chinese affairs are somewhat surprised at the similarities they find between the Chinese and Korean methods. It should be kept in mind, however, that for various reasons many of these methods were often put into practice earlier in Korea than in China.

One explanation for the speed and efficiency characterizing the execution of new policies in Korea, as compared to some of the difficulties encountered in China, may be geographical differences—such as the size of these two socialist countries. All other things being equal, it certainly must be easier to carry out innovations in policy in a small country than in a country of over 700 million inhabitants. A more important difference, however, is a political one, having to do with agreement and dissension within the leadership of the country. In Korea, policies decided upon by the leading organs were not consistently sabotaged at all levels of the Party, including the highest, as appears to have been the case in China. That such uniformity may in certain cases have been attained through purges at the top does not alter the fact that both in theory and practice there seems to have been a great deal of unanimity within the Korean leadership. The geopolitical position of Korea no doubt made it a particularly urgent matter to overcome the factionalism which had plagued the Korean revolutionary movement throughout its history. The result has been a very striking singleness of purpose. How many political leaders can say with equal conviction what Kim Il Sung has said? "Once a policy had been formulated, our party never retreated in any complex and difficult conditions. With unflagging tenacity it carried out its policy and line to the end."[30]

In China, on the contrary, dissension over economic policies surfaced as early as the time of the "Great Leap Forward" and the establishment of the people's communes. Some of these disagreements were sharpened by Soviet pressures and their influence on some elements within the Chinese Communist Party. Such was the case, for example, with the struggle around the introduction of the so-called Anshan Charta in the field of industrial management in the early 1960s.[31] Hence, the Cultural Revolution was among other things a struggle between at least two principal lines within the Party. One line favored socialist advances on the level of both economic base and superstructure, while the other, the so-called "bourgeois political line," opposed transformations that could reduce the influence of elitist elements in the economic and ideological spheres. The crux of the matter was whether Party policies should take the offensive or remain passive and fatalistic. This struggle between the two lines resulted in a new period of activism: "Between 1960 and 1966, the adherents of Liu Shao-chi's line had tried to undermine the economic and social changes initiated in the countryside during the Great Leap Forward. The Cultural Revolution that followed was to provide the impetus for a massive socialist counter-offensive...."[32]

To return to Korea, once the initial difficulties of setting the economy in motion had been overcome, the sociopolitical problem of creating the institutional foundation for a new social system became sharply apparent. Indeed, there seems to be a direct relation between the speed of economic progress and the urgency of the need to tackle this problem. This is because old production relations can only contribute toward the new social order up to a certain point; after that they increasingly become an obstacle to further development. In the words of the Korean leader:

> Following the completion of the socialist transformation of productive relations and the establishment of a socialist system, the successful building of socialism and communism depends largely on how the socialist production relations are adapted to the constantly developing productive forces and how they are perfected; on how the superstructure is perfected to suit the established base; and finally on how the reverse influence of the superstructure on the foundations is to be stimulated.[33]

While such interrelationships take shape more or less spontaneously under capitalism, they require a conscious strategy under socialism. This is where politics have to take command, regulating and transforming society.

> Under the socialist system, these interrelations should be planned and purposeful. The slightest error may cause grave damage to the revolution and to construction. To form such interrelationships correctly, it is necessary scientifically to analyse the changing and developing situation and to apply the *Juche* principle. Several socialist countries suffered confusion and grave losses from failure to solve this question correctly.[34]

The fact that the leadership of the DPRK had such an early awareness of these intricacies in the construction of socialism was due to internal conditions as well as to the

The Need for a Socialist Political Economy 321

possibility of studying the example of other socialist countries.

In this context it is interesting to note that the Korean method represented a radical departure from the reform movement in Eastern Europe. The measures taken by this movement—granting greater independence to enterprises, reducing planning to a system of macroeconomic indices, giving priority to economic criteria, and putting the emphasis on profits and individual material incentives—all tend to permit the market to play a more important role. Even some of these "reformists" themselves recognize the fundamental contradiction between their policies and the basic aim of socialism. Thus the Polish economist Wlodzimierz Brus, although a firm spokesperson for the "reform" movement, reaches such a conclusion when he unequivocally states that "the conviction that the socialist economy is a centrally planified economy is profoundly anchored in the theoretical and ideological attitude of the revolutionary labor movement." He points out that "this is true not only in the general sense of the term, but in all its elements, and in that respect the market mechanisms in the socialist economy constitute a foreign body which will have because of necessity to be tolerated for a certain time, but which will have to be eliminated as rapidly as possible with the greatest efforts."[35] Practice in Eastern Europe, however, has been going against precisely this "theoretical and ideological attitude of the revolutionary movement." Korea, on the other hand, in the spirit of the original socialist conception, sought a way out of these difficulties through a mass movement to renovate its systems of economic management and planning—in other words, putting politics in command without ignoring economic realities.

Finding the right combination of these two elements is of decisive importance at all the different stages of socialist construction. If either one is emphasized at the expense of the other, it can lead to negative results. "In the same way that 'economism' tends to 'fuse' the political and the economic level, 'voluntarism' tends to 'reduce' the economic to the political level, practically ignoring its existence, its laws, and, in the last instance, its determining action."[36]

Notes

1. Oskar Lange, "Political Economy of Socialism," in Oskar Lange, ed., *Problems of Political Economy of Socialism* (New Delhi, 1965), p. 1.
2. Adam Kaufman, "The Origin of 'The Political Economy of Socialism,' An Essay on Soviet Economic Thought," in *Soviet Studies* 4 (July 1952): 243.
3. Rosa Luxemburg, "Einführung in die Nationalökonomie," *Ausgewählte Reden und Schriften* 1 (1955): 491.
4. N. Bucharin, *Oekonomik der Transformationsperiode* (Hamburg, 1922), pp. 1-2.
5. Cf. Kaufman, "Origin of 'The Political Economy of Socialism,' " p. 244.
6. Quoted in ibid.
7. This was the attitude implicit in the Che Guevara's rejection of commodity categories and other mechanisms of capitalist production:

    I am against material incentives because I regard them as incompatible with socialism. . . . The law of value is meaningful in a capitalist society in which the economy is based on profit. It is meaningless in a socialist society. We have no reason . . . to conform to the economic laws of capitalism as if our aim were merely to run the old system more efficiently.

    [Quoted by Ronald Radosh, "Incentives, Moral and Material," *Monthly Review* 25, no. 10 (March 1974): 62.]
8. Paul A. Baran and Paul M. Sweezy, "Economics of Two Worlds," in John O'Neill, ed., *The Longer View* (New York: Monthly Review Press, 1969), p. 84.
9. Lange, "Political Economy of Socialism," p. 5.
10. Charles Bettelheim, *Economic Calculation and Forms of Property* (New York: Monthly Review Press, 1975), p. 81.
11. Paul A. Baran, *The Political Economy of Growth* (New York: Monthly Review Press, 1962), p. viii.
12. Mao Tse-tung, "Introducing a Co-operative," April 15, 1958, in *Se-*

The Need for a Socialist Political Economy 323

lected *Readings From the Works of Mao Tse-tung* (Peking: Foreign Languages Press, 1971), p. 500.
13. Bettelheim, *Economic Calculation,* p. 139.
14. V.I. Lenin, "Report On War and Peace," in *Selected Works in Two Volumes,* vol. II, part 1 (Moscow: Progress Publishers, 1952), p. 419.
15. Although Marx often expressed the opinion that Europe's reactionaries would eventually be confronted with progressive forces in Asia, it is ironic that the founder of scientific socialism on one occasion voiced his fear of the danger capitalism in the vast areas of Asia might pose to European socialism. "The difficult question for us is this: on the Continent the revolution is imminent and will immediately assume a socialist character. Is it not bound to be crushed in this little corner, considering that in a far greater territory the movement of bourgeois society is still in the ascendant?" [Marx to Engels, October 8, 1858, in K. Marx and F. Engels, *On Colonialism* (Moscow: Progress Publishers, n.d; rep.ed., 1975), p. 318.]
16. Lange, "Political Economy of Socialism," p. 11.
17. Charles Bettelheim, *La transition vers l'économie socialiste* (Paris: Maspero, 1968), p. 7.
    Whereas the notion of state capitalism was conceived by German Social Democrats before World War I as a stage in which the centralized state apparatus of monopoly capitalism would play a decisive role—and considered it a tool the proletariat could use for socialist construction—Lenin, in his writings of 1917 and 1918, used the term to describe the situation after nationalizations and establishment of state control. Later he termed as state capitalism the period of state concessions to private capital, the development of cooperatives under state control, the use of "bourgeois specialists" in the state sector, and the utilization of monetary and financial relations between state enterprises—i.e., largely a description of the initial part of the transitional period. (For a discussion of this definition, see Bettelheim, *Economic Calculation,* pp. 87-88.)
18. Kim Il Sung, *On the Questions of the Period of Transition from Capitalism to Socialism and the Dictatorship of the Proletariat,* May 25, 1967, (Pyongyang, 1969), p. 11.
19. Kim Byong Sik, *Modern Korea* (New York: International Publishers, 1970), p. 72.
20. Bettelheim, *Economic Calculation,* p. 142.
21. Oskar Lange, "The Role of Planning in Socialist Economy," in *Problems of Political Economy of Socialism,* p. 17.
22. Ibid., p. 19.
23. R. Richta, "Models of Socialism," *Rude Pravo,* July 11, 1968 [quoted in E.L. Wheelwright and Bruce McFarlane, *The Chinese Road to Socialism* (New York: Monthly Review Press, 1970), p. 149].

24. Joan Robinson, *Economic Management in China 1972* (London: Anglo-Chinese Educational Institute, March 1973), p. 4.
25. Elizabeth Windsor, "Hungary Acts Against Wealthy," *Financial Times,* London (May 14, 1974).
26. Paul M. Sweezy, "Reply," *Monthly Review* 20, no. 10 (March 1969): 13. This is part of a discussion with Charles Bettelheim on transitional problems, which was later published in book form.
27. Cf. Alain Bouc. *Le Monde,* June 23, 1973. "It is in a certain sense natural that the struggle against the excessive enthusiasm of the extreme left results in a certain depolitization of opinion."
28. V.I. Lenin, "Preliminary Draft of Theses on Agrarian Questions," in *Selected Works in Two Volumes,* vol.II, part 2 (Moscow: Progress Publishers, 1952), p. 457. (Emphasis added.)
29. Kim Il Sung, *On Immediate Political and Economic Policies of the Democratic People's Republic of Korea and Some International Problems,* January 10, 1972 (Pyongyang, 1972), p. 21.
30. Kim Il Sung, "Report to the Fourth Party Congress," in *Selected Works,* vol. II (Pyongyang, 1965), p. 163.
31. Among the main aspects of this attempt at reforming relations in industry, as formulated by Mao-Tse-tung in 1960, were the following: politics in command, strengthening of Party leadership, mass movements, worker participation in management and vice versa, reform of outdated rules and regulations, and close cooperation among workers, cadres, and technicians. During the Cultural Revolution it was revealed that an important wing of the leadership under Liu Shao-chi sabotaged its implementation: "They resisted it and energetically pushed the 'Magnitogorsk Constitution' (Soviet model of industrial management). They advocated such counter-revolutionary revisionist fallacies as 'let specialists run factories,' 'production first,' 'put profit in command,' and 'material incentives,' and put down the vigorous mass movements so as to misdirect the Anshan Iron and Steel Company onto the capitalist road." (" 'Constitution of the Anshan Iron and Steel Company' Formulated by Chairman Mao Stimulates Revolution and Production," *New China News Agency* (NCNA-English), Shenyang, March 23, 1970.)
32. Charles Bettelheim, *Cultural Revolution and Industrial Organization in China* (New York: Monthly Review Press, 1974), p. 8.
33. Kim Il Sung, "The Democratic People's Republic of Korea is the Banner of Freedom and Independence for Our People and a Powerful Weapon for Building Socialism and Communism," 20th anniversary of the founding of the DPRK, September 7, 1968, in *Selected Works,* vol. V (Pyongyang, 1972), p. 158. (The wording of this edition varies slightly from the original translation, the one we used.)
34. Kim Byong Sik, *Modern Korea,* p. 112.

35. Wlodzimierz Brus, *Problèmes généraux du fonctionnement de l'économie socialiste* (Paris: Maspero, 1968), pp. 45-46.
36. Bettelheim, *Economic Calculation,* p. 135.

Chapter 9
Administration and Planning in the DPRK

A. ORGANIZING SOCIALIST AGRICULTURE

The problem of the reorganization of economic administration and planning took on immediate importance in Korea upon the completion of the cooperativization of agriculture, handicraft, and small trade in August 1958. This date is considered to mark the first stage in the reorganization of production relations.

In a country such as Korea, it is not surprising that the rural economy was always given special attention. Pragmatically speaking, the reason for this was that after the division, the North, poorly endowed from the point of view of agricultural resources, faced a serious food problem. The war in 1950-1953 only reemphasized the vulnerability of this sector. In a more general sense, the failure to solve the rural question could, according to the Koreans, not only have paralyzed the national economy, but also handicapped the construction of socialism.[1]

Administrative Changes

Soon after the reorganization of production relations in the rural economy through cooperativization, the disparity between the new units of production and the old system of administration became apparent. This was because the administration had originally been organized after the agrarian reform, at a time when the private farm had become the dominant economic unit.[2] The one measure following cooperativization which did most to give Korean agriculture its present physical appearance was the 1958 merger movement. Within two months of the date of its inception in August 1958, this movement reduced the number of cooperative farms to about 3,843, each comprising 275-300 households with a 130-500 hectare average.

Economically, this consolidation was an important prerequisite for the promotion of land adjustment; the introduction of modern farming techniques, permitting a more rational utilization of human and natural resources and the elimination of waste; the planning of rural construction; and the diversification of production. Administratively, it paved the way for a streamlining of the local structure and a simplification of central supervision and control. It also facilitated the standardization of policies emanating from the center to the localities. Finally, the reduction in the number of production units permitted more efficient utilization of technicians at a time when they were in short supply.

To reap the full advantages of this new situation an administrative change was introduced at the most basic level, with the head of what was formerly the *ri* people's committee now assuming the functions of chief manager of the cooperative farm. Thus, rather than remaining a purely administrative body, the *ri* became a production unit with special ties to the higher administrative county level. This reform had the advantage of linking the local administrative organ more closely to the process of production, strengthening its leading role in the economic and cultural life of the countryside.

As we have seen, in the second half of the 1950s the number of local industries in the rural areas was growing, while at the same time, there was increasing mechanization of agriculture. This development of a more modernized agriculture with closer links to industry demanded the introduction of a more scientific, industrial type of management. In and of itself, of course, such a process is hardly unique to socialist agriculture: "In capitalist countries, too, all large farms worked by machines are run by such methods. This shows that although the capitalist and the socialist economy are fundamentally different economic formations, technically advanced large-scale agriculture, of whatever kind, can after all be managed and run only by the industrial method of management."[3]

To cope with these changes, a new administrative unit for agriculture had to be chosen. Previously the private, individual farms had been administrated through the *ri* people's committee. But when the *ri* was transformed into a production unit, a cooperative farm, a change became necessary. The cooperatives were considered too limited in size to serve as directing organs in rural areas, while the province, on the other hand, was too large. As a result, the *county*—with its approximately 10,000 *chongbo* of farmland, access to a considerable number of technical and management cadres, plus control over the necessary local state enterprises such as machine stations, repair shops, irrigation control offices, etc.—was chosen to become the responsible unit for the agricultural production of the collectivized associations, now organized into *ri*. On the average each county people's committee was given jurisdiction over twenty *ri*. But since the committee was also responsible for such activities as industry, trade, education, cultural affairs, and public health in its administrative area, it could not function efficiently as the managing organ for the cooperative farms. In order to resolve this problem, county cooperative farm management committees were established independently of the county people's committees. At the same time, but on a higher level, provincial rural economy committees were created as leading organs for the county cooperative farm management committees. This system has since become the backbone of agricultural administration in the DPRK.

This reform strengthened the functioning of state organs in the management and planning of the entire economy. Formerly, the people's committees had dealt with the private sector of the economy, assuming responsibility for controlling and adjusting its development. But with the establishment of socialist relations of production and the development of local industries, the situation demanded that all aspects of the local economy, both its agricultural and industrial sectors, be directed and coordinated according to a plan. In addition to their planning functions and their duties of municipal administration, the new committees became responsible for the organization of material supplies for the local working people as well as for education, health, and cultural activities.[4]

Similarly, the expansion of industry generally, and of local industries in particular, proved incompatible with the old system of administration. To cope with the new problems a reform movement was started to shift some of the administrative responsibility from the central organs to a level closer to the local production units themselves. "In order to bring the guidance of industry by the state organs closer to the production sites and to guarantee concrete and flexible guidance it was necessary to relieve the ministries and bureaus of their burdens to a considerable extent and definitely strengthen the local organs of industrial management."[5]

Thus the administration of local industry and construction in the rural areas, formerly controlled by the central authorities (ministries and bureaus), was now transferred to provincial management organs. The central organs themselves were reorganized and streamlined, making it possible to send surplus managerial and technical personnel to local areas. Even though this reform resulted in a certain degree of "decentralization" on a national scale, it simultaneously meant a more efficient central administration of the provinces. "The reorganization of the industrial management system has led to the strengthening of centralized, unitary guidance in industrial management and, at the same time, to the heightening of the role of the provinces and the further extension of democracy."[6]

The granting of greater responsibilities to local state organs left the central ministries free to concentrate on the larger-scale, national industries. It also promoted the development of local industries, for the economic effect of the establishment of provincial economic organs and the degree of independence and initiative it conferred on the provinces allowed a more rational utilization of the resources and potentialities of local communities. Politically speaking, this had the advantage of rendering the responsibility for production and distribution more concrete. Whereas overcentralized administration tends to give people a sense of impotence vis-à-vis what seems to be an abstract and distant decision-making body, usually located in the capital, the enhancement of the role of local organs, with direct contact between the administrators and the administered, strengthens the democratic, self-governing aspect of the system.

Relationship Between Cooperatives and State Organs

As far as agriculture proper is concerned, the administrative reforms had a variety of consequences. Even though a collectivized socialist economy is still semiprivately owned, under the present Korean system cooperative farms are organically linked to the state economy, thus eliminating some of their fundamental weaknesses. Under the administration of the county cooperative farm management committees all cooperatives are able to maintain mutual ties and work out production plans correctly, taking all the resources of the region into account. Previously, there had been little coordination between cooperatives; and since they were unable to evaluate the availability of water, machinery, and power, the planning of production was plagued by uncertainty.

The new administrative arrangements also made it possible to improve the management of individual cooperative farms. In the past each had to rely on its own resources in administering the affairs of its dependent households. Difficulties arose in the handling of labor administration, the management of finances and property, the establishment of the ratio of accumulation of consumption, and the drawing up of plans. Through the county cooperative farm management committees a superior method of management has been introduced. Each committee includes a chief engineer who is in charge of planning and other technical aspects of production, and a deputy chairman who sees to it that all communities have sufficient supplies. Not only does the new system assist in the administration of the individual cooperatives, but it works to integrate them more fully into the activities of the area. During our visit to the Chongsan-ri Cooperative, we were told that the previous year (1970) three hundred members had gone to help relieve a critical situation at another farm in the region. During the same year a number of surplus laborers, their jobs made redundant by agricultural mechanization, had been sent to assist local industries. "Before, industry helped agriculture with its products, now agriculture is able to help industry," we were told with a big laugh, probably indicating that this statement is still considered somewhat of an exaggeration.

It is anticipated that with the further mechanization of agriculture and a corresponding reduction of labor intensity in that sphere as well as in industry, resulting in increased material benefits for all, the cooperative economy will undergo a radical shift toward public ownership. For the Koreans, the transition to a socialist formation would be inconceivable without the conversion of all property relations to ownership by the whole people. "Some people hold that the transition to communist society is possible even if the co-operative economy is retained, and go so far as to say that transition to communism is feasible even if the private economy is left intact. That is all wrong."[7]

Even though the transformation of ownership already seems to be a realistic possibility, the policy at present is to move with caution. The next step will probably depend on the fulfillment of the tasks set by the current Six Year Plan, which is said to be going very well. It is expected that as the cost-accounting system is introduced in the countryside and further progress is made in the technical revolutionization of the rural sector, the peasantry will become increasingly receptive to more progressive working-class ideology. With the narrowing of the gap between the productive forces in industry and agriculture, and the peasantry's attainment of a level of material well-being and culture approaching that of the industrial work force, the distinction between city and country will further decrease, permitting the transition to the higher form of state ownership.

This process, however, is not seen as the inevitable outcome of a set of economic determinants. In this connection another important side effect of the county cooperative farm management system is the link it forges between state and cooperative ownership, which works to strengthen the leading role of the state in the cooperative economy. With their unified control over local state-owned enterprises serving agriculture—including technological resources and means of production in such forms as repair shops, farm machinery factories, irrigation control offices, and livestock inoculation centers—these management committees are becoming an indispensable element of the rural economy. In the course of administrative activities each committee introduces modern methods and promotes the development of interdependence between the two existing forms of ownership. Each one "uses industrial management techniques to direct cooperative farms, and, in this way, links state and cooperative ownership in an organic way in production so that the technical and economic assistance of the state to cooperative farms may be increased decisively."[8]

It is interesting to recall that the creation of such a link has ever been a prime concern of socialist experiments in agriculture. In most socialist countries it has been mainly through the machine and tractor stations (MTS) that the connection between the two types of economy has been carried out. The state assisted collectivized agricultural units and promoted the technical revolution in the countryside through these state-owned MTS. But although they gave assistance to the peasantry, the MTS did not guide the productive activities of the farms and remained unintegrated into the socioeconomic development of the rural sector. More recently, however, the MTS in many countries have been reorganized into simple tractor repair shops, passing on to the collectivized farms the burden or the privilege (depending on the way one looks at it) of buying tractors and machinery at their own expense. In the Soviet Union this step signaled a radical departure from former agricultural policies. When in 1958 Nikita Khrushchev dissolved the MTS and transferred the ownership of their means of production to the collective farms, he was doing something which had previously been considered a step backwards toward capitalism.[9] In a debate not long before his death, Stalin had criticized the proponents of conversion of state-owned MTS into collective-farm property, reminding his audience that a trial experiment in the 1930s had demonstrated the inadvisability of such a policy. From a socialist viewpoint, he concluded, it would mean a step in the wrong direction. "The outcome would be first, that the collective farms would become the owners of the basic instruments of production; that is, their status would be an exceptional one, such as is not shared by any other enterprise in our country, for, as we know, even the nationalized enterprises do not own their instruments of production."[10] Such a move would also affect the national economy, in the form of "an extension of the sphere of operation of commodity circulation, because a gigantic quantity of instruments of agricultural production would come within its orbit."[11]

It is interesting to note that while this reform was being introduced in the Soviet Union, Korea was moving in precisely the opposite direction, stepping up collectivization of the agricultural sector[12] and consolidating the state-owned MTS. In Korea it was thought that a transfer of machines and tractors to the cooperatives would weaken "all people ownership" and give the advantage to the more well-to-do cooperative farms at the expense of those with weaker economic foundations.¹³ Such a course would run counter to the entire political project of socialism; in fact, the Korean management system is expressly designed to avoid any such unnecessary differentiations. "In capitalist society where all the means of production are owned privately by the capitalists and the dollar is almighty, the capitalists can buy tractors for their farms and have no alternative but to do so. But we cannot follow the example of the capitalists, for ours is a socialist collective economy."¹⁴ Besides, in a country like Korea, with an increasing but still limited quantity of qualified technical personnel and farming equipment, it would put additional strain on the supply of both if each and every cooperative had to take care of its own needs. This could give rise to an element of competition quite different from the principle of socialist emulation. As it is, the fact that tractors and trucks are not the property of the individual cooperatives permits more efficient utilization of such machines, since outside of the busy agricultural seasons they may be put to work elsewhere, in local construction, transportation, or the like. Such a diversified pattern of utilization might present certain complications if the machine stations were not public property.

In some countries state ownership of the MTS led to practical difficulties, because the state-employed personnel did not always work smoothly with the farmers. As a consequence, a system was introduced whereby a farmer's payment was made in the form of a share in the harvest. Although some friction between MTS and cooperatives was also a problem in the DPRK, such a form of payment was not introduced. Farms pay a certain fee for the use of machines (including wages to operators), but no share of the harvest.

While the relationship between the state and the collectivized agricultural sector is cemented through the agricultural machine stations and the county cooperative farm management committee, the latter organ is but the lowest in a nationwide hierarchy of state bodies. In the administrative reorganization of agriculture the provincial rural economy committee plays a multi-faceted and significant role. With its control over machine factories and certain repair shops, it assists the county cooperative farm management committee and thereby oversees all activities related to agricultural production within the province. It is this provincial organ which draws up the production plans and supervises their implementation. It supplies the counties with items necessary for agricultural production—machinery, spare parts, fertilizer, chemicals, etc.—and is responsible for the scientific selection of crops and seeds. A fertilizer application system has also been established under its supervision. It is further responsible for any adjustment in the labor force. On the administrative scale, the provincial rural economy committee is subordinate to the central agricultural commission and the Administration Council (Cabinet) with respect to the fulfillment of production. The provincial committee has thus taken over the functions formerly accomplished by the ministry of agriculture. This leaves the more important tasks of working out long-term measures for agricultural development to the highest organ of agricultural administration, i.e., the central agricultural commission. Its functions include responsibility for programs related to the general development of agriculture, such as upgrading of rural technology and machinery, better seed selection and experimentation, land improvement, long-term perspectives for land reclamation, soil and fertilizer analysis, improvement of animal stock and stockbreeding as well as measures for the development of other activities in the countryside. This central commission is under the direct authority of the Party Central Committee and the Administration Council and is responsible to these organs for the long-range planning of rural affairs, including the training of engineers and scientists and large-scale land reclamation.

This division of administrative functions between the central agricultural commission, the provincial rural economy committees, and the county cooperative farm management committees raises agriculture to the level of industry. It links the cooperative economy to the national economy and makes it possible to coordinate more immediate tasks with more long-term development.

The Chongsan-ri Spirit and Method

Since the problems of socialist construction are of a political nature the reorganization of administrative organs should not obscure the fact that the Party plays a dominant role on all levels, from the highest to the lowest, as Kim Il Sung has made clear: "Just as the Presidium of the Party Central Committee leads at the center and the Provincial Party Committee leads in the province, so the County Party Committee must exercise overall leadership in the socialist revolution and socialist construction in the county, and all establishments and organizations in the county, without exception, must come under the leadership of the County Party Committee."[15]

In other words, the county people's committee relies on the collective leadership by the county party committee for the formulation and implementation of policies. Below this level there are no central Party organs but only the Party organizations at the *ri* level, which are considered political cells under the direct leadership of the county Party committee. In this way the Party remains in contact with the masses on the various collective farms, thus enabling it to gauge public opinion on issues affecting the policies of the county people's committee as well as to propagandize for its own policy. This conforms with the Korean conception of the mass line:

> Dynamic and creative wisdom, as a rule, is found among the masses. Fragmentary and immature as the opinions of the masses may be at first, it is the duty of Party workers to grasp them in good time, and supplement and systematize them through collective discussions. The Party's leading organs should then disseminate among the masses the opinions

which have thus been summarized and systematized, and lead the masses to put them into practise. This is precisely what constitutes political leadership, living leadership.[16]

Through the Party organizations, policy decisions made at the administrative level are supported and encouraged by all Party members down to the local cells and the work teams. True, there is a pattern of direct dependency in the relationship between masses and Party, but this is because both discipline and a sense of proportion are considered necessary in order to avoid chaos: "That cadres should learn from the masses does not mean that everyone may offer a conclusion in his own way, which will lead to a state of anarchy."[17]

Because of the constant new developments within the agricultural sector, the system of coordinated guidance had scarcely come into being before it needed to be revised. Many Party cadres and administrative officials were at first politically and practically unprepared to cope with the new and complicated problems. Only through a change in the system of work and method of direction could these weaknesses be overcome. In February 1960, during an "on-the-spot guidance" session by President Kim Il Sung at Chongsan-ri in Kangso county, a new method and system of direction for Party and state functionaries was introduced.

The main feature of this "Chongsan-ri spirit and method," as it is called, was the introduction of a system of relations between higher and lower organs, with the emphasis on political work and mass involvement. These new principles of guidance were later extended from agriculture to the industrial sector.

> The essentials of the Chongsan-ri method are that the higher organ helps the lower, the superior assists his inferiors and always goes down to work places to have a good grasp of the actual conditions there and to find correct solutions to problems. [This method] gives priority to political work or work with people in all activities, giving full play to the conscious enthusiasm and creative initiative of the

masses so as to ensure the fulfillment of the revolutionary tasks. This is not only a powerful method of work, enabling us to carry out immediate revolutionary tasks successfully and substantially, but a powerful method of education that enhances the ideological and political levels and the practical ability of the functionaries and revolutionises the masses.[18]

In this manner the center assists the provinces, the province assists the counties, and the county assists the agricultural units. This system also initiated internal Party reforms aimed at getting rid of formalistic administrative and bureaucratic procedures in day-to-day work. Priority was to be given to political work, and here too there was a descending order of guidance, from the highest to the lowest levels. The basic approach was to persuade and to educate rather than simply to give orders through administrative decree. "By giving precedence to politics, which is what we have been calling for, we mean doing the political work first, followed by other work. When political work is done well, administrative work will naturally go well, too."[19] Through collective consultations with Party organs, activists receive guidance in their daily work of organizing and encouraging all workers to meet and overfulfill the production targets.

But the administrative reorganization and the improved system of political guidance for the producers by no means meant that the question of material motivation could be disregarded. As Kim Il Sung put it, "To make light of the principle of material interest, while claiming that we are building socialism is the violation of the elementary principles of Marxism-Leninism. We must resolutely combat such a phenomenon."[20] This is a very important question in the rural sector. To stimulate the efforts of the peasantry, the principle of socialist distribution, i.e., to each according to the quantity and quality of work, was enforced. On the one hand, socialist distribution is considered a major step toward democratization. On the other hand, it is also acknowledged to be a kind of concession to the remnants of a capitalist mentality. But given the present subjective consciousness of the people, any other policy would tend to encourage their desire for an easy, idle life, causing a decrease in productivity.

Apparently, due to administrative deficiencies, this principle was in some cases applied in a negative manner —as when people with special skills were given more work points for their labor than were the laborers in the fields, who worked longer hours.[21] A policy of rewarding skills instead of actual work, if allowed to continue, could produce differences within the cooperative communities and undermine their solidarity. In the struggle against this tendency there is an attempt to involve the whole collectivity, thus ensuring that the problem would be resolved to the satisfaction of the majority. "Work-points should be appraised not by any individual at his own will but by several people collectively, strictly in keeping with the norms. It is necessary, in particular, to listen to the unbiased opinions of the masses. And the assessment of work-points should be made each day on the work site, not in the offices as in the past."[22]

In this policy of stimulating productive activity, overfulfillment of planned targets was rewarded through a bonus to the work team. This favored a kind of collective emulation drive for increased production: "Of course, it is most important of all to enhance the voluntary enthusiasm of the working people by educating them in communist ideology. But this must be coupled with a material stimulus to raise their enthusiasm and increase the output. Apart from this, emulation is unthinkable. The working people will not be very enthusiastic about emulation that brings them little benefit."[23] This question of motivation is equally relevant to industry and will be discussed in a special section below.

The Group Management System

Because agriculture still remains under a semisocialized form of ownership, from the Koreans' point of view the rural question has not yet been fully resolved. This explains the constant movement of reforms and administrative innovations in this sector. In 1966, for example, the *group management system* was introduced, giving new strength and direction to agriculture. Previously the primary production unit had been the cooperative farm work team, consisting of five or six subteams with fifteen to twenty-five laborers each. Both work teams and subteams were frequently shifted from one field or task to another, a method hardly conducive to the farmers' development of an individual sense of responsibility.

The new "small work-group contract system," approved at the Fifteenth Plenum of the Fourth Central Committee in November 1965, organized groups of ten to twenty-five farmers into production units, each of which was then put permanently in charge of a certain area of land, a certain task, or a certain instrument of production. This arrangement has given a greater sense of responsibility to the group and is more gratifying to the team members. Now they can see the concrete results of their collective labor, whereas before they were shunted around to so many fields and assignments in the course of a year that they could never follow through on any one job. The political advantage of the system is described as permitting greater cohesiveness to develop within the group participating in collective labor and thus facilitating political work at the production site itself. It also gives the peasants an opportunity to participate more actively and concretely in the management activities of the farms and the conduct of local affairs. Within a limited group assuming mutual responsibility for the most efficient utilization of labor and the maintenance of various tools and other resources, an individual is more likely to have a voice in decision-making. This serves to enhance his or her sense of responsibility for common property. In other words, through this latest arrangement the individual member of a cooperative farm probably becomes more involved socially, politically, and economically in the affairs of his or her production unit.

Having been furnished with the necessary means of production and labor force, the subteam is responsible for the fulfillment of a work plan covering the entire year as well as for a certain yield per hectare of cultivated land. The plan is drawn up by the county cooperative farm management committee, approved by the work team leader, and discussed by the members of the subteams. In this manner, the state agricultural macroplan is broken down into microplans, enabling each cooperative farm member to understand his or her concrete functions in the light of the overall tasks assigned by the state plan. This is how the centralized and detailed planning system of the country is carried out in the rural sector.

As far as distribution is concerned the group management system should make it possible to define work norms and evaluate work days in a more direct and democratic manner. A per-*chongbo* quota is set for each group in accordance with the plan, and the number of work days is calculated in relation to the average quantity of work done by the members. Once the number of work days has been determined, the matter of payment is assessed on an individual basis, taking into account the efforts he or she has displayed during the production cycle, and is finally decided through discussions. In cases of severe disability or illness, the entire community assumes financial responsibility for the worker's family. The amount of support corresponds to the average previous income formerly earned by the worker and is paid out of a common fund. Minor, temporary illness, however, is usually the responsibility of the individual.

Capitalist Remnants in Socialist Agriculture

Both the system of ownership and the form of income (payment in kind) prevailing in the countryside indicate that from the point of view of socialism the rural sector has not yet completely been purged of presocialist characteristics. As we have already mentioned, during the formation of cooperatives each farmer was given individual proprietorship of a small plot of land—and this, incidentally, is the last remnant of private ownership of means of production in the entire economy. In these small kitchen gardens surrounding peasant houses vegetables are cultivated and a few chickens and pigs may be raised either for sale or for private use. The small size of the plots—thirty to fifty square meters, depending on the quality of the soil—was part of a conscious policy to avoid the creation of material conditions that might retard the ideological education of the farmers.

> If co-operative farmers are given large kitchen gardens, they may be interested only in them instead of taking an active part in the co-operative farm work and their selfishness will grow. Therefore, we intentionally allotted small private kitchen gardens to our farmers so that they might rid themselves of egoism and small proprietor mentality, develop the collectivist spirit and whole-heartedly participate in collective labour on the co-operative farms.[24]

In comparison with other socialist states the DPRK's private plots are of limited size and significance. In the Soviet Union they made up 4 percent of the cultivated land and accounted for more than 20 percent of agricultural production prior to World War II.[25] In China, too, the private plots have been considerably larger and have played a bigger role in household income.[26] It is perhaps no exaggeration, therefore, to say that Korean agriculture is one of the most politically advanced of all the different socialist countries.

But this is not the same as saying that the socialist objective has already been reached in Korea. For example, the farmers are allowed to sell their surplus produce on the "free peasant market" at prices which are, to a certain extent, still determined by supply and demand. Since Korean society is in a transitional phase, the peasant market is seen as a capitalist remnant which, under present conditions, performs a necessary function. Its main justification is that it fills certain consumer demands which are not yet entirely covered by the socialist sector.

Should the peasant market be abolished prematurely it is feared that it would lead to black marketeering and unnecessarily incriminate or throw suspicion upon a fairly substantial segment of the population. Consequently, the solution is not to be found in radical administrative measures. The "leftist" tendency to ignore the concrete conditions must be restrained and a moderate policy adopted, even though the long-term objective is still the elimination of this phenomenon. It is foreseen that two basic factors will contribute to progress toward this goal: (1) the development of industry and technology, resulting in an abundance of all types of consumer goods at state-owned shops; and (2) the shift from cooperative to state ownership. Under such conditions, "sideline" production and the related peasant market will lose their economic justification. The dialectical development of the productive forces and the transformation of the forms of ownership in the rural economy will thus bring the entire system of distribution further into line with the ideals of socialism. "Therefore, when the two sorts of ownership are welded into the single ownership of the entire people, the individual sideline economy will vanish, due to the developed productive forces, and consequently, the peasant market will disappear and the circulation of commodities as a whole will become unnecessary. Then, products will be distributed under a supply system."[27] Furthermore, the abolition of commodity production itself is clearly one of the goals transitional societies must reach on their way to a higher form of society.

The kitchen garden may supply the farmer's household with additional revenues, but his main income, in the form of cash as well as grains and other natural products, is derived from participation in collective labor on the farm. Usually, collective distribution takes place following the harvest; the incomes may vary over the country as a whole, since some cooperative farms are better off than others. From our study of several cooperative farms during a visit in 1969 it could be deduced that in 1968 each household had averaged 3.5 tons of rice and 800 *won*. (The average yearly per-capita consumption of rice is calculated to be about 200 kilograms. After the harvest the working cooperative farmers are allowed to keep 400 kilograms, elderly people and children somewhat less. The surplus, which probably depends on the size and composition of the household, may be sold to the state at the above-mentioned highly subsidized price.) On a return visit in 1971 we asked cooperative farmers the same questions as before, and their answers indicated increased revenues. In Chongsan-ri, which is probably somewhat of a model, in 1970 the average cash revenue had been 1,420 *won* per family, plus 4.3 tons of rice. In 1971 it was calculated to amount to 5 tons of rice and 1,500 *won*. If these figures are correct, they indicate a rapidly increasing income for the rural population. This trend was confirmed with the announcement in 1974 that real income in the countryside had grown about 70 percent, from 1970 to 1973 (for industrial workers the corresponding figure was 60 percent).

In order to get a true picture of the standard of living of the cooperative farmers it must be recalled that besides inexpensive housing, heating, and electricity they have access to a wide range of social and cultural benefits. Everybody has fourteen days of paid vacation, while old people or people with special needs get thirty days, including free stays at sanatoriums. All cooperatives include shops whose selection of consumer goods seems as good as that available to city dwellers. Each cooperative has its own nurseries, kindergartens, and schools; each has several cinemas, a house of culture, laundries, and a small hospital. A high percentage of farmers take correspondance courses, and every adult attends some kind of political study group. Today it is already becoming difficult for the foreigner to distinguish the young farmer from his counterpart in the cities. In outward appearance—clothes, mannerisms, education—they seem very much alike.

The development of the productive forces to solve the question of socialist agriculture and the immense effort to raise the cultural level of the peasantry have been accompanied by an ongoing attempt, using noneconomic means, to influence the rural population in the ideological sphere. Failure to do this may retard development and cause great harm to the process of socialist transition. "If the peasants are not awakened ideologically, feudal-Confucian ideas may revive in the countryside and capitalist ideology may readily infiltrate. In other words, the backwardness of the countryside paves the way for the penetration of all kinds of virulent ideological poison and provides a hotbed for its growth. It is a serious obstacle to the building of socialism."[28] Certainly many remnants of feudal behavior still exist in the Korean countryside; sometimes elderly workers may be seen taking off their caps when a superior cadre approaches; some women still adopt an exaggerated attitude of submissiveness. Some signs of paternalism may also be noticeable to the foreign visitor. Nevertheless, in the Party's policy toward the rural sector it is emphasized that no rash measures ought to be taken, as an infringement on the farmers' interests would bring not only political losses but economic ones as well.

B. TRANSFORMING RELATIONS OF PRODUCTION IN INDUSTRY

It is true of all socialist countries that because of the more advanced form of ownership in industry, production relations in this sector are inherently more socialist than those in agriculture, where cooperative ownership is still dominant. Empirical evidence has shown, however, that nationalization of industry and the development of the productive forces are not by themselves sufficient preconditions for the establishment of a socialist system. As the recognition of this fact is of rather recent origin it may be of interest to discuss the question on a more general level as well as in relation to the practical solutions employed in the DPRK.

The Scope of the Problem

The elaboration of any realistic policy of socialist industrialization presupposes a recognition of the underlying mechanisms of the capitalist mode of production. The dominant feature of industrial capitalism is that the means of production are controlled by capitalists, whose existence and survival as a class is connected to their ability to satisfy an inherent drive for profit. This profit, usually described as the return on invested capital, is in reality the surplus value created by the labor of the producers. The main motivation of management, planning, control, and organization in capitalist enterprises thus consists in the creation and increase of this surplus value. Industrial management under such a system must by definition reflect this concealed and unwritten law of the capitalist mode of production.

Technically speaking, this socioeconomic formation may be characterized as a system in which a socialized work process coexists with individual or private appropriation of the collectively created wealth—i.e., in which no control or voice in the utilization of this wealth is accorded to the majority, to the producers themselves. Since the workers are cut off from any decision-making about the production process (organization of work, quantity or quality of the products, utilization of the surplus, etc.) they have a very limited interest in the unit's overall economic performance. Furthermore, because they are aware of the fact that any improvement of the management system is invariably translated into intensified exploitation of the producers, they tend to develop various forms of defensive reactions.[29] The political antagonism which exists in this type of society may be said to be the direct result of the contradiction between socially created value and its private appropriation. Under capitalism, this usurpation of the product of other people's labor is legitimized by the existing form of property relations, which bestows this privilege on the capitalists by virtue of their ownership of capital and means of production.

However, although this element is basic to it, the capitalist mode of production is much more than a simple question of property relations.

> ... capitalism is not only the ownership of the means of production. This private property reflects a complex process: by it man loses the ownership of his own labor through alienation, the parceling out and the rigidity of the productive cycle, which in turn implies a technical and hierarchical division of tasks, and which in turn presupposes a certain type of priorities in the development of productive forces, development which creates a certain science, a certain culture and a certain type of reproduction of science and culture, of competence and roles.[30]

The recognition that many of these secondary aspects of the capitalist mode of production do not disappear automatically with the transformation of the ownership of the means of production is a vital point in the understanding of the problem of socialist transition.

The main reason for this state of affairs has to do with the historical development of the productive forces themselves. Since industry was historically developed under capitalism, the capitalist mode of production has become so intrinsic to industrialization that without a conscious struggle, capitalist forms will tend to survive and reproduce themselves in both the economic and ideological spheres. The scope of this phenomenon and the tasks incumbent on a socialist strategy are summarized by Charles Bettelheim:

> Thus, capitalist relations of production took shape before machine industry; the latter develops under the domination of capitalist relations of production, to form the specifically

"capitalist" *mode of production*. In the same way socialist relations of production begin by exerting their action on historically given productive forces; it is through a definite transformation of these forces that the specifically socialist mode of production can be constituted.[31]

The problem in a transitional economy is that even though private capitalist ownership of the means of production has ceased to operate, elements of the old system may still survive in the sphere of industrial relations. Unless this situation is remedied, such remnants will tend to reproduce conditions similar to those existing in presocialist society. The results may be politically damaging to the project of socialism as well as detrimental to economic development. Complicated as the problem may appear, the implications are quite clear. As a leading member of the Party factory committee at the Daean Electrical Plant in Korea put it, "Without destruction of the old management system we cannot display the superiority of socialism." For Marxists this will seem strikingly analogous to the theory of the need to destroy the capitalist state machinery in order to construct a socialist society. The remarkable thing about Korea is its surprisingly early recognition of this complex problem, as well as the solutions it prescribed.

During the reconstruction period following the Korean War the old production relations based on individual management had still proved capable of generating effective economic growth. This was due partly to the simpler administration required in an unsophisticated economy, and partly to the massive efforts stimulated by the Chollima Movement, with its political mobilization of all producers. Nevertheless, it is interesting that in a discussion with the authors a Korean industrial cadre described the pre-1961 system as one of "handicraft management."

With the complexities involved in managing an expanding and increasingly diversified economy, basic weaknesses began to appear signaling the urgent need for an adjustment of production relations. Indeed, as one observer points out, in these conditions, "it became all the more evident that a system of control and administration of a factory at the discretion of a manager or a group of several specialists did not fit in with the new circumstances."[32] This was accentuated in those cases where the Party failed in the correct performance of its control functions. Arbitrary methods became a more common feature of management.

As far as the producers were concerned, they tended to react to this situation by losing interest in the production process, considering their work a necessary evil, merely a means of earning a livelihood. If such a frame of mind were allowed to become dominant, the possibilities for stimulating their initiative and enthusiasm would become correspondingly limited. The scope of the problem is vividly described by Kim Il Sung:

> It must be admitted that the old system of factory management, though it was a socialist one, still retained capitalist elements in many respects. Elements of bureaucracy, departmentalism, and individualism were found in a large measure in that system. Superiors used to shout commands at their subordinates in a bureaucratic manner, instead of going down to the lower units to help them; the spirit of cooperation between workshops was lacking; and among some people there was a tendency towards individualism of the "You attend to your business, and I'll do mine!" variety. Therefore, under the old system of work it was not possible to give full play to the activity and creative initiative of the workers, people busied themselves for nothing, and no achievements were made in production.[33]

Besides affecting the rate of economic growth, such differences among the people may lead to antagonistic contradictions with grave political consequences. In a discussion of the events in Poland in December 1970, when riots by workers took place in various cities, the editors of *Monthly Review* recognized the importance of the workers-versus-managers contradiction in an economy where capitalist ownership may have been transformed but industrial relations have remained more or less unchanged.

> *The managers operate according to what are essentially capitalist standards.* Their economic thinking and decision-making are directed to the goals of production, productivity, competitiveness in international markets: these are seen as ends, not as means. And the means to these ends are precisely the workers who are to be manipulated by propaganda, incentive schemes, fear of loss of income, dread of unemployment, etc. This not only *resembles* the economic ideology of capitalism, it *is* the economic ideology of capitalism.[34]

From a middle- or long-range perspective, to remain at such a stage—or even, perhaps, to prolong it by strengthening the role of the managerial elite—can, despite the absence of private ownership of the means of production, mean a survival or revival of capitalist forms contrary to the project of socialism. The existence of such a possibility during the transition period testifies to the complexities of the capitalist mode of production, and thus to the importance of correct analysis of the interaction of social production relations in laying the foundation for a new socioeconomic system.

> As such means, state capitalism and nationalizations—even those put into operation by a workers' state—still do nothing more than displace the effects of the contradictions that result from the "private" character of the possession of the social means of production. If the change in the class character of political domination *opens the way* to the elimination of these contradictions, it is because it *opens the way to the elimination of the enterprise,* initially by "limiting" its autonomy, and then by making possible its "revolutionarization."[35]

In other words, if the capitalist mode of production is to be displaced entirely, the transformation of property relations in the industrial sector must be followed by a "revolutionization" of the nature of the "enterprise" as it took form under capitalism, a radical change in the direction of the establishment of socialist relations.

The Daean Work System

The framework for such a transformation, implying a limitation of the autonomy of enterprises, is first of all *appropriate planning,* combined with what is known as the *mass line*—that is, a line which is both the cause and effect of the politicization and involvement of the masses in the process of economic development and socialist construction. Far from obstructing production, such a line favors greater output. This understanding seems to have been a basic component of the Korean socioeconomic experiment: "We can say that whether or not we can build socialism and communism faster and better depends after all on how we bring the creative ability and talents of the working people into play, how we organize and use social labour and how speedily we raise labour productivity."[36] The new system of industrial administration was inaugurated in December 1961, during a visit by Premier Kim Il Sung to the Daean Electrical Machine Factory, and was given the name of the Daean work system.

It is the special Korean political style for most new policies to be introduced through "on-the-spot guidance" sessions during visits by the Korean leader to agricultural cooperatives, industrial enterprises, or other institutions. After a series of meetings, virtual "teach-ins" often lasting several days and sometimes going on for weeks, there is a generalized application of the policy in corresponding units throughout the country. Such a procedure not only facilitates the presentation of new policies to the country but also reinforces the Chongsan-ri spirit in administration, with superiors helping inferiors in a nonbureaucratic way. "In giving on-the-spot-guidance, the Party has always solved the main issue and created a model in one place and systematically popularized the practical experience gained there. Thus, it has combined general and specific guidance and has successfully overcome subjectivism and formalism in guidance."[37] By creating a model which is widely publicized, a living example is provided for general emulation.

As far as the Daean work system is concerned, its main characteristic is the application of the Chongsan-ri spirit and method to the field of industrial management. Its essence is that industrial relations should relate more directly to the nature of socialism and overcome the nonsocialist deficiencies previously present in the system. In the words of a Korean observer, the Daean work system means "to embody the mass line in economic control; to get rid of survivals of capitalism in economic management such as bureaucracy, over-centralization and individualism, and to implement the Chongsan-ri spirit and method, enabling workers to contribute to the maximum in accelerating socialist construction."[38] ("Overcentralization" here refers to the concentration of responsibility and decisions in the individual management system.)

The concrete measures involved in overcoming the shortcomings included: (1) abolition of individual management and its replacement by collective management in the form of the Party factory committee; (2) an improved system for supplying materials to the production site and providing for the welfare of the producers; (3) the creation of a method of unified and detailed planning accompanied by a nationwide guidance system involving the active participation of workers at the production level.

Formerly, the ministry of industry appointed the manager of each enterprise, usually a Party member. The manager made all decisions and was solely responsible for planning and production at the factory. With the increasing complexities of a modern economy, however, this form of management was leading to excessive subjectivism, causing harm to production and endangering the socialist project.

The new system is described as an attempt to remedy this situation. The Party factory committee assumes the highest authority at the level of the enterprise. Ways of solving questions affecting production and workers' activities, as well as methods of carrying out decisions, are arrived at through collective discussions within the committee, whose members are elected by the factory's Party members. To be effective this committee has to be relatively small, its precise numbers depending on the size of the enterprise. At the Daean Electrical Plant, with a labor force of 5,000, the Party factory committee is made up of 35 members who meet once or twice a month, while the 9 members of the executive board keep in continuous contact. Sixty percent of its members are production workers, with the remainder representing a cross-section of all factory activities, including functionaries, manager, deputy managers, engineers, technicians, women's league representatives, youth league members, trade union members, and office employees. Its composition thus gives it access to all socioeconomic aspects of the enterprise and the lives of its workers.

This committee has become what is called the "steering wheel" of the industrial unit, conducting ideological education and mobilizing the workers to implement the collective decisions and to fulfill the production target. Through its connection to the Party it has a clear picture of overall policies and aims as well as the exact function of the individual enterprise in the national context. In other words, this setup ensures that politics are given priority. According to Kim Byong Sik, "The basic content of the Daean work system is to strengthen the leading role of the Party in the economy, to draw broad working masses into active management and control of factories, and to encourage them to display their creative capacity and talent to the fullest extent."[39] The Party factory committee acutally represents only the highest level of a whole structure within each enterprise which eventually—through the work-team leaders and the Party cells—reaches every single worker. As it was explained to us, all Party members are concerned with the work of the committee, the manner in which it carries out the political lines and conducts its activities.

Wherever one goes, it seems people have a clear understanding of problems and the significance of their efforts in the light of the entire socioeconomic context. This provides for a strong sense of motivation. Thus, at iron plants the visitor will be told about the importance of iron in the building of industry. At the cooperatives the slogan of "rice is socialism" will be quoted. The food-processing factory will explain the efforts to "alleviate the burden of women" and talk at the textile factory will be about the necessity of making the entire people "equally well dressed." And so forth.

The fact that the managers and engineers, responsible for the implementation of the collective decisions of the factory committee, likewise belong to it, allows for close coordination at the highest level of the enterprise, enabling political, administrative, and economic work to be carried out in a more coherent and purposeful manner. The collective leadership practiced through the Party factory commitee is considered a defense against subjectivism, enabling the combined wisdom of workers, technicians, and administrators to play a determining role.

A second important innovation was the establishment of a "general staff" under the leadership of the chief engineer, who in turn is directly responsible to the factory director. Thus the chief engineer, previously responsible only for the technical department, is now the "chief of staff" of a "headquarters" encompassing all planning, technical, and production departments of the enterprise. Due to his technical knowledge and experience the chief engineer is said to be best able to supervise these vital functions and to become the first assistant to the manager. He is also a member of the Party factory committee. This new organization of all the departments directly involved in the production process under a kind of strategic "headquarters" has facilitated what is described as "unified and concentrated guidance combined with collective leadership." This was a departure from the old system where there were no close connections between the technical, planning, and production departments: "In the old work system, many production processes were separated from each other and there was no general staff that could direct production in an integrated way."[40] Experience had shown that in drafting work plans many cadres had little contact with those who were supposed to carry them out. In some cases officials only signed documents, while producers had to rely on their own initiative in order to acquire the different materials necessary to fulfill the directives. When difficulties arose in the production process, the blame was generally passed down the line. With the new system this bureaucratic method of work is said to have been replaced and superior cadres are now supposed to go down to the production sites, where the work plan is drafted and carried out, so that knotty problems may be worked out in close collaboration with the inferior cadres and workers. Further, not only are the different production departments combined in an organized manner, but supporting functions not directly connected to production are integrated into the collective factory administration.

Departments for these supporting functions have been systematized under the following categories: (1) material supply, (2) labor administration and financial affairs, and (3) welfare work. Each is put under the leadership of one to three vice-managers (their number depending on the size of the enterprise) who work under the authority of the manager and are members of the Party factory committee. Even though not directly related to production, these departments serve it by creating an environment in which producers at all levels can concentrate their efforts on output. A consistent attempt seems to be made to eliminate any worries or material shortages the producers may encounter at work or at home.

The *material supply department* fulfills the following

duties: (a) responsibility for the detailed plan of supply for the entire factory; (b) responsibility for bringing material to workshops so that the producers do not waste their time searching for it; (c) management of store rooms, using materials as economically as possible; (d) control of material consumption; (e) shipment of finished goods out of the factory as well as internal transportation between the different workshops.

The *labor supply and financial department* is responsible for labor allocation plans that can anticipate needs for increased labor or for redistributions of labor within the factory. It organizes the work shifts and workteams, gives political education to the workers, and is responsible for increasing labor productivity. It is also responsible for the administration of wages. The financial department, which is often included in this division, assumes the responsibility for the financial plan and the calculation of production costs as well as for the control of monetary affairs.

One of the most interesting innovations of this industrial reorganization has been the formation, under a deputy manager, of a supply committee responsible for the *welfare* of the personnel. In the case of very large enterprises the main sphere of this committee's activities is the *ku* area (the neighborhood where factory personnel live). In this neighborhood a *ku* management committee has been established with the factory deputy manager serving as chairperson and with a membership including representatives of the *ku* municipal committee, the heads of schools, kindergartens, and nurseries, the director of the local hospital, the heads of the central shops, etc. This *ku* committee is responsible for all aspects of the lives of the workers and their families: housing, fuel, deliveries of consumer goods, various services, education, health, laundry, dining halls, cinemas, houses of culture, etc. Agricultural supplies are guaranteed by the allotment to the *ku* of a certain area of land on which workers may engage in an informal sort of farming. At the Daean plant this committee has charge of 70 *chongbo* of vegetable fields, a chicken farm with a daily capacity of 45,000 eggs, a pig farm, and an orchard of 80 *chongbo* of fruit trees. Any further supplies needed for the 5,000 workers employed at this plant are obtained through arrangements with nearby cooperative farms, although these cooperatives are not directly connected with the *ku*.

As in the case of the administrative reorganization of the countryside, this system serves to make local administration more flexible and democratic. Mistakes and failures, minor everyday nuisances which if left untended, might develop into real sources of resentment—all these may be solved on the spot by people who are well known to everybody. When the local organs of administration assume the responsibility for any shortcomings, it is difficult to put the blame on some distant and unknown body of administrators and, in the final analysis, on the system of socialism itself, as has increasingly been the case in countries with extreme centralization. Indirectly, socialism comes out reinforced. Although such considerations may not be acknowledged explicitly, they are nevertheless implicit in the Korean method of administering a modern socialist economy.

The Daean work system's concrete contributions to industrial relations may be summarized as follows: (1) management of the enterprise is now conducted through the collective leadership of the Party factory committee which assumes direct and indirect responsibility for the functioning of the plant; (2) politics are given priority, with the masses mobilized to resolve all questions relating both to production and to the conditions of the producers; (3) a system of mutual assistance, with the more experienced helping those who are less so, has been institutionalized as part of the struggle against bureaucratic methods of work, while responsibility is encouraged; (4) industry is managed in a more scientific and rational way.

Struggle Against Bureaucratism

By 1962 the Daean system was fully implemented on a national scale, not only in industry but in agriculture as well. The Koreans describe this form of industrial management as representing the "mass line combined with scientific methods." In their opinion, it is precisely the mass line which ensures the scientific principle, as "science without the mass line is useless."

Accordingly, it is only through mutual contacts between producers and industrial cadres that problems of an administrative and technical nature can be solved efficiently. Such cooperation tends to focus increased attention on the concrete, objective conditions, while minimizing elements of subjectivism. Further, the introduction of a method of collaboration whereby senior cadres help junior cadres, technicians help nontechnicians, those with knowledge teach those who lack it, and workshops assist each other in a spirit of "one for all and all for one," not only ensures that knowledge is not monopolized, but is said to encourage the emergence of a mentality more conducive to socialism and communism. The establishment of scientific management and planning under Party leadership and on the basis of the mass line, is described as a precondition for policies contributing objectively and subjectively to the creation of a new society. "The Daean work system, which basically and decisively strengthens the leading role of the vanguard party and the socialist state in the economy and realizes the principle of democratic centralism in economic management, is of great importance in strengthening the function of the dictatorship of the proletariat."[41]

The variable element in this entire system and its weakest link, is the extent and success of the struggle against a bureaucratic mentality through the institutionalization of the principle of mutual assistance. The implementation of the Chongsan-ri spirit and method is based on the recognition that—in the last instance—the strength of any system depends on the people involved: "The management structure can be made to demonstrate its strength only when it is combined with a corresponding method of work. Repeated reorganization of the management structure will be of no use where work is conducted bureaucratically."[42]

The struggle againt bureaucratism is a long-term process and it is difficult for visitors to get an absolutely clear picture of whether the reforms in agriculture and industry are having the expected results. But the awareness that there is a problem, and will be for some time to come, seems to be a precondition for its elimination. The main responsibility for the struggle against this phenomenon is assumed by the political party, which must prevent such tendencies from emerging within its own ranks.

> In its method and style of work, a ruling party should always guard against the tendency to wield party authority and practice bureaucratism. After a party has come into power, the danger of putting on airs and violating the mass line increases among some functionaries who are not armed firmly with the Marxist-Leninist world outlook. That is why the party should constantly improve its method and style of work in order to implement the mass line and ensure proper leadership for the revolution and construction.[43]

This means that Party cadres carry a special obligation to implement this antibureaucratic line in their work both inside the Party and outside of it—that is, in the production process itself. In this respect it is generally felt that the cadres must possess qualities which can only be acquired through organizational work and contact with the masses. Similarly, it is of the utmost importance to the attitude of cadres that they accept the principle of criticism and self-criticism.[44]

Certain Korean documents in which Kim Il Sung criticizes such attitudes as bureaucratism and subjectivism among functionaries, make it clear that problems still exist. Yet the case of the Chinese Cultural Revolution, which came as a surprise to all the so-called China experts, should have taught observers of socialist experiments a certain restraint with regard to any conclusions. An outsider can never truly grasp the internal dynamics of a social system. Nevertheless, one is tempted to conclude that in Korea, with the implementation of collective leadership in factory management, under the guidance of the Party and the mass line, progress has been made in the correct direction.

Generally speaking, the new management system seems to have eliminated an important capitalist remnant in the realm of industrial administration, and industrial relations are now more in harmony with the law of development of a socialist economy. According to the latter, the greater the scope of the economy and the more advanced the development of production, the more rapid the rate of economic growth will be.

> The decisive significance of the Daean work system lies in the fact that it is based on this objective law of development and that it is adapted to socialist production relations—the economic management system best suited to the expanding productive forces—and that it perfects the superstructure, the administrative system of the Party, state and economic organizations in such a way that these may be adapted fully to the established base.[45]

Furthermore, since a Korean industrial enterprise has its own political and affiliated organizations, its own educational institutions, and its own supply and social welfare systems it ceases to be purely a production unit in the restricted sense of the word. This is emphasized still further by the existence at all major enterprises of a system of workers' militias called the worker-peasant Red Units.[46] Experience has shown, as will by now be abundantly clear, that giving priority to political aims is not in conflict with the demands of the economy but rather leads to positive economic results.

C. THE TASK OF SOCIALIST PLANNING

The influence of the Daean work system was an important factor in the introduction of improved unified and detailed planning system on the national scale. This system operates under the leadership of the Party and the state while at the same time involving the active participation of the masses.

"Socialism" and "planning" are terms which have become almost synonymous. This is due to the fact that in a socialist economy, based on the social ownership of the means of production, the spontaneous forces of competition among individual capitalists are lacking; thus, were it not for the plan the economy would remain static and there would be no means of setting the economic system in motion. At the same time, the plan, in addition to being an economic operation, fulfills the sociopolitical function of resolving social contradictions.

Under socialism all the means of production, resources, raw materials, and labor power are thus set in motion through a plan dealing directly or indirectly with all aspects of socioeconomic activities. In this respect, it is a task of paramount importance in socialist construction to show constant concern for the interests of the population. Economically, this is done by striking the correct balance between accumulation and consumption—i.e., the need to combine expanded future reproduction (which is likewise future consumption) with short-term human requirements. In addition, there are problems to be solved in charting a course of balanced development between city and country; between agriculture and industry; and between various branches of industry (heavy and light industry, ore-extracting and processing industries, and so on). Dissension may even arise between provinces. All these potential conflicts of interest, which fall into the category of "contradictions among the people," need not be antagonistic if they are resolved in a way that contributes to the realization of the political project of socialism.

The socialist state has only one socioeconomic means of resolving these contradictions—the plan. "As we always point out, planning is one of the key issues that influence the success of socialist economic construction."[47]

Overcoming Previous Weaknesses

Through such measures as the land reform, the nationalization of industries, and the various economics plans (beginning in 1947), a certain amount of experience was acquired in the DPRK. Even during the Korean War the wartime economy was run in a planned manner. But by the early sixties, as we have seen, with the expansion of production and technological development some shortcomings became apparent. This was partly because the previous planning process had been modeled on foreign systems, in what Korean economists and leading functionaries now consider to have been a "dogmatic" fashion. Due to this weakness, difficulties were created by the subjectivism of the personnel involved in both planning and production. Thus, basic differences of interest manifested themselves between the demands of state-planning functionaries and the producers. Central planners asked for maximum output from production units without being able to guarantee more than a minimum of material supplies. At the production level the opposite tendency could be observed, namely to devote a minimum of effort to output tasks while requesting maximum supplies. These problems were not unlike those which arose in Eastern Europe at approximately the same time.

A second, closely related source of difficulties was the fact that while the planners at the center had exhaustive knowledge of the economic life of the country as a whole, as well as of the prospects for economic development, they were often relatively unaware of the objective reality at the production level such as the output potential specific to each plant. The producers, on the other hand, were fully acquainted with their own particular conditions, including the production reserves of their enterprises, but generally lacked awareness of the economic life of the country and the prospects for national development. As the Koreans point out, these contradictions revealed themselves to be the result of subjectivism on the part of state planners on the one hand, and departmentalism and local patriotism among the producers on the other. If left unremedied such a situation was bound to become a real hindrance to realistic and scientific planning.

In order to be effective the solution had to ensure that central planners were given access to a complete evaluation of objective conditions on the local level, including production reserves. But these factors are extremely numerous and complicated and it seemed impossible for the planners to grasp them fully without assistance from below. Since the Daean work system had secured the involvement of the producers in the management of the enterprises, it followed logically that the question could best be solved by letting the working masses participate actively in planning, thus permitting their creativity and hidden talents to be further unfolded. This idea became the driving force behind the method known as the *unified and detailed planning system*, established in 1964.

Parallel with the development of a system whereby the masses could be drawn into the planning process, a national administrative reorganization was undertaken. Regional planning commissions were established in the country's provinces under the direct supervision of the state planning commission. Similar state planning organs were set up in cities (district level) and counties, with corresponding sections at factories and enterprises.

On none of these levels are such state planning organs in any way affiliated with the corresponding unit of local government. The same applies to state planning sections at the factory and enterprise level, which function as local branches of the regional state planning commissions.

With the establishment of this network of state bodies, operating at a number of different levels yet kept separate from the pre-existing local planning bureaus, the state planning commission is able both to take root in localities and, at the same time, to serve the national interest by performing a sort of "checks and balances" function for units of local administration. Such coordination of regional and national affairs did not exist in the past. At present, the tasks of the state planning organs basically involve supervision of the planning at their respective levels: controlling and investigating production reserves as well as providing guidance and assistance in the establishment of the plans. These bodies also report any shortcomings (failure to organize production rationally, waste of labor and materials, etc.) to their superiors, right on up to the highest state institutions. In this manner a unified administration, coordinating the planning of the national economy from the center down to localities and production units, has been introduced.

Any system, however, depends in the last analysis on the human element and the style of work employed in carrying out the tasks. Only the implementation of the mass line—the essence of the Chongsan-ri spirit and method and the Daean work system—can, according to the Koreans, assure objective and scientific plans. Bureaucratism and formalism are incapable of marshaling all the available reserves and potential of the national economy. Only after it has been discussed by the masses is it possible for the plan to reflect, scientifically, the factors of production, and only when political work has been carried out among the producers can the plan successfully be carried out. A certain interrelation has to be established between the capacities of the producers and the projects of the planners. Because of their limited knowledge and perspective, functionaries at local levels are not always able to take advantage of existing resources. Sometimes they reflect the narrow interests of their institution or region rather than the national objectives. Therefore, guidance and assistance by the state planners is of decisive importance in making the plan active and not allowing it to sink into inertia.

Planning Through Producers' Participation

Under the present comprehensive system, planning has developed into a sociopolitical procedure rather than an exclusively economic one. Its broad scope allows both producers and planners to participate, giving more positive results than could be achieved by an arbitrary determination of the various goals. The actual process through which this plan is established consists of three distinct stages: (1) the calculation of preliminary figures; (2) the definition of control figures; and (3) the determination of target figures.

Formerly, the planning process started with control figures being sent by the state planning commission down to ministries, bureaus, and enterprises, which would then adjust their draft work plans accordingly. Often the control figures did not correspond to the existing possibilities. Since control figures are now arrived at on the basis of the preliminary figures worked out at the enterprises themselves, these basic weaknesses have in principle been eliminated. Today, in fact, the planning process begins at the factory level with mass meetings and discussions at workshops. The producers democratically arrive at decisions about the quantity and quality of what they can promise to produce given a certain availability of materials, technology, and labor. This preliminary decision is then conveyed upward through two parallel routes (local, regional administrative bodies and ministries on the one hand, and state planning organs on the other) passing through each of the higher administrative organs in turn on its way to the central planning authorities. At all levels comments and suggestions are added. The state planning commission compares the drafts received and arrives at a set of control figures, taking into consideration the Party line on economic construction. After these figures have been examined and discussed by the Administrative Council (formerly called the Cabinet), they are presented for approval and signature by the Politburo of the Central Committee of the Workers' Party. Following this evaluation at the highest political level, the control figures are first sent back to the state planning commission, then passed down to the lower organs along the same two routes utilized on the way up.

These figures now represent the aim of the Party and take on a quasi-legal status. They form the basis upon which target figures are elaborated, following renewed widescale discussions by workers in factories and enterprises, where Party members conduct political work and explain the Party's aim. Often, it is said, the target figures are set higher than the original control figures. These target figures are again sent up to the state planning commission where they are reexamined before being sent to the Administrative Council. This latter body sometimes has to settle cases where there is a divergence between the state planning commission and the ministry of planning department. After it is passed by the Administrative Council, the plan is submitted to the Central Committee of the Party for final approval. All that remains is for the Administrative Council to work out a more detailed version of the plan. When this procedure is completed the plan takes on the status of a state law that no one has the right to revise or violate. This process, involving all the producers and different organs, is considered an effective means of resolving most planning problems. As a Korean planning expert explained to us, "Drawing up plans through this procedure enabled us not only to realize the detailed planning but also to solve the problem of combining democratic centralism with the mass line in planning more elaborately."[48]

One technical weakness which had formerly existed was that the state plan concentrated on major items such as volume of ore or steel, number of tractors, etc., while ignoring minor but essential supplies (screws, nails, bolts, cogwheels, bearings, and the like). Shortages or lack of such items could result in serious dislocations in the production process. The actual provision of these items was left to the appropriate ministries, on the basis of what had been called a "moral plan." "A moral plan," we were told somewhat sarcastically by the same planning functionary quoted above, "meant one by which each partner may or may not carry out the request of the other." Such arbitrariness has now been overcome by including all industrial products in the state plan, thus replacing the "moral plan" for secondary items with a definite plan having the force of law. Besides, since self-reliance is an important element in the production process of most enterprises, many of them are now able to manufacture their own machines or spare parts, thus reducing their dependence on outside supplies.

Another advantage under this system is that the state planning agencies can better coordinate the general economic development of the country with the management system of every single factory. This ensures that the plans will be geared to actual conditions in all branches of the economy, localities, and enterprises, with all indices aligned down to the smallest detail, and all organs and cells set in motion by the precise implementation of the plan. It should be emphasized, though, that none of these institutions can be expected permanently to retain its present form. Adjustments will have to be made in accordance with current technological and productive developments in order to fulfill future tasks. This need for constant improvement is stressed in Korea: "It is by no means an easy thing, however, to have everything correctly planned. We have been carrying on a planned economy for over 20 years and we have kept on emphasizing that the plans must be objective. But planning is still not quite in order."[49]

At a time when most Eastern European countries are encountering difficulties in running their economies, Korea has taken a leading position in the development of its own socialist management and planning. As Kim Il Sung points out, there were no ready-made formulas:

> I have read the works of Marx, Engels and Lenin. I have read also the works of Stalin who had the experience in personally leading socialist economic construction. I have studied many foreign planning systems as well. But no reasonable system of planning suitable for our specific conditions was to be found in any Marxist-Leninist classics or in books written by foreigners. We had no alternative but to develop the universal Marxist-Leninist theory on planning in conformity with our country's reality and to perfect the planning system of our country with our own brains.[50]

Perhaps the most noteworthy feature of the unified and detailed planning process instituted by the Koreans is its originality. But even though their methods may not serve as a model, in the sense of being copied by others, the Koreans do seem justified in considering their efforts a contribution on both the theoretical and practical level to the construction of socialism.

Notes

1. "If a socialist state fails to put great stress on rural construction, its countryside will be left behind, and eventually it will be compelled to buy even grain for food from other countries. In such a case the complete victory of socialism would be impossible, and the country indefinitely lamed." [Kim Il Sung, "Speeding Up Construction of Socialism in the Countryside," September 24, 1968, in *Selected Works*, vol. V (Pyongyang, 1972), p. 202.]
2. Even in the immediate postwar years the need had been felt for an administrative system whereby closer guidance could be given to units on the lower levels, thus speeding the carrying out of state policies. Previously, the countryside (beyond the hamlet level) had been administratively divided into three political levels: the *ri*, the township, and the county. A reform was introduced in 1953 through which the number of *ri* was reduced from 10,666 to 3,772 and the intermediate township unit was abolished altogether. Above the

ri, the counties—which had increased in number from 97 to 173—remained under the jurisdiction of the once 8, now 9, provinces. (Cf. Robert A. Scalapino and Chong-Sik Lee, *Communism in Korea,* vol. II (Berkeley, Cal.: Univ. of California Press, 1972), pp. 1062-1063.
3. Kim Il Sung, "On Further Strengthening and Developing the County Co-operative Farm Management Committee," November 13, 1962, in *Selected Works,* vol. II (Pyongyang, 1965), p. 394.
4. Kim Il Sung, "Report to the Fourth Party Congress," September 11, 1961, in *Selected Works,* vol. II, p. 173.
5. Ibid.
6. Ibid. Koreans do not use the term "decentralization" to describe these changes, since in fact they strengthened centralizedleadership, in contrast to the process in Eastern Europe.
7. Kim Il Sung, "On Further Strengthening and Developing," p. 399.
8. Kim Byong Sik, *Modern Korea* (New York: International Publishers, 1970), p. 142.
9. Cf. Bo Gustafsson, "Socialkapitalism eller socialism?" in Bo Gustafsson, ed., *Socialkapitalismen, En kritik af sovjetekonomin,* (Stockholm, 1971), pp.10-11.
10. J. V. Stalin, *Economic Problems of Socialism in the U.S.S.R.* (Moscow, 1952; Peking: Foreign Languages Press, 1972), p. 95.
11. Ibid., p. 96.
12. In China, of course, this was the period when the Great Leap Forward was launched. And in Vietnam an intensivation of agricultural socialization took place almost simultaneously. A resolution adopted at the Fourteenth Session of the Central Committee of the Party, toward the end of 1958, foresaw the gradual growth of agricultural cooperation in the form of a mass movement, the collectivization of the means of production, and the further development of technical expertise and ideological education. [Cf. Le Chau, *Le Viet Nam socialiste* (Paris: Maspero, 1966), p. 184.]
13. Scalapino and Lee seem to commit a serious factual error when they state that this Soviet policy was followed in the DPRK: "Some Soviet actions, such as . . . the abolition of the independent machine tractor stations, were incorporated into North Korean policy almost immediately." (*Communism in Korea*, p. 1134). What happened was that in 1960 the MTS within *state farms* were abolished and the equipment given to the work brigades. From then on the MTS had the sole mission of assisting cooperatives. By 1960 most of the tractors under the control of the machine stations were assigned to the cooperative farms for stationing, but ownership remained with the machine stations. Operators are paid on the basis of work points and work standards set by the MTS. [Cf. Joseph Sang-hoon Chung, *The North Korean Economy* (Stanford, Cal.: Hoover Institution Press, 1974), pp.36-37.] In China the policy oscillated between two solu-

tions: after the transfer to communes in 1958, the policy was repudiated and ownership of the machine stations restored in the 1960s; these again became the possession of communes during the Cultural Revolution. [Cf. Kjeld Allan Larsen, *Den kinesiske lokalindustri på xian-niveau under og efter kulturrevolutionen* (Copenhagen: Statens trykningskontor, 1975), pp. 152-153.]
14. Kim Il Sung, "On Further Strengthening and Developing," p. 396.
15. Kim Il Sung, "On the Lessons Drawn from Guidance to Kangso County," February 23, 1960, in *Selected Works,* vol. II, pp. 61-62.
16. Ibid., p. 64.
17. Kim Il Sung, *For the Correct Management of the Socialist Rural Economy,* February 8, 1960 (Pyongyang, 1969), p. 29.
18. Kim Il Sung, "On the Occasion of the 20th Anniversary of the Workers' Party of Korea," in *Selected Works,* vol. II, pp. 582-583.
19. Kim Il Sung, "On the Lessons Drawn from Guidance," p. 56.
20. Ibid., p. 74.
21. The inherited cultural conditions of inequality in the villages are thrown into sharp relief in this description of the problem by Kim Il Sung: "All the shrewd and sleek people in the co-operative have surreptitiously quit the principal work and joined the so-called skilled work, which is more leisurely while bringing in more workpoints. The result is that farm work is left to hard-working and less articulate women." ("On the Lesson Drawn from Guidance," p. 72.) Elsewhere Kim Il Sung describes the women as the "most exploited" in Korean society. More than half the labor force today consists of women and due to their traditional tasks as mothers and wives they often do a double day's work. Even though much is done to alleviate women's burdens and to ensure that they are equal in practice, not just on paper, in Korean society men still occupy most of the important leadership positions.
22. Kim Il Sung, "On the Lessons Drawn from Guidance," p. 72.
23. Ibid.
24. Kim Il Sung, *On Some Experiences of the Democratic and Socialist Revolutions in Our Country,* October 11, 1969 (Pyongyang, 1973), p. 27.
25. Scalapino and Lee, *Communism in Korea,* p. 1000.
26. Ibid., p. 1156.
27. Kim Il Sung, *On Some Theoretical Problems of the Socialist Economy,* March 1, 1969 (Pyongyang, 1969), p. 33.
28. Kim Il Sung, "Speeding Up Construction of Socialism," p. 202.
29. In modern capitalist societies many attempts are made to overcome this inherent weakness: efficiency experts are invited to study each and every movement of the workers during the job in order to increase their productivity; union leaders agitate for "participation"

and "democracy" at the work place in order to get the workers personally involved and motivated. All these activities are of course of limited value, as the workers know only too well that doing their job faster and better invaribly leads to a decreased number of jobs and the further enrichment of their employer.

30. Rossana Rossanda, "Le Socialisme en marche avant," *Le Nouvel Observateur,* no. 299 (August 3-9, 1970).
31. Charles Bettelheim, *Economic Calculation and Forms of Property* (New York: Monthly Review Press, 1975), p. 79.
32. Kim Byong Sik, *Modern Korea,* p. 123
33. Kim Il Sung, *On Further Developing the Daean Work System,* November 9, 1962, in *Selected Works,* vol. II, p. 376.
34. Harry Magdoff and Paul M. Sweezy, "The Lessons of Poland," *Monthly Review* 22, no. 9 (February 1971): 11.
35. Bettelheim, *Economic Calculation,* p. 77.
36. Kim Il Sung, "Let Us Embody the Revolutionary Spirit of Independence, Self-Sustenance and Self-Defence More Thoroughly in All Fields of State Activity," December 16, 1967, in *Selected Works,* vol. IV (Pyongyang, 1971), p. 587.
37. Kim Il Sung, "Report to the Fourth Party Congress," p. 234. Koreans further characterize this method as one of "detecting the main link, concentrating effort on it while giving attention to other links and thus ensuring success in the work as a whole and the steady upswing in the revolution and construction." (Kim Yun Sik, "Great Chongsan-ri Spirit and Chongsan-ri Method Brings About Radical Change in Improvement of Our Party's Style of Guidance and Method of Work," *The Pyongyang Times,* February 20, 1971.
38. Kim Byon Sik, *Modern Korea,* p. 120.
39. Ibid., p. 129.
40. Ibid., p. 130.
41. Ibid., p. 134.
42. Kim Il Sung, "On Further Developing the Daean Work System," p. 377.
43. Kim Il Sung, *Report on the Work of the Central Committee to the Fifth Congress of the Workers' Party of Korea,* November 2, 1970 (Pyongyang, 1970), p. 137.
44. Ibid., p. 144.
45. Kim Byong Sik, *Modern Korea,* p. 133.
46. What Charles Bettelheim found to be one of the most interesting results of the Cultural Revolution had thus already been introduced in the DPRK by 1962: "In China, factory management is primarily *political* management, which gives priority to the *political* objectives of socialist construction and not to narrow economic objec-

tives." [*Cultural Revolution and Industrial Organization in China* (New York: Monthly Review Press, 1974), pp. 76-77.]
47. Kim Il Sung, "Unified and Detailed Planning," September 23, 1965, in *Selected Works,* vol. IV, p. 254.
48. Lecture given us in Pyongyang by Chong Hae Sung, director of study of economics, state planning commission.
49. Kim Il Sung, *On Some Theoretical Problems,* p. 22.
50. Kim Il Sung, "Unified and Detailed Planning," p. 267.

Chapter 10
Contributions to Theoretical Questions

One of the guiding principles of economic thinking in the DPRK is the conviction that socialism is the mode of production most conducive to rapid economic development. From the foregoing chapters it will be clear that Koreans see development not as an automatic outcome of an increase in the national product but in terms of structural changes. Actually the "growth" formula much in vogue with Western economists often seems to be a prescription for more of the same—which in the context of the Third World means continued underdevelopment. As a matter of fact, some of the so-called high-growth Third World countries—including South Korea—demonstrate a consistent pattern of economic dependence and lack of internal sectoral integration.

Looking back on the many changes implemented in North Korea, one feels inclined to conclude that it was precisely the background of structural underdevelopment which forced it to develop an early understanding of the necessity to revolutionize not only the economic base but also the superstructure. The material point of departure probably didn't leave any margin for neglect.

According to the *Juche* principle, Koreans view economic development as a transformation of the relations of production generated by underdevelopment, whereby the economy is made to move increasingly in the direction of satisfying internal needs. Whereas underdevelopment may be characterized as a situation of structural nonconvergence of internal needs and resource utilization, the *Juche* approach implies, as we have seen, precisely the opposite: to make internal resource utilization converge with internal needs.

Internationally speaking, Korean socialists believe that ultimately all countries will have to build their economies on such an internally integrated pattern of self-reliance. Moreover, such a process is seen by them as the only sure method to abolish the unequal international division of labor and to establish equality among states.

On the more theoretical level, this way of thinking is related to the socialist project of gradually moving away from the domination of market mechanisms. An important prerequisite for reaching such a goal would seem to be a policy of increased equalization of distribution. Particularly in Third World countries, where demand (in terms of purchasing power) has often been extremely unevenly distributed, a great discrepancy exists between on the one hand, "demand," and on the other hand, basic human needs—the majority barely having the means to subsist. A more equal distribution of buying power would open the way to increased convergence of demands and needs, whereby the domestic market becomes activated to such a degree as to be able to stimulate a more balanced internal development of the economy (breaking the relations of dependence). Furthermore, such a strategy is the material precondition for the continuous political mobilization of the masses.

Because of its former colonial status the DPRK is still employing itself in the rapid development of its productive forces. According to Koreans, the historical reason for their country's colonization was the feudal system's inability to develop the economy. In discussing the question with us, one official put it this way: "In the 1860s, the Meiji bourgeois restoration in Japan initiated the construction of railroads and the manufacture of heavy weapons. At that time our feudal lords were still riding horses and using bows and arrows!"—the implication being that imperialism could exploit the country's weakness. Korean socialists are determined to avoid any reoccurence of this state of affairs. Besides, the nation is still divided and it is that through its economic achievements the regime in the North promotes the process of reunification. Finally, the DPRK feels a responsibility toward the Third World: Through its economic advances, the country enhances the appeal of socialism in those geopolitical areas which capitalism has been unable to develop.

But this is not to deny the fact that a stage will be reached in the development of the productive forces where a radical break will be necessary in order to fulfill the aims of classical socialist thinking. The scope of this future change was expressed in a rare prediction by Karl Marx: "The true wealth being the full productive power of each individual, the scale of measure (for social wealth) will no longer be labor time, but disposable time."[1] This formulation implies not only the fullest development of science and technology but also a total revision of all previous socioeconomic norms. Instead of measuring efficiency by the ability to produce as much as possible in a process of endless growth, the true measure of rationality in such a future society would rather be to produce only what was necessary for the fullest human expansion of all individuals. From a somewhat different angle, modern ecological studies tend to project such a vision not only as a politically determined choice, but as a necessity imposed by nature. Such speculations about long-term perspectives are not yet the order of the day in any socialist society, including the DPRK. Nevertheless, the present pattern of trends and priorities may have a decisive influence on future possibilities.

Against Revisionism in Economic Thinking

For many years it had been an accepted fact among most socialist economists that the rate of economic development at the beginning of the socialist process was far superior to that of capitalism. However, in the last decade or so, new theories have emerged, maintaining that after an initial period of relatively rapid growth, development tends to stabilize at a moderate rate. Empirically, the rate of growth of agricultural and industrial production slowed down in the DPRK during the 1960s (mainly, we think, due to factors external to the Korean development "model"). Nevertheless, this line of argument is vehemently denounced as antisocialist by the Koreans:

> To deny the rapid development of the large-scale socialist economy is a revisionist economic theory ignoring such lawful demands of the socialist economy. It is nothing but a sophistry brought forward by some people to justify the fact that their technical progress is slow and their economy stagnant because they, talking about "liberalization" and "democratic development," did not educate their working people and, as a result, the latter is ideologically so slackened as to fiddle about and loaf on the job. If one wants to develop production constantly at a high rate by giving full play to the superiority of the socialist system, one must oppose revisionism which introduces the capitalist way of enterprise management into socialist economic management, refusing the dictatorship of the proletariat and crying for "democratic development" and "liberalization."[2]

Korean socialists feel that in order to bring out the superiority of the system, a proper correlation of the following factors is essential: (1) the planned and balanced development of the economy, (2) the planned and rapid development of technology, and (3) the revolutionary enthusiasm and creative initiative of the masses. This last element, considered the most decisive, depends in the last analysis on correct political work: "The essential excellence of the socialist system lies in the fact that *the work-*

ing people freed from exploitation and oppression, work with conscious enthusiasm and creative initiative for the country and the people, for society and the collective, as well as their own welfare."[3] For socialism, therefore, the problem is to find a method of breaking down all the economic, organizational, and ideological constraints on mass initiative. In fact, this may be considered one of the key strategic questions during the construction of socialism.

What this implies is that political considerations are of the greatest importance. The Korean emphasis on politics is based on the Leninist formulation that "communism is Soviet power plus electricification." Kim Il Sung poses the question, "What is meant by the Soviet power, mentioned by Lenin?" and goes on to offer the following interpretation:

> It means no less than the dictatorship of the proletariat. It, therefore, means that the state of the working class should continue the class struggle and carry out the ideological and cultural revolutions to remould the consciousness of the people and enhance their technical and cultural level, and accomplish the task of *working-classizing* and revolutionizing the whole society. By electrification it is meant that technology should be developed to such a high level as to be able to make all the production processes automatic and the material-production basis of society be greatly consolidated.[4]

Only when what the Koreans call the ideological and material fortresses have been captured, can the march toward socialism and communism be completed.

Since Lenin died before this theory could be implemented, the question of a correct correlation between politics and economics was left open to various interpretations. In Korea it led to an ideological confrontation with "economism" — the tendency to give predominance to economics at the expense of politics in the sphere of social relations:

> Some people . . . refuse to correctly understand and put into effect this proposition of Lenin's. We must categorically oppose Right opportunism in the field of economic theory in order to accelerate socialist construction at a higher rate. If we do not take issue with the Right deviation in the economic field, weaken the proletarian dictatorship, do not conduct political work, foster individual selfishness among the people, and try to make the people move merely with money, we cannot call forth their collective heroism and heuristic initiative and, accordingly, we cannot successfully carry out the tasks either of technical revolution or of economic construction.[5]

As we have seen, the nationalization of the means of production is only the first step in a long process of transforming the entire structure and direction of production away from market relations. Moreover, the very existence of enterprises as separate economic units has a tendency to reproduce capitalist social relations. In this light, the Korean effort to revolutionize the enterprise by developing new systems of management, supply, and planning which draw the masses into the decision-making process, is an attempt to eliminate capitalist remnants in the superstructure.

But at the same time, such capitalist categories as commodity production, the law of value, and a certain degree of monetary calculation—all remnants of the market economy—continue to operate after the installation of people's power. As pointed out by Charles Bettelheim, a whole series of ideological and material preconditions have to be met before they can be eliminated: "The notion of a 'direct' and 'immediate' abolition of market relations is as utopian and dangerous as the notion of the 'immediate abolition' of the state, and is *similar in nature:* it disregards the specific characteristics (i.e., the *specific contradictions*) of the period of transition which constitutes the period of the building of socialism."[6] Nevertheless, the attitude taken toward these matters is decisive for the analysis of the entire social process.

Capitalist Categories in Transitional Societies

What, then, is the significance of commodity production and the law of value in the transitional process? And why are they in fact accorded special attention in Marxist analyses? It must be recalled that under capitalism commodity production and the law of value constitute the mechanisms that make it possible for the owners of the means of production to obtain their profits; they are, in a way, the very sinews and muscle of capitalist relations. Historically, it is more than probable that people originally produced things only for their own use or, at most, for purposes of simple barter. But with increased productivity and the division of labor production begins to be carried out by independent, separate units for the purpose of exchange—the products, in other words, take the form of commodities. The *value* of these commodities is determined by the labor socially necessary for their production and is realized through exchange, i.e., sale. What is known as the "value" of commodities, therefore, is nothing but disguised labor. Under conditions of commodity production the law of value conceals the true content of social relations—the private appropriation of social surplus labor. Commodities become fetishized and the producers alienated from their products.

On the macroeconomic level, other, related mechanisms are worth mentioning. Under capitalism the prices of commodities tend to fluctuate around their value; it is these fluctuations, indicating effective demand, by which production is regulated. Consequently, the utility of production (and labor) under capitalism is measured not by its ability to fulfill human needs, but its capacity to produce surplus value in the form of profits. In this manner the law of value conditions the development of the means of production, affecting all operations of production and circulation in a blind and anarchic manner. The result is unequal development and social distortions both within and between nations. Economically, the competition between separate producers and the anarchy of production inherent in a private commodity system result in waste and destruction of both labor and material. The law of value as it operates in private commodity production may be said to constitute the very mechanism which originally led to the birth and development of capitalist relations.

In the context of socialism, the existence of commodities and the law of value is clear evidence that the social formation in question is not yet a mature socialist society, but is in a process of transformation. The aim of production is no longer the private appropriation of social surplus labor in the form of profits, but its social accumulation and utilization to satisfy various social needs. Under these modifying circumstances the question must be: How do these categories affect socialist construction? As long as capitalist categories remain in existence, the danger persists of introducing or maintaining concepts foreign to socialism, i.e., of reverting to the supply-and-demand criteria of market relations and allowing planning to be overly influenced by monetary calculations based on such relations.

Accordingly, it is only to the extent that socioeconomic functions are given conscious political direction that such dangers may be averted. By pointing to these basic issues and comparing the classical Marxist theory with the practice of different socialist countries, Charles Bettelheim may well have discovered new tools for analyzing the problems of transition.[7] The interesting aspect in the present context, however, is that Korean theoreticians seem to have themselves been aware of the problematic and have gone back to original Marxist concepts in order to work out a strategy in the spirit of *Juche*.

In their analysis of transitional societies, Marxist economists often refer to certain remarks by Friedrich Engels on the society of the future. According to Engels, planning in a socialist formation would be based on *economic* calculations rather than the *monetary* calculations that typify nonsocialist societies. In his opinion, such economic calculations would have to be based upon a comparison of the use values of different objects in relation to the labor involved in their production. It would thus be a more direct form of calculation, and not—as in the case of capitalism—an indirect evaluation through the intervention of commodities and value measurements. "The useful effects of various articles of consumption, compared with one another and with the quantity of labor required for their production, will in the end determine the plan. People will be able to manage everything very simply, without the intervention of much-vaunted 'value.' "[8]

One of the reasons this prophecy has not yet been fulfilled in any country calling itself socialist, is probably that the process of socialist transformation took place first in economically underdeveloped countries and not, as predicted, in the highly industrialized ones. That, in any case, is the explanation offered by the Koreans. "Engels, on the supposition that socialist revolutions would triumph almost simultaneously in highly advanced capitalist countries, presented the proposition that commodity production would be abolished when private ownership of the means of production was replaced with social ownership."[9] This of course does not imply that highly developed countries would not need a transitional period of ideological transformation. But at least the material basis—the relatively low incidence of small-scale and/or artisanal production—might make it possible to pass more directly to a unitary form of ownership, skipping the stage of small peasant ownership or even, perhaps, of collectivization.

In Korea, consumer goods are all considered commodities. Only when determining the nature of the means of production does an analytical differentiation become necessary. In a socialist society, according to the North Koreans, the means of production must be considered commodities when: (1) goods produced by the state sector are acquired by cooperatives, resulting in a transfer from public to cooperative ownership; (2) the produce from one cooperative is sold to another, again leading to a change in ownership; and finally (3) enterprises produce for trade with foreign countries.

This explanation is quite different from the one given by Soviet socialists like Preobrajensky in the mid-1920s and by Joseph Stalin some twenty-five years later. Although acknowledging the existence of commodity categories in the Soviet Union's commercial relations with capitalist states, Stalin denied that they actually functioned in domestic exchange. Although they did exist as *forms,* this, he maintained, was dictated by the need for enterprises to keep a strict accounting of their production costs.

> It therefore follows that in the sphere of foreign trade the means of production produced by our enterprises retain the properties of commodities both essentially and formally, but that in the sphere of domestic economic circulation, means of production lose the properties of commodities, cease to be commodities and pass out of the sphere of operation of the law of value, retaining only the outward integument of commodities (calculation, etc.).[10]

Although helpful for an understanding of the problem, this definition is not entirely satisfactory. The Koreans, in contrast, maintain that the means of production assume the character of commodities in all internal exchanges involving a transfer of ownership. In the case of exchanges between state enterprises, however, the means of production are not considered to *be* commodities in the proper sense of the word, but only to be assuming the *form* of commodities. No actual change of ownership takes place, but simply a transfer from one productive unit of the state sector to another, according to the plans of equipment and material supply. In such cases, as we shall see, the commodity form and the law of value are used in the system of "social accountability" which, in the transitional period, is necessary to implement the political project.

From a socialist point of view, the recognition of the existence of value/commodity categories is useful only if it reveals the extent to which such capitalist remnants survive—and uses this knowledge to eliminate them. This involves not only a transformation of ownership relations but superstructural changes in the direction of mass participation which, combined with ideological remolding, may lead to a higher stage of social development in which a whole set of new mechanisms will prevail. This long-range evolution, as Kim Il Sung sees it, is very much along the lines of Engels' prediction: "Later, when the transition period is over and co-operative property is turned into property of the entire people so that a unitary form of ownership is established, the produce of society, if foreign trade is not taken into consideration, will be called not by the name of commodity but simply called means of production and consumer goods or by some other names." At this time, Engels asserted, "the law of value will also cease to operate."[11] A failure to comprehend this question, as well as the future vision it implies, may lead to various kinds of erroneous practice during socialist construction. Aware of the problems of deviation, the Koreans identify two main types of errors as the ones most apt to be committed:

> At present, right opportunists, defining all the means of production in a socialist society indiscriminately as commodities, are trying to carry out economic management in a capitalist way, while overestimating the significance of commodity production and the law of value. On the other hand, left opportunists, ignoring the transitional nature of a socialist society, are unable to rationalize the management of socialist enterprises and are wasting substantial quantities of means of production and labor power because they refuse completely to recognize the role of commodity production and the law of value under socialism.[12]

The Utilization of the Law of Value

According to Korean economists, under conditions of socialist transition, commodity production is carried out not for profits but—due to the political power and regulating force of economic planning—in order to satisfy the material and cultural needs of the people. When the state controls the functioning of the economy with such a purpose in mind, the law of value no longer operates as it used to, in blind and unrestricted fashion. Indeed, through a planned approach to such categories the state can employ them as a socioeconomic lever for effective management. Thus in their view, the correct use of capitalist survivals in a noncapitalist environment may—within limits—even be conducive to the change in production relations during the process of transition.

The independent management of enterprises and the cost-accounting system are two more survivals; their continued existence, according to the Koreans, is related to the special characteristics of a society in transition. Production is not yet developed sufficiently to meet overall demand. Remnants of the old ideology continue to exert a certain influence on functionaries, manifesting itself in disregard for state property, in egoism, and in departmentalism. Collectivism is not yet the prevailing mentality; nor do enterprises fully identify their own interests with those of others. Labor is not yet considered the primary requirement of the people; moreover, a division persists between light and heavy work, and between physical and mental labor. Because of this situation, the cost-accounting system between enterprises is considered to have an important role to play during the transitional phase. As Kim Byong Sik puts it, "Under limiting conditions resulting from the transitional nature of a socialist society, or when people do not yet work consciously and devotedly both for the society and their own welfare without social compulsion, the use of the commodity and commercial forms is an inevitable social and economic regime for national control and management of socialist state enterprises."[13]

As a result, products have to be exchanged in a commercial form, in accordance with the law of value and in conformity with the principle of socialist distribution. Moreover, given the special circumstances of the transitional period, the utilization of the law of value (though a mere formality in the case of exchanges between state enterprises) is considered necessary to secure an adequate accumulation of funds: "A proper use of the commodity form and the commercial form in the production and circulation of the means of production is of definite significance in methodically increasing the profits of enterprises and the accumulations of the state by eliminating the wastage of social labour and strengthening the save-and-spare regime."[14] For this method to be effective, the enterprise cannot be autonomous to the extent of choosing its own line of production or determining the prices of its products. Prices are established by the central authorities on the basis of a single price system encompassing the entire country. The state pricing commission is under the direct guidance of the Central Committee of the Party as well as of the Administrative Council. The Koreans feel that if price setting were liberalized and decentralized, it would make planning more difficult.

In this manner industrial plants are made to economize as much as possible by producing more with less material and by generally lowering their production costs. Further, as control of production is exercised not only through mass participation and political guidance, but through financial means as well, the law of value—in the exchange of goods and in the use of precise calculation—serves as a system of checks and balances. Thus, if an enterprise wastes materials, this may be observed through the increase of its production costs and a decreasing amount of "pure income." Since salaries are fixed by the state, such a budgetary deficit cannot be hidden and the economic weakness may be detected at an early stage. Were salaries fixed by individual enterprises, it is feared that the law of socialist distribution (to each according to his or her efforts) would be violated. Where an enterprise shows a consistent deficit, either various measures are taken to overcome the deficiencies, or—if the activities or production in question are deemed important for overall development—the state underwrites the deficit, absorbing it as a necessary loss.

It is important to realize that even though industrial enterprises are in no way self-financing—that they are, in fact, entirely dependent on the central authorities—this does not mean that the principle of "profitability" is disregarded. This aspect is related to the macroeconomic functioning of the economy. This so-called pure income of state enterprises is the primary source of accumulation, providing the funds used for reproduction and for the running of the state, as well as for new investments. Through the *overall* profitability of state enterprises the introduction of new branches of production, as well as the *equalized* development of the economy as a whole, can be guaranteed regardless of the initial unprofitability of particular sectors.

With this in mind, Korean economists warn that narrow profit-seeking on the microeconomic level would interfere with the construction of socialism. One possible result of such a line is the supposed "liberalization" of the economy, bringing pronounced decentralization and the gravitation of the labor force toward the enterprises making the largest profits. Such a phenomenon, in Korean eyes, is tantamount to the capitalistic pursuit of surplus value.[15] In Korea, the aim is not primarily accumulation of profit, but the direction of all economic activities toward increased self-reliance. Thus the fulfillment of production quotas is considered imperative not because they promise financial gain but because they are assigned by the plan —itself the product of a consensus among the producers— and represent certain social priorities. Under a different method there might be an inclination to invest primarily in the sectors already developed, leaving the less developed areas behind and producing a growing lopsidedness in the economy.

Under the guidance of political considerations and institutions on the one hand, and planning and management systems on the other, the law of value should be employed actively in the struggle against ideological remnants (egoism, individualism, departmentalism) and for the promotion of collectivism. The feeling is that unless certain positive social efforts are made, negative influences will survive, endangering the building of socialism and communism. From a political point of view the elimination of outdated attitudes is considered an extremely important aspect of socialist transition. From an economic viewpoint, too, the reciprocal relations between political institutions and economic laws strengthen the "save-and-spare" regime.

Thus, according to the Koreans, the utilization of the law of value in a socialist way means putting it at the service of the planned socialist economy. For example, in setting prices the aim is to combine the basic law of socialist construction (producing to meet human needs) with a proper use of the law of value (the labor socially necessary to produce the goods). In other words, prices reflect both political and economic considerations: the interests of the people, on the one hand, and the amount of labor power and materials consumed in the production process, on the other. The result is a decreasing sphere of market relations and an increased level of social and collective consumption: health care and education are being met free of charge, while housing and an increasing number of daily necessities and services are available at very low prices. Similarly, prices on mass consumer goods are continually being lowered sometimes even in disregard of their actual value—the socially necessary labor they require. Luxury items on the other hand, still in short supply, are priced relatively high. The Koreans consider this procedure consistent both with the criteria of socialist construction and with the proper use of the law of value during this process:

> This is not meant to ignore the law of value, but to apply it correctly in a socialist society. Thus, while it is necessary to

fix the prices of commodities in the direction of making them coincide with their values on the basis of the law of value, it is also necessary for prices of commodities to differ from their values in accordance with the requirements of the basic economic law of socialism. This is the correct use of the law of value in a socialist society.[16]

Thus, whereas *indirect monetary calculations* (based on commodity and value categories) still exist in the DPRK, one may say that a process has been started through which *direct economic calculations,* in Engels' sense, may eventually gain predominance.

Questions of Coercion and Motivation

Closely related to the problem of monetary/economic calculations during the transitional phase of socialist construction is the policy on wages and incentives. Because of the relatively low level of productivity which does not yet permit distribution according to needs, and a consciousness level which still prevents efforts according to ability, transitional societies make use of mechanisms which would otherwise be ideologically and politically unacceptable to them.

Due to this state of affairs great care must be taken to determine the proper degree of emphasis to be put on moral and material incentives. Such motivational problems are not peculiar to societies engaged in socialist construction. Even in Western industrial states where materialism seems to be the primary incentive, many managers, engineers, intellectuals, or workers identify with the aims and content of their occupations to a larger degree than can be accounted for by the size of their salaries. Where the two types of societies do differ, however, is in the utilization of negative stimuli. This was pointed out very forcefully in a speech to a Cuban trade union mass meeting by Fidel Castro: "The capitalist and the capitalist system operate through very powerful incentives. In the first place, capitalism has a labor reserve, the army of the unemployed. There is no more effective whip than the fear of losing your job. . . . "[17]

Such coercive means of imposing work discipline are by definition antithetical to a socialist formation. In fact, a socialist society solves for the workers many of the problems they must face on their own in nonsocialist societies. Thus much of the insecurity attached to questions of unemployment, illness, old age, risk of accidence, child care and education, taxes and rents, is reduced or eliminated relatively early in the transition period.

> With socialism, the people, the workers and their families, are guaranteed all these things. Under capitalism, the thing uppermost in man's mind is survival, health, his children. If he's the head of a family, if one of his loved ones is sick, he's haunted by the thought of not having any money, he's haunted by all the fears on which capitalist labor discipline is founded. In other words, under capitalism it's the subhuman standard of living that disciplines the workers.[18]

This argument, raised in a Latin American context by Fidel Castro, seems equally applicable, material differences aside, to the situation in the Scandinavian "welfare state." There, despite one of the highest average living standards in the world, social insecurity is as pervasive as ever. According to studies done in Sweden and Denmark during an unprecedented economic boom period in the 1960s, among the higher paid workers one out of five loses his or her job within a year; in the lower income categories the percentage is even higher.[19] Thus, people continue to be haunted by the constant fear of unemployment and related specters. The responsibilities placed on the shoulders of the individual work as a psychological force that dominates social activities in these societies.

These observations should make it clear that even in highly developed capitalist nations the problem of coercion is very much present. This does not imply that no social inducements are used in societies constructing socialism. The long-term objective of the socialist project, however, is a politically and ideologically self-motivated society in which neither negative nor positive stimuli will be necessary.

Moral versus Material Incentives

In the DPRK, unemployment is nonexistent. All individuals are given an occupation and paid a "living fee" —a term used by the Koreans to indicate the qualitative distinction between socialist labor and the wage labor of capitalist societies. The wage system itself is based on the principle of socialist distribution—i.e., "to each according to his work." This may be measured either in terms of labor time or in terms of quantity and quality of work accomplished. At present, the latter form is predominant. Although at times this approach may seem very close to a "piece-work" system, it does not seem to have the same negative effects as in capitalist countries, since people are paid as part of a collective group, the work team, rather than as individuals, and quotas are adjusted so that workers with less modern machines are not discriminated against. In practical terms, the lowest wages seem to be paid to the young workers, still lacking in experience and skill. There is a uniform wage scale for the entire country. Although this system is seen as an aspect of material incentives, it is considered necessary in the present phase.

The general line followed is to give preference to political inducements but not to neglect material rewards. In both the industrial and agricultural sectors collective material incentives are favored, with the whole work team rewarded for its efforts in fulfilling or overfulfilling the planned target. Members of work teams may occasionally be singled out for awards as well. In cases where an entire factory overfulfills the plan, all personnel receive a bonus. More rarely, collective benefits are awarded in the form of increased services or more cultural centers for the enterprise. It is felt that such a policy might increase inequalities between conditions in the different units. At present, such services are introduced independently of special rewards, depending on both the central plan as well as on the enterprise itself, which may use accumulated funds for such purposes. Even though the use of material incentives is an important reality, the need to combine them with moral or political motivation is fully recognized: "If we allow people to become mercenary, it will be impossible to realize the transition to communism."[20]

Besides the political aspects, there are also "sound economic reasons" against an exclusive emphasis on material incentives. First of all, they are less economical: once you start with the promise of a reward for a certain effort, more will be necessary the next time, and so forth. In the context of a former underdeveloped society engaged on the road to socialism, where consumer goods production still exists only on a small scale, such an approach has definite limitations. In addition, overemphasizing material incentives might have unintended consequences. As pointed out by Clive Thomas:

> Material incentives work against efforts to expand the public consumption of goods, since for material incentives to mean anything, they have to be accompanied by support to individual choices to govern consumption. In this way, therefore, they strengthen the role of the market in the transition period and further remove us from being able to establish *need* as the basic distributive principle. This is true because material incentives pander to the commercialization and mercenariness of social intercourse, negating most of the ethical and moral principles of socialism, and fostering the alienation of the worker from his work and life situation.[21]

Accordingly, in Korea daily necessities are very inexpensive, therefore, and although luxury goods of a sort are increasingly available, even the most highly paid workers would be unable to buy their own private houses or cars, jewelry, antique furniture, etc. In Korea hardly any individual has access to special consumer goods which are unavailable to others. The general rule is for new products not to be put in circulation before they can be made available in great quantities. In such an environment monetary incentives cannot serve as a very potent motivating force.

In addition, social insecurity has been eliminated as a compelling inducement to work. The result is similar to the situation in China described by Carl Raskin: "While the broad range of socially provided goods and services dulls the negative spur of feared deprivation, the relative modesty of the maximum income to which the worker can aspire puts a severe damper on personal income as an active source of work motivation."[22]

The nonmaterial incentives used in the DPRK first of all take the form of political work at the shop level. Party members exert their influence in discussions on the elaboration of production targets and in meetings called to find ways of surpassing the goals set by the plan. The Chongsan-ri method and spirit as well as the Daean work system have institutionalized the mass line—direct participation in decisions and greater responsibility on the part of the producers—both in industrial enterprises and in agricultural units. This system has had a definite influence on the mentality of the producers, motivating them in a way which transcends the monetary gains derived from labor. During visits to various workplaces our questions about wage differences were often met by angry retorts: "We are not working for money," or "we are not salary-people." Perhaps these reactions were somewhat exaggerated; still, the impression remains that an attitude is cultivated whereby work in itself becomes a rewarding and important part of the worker's life.

Another stimulus to increased efforts are President Kim Il Sung's frequent visits to production units and institutions. In the beginning these were principally intended as a method of initiating and popularizing new policies. But they also served to provide higher functionaries with concrete examples of the application of the Chongsan-ri spirit and method, thereby encouraging struggle against the bureaucratic habit of directing public affairs from a writing desk. And in time the visits became a kind of reward in themselves for production units that had accomplished their assignments in a more than satisfactory manner. During such visits Kim Il Sung makes suggestions and gives a kind of "on-the-spot guidance." These talks, full of concrete observations concerning the unit's particular problems, are later studied and discussed by the workers. In special cases the visits provide the occasion for launching a nationwide campaign and the speeches, containing general directives as well as specific examples, are widely published and studied. The result of this political contact with the grassroots seems to be a deeper general understanding of common problems and tasks, encouraging an energetic and responsible attitude among peasants and workers.

Such efforts are further spurred by a multitude of campaigns, the results of which are publicized on charts outside factory buildings or in the newspapers. At one plant we visited they were just completing the "One Hundred Day Battle" for production; elsewhere we were confronted with the "Red Machine Movement," which turned out to be a drive for innovations to increase the productivity of existing machines and material. In autumn 1971 a so-called "Great Upsurge" was widely publicized. The purpose of this campaign was to achieve the production goals of the first two years of the Six Year Plan before April 15, 1972 (the sixtieth birthday of the president).

Many campaigns are infused with a distinctly socialist perspective: increasing the equality and well-being of the population; the *Juche* slogan of self-reliance and "showing a master's attitude." It struck us, however, during our visits in 1969 and 1971, that quite a number of them derive their inspiration from celebrated feats during the anti-Japanese armed struggle or the Great Fatherland Liberation War (Korean War). Many leading cadres in fact got their most intensive "training" in organizational work during such struggles, and slogans which compare the "battle" for production or for constructing a dam to, say, the capture of the Height 1211—a famous strategic point during the Korean War—have singular mobilizing effects. A campaign is usually well-defined in terms of its time limit and target. When it is completed, a certain interval is allowed for material and ideological preparations for the next "battle." Military terms are often adapted to the realm of production—as, for example, in the terminology of industrial organization ("headquarters," the "chief of staff," etc.). Leading cadres' former experiences as partisans may also be reflected in strategies of reconstruction and economic development. An atmosphere of political militancy seems to prevail at all major places of work, emphasized by anti-imperialist slogans and posters. The latter often picture the Korean worker, producing at top speed, side by side with the armed partisans of Asian, African, and Latin American liberation movements.

A closely related system of political motivation is the Chollima Rider Movement, designed to stimulate members of production units to contribute to technological, administrative, or other types of innovations at their places of work in order to increase productivity. In this "socialist emulation" movement, the honored workers usually have their machines decorated, while in the case of work brigades or work teams the entire work area is decorated. The presence of a few such workers in a production unit will inspire the others to follow their example. When an entire cooperative farm or factory is singled out, Kim Il Sung himself often presents the award, and wide publicity, praising the merits of the unit, is given to the event in the media. Indirectly this serves to encourage initiative and innovations and breaks down undue and abstract respect for expertise.

Another means of political mobilization is the appeal to Korean nationalism. The Koreans feel that through hard work and frugality, they can promote the reunification of the country. National unity is a constant preoccupation with the people, many of whom have relatives in the South. Under the slogan "The U.S. agressors must leave South Korea and the country [be] reunified by its own people without foreign interference," a movement has developed to put money aside in savings accounts for the purpose of helping relatives in the South once contacts are reestablished.[23] Although its main function is political, this movement has the indirect advantage of holding back immediate consumption, thereby furthering increased productive investment.

The Policy of Socialist Distribution

The use of material incentives is closely related to the principles of socialist distribution. The policy with regard to the "living fee," as explained to us in Korea, is based on two things. (1) The recognition that differences in wages among various economic branches and fields of endeavor are still necessary at this stage. Distribution, therefore, corresponds to the skill and quantity of labor. (2) The need to demonstrate the intrinsic superiority of socialism through its capacity to equalize and improve the living standard of the people, with the aim of providing "the same happy life to all."

With regard to differences in income due to variations in skill, it is felt that with the development of technology and mechanization, differentiations between various kinds of labor will gradually decrease. Simultaneously, the level of education, culture, and living standards will also tend to become more and more uniform. On the level of economic policy, this means making a growing quantity of daily necessities available at low and decreasing prices, with many services entirely free of charge, while at the same time raising the minimum income level. It is interesting to note that although increased labor productivity does lead to wage increases, there is no automatic link between the two since in most cases greater productivity is a result of state investment in material and machines. Innovations, likewise, are not necessarily rewarded by higher wages, but often simply a one-time bonus and a political citation. The quotas are adjusted so that wages are paid in terms of the amount of labor exerted rather than the level of productivity. Otherwise, workers in the modern sectors of the economy would tend to be favored at the expense of the great majority, still working with old machines and hence showing lower productivity. Politically such a course would tend to divide the working class.

Quite a few of the problems Korea has had to resolve derive from the fact that the transition process started from a very low level of development of productive forces. In order to replace the principle of socialist distribution—"to each according to his work" (which fundamentally is a bourgeois right)—with the communist principle of "from each according to his ability and to each according to his needs,"[24] a higher form of society will have to be reached. Political factors will play a crucial role in attaining this goal, even though the determining elements will still be economic ones. It is expected that as production increases in response to the demands and needs of the people, many of the above-mentioned remnants of capitalism will disappear. But this, of course, all depends on the application of correct policies in successive stages of the country's progress toward its goal.

Cases of excessive revolutionary zeal, in the form of a desire to bypass the stage of socialist distribution, are not infrequent in the experiences of socialist countries. Thus, during the Great Leap Forward in China, in some instances the free distribution of food was prematurely introduced. This was partly due to the exceptional harvest of 1958:

> The peasants thought it then possible to realize a dream of generations of starving peasants: "To give everybody equally abundant nourishment." During the following difficult years, accompanied by a procession of natural calamities, the peasants understood that it was not possible to continue to apply this principle without restriction and a

stricter interpretation of the principle, "To each according to his work," was reinstated. In this manner each may establish a narrow link between the result of his work and personal interest and the development of production, between individual and collective interests. One may likewise "ascertain inequalities, combat egalitarianism, reenforce the unity of the peasants, educate the lazy, reeducate the old exploiters."[25]

At the time political forces at the highest level of the Chinese political structure, bent on sabotaging the achievements of the communes, encouraged the peasants' illusions, knowing full well that the objective conditions were not ripe for such social innovations. Moreover, during the Cultural Revolution, measures disregarding objective conditions were promoted by certain elements: "Ultra-leftist activity undermined the revolutionary unity of the masses with respect to many other questions . . . ; for instance, it tried to force some people's communes . . . immediately and completely to give up private individual plots of land and farming, before they were ready for this."[26] In Cuba, as well, a somewhat idealistic course was followed with respect to the question of material incentives. The error of this path—the premature elimination of the principle of socialist distribution—has since been acknowledged:

> When we said on the 26th of July, during the celebration of the twentieth anniversary, that we would have the courage to correct the idealistic mistakes we had made, that meant that if, in certain cases, we had tried to make more headway than we were prepared for, this called for a reappraisal of the situation. If you try to go farther than you can, you are forced to retreat. Fortunately, in this case, it's a matter not of retreating, but of correcting our errors.[27]

In such cases there may be a tendency to go to the opposite extreme, which is equally to be avoided.

Socialist Perspectives

While on the economic level the elimination of presocialist mechanisms is perhaps the most complex problem, on the ideological front it is the sociopsychological question of motivation which demands the most protracted struggle. In this respect, socialist distribution, though a bourgeois remnant, is nevertheless the cornerstone of transitional socialist societies. The preconditions for its disappearance include not only the development of the productive forces but the emergence of a new type of individual—one to whom work becomes identified with the realization of his or her own personality. According to Lenin, a higher stage of society will be reached when a new work ethic has been assimilated by the people. Thus will it become possible (assuming of course, that imperialism has ceased to exist) for the state power to fade away.

> It will become possible for the state to wither away completely when society adopts the rule: "From each according to his ability, to each according to his needs," i.e., when people have become so accustomed to observing the fundamental rules of social intercourse and when their labour becomes so productive that they will voluntarily work *according to their ability.* "The narrow horizon of bourgeois right," which compels one to calculate with the coldheartedness of a Shylock whether one has not worked half an hour more than somebody else, whether one is not getting less pay than somebody else—this narrow horizon will then be crossed. There will then be no need for society to regulate the quantity of products to be received by each; each will take freely "according to his needs."[28]

What is really at issue here is the creation of a kind of social formation which bourgeois social scientists, unable to grasp that a society can function without any form of compulsion, have termed "utopian." But is it really so farfetched to consider human beings capable of living by different norms (different, that is, from those of a highly industrialized capitalism) in a society where the material conditions permit a different kind of distribution system? The "pessimistic" attitude toward this question rests on the same ahistorical view of human "nature" which Marx so emphatically rejected. Marx affirmed the possiblity of transforming both socioeconomic mechanisms and the human element through a process of constant interactions:

> If man draws all his knowledge, sensation, etc., from the world of the senses and the experience gained in it, the empirical world must be arranged so that in it man experiences and gets used to what is really human and that he becomes aware of himself as man. . . . If man is shaped by his surroundings, his surroundings must be made human. If man is social by nature, he will develop his true nature only in society, and the power of his nature must be measured not by the power of separate individuals but by the power of society.[29]

In this discussion of material and political incentives, there are some further perspectives which deserve mention. Although these have not yet become immediately relevant in the context of any contemporary socialist experiment, they may take on increasing urgency with respect to socialist transitions in *industrialized* societies. In his analysis of the contradiction between the development of the means of production and the outdated social norms of the mode of production, Marx made certain observations that have often been overlooked or dismissed as utopian visions. We have already mentioned how his studies on the development of the means of production and the social relations prevailing under capitalism led him to believe that human labor would tend less and less to be the primary measure of wealth. Such a perspective would imply the transformation even of the so-called economic laws that operate in industrial societies. In the meantime, capitalism's contradictions grow steadily deeper, with capital on the one hand constantly attempting to reduce labor time to a minimum, while on the other still using labor time as the only measure and source of wealth. In order to make the wheels go round, capital consequently "reduces labor-time in the form of the necessary, only to multiply it in the form of the superfluous; thereby increasingly placing the superfluous as a precondition—question *de vie et de mort*—for the necessary."[30]

As we interpret it, the modern "consumer society" offers precisely such a case of the superfluous becoming a precondition for the necessary. This may be one of the basic reasons why, in a milieu of great technological and scientific progress, we find a mode of social organization that seems increasingly irrational. In a society where the development of the means of production has made useful employment a scarce commodity, producers find themselves trapped in monotonous and tedious jobs that offer no means of self-realization. Alienation and neurosis are reaching alarming proportions; leisure time, once providing an outlet for some personal happiness and growth, is now largely a matter of passive consumerism. Furthermore, in capitalist industrial society, despite its overwhelming productive capacity and massive material wealth, social insecurity and real poverty not only persist, but may even tend to increase.

In order to avoid the pitfalls associated with the continued definition of social wealth in terms of labor time—which is only another aspect of "economism"—socialist society would have to embark upon a new road. Provided the means of production are sufficiently developed, this would imply that the "free development of the individual" should be promoted, as Marx put it, by "reducing to a minimum society's necessary labor," thus liberating the time and resources necessary for the "artistic, scientific, etc. education of the individual."[31] One important step in accordance with this vision is the aforementioned process of converging needs and demand.

But whether socialism will be able to cope with this problem is as yet undermined. Is it possible, for example, to picture a future society where labor will no longer be performed as a duty but as a natural requirement? An environment where such terms as "labor" and "leisure" are no longer even meaningful? And how does such a perspective relate to the aims of Korean socialist construction? One indication may be the changes that have already occured. Thus the relations of production originally formed under the international division of labor (making Korea a colony) have been radically transfomed. Although we hesitate to make predictions concerning the future of Korean socialism, it seems to us that it will basically involve a choice between two political lines: one could be defined as "economism" and the other as putting "politics in command." Examples of the latter may include: low and decreasing prices on widely used consumer goods; educational, health, and cultural services made available on a mass basis, free of charge; efforts to conserve resources; an attitude of respect for human labor. Such material manifestations may be taken as a sign that the yardstick for social wealth is already changing in the DPRK. It is no longer measured exclusively in terms of things and goods—i.e., labor time—as is the case under capitalism, but rather in terms of human development in the larger sense. Under present circumstances, with the Korean people not fully liberated from the hardships of economic underdevelopment and their liberation still contingent on the development of the productive forces, these material and nonmaterial aspects are very closely interconnected. But because the emphasis is already radically different from that of the capitalist system, possibilities for doing away with capitalist norms seem to be opened up.

In the process of becoming an industrialized society, the DPRK does not yet seem to have experienced what were until recently considered the "natural costs of industrial development." Marxists have maintained that the construction of a socialist society would open up new opportunities to solve or eliminate the contradiction between "Gemeinschaft" and "Gesellschaft" (i.e., village, tribe, or family community versus modern urban society), and the alienation associated with it.[32] In this respect it is interesting that according to Scalapino and Lee, the rural-urban gap is narrower in the DPRK than in the Soviet Union and China.[33] Conscious attempts are made to ensure that with modernization, individuals will not lose all feelings of attachment to their community, fellow workers, and neighbors. Along the same lines, there is an effort to make the administrative apparatus more tangible to the people, both at the workplace and in the neighborhood. In addition, everybody belongs to a political organization of one kind or another. Participation in the people's militia further enhances a sense of belonging. In other words both organizational structures and productive functions serve to incorporate the individual into the social life of the country, thus minimizing the alienation that is so characteristic a feature of developed industrial societies.

However, whether the future socioeconomic mode of production of the DPRK will fulfill the Marxist vision will depend on the politics of Korean socialism in the coming decades. The eventual reunification of the country, for example, represents an important challenge requiring new and flexible politics. It should be noted that for the Koreans, national liberation will not be complete until this task has been fulfilled. A further influence on Korea's future progress will be the experience of socialist development in other countries. Thus, the struggle of each country to promote socialist construction becomes a source of strength and support for all such countries.

The Role of the Dictatorship of the Proletariat

The Koreans believe that in order for a former colony to attain a higher type of society—one transcending the principle of socialist distribution—certain stages of development need to be respected. Each phase corresponds to a concrete situation, and each demands specific and limited treatment. Thus the tasks of the period of the people's democratic revolution are different from those of the phase of socialist revolution. Under the people's democracy—based on the worker-peasant alliance and a broad united front that includes national capitalists—priority must be given to building a political force capable both of withstanding any imperialist onslaught and of eliminating the footholds of foreign powers in the country: "In short, in the stage of the people's democratic revolution, liquidation of the capitalist class in general is not a prerequisite; the important task is elimination of the comprador capitalists who are in collusion with imperialist forces."[34]

With the completion of this task the way is opened for the establishment of the dictatorship of the proletariat. Its particular mission is to guide the long-term process of transition, including the socialist transformation of production relations and the development of the productive forces, as well as socialist construction and industrialization.

This process also involves the education and remolding of the people, with the ultimate goal of abolishing class differences—of transforming everyone into socialist working people. Further objectives include the elimination of differences between types of ownership as well as those between city and country. Once these transformations have been won through class struggle the transition period, according to the Koreans, will have reached a qualitatively new stage: "When we advance socialist construction and thoroughly win over the middle classes to our side, when we eliminate the distinction between the working class and the peasantry and build a classless society, we shall be able to say that the tasks of the period of the transition from capitalism to socialism have been accomplished."[35]

As we have already noted, in their rather schematic discussions of the transition period the fathers of scientific socialism were thinking chiefly in terms of the industrially developed societies. Therefore they perceived the transition as a relatively brief period more or less coinciding with the stage of proletarian dictatorship. This theory was based principally on Marx's expectation that the proletarian revolution would break out simultaneously in the major capitalist centers of Europe. "Proceeding from such premises, Marx thought that the period of transition from capitalism to socialism would be a comparatively short historical epoch, and further provided that the dictatorship of the proletariat would correspond to the transition period in terms of time, i.e., that the transition period and the dictatorship of the proletariat would be inseparable."[36] The Koreans have given serious consideration to Marx's perspective in developing their own theories on the problem of the transition period; they have concluded, however, that from an historical perspective, to stick with such a position would be contrary to the Marxist method of analysis.

Lenin, working in a backward country like Russia, had already reached the conclusion that the transitional period would be longer than anticipated and that it would continue to be characterized by class struggle until class differences were eliminated. Today, because of the new historical situation and the problems confronting the construction of socialism, the Koreans think that—though correct in relation to conditions at the time—Marx's definitions are in need of undogmatic reexamination. Under present circumstances, as they see it, to expect the dictatorship of the proletariat to coincide with the end of the transitional period would be realistic only if the revolution could simultaneously be generalized on the world scale. If this were the case, "the transition period and the dictatorship of the proletariat would coincide with each other, and with the termination of the transition period the dictatorship of the proletariat would also cease to exist and there would come the fall of the state."[36]

But if a differentiation is made between the transition period and the dictatorship of the proletariat, it is considered not only feasible but desirable to strive for or to establish a more advanced socioeconomic formation while not abandoning the political weapon—i.e., the dictatorship of the proletariat—for an indefinite period of time. "And yet, if socialism has been built and a classless society materialized in one country or in some areas, the transition period should be regarded as terminated there even though the revolution has not won the victory on a world-wide scale. As long as capitalism remains in the world, however, the dictatorship of the proletariat shall not vanish and we cannot even talk about the withering away of the state."[38] In developing their conception the Koreans have rejected what they consider to be a rightist theory of the transitional period: its start is identified with the taking over of power by the working class and its end with the victory of the socialist system—which supposedly coincides with the termination of the dicatatorship of the proletariat. "This results in emasculating the functions of the dictatorship of the proletariat as the most powerful weapon of class struggle and for building socialism and communism, the most essential functions of a socialist state, and is, in effect, an abandonment of the revolution."[39]

This theory, according to the Koreans, has its ideological roots in an attitude which, on the domestic level, abandons the class struggle, while in the international sphere it seeks an accomodation with imperialism at the expense of the world revolution. The Koreans likewise keep their distance from what they perceive as a "leftist" error: the tendency to see the transition period as a process lasting many generations, until the final attainment of the highest communist stage. Further, they consider it false to argue that communism cannot be realized in a single country. Their reasoning is based on a differentiation between the concept of the dictatorship of the proletariat on the one hand, and the transitional period on the other; the classless society, in turn, is set off by the boundaries of the transitional period. In this way Korean socialists distinguish themselves from what they consider rightist and "leftist" conceptions. Yet they also recognize the need for further research into this fundamental problem. Kim Il Sung, speaking to an audience of Party ideologists, declared that "This is not the final but a preliminary conclusion reached by us. It is desirable that you make further studies in this direction."[40]

The Question of Leadership in the Framework of Proletarian Dictatorship

While disagreements exist concerning the role of proletarian dictatorship in relation to the transitional period, there is relative unanimity as to the principle itself. According to Marxism, all presocialist societies are class societies, with one class dominating the others. During the socialist revolutionary process the working class, regardless of its numerical strength or weakness, must assume leadership. Its special position within the production process has made it more disciplined and militant than other segments of the population; in addition, there is the fact that workers, in the famous phrase from *The Communist Manifesto,* "have nothing to lose but their chains." In other words, it is the class with not only the ability but also the will to become the agent of change. Finally, the working class is considered the only one which by emancipating itself can fundamentally transform social relations, thus liberating the majority of the people, making them masters of the fruits of their own productive efforts.

However, the working class is neither entirely homogeneous nor immune to internal economic competition. If it is to organize itself into an agent of change, it must be unified and guided by its most advanced section. This nucleus, which may comprise intellectuals and other political persons who identify themselves with the working class, is considered the vanguard. It becomes institutionalized in the form of the political party.

Such an organization needs capable leadership, and structurally this is provided by the Central Committee of the Party, which in turn is headed by its most influential and farsighted member. This individual must have great leadership ability and experience, as well as a thorough understanding both of the changes needed, and of the concrete demands of the people. It goes without saying that if the masses were able spontaneously to organize themselves and effect necessary changes, there would be no need for a vanguard. From the beginning, therefore, Marxism-Leninism has maintained the need for a strong leadership capable of rallying the masses and waging protracted struggles. This approach to the question of social change has not been unique to socialist doctrine. The role of personal leadership has always been recognized as a fundamental element in social transformations: "Western theorists from Plato to Rousseau, Marx, Weber, and Lenin, have all recognized that a great leader or vanguard is essential to radically transform existing society."[41] Nevertheless, social scientists in our part of the world have continually refused to acknowledge the necessity for a vanguard in their analysis of present-day socialist societies.

Starting with the first socialist state, it is difficult to find examples of authentic revolutionary change during this century which have not been characterized by a highly personalized leadership within a certain political structure. It is hardly mere coincidence that nations with very different cultural and historical backgrounds have all experienced the need for an individual leader—one able to serve as a unifying element during the extremely complex transformations of their societies.

A dialectical interaction of various elements is usually responsible when one particular individual acquires such enormous importance in a given historical period. As one scholar wrote at the turn of the century, when socialist transition was still purely in the realm of speculation:

> While his appearance at a particular moment appears to us a matter of chance, the great man influences society only

when society is ready for him. If society is not ready for him, he is called, not a great man, but a visionary or a failure. It is to him that progress seems to be, and in fact often is, in large measure due. But we must not forget that even then the great mass of his characteristics are those of the society about him, and that he is great because he visualizes more truly than any one else the fundamental tendencies of the community in which his lot is cast, and because he expresses more successfully than others the real spirit of the age of which he is the supreme embodiment.[42]

The most important question during socialist transition, namely that of *how to combine strong and unifying leadership with the mass line,* has only found a preliminary solution in Marxist theory and practice. However, in the context of the present discussion, the problem for socialists has not been the question of personal leadership as such, but of how to find the individual best suited for this function. At times of great social and national crisis such great leaders may or may not appear, and this element can be decisive for the entire process of change.

In a society engaged in socialist transition, the exceptional leader does not function in a vacuum but is part of a social movement and the political structure it generates to carry out the process of change. In the context of the proletarian dictatorship, his or her role is closely connected to the Party organization. In the words of one such leader, " . . . a genius is after all only a person that is a little more intelligent than the others. A genius cannot succeed alone but only with the support of others. A genius must rely on the Party which is the vanguard of the proletariat. A genius depends on the mass line and on the wisdom of the masses."[43]

During the first half of this century it was to be expected that ideological opponents of socialism, hoping to weaken the dictatorship of the proletariat, would concentrate their attacks on the leadership of the Soviet Union. Such criticisms, however, had little impact in comparison with the great event at the Twentieth Congress of the CPSU in 1956 which witnessed the condemnation of Joseph Stalin by Nikita Khrushchev. A serious attempt at critical analysis of a whole era of socialist construction, especially coming from the very center of world socialism, would have been beneficial to the international movement. But these denunciations, rather than clarifying crucial issues, served to sow great doubts among adherents of socialism: "Indeed, it wasn't long before seeing the official criticism of 'Stalinist' deviation through the 'cult of the personality' produce in this connection its inevitable ideological effects. After the Twentieth Congress, an openly rightist wave expanded among Marxist and Communist 'intellectuals,' to speak only of them. And this took place not only in capitalist countries, but also in socialist countries."[44]

Given the effects of this historic stigmatization, it is questionable whether the very concept of "personality cult" is an appropriate tool for social analysis. One obvious result was the creation of a lot of confusion around the role of personalized leadership within the framework of proletarian dictatorship. Many—especially Western—communist parties, have tended more and more simply to abandon the goal of establishing the proletarian dictatorship both in their political programs and in practice. Some organizations, in order to avoid identification with socialist countries and placate nonproletarian elements in their own societies, no longer even call themselves communist parties.

Similar ideological influences are at work in certain purportedly Marxist attempts to account for the role of the individual during socialist construction. Such analyses often amount to little but defensive rationalizations. Moreover, they use a strange methodological procedure that makes advanced bourgeois society the standard of comparison, treating it as something permanent and static, and thus failing to give proper weight to certain historical experiences. Even a distinguished social scientist like Oskar Lange, in analyzing this phenomenon and its role in the Soviet Union, saw it as the result of the special conditions of nonindustrial societies:

> In studying this period a certain important sociological factor has to be taken into account, and that is the weakness of the working class in an underdeveloped country. It seems to me that it is on the basis of this weakness of the working class, under conditions of underdevelopment, that the bureaucratic state machine gains importance, and phenomena like that of the "cult of the personality" develop. It substitutes, in a certain sense, for the spontaneous activity of the working class.[45]

This viewpoint disregards the historical evidence that highly personalized leadership is not uniquely the result of proletarian dictatorship in countries with weak industrial working classes. Perhaps the classical example would be that of Nazi Germany, where an advanced organized working class was made to accept a type of leader who both in theory and practice was very far removed from anything resembling collective leadership or the mass line. Lange's comments also reflect the confusion surrounding the concept of "spontaneous activity of the working class." This line of thinking would seem to undermine completely the Marxist principle of proletarian dictatorship as well as the need for organization during the transitional period. In sum, such attempts to analyze the USSR—the first substantial experience with proletarian dictatorship—fall victim to idealism at the risk of abandoning the entire idea of socialism. Furthermore, focusing exclusively on the problem of personalized leadership often means running the risk of overlooking the more important questions related to it—i.e., the historical and material conditions, and above all the social forces, of which such leadership is the historical instrument. Following the so-called "de-Stalinization" process, Asian communist parties voiced disagreement with some of the criticisms leveled against the Soviet leadership. Kim Il Sung, reviewing the former Soviet leader's accomplishments and weaknesses, expressed what was probably a widespread opinion among fraternal Asian parties at the time:

> We Communists criticise [Stalin] for his violation of Leninist collective leadership and Marxist-Leninist ideology. This does not mean that we deny the role of the individual in history. Marxism-Leninism recognizes the important role of leaders in history.
>
> Stalin was a strong Marxist-Leninist who made a significant contribution to the international proletarian movement and played a historic role in the construction of socialism in the Soviet Union, the victory of the socialist revolution and the defeat of Fascism, thereby achieving great fame.
>
> Nevertheless, he became excessively conceited during the last stage of his life and consequently inflicted considerable damage upon the Party as well as the government by violating Leninist principles of collective leadership. It is entirely proper, therefore, for the CPSU to expose and criticize his errors vigorously while recognizing his great contributions.[46]

Despite their qualified acceptance of the criticism of Stalin, many parties refused to follow the rightist trend implied by the process of "de-Stalinization." They recognized that by relying on individual leaders with great popularity among the masses, a certain protection could be secured from both internal factionalism and external interference. As we have seen in the case of Korea, during the Third Party Congress the new Soviet leadership, under the guise of encouraging collective leadership in independent socialist countries, tried to impose a change of policies within the international movement. The Koreans had to take a clear position on a question which was virtually forced upon them:

> It is more impermissible to try to force the "antipersonality cult" campaign on other parties, and behind this smokescreen interfere in the internal affairs of brother Parties and even scheme to overthrow their Party leadership. Is it not

true that precisely because of the "antipersonality cult" clamors, many fraternal Parties suffered from unnecessary "fever" and the international Communist movement sustained serious losses?[47]

While the Korean Workers' Party vehemently rejects the concept of "personality cult" it also denies that personalized leadership is inherently opposed to collective leadership. Indeed, to assume mechanically—as some countries have done—that the two are contradictory, is considered a counter-revolutionary attempt to discredit and weaken the entire structure of proletarian dictatorship. According to Korean socialists, the unity and smooth functioning of collective leadership may very well depend on the individual leader, who commands a respect that transcends any temporary political disagreements. Of course such a leader must himself respect the principle of collective leadership and must follow the mass line—i.e., fully grasp the demands and the will of the masses, shape them into a political line, and mobilize the people to carry out the requisite tasks.

According to the Koreans, to determine whether or not the political leadership of a given country embodies the mass line, one must look not only at the leaders themselves but at the political priorities and general direction of the society in question. Should such analyses reveal a violation of the collective leadership and the mass line, there is danger of a leader's becoming a kind of political power unto himself, and criticisms should be raised within the country in question. In Korea, however, the unity between Party, people, and leader is very strong and for this reason it is felt that in the future too the leadership of the proletarian dictatorship may be organized in a similar way.

Nevertheless, some Western visitors sympathetic to the DPRK misinterpret the public manifestations of veneration for Kim Il Sung; they have difficulty adjusting to a phenomenon which they are politically and ideologically unprepared to comprehend. In this connection it should be kept in mind that any comparison with leadership in nonsocialist countries is out of the question. Under socialism the leader is or should be the supreme embodiment of a mass desire for changes that will benefit the majority of people. Another case of Western misinterpretation is the assumption of similarities between the Soviet Union under Stalin and Korea, because of the role of the individual leader in both societies, and also because of the respectful appreciation of Stalin frequently voiced in the DPRK. This line of thinking mechanically emphasizes similarities, while completely disregarding basic differences in content. In the Soviet Union, where the construction of socialism took place at a very difficult time, an overemphasis was put on the development of the productive forces through an underestimation of the sociopolitical elements. As we have stressed throughout our discussion of Korean socialism, its practice—starting with a capital accumulation based on political mobilization and institutionalization of the mass line—constituted a break with what has been called the "economic deviation" of the Soviet Union, which was probably the material basis for the excesses and mistakes of the Stalin period.

In considering the progress made under the present regime—with the Korean people, once living under conditions of extreme hardship, now on the march toward the twenty-first century—one should not underestimate the general feeling of respect and affection for the individual who personifies this transformation. A sophisticated observer like Joan Robinson does not hesitate to use the term "messiah" to describe the role of Kim Il Sung. Addressing herself to Westerners, she adds: "To us old cynics it sounds corny. But imagine a people hurled suddenly from a blank colonial past, without a clue, into socialism and into the twentieth century. He gives them a coherent and practical vision of what they are to be. No deviant thought has a chance to sprout."[48]

The role of the Korean leader is also connected to the fact that in a political process, it may be more difficult for the masses to identify with a political program presented in terms of apparently impersonal institutions or abstract ideological considerations. In other words, it is easier to relate to a person whose example and background form a direct link with the people, than to a host of new values and ethics which may be difficult for the average person to grasp without preparation.[49] The time factor—the transformation of both the society and the mentality of the people within a limited historical period—lends such a personality additional weight in symbolic terms. It is acknowledged even among critics of the regime that peasants, workers, and intellectuals are loyal to the person of Kim Il Sung and through him to the Workers' Party. In the eyes of the people the two are almost identical. Thus the respect and veneration shown the Korean leader is a way simultaneously to unite the people around a coherent political line and to mobilize them to carry it out. Since Kim Il Sung's public statements all reflect the decisions of the Party Central Committee, rank-and-file Party members base most of their political education on the study of the revolutionary writings of their president. Leading cadres often attribute the achievements of socialism to precisely this unity of ideology and action around the Korean leader.

The person of Kim Il Sung—quite apart from his historical accomplishments and theoretical contributions—thus fulfills several vital functions in the political life of Korea. With his background in the anti-Japanese liberation movement and his central role in all subsequent important events, he is a political figure of truly historical dimensions. As such he is respected by patriotic Koreans everywhere, not just north of the 38th Parallel. It should be recalled, for example, that the majority of Korean nationals living in Japan nurture the same sentiments toward Kim Il Sung and identify themselves with the system in the DPRK.

Even though the form of political propaganda emanating from the North may often seem unlikely to convince the sceptical Westerner, it should not be taken for granted that the South Koreans, at present denied any true possibility for expressing themselves, would react the same way. One important difference is the cultural and historical background they have in common with the North.[50]

In a certain sense the Korean leader thus symbolizes the special situation of the nation, characterized by the fact that the peninsula has not yet been completely liberated. On the one hand he is the supreme organ for the proletarian dictatorship during the process of socialist construction; on the other he is the national hero whose past and present dedication to the cause of the country can win the respect of nonsocialist nationalists.

Political cadres in North Korea insist that without the leadership of Kim Il Sung many of the accomplishments of the last three decades would not have been possible. Although the authors of the present study are wary of adopting such an absolute view, we do agree that had it not been for the policies in the fields of economic development and socialist construction put into effect under the present leadership, the concrete realization of most goals would not yet have been achieved. In this respect it should be remembered that the strong personality of Kim Il Sung did much to overcome the weaknesses resulting from Korean communism's history of chronic fragmentation. In a recent study of the leadership of the DPRK a liberal Korean intellectual living in the United States made the following relevant observations:

> The intense growth of factionalism might have developed into sheer internecine competition, factional loyalty taking precedence over party loyalty, the preoccupation with the struggle causing less concern among the members of factions towards society as a whole and blinding them to the external threats which the regime had to deal with from its early years until the end of the Korean War. Had such severe factionalism split into the society, North Korea would have been plagued by continuous political instability and social unrest, all of which would have hampered its socioeconomic

growth. . . . Thus the emergence of strong-man rule in North Korea was a necessity for the nation's survival as a communist state.[51]

Without its present leadership the independence of the DPRK would most certainly have been in grave jeopardy, and for this reason Kim Il Sung will undoubtedly go down in the history of this proud nation as one of its most heroic sons. For his success in solving the urgent and difficult problems of underdevelopment which afflicted his country, Kim Il Sung deserves the esteem and attention of all men and women who are struggling against the evils of such a condition throughout the Third World.

Notes

1. Karl Marx, *Grundrisse der Kritik der Politischen Ökonomie* (Berlin, 1953), p. 596 (our translation).
2. "Let Us Uphold the Dictatorship of the Proletariat and Proletarian Democracy," *The Pyongyang Times,* February 8, 1971.
3. Kim Il Sung, *On Some Theoretical Problems of the Socialist Economy,* March 1, 1969 (Pyongyang, 1969), p. 4. (Emphasis added)
4. Ibid., p. 10.
5. Ibid., p. 11.
6. Charles Bettelheim, "On the Transition Between Capitalism and Socialism," *Monthly Review* 20, no.10 (March 1969): 5.
7. See especially the theoretical work by Charles Bettelheim, *Economic Calculation and Forms of Property* (New York: Monthly Review Press, 1975).
8. Friedrich Engels, *Anti-Dühring - Herr Eugen Dühring's Revolution in Science,* 3rd ed. (Moscow: Progress Publishers, 1962), p. 425.
9. Kim Byong Sik, *Modern Korea* (New York: International Publishers, 1970), p. 174.
10. J.V. Stalin, *Economic Problems of Socialism in the U.S.S.R.* (Moscow, 1952; reprint ed., Peking, 1972), p. 54.
11. Kim Il Sung, *On Some Theoretical Problems,* p. 14.
12. Kim Byong Sik, *Modern Korea,* p. 175.
13. Ibid., pp. 182-183.
14. Kim Il Sung, *On Some Theoretical Problems,* p. 19.

15. "Let Us Uphold the Dictatorship."
16. Kim Byong Sik, *Modern Korea*, p. 184.
17. Speech by Fidel Castro reprinted in *Granma*, November 25, 1973.
18. Ibid.
19. Cf. Bent Hansen, *Velstand uden velfærd (Wealth without Welfare)* (Copenhagen, 1969). The author is editor-in-chief of the Danish social-democratic daily newspaper, *Aktuelt*. Investigations in Sweden and Norway reached similar results: Cf. Gunnar og Maj-Britt Inghe, *Den ofärdiga välfärden* (Stockholm, 1967) and Lars Gunnar Lingas, ed., *Myten om Velferdsstaten. Søkelys på norsk socialpolitikk* (Oslo, 1970).
20. Kim Il Sung, "On Further Developing the Daean Work System," November 9, 1962, in *Selected Works* (Pyongyang, 1965), vol. II, p. 377.
21. Clive Y. Thomas, *Dependence and Transformation: The Economics of the Transition to Socialism* (New York and London: Monthly Review Press, 1974), p. 292.
22. Carl Raskin, "Maoism and Motivation: Work Incentives in China," *Bulletin of Concerned Asia Scholars* 5, no. 1 (July 1973): 20.
23. During visits to various enterprises we were told that the country is building up its stock piles in anticipation of the demands reunification would place on the nation's resources. Of course, this serves simultaneously as a preparation against natural calamities or war.
24. Karl Marx, *Critique of the Gotha Programme,* in K. Marx and F. Engels, *Selected Works in Two Volumes,* vol. II (Moscow: Progress Publishers, 1958), p. 24.
25. Hélène Marchisio, "Les systèmes de rémunération dans les communes populaires," in Charles Bettelheim, Jacques Charrière, and Hélène Marchisio, *La Construction du socialisme en Chine* (Paris: Maspero, 1965), p. 89.
26. Charles Bettelheim, *Cultural Revolution and Industrial Organization in China* (New York: Monthly Review Press, 1974), p. 107.
27. Castro, speech in *Granma*, November 25, 1973.
28. V.I. Lenin, *The State and Revolution*, in *Selected Works in Two Volumes,* vol. II, part 1 (Moscow: Progress Publishers, 1952), pp. 299-300.
29. Karl Marx, in K. Marx and F. Engels, *The Holy Family—or Critique of Critical Critique* (Moscow: Progress Publishers, 1956), p. 176.
30. Marx, *Grundrisse,* p. 593 (our translation).
31. Ibid.
32. Ferdinand Tonnies,*Community and Society (Gemeinschaft und Gesellschaft)* (East Landing: Mich. State University, 1957).
33. Robert A. Scalapino and Chong-Sik Lee, *Communism in Korea*, vol. II (Berkeley, Cal.: Univ. of California Press, 1972), p. 1153.
34. Kim Byong Sik, *Modern Korea*, p. 79.

35. Kim Il Sung, *On the Questions of the Period of Transition From Capitalism to Socialism and the Dictatorship of the Proletariat*, May 25, 1967 (Pyongyang, 1969), p. 15.
36. Ibid., pp. 4-5.
37. Ibid., p. 6.
38. Ibid., pp. 6-7.
39. Kim Byong Sik, *Modern Korea*, p. 89.
40. Kim Il Sung, *On the Questions of the Period of Transition*, p. 16.
41. Richard M. Pfeffer, "Serving the People and Continuing the Revolution," *The China Quarterly* 52 (October-December 1972): 620.
42. Edwin R.A. Seligman, *The Economic Interpretation of History*, 2nd ed., rev. (New York: Gordian Press, 1966), pp. 97-98.
43. Document in *La Nouvelle Chine*, no. 10 (October-November 1973): 13.
44. Louis Althusser, *Rèponse à John Lewis* (Paris: Maspero, 1973), p. 85.
45. Oskar Lange, "Role of Planning in Socialist Economy," in *Problems of Political Economy of Socialism* (Delhi, 1965), p. 20.
46. Kim Il Sung, press interview with V.V. Prasad, *Rodong Sinmum*, May 31, 1956 (quoted in Scalapino and Lee, *Communism in Korea*, pp. 510-511).
47. "Let Us Defend the Socialist Camp," *Rodong Sinmum*, October 28, 1963 (quoted in ibid., p. 630).
48. Joan Robinson, "Korean Miracle," *Monthly Review* 16, no. 9 (January 1965): 548 and 549.
49. In fact, this is a well-known phenomenon even in highly industrialized "democracies," where "baby-kissing," the "winning smile" on the TV screen, etc., form a familiar part of any electoral campaign, almost to the exclusion of political programs and principles (which might have only temporary validity anyway—until the next election!). In the United States even film stars have been known to become instant politicians, with little more than their recognizability to recommend them.
50. Bruce G. Cumings draws attention to the fact that there seems to be a tradition in Korea of veneration of leaders and hagiography. ("Kim's Korean Communism," *Problems of Communism*, March-April 1974, p. 34, note 41.)
51. Koon Woo Nam, *The North Korean Communist Leadership (1945-1965)* (University, Ala.: Univ. of Alabama Press, 1974), pp. 141-142.

Appendix

*The Ten Point Program of the Association
for the Restoration of the Fatherland
(1936)*

1. To mobilize the entire Korean nation and realize a broad-based anti-Japanese united front in order to overthrow the piratical Japanese imperialist rule and establish a genuine people's government in Korea;
2. To defeat Japan and overthrow its puppet state "Manchukuo" by the Koreans resident in Manchuria through a close alliance between the Korean and Chinese people, and to effect full autonomy for the Korean people residing in Chinese territory;
3. To disarm the Japanese armed forces, gendarmes, police and their agents and organize a revolutionary army truly fighting for the independence of Korea;
4. To confiscate all enterprises, railways, banks, shipping, farms and irrigation systems owned by Japan and Japanese and all property and estates owned by pro-Japanese traitors, to raise funds for the independence movement, and to use part of these funds for the relief of the poor;
5. To cancel all loans made to people by Japan and its agents and abolish all taxes and monopoly systems; to im-

prove the living conditions of the masses and promote the smooth development of national industries, agriculture and commerce;

6. To win the freedom of the press, publications, assembly, and association, oppose terrorist rule and the fostering of feudal ideas by the Japanese imperialists, and to release all political prisoners;

7. To abolish the caste system which divides the *ryangban* (nobles) and the common people, and other inequalities; to ensure equality based on humanity irrespective of sex, nationality or religion; to improve the social position of women and respect their personalities;

8. To abolish slave labor and slavish education; to oppose forced military service and military training of young people; to educate people in our national language, and to enforce free compulsory education;

9. To enforce an eight-hour day, improve working conditions, and raise wages; to formulate labor laws; to enforce state insurance laws for the workers, and to extend state relief to the unemployed;

10. To form a close alliance with nations and states which treat the Koreans as equals and to maintain comradely relations of friendship with states and nations which express goodwill and maintain neutrality toward our national liberation movement.

The Twenty Point Platform (March 23, 1946)

1. To thoroughly liquidate all the remnants of Japanese imperialist rule from the political and economic life of Korea;
2. To wage an implacable struggle against reactionary and antidemocratic elements at home and strictly ban the activities of fascist, antidemocratic political parties, organizations, and individuals;
3. To grant the entire people freedom of speech, the press, assembly, and religion. To provide conditions for free activities to democratic political parties, trade unions, peasants' associations, and other democratic social organizations;
4. To see to it that the entire Korean people have the right and duty to form people's committees—the administrative organs responsible for all local affairs—through universal, direct, and equal suffrage by secret ballot;
5. To grant equal rights to all citizens in political and economic life, irrespective of sex, religion, or property status;
6. To assert the inviolability of persons and their residence and protect by law the property of citizens and their private possessions;
7. To abolish all laws and judicial organs which were in operation during the rule of Japanese imperialism and still retain their aftereffects, elect the people's judicial organs on democratic principles; and grant the citizens at large equal legal rights;
8. To develop industry, agriculture, transport, and trade for the enhancement of the people's welfare;
9. To nationalize big enterprises, transport services, banks, mines, and forests;
10. To allow and encourage free activity in private handicrafts and trade;
11. To confiscate the land belonging to Japanese, the Japanese state, the traitors, and landlords who continue to rent out their land; abolish the tenant system and distrib-

ute among the peasants, free of charge, all the confiscated land, making it their property. To confiscate without compensation all irrigation facilities and place them under state control;

12. To fix market prices for living necessities to combat speculators and usurers;

13. To institute a system of uniform, equitable taxation and introduce a progressive income tax system;

14. To introduce an eight-hour working day for factory and office workers and fix minimum wages for them. To prohibit employment of children under thirteen years of age and institute a six-hour working day for children of thirteen to sixteen;

15. To institute life insurance for factory and office workers and set up an insurance system for workers and enterprises;

16. To introduce a system of universal compulsory education and widely increase primary, secondary, and specialized schools and colleges to be run by the state. To reform the system of public education in line with the democratic state system;

17. To actively develop national culture, science, and the arts, and increase the number of theatres, libraries, radio broadcasting stations, and cinema houses;

18. To set up special schools on a wide scale for training the personnel required in state organs and in all fields of the national economy;

19. To encourage scientists and artists in their work and give them assistance; and

20. To increase the number of state-run hospitals, stamp out epidemics and provide free medical care to the poor.

Charts

I. The Planning System

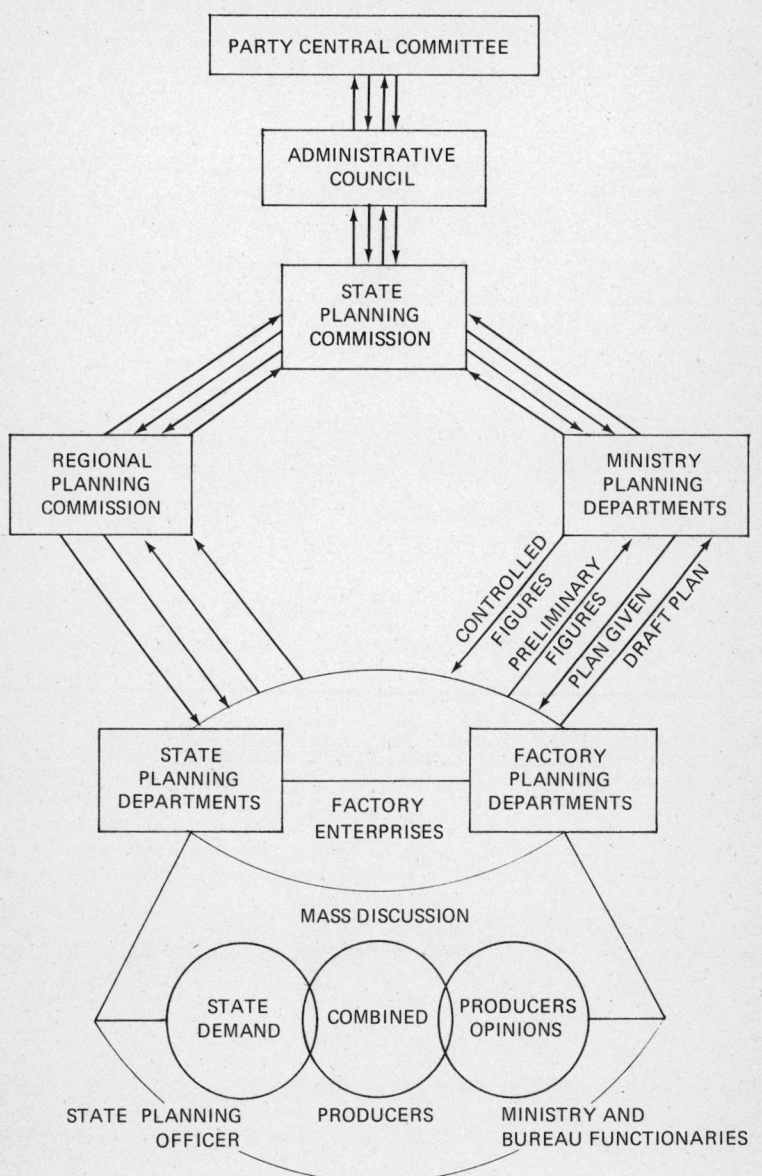

II. The Material Supply System

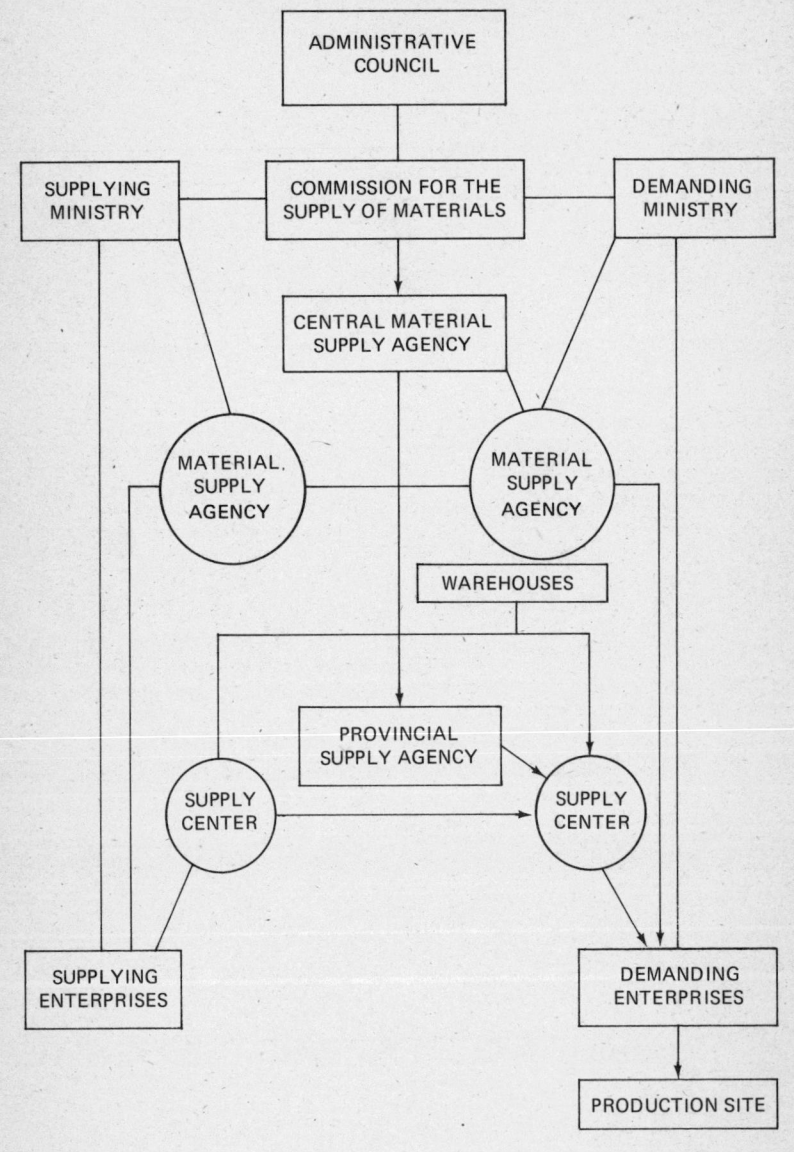

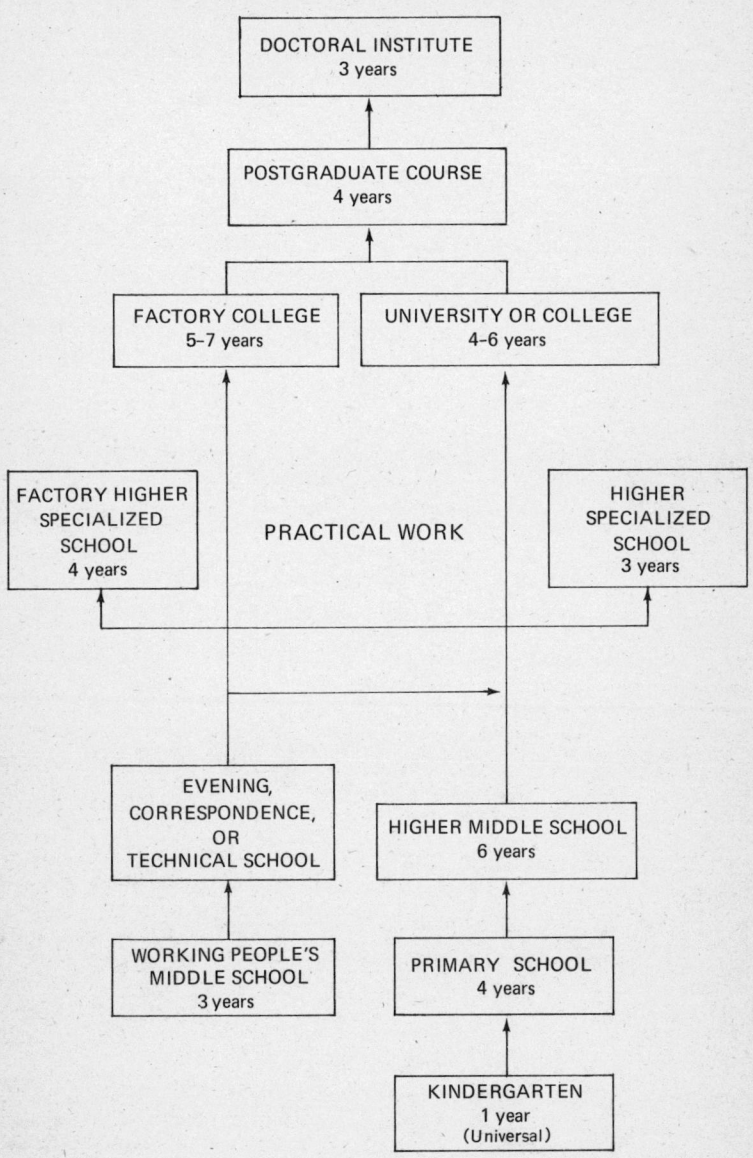

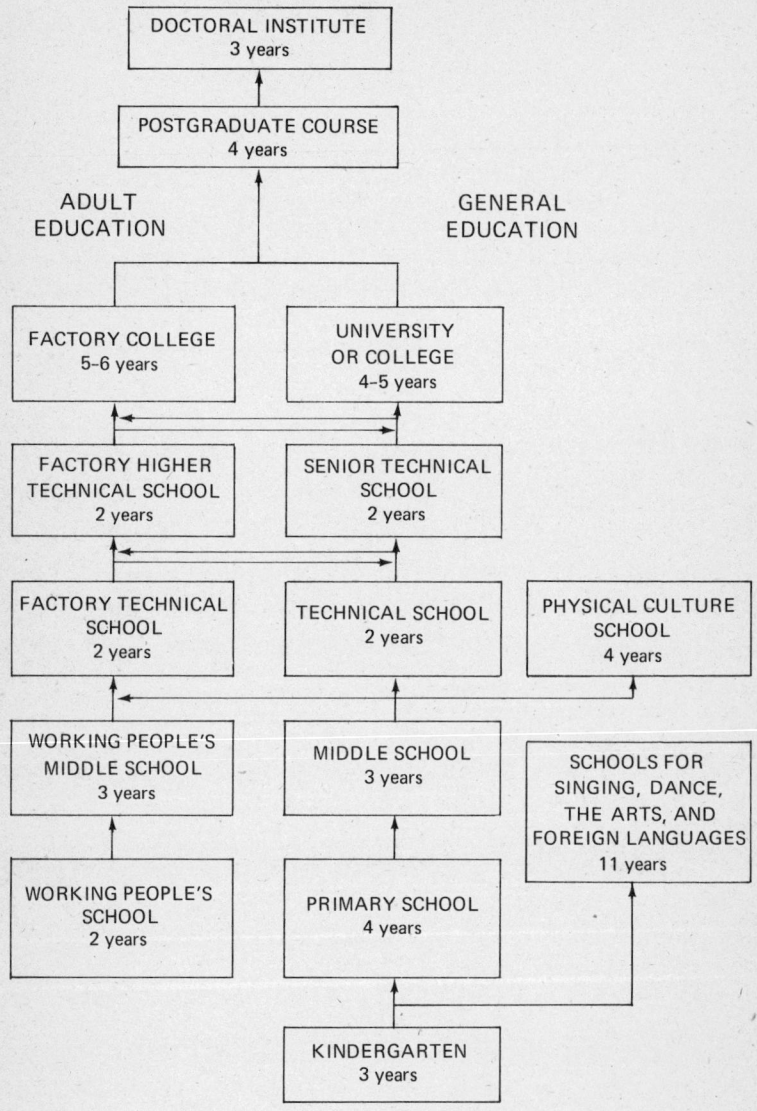

V. Old Agrarian Guidance System

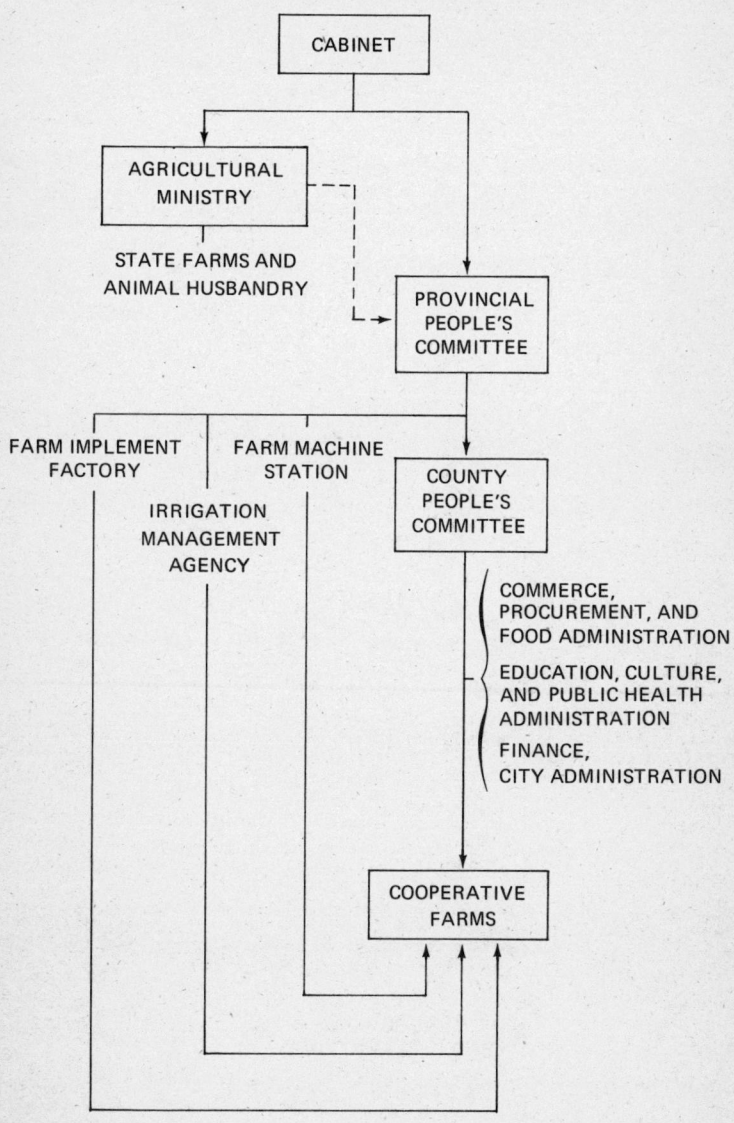

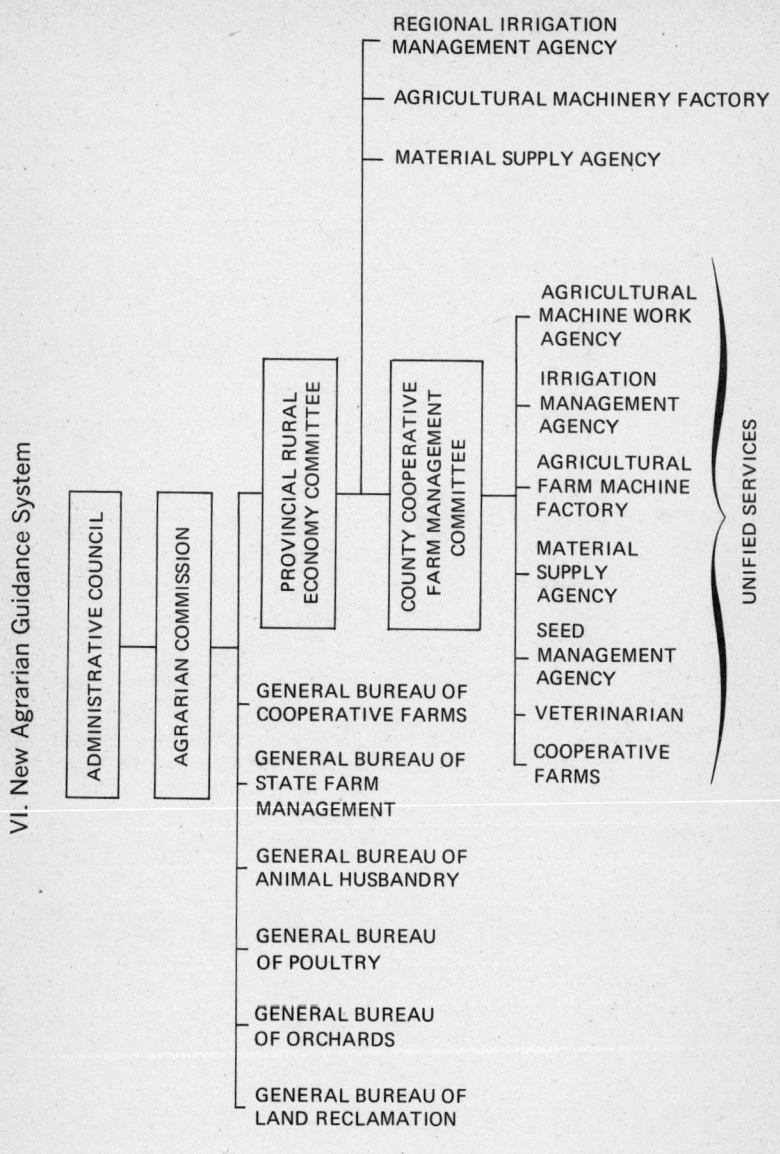

VI. New Agrarian Guidance System

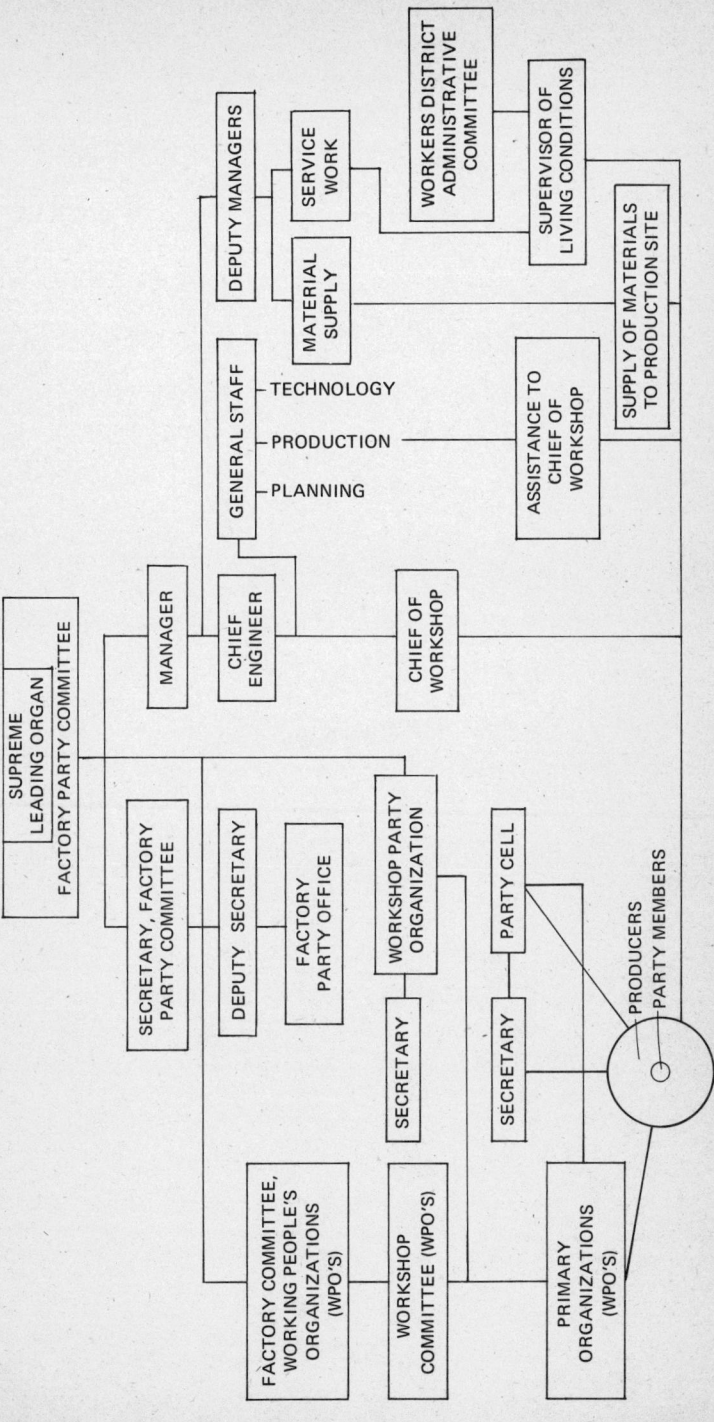

VII. Daean Work System

VIII. Superstructure

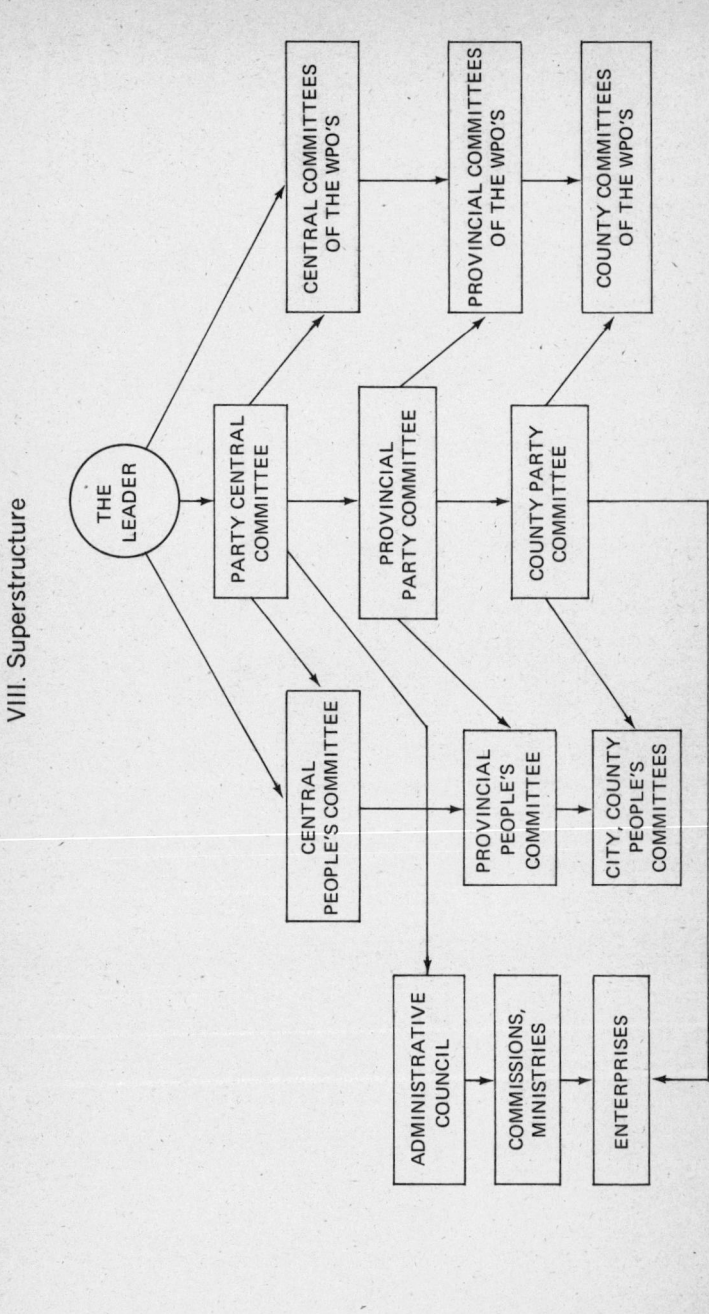